Also available from Hungry Minds

the Unofficial Guide® to London

2nd Edition

the Unofficial Guide® to London

2nd Edition

Lesley Logan

Hungry Minds™

Best-Selling Books • Digital Downloads • e-Books • Answer Networks • e-Newsletters
Branded Web Sites • e-Learning

New York, NY • Indianapolis, IN • Cleveland, OH

Please note that price fluctuate in the course of time, and travel information changes under the impact of many factors that influence the travel industry. We therefore suggest that you write or call ahead for confirmation when making your travel plans. Every effort has been made to ensure the accuracy of information throughout this book and the contents of this publication are believed correct at the time of printing. Nevertheless, the publishers cannot accept responsibility for errors or omissions or for changes in details given in this guide or for the consequences of any reliance on the information provided by the same. Assessments of attractions and so forth are based upon the author's own experience and therefore, descriptions given in this guide necessarily contain an element of subjective opinion, which may not reflect the publisher's opinion or dictate a reader's own experience on another occasion. Readers are invited to write to the publisher with ideas, comments, and suggestions for future editions.

Your safety is important to us, so we encourage you to stay alert and be aware of your surroundings. Keep a close eye on cameras, purses, and wallets, all favorite targets of thieves and pickpockets.

Published by Hungry Minds, Inc.
909 Third Avenue
New York, NY 10022

Produced by Menasha Ridge Press

Unofficial Guide is a registered trademark of Hungry Minds, Inc. All other trademarks are property of their respective owners.

ISBN 0-7645-6449-8

ISSN 1521-4907

Manufactured in the United States of America

10 9 8 7 6 5 4 3 2 1

Second edition

Contents

Part Ten **Shopping in London 332**

Part Eleven **Exercise and Recreation 355**

Index

List of Maps

About the Authors and Contributors

Lesley Logan is a freelance writer who has worked in publishing over the years as a nonfiction ghostwriter, publicity copywriter, and editor. Originally from New York, she has lived in London for many years with her husband Tom and daughter Nora.

Richard Ehrlich, who wrote the chapter on dining, has been writing about food and drink in major United Kingdom magazines and newspapers since 1988. His work appears regularly in The Independent on Sunday, The Guardian, and Time Out. An American, Richard has lived in London since 1974.

Delilah Durrant is a freelance writer who worked on the updated edition of this book, expanding the chapters on exercise and recreation, children, and entertainment. She also did the hard work of fact checking. She has lived in London her entire life and lives there still with her daughter Erell.

Andy Craft, a native Londoner, wrote the chapter on exercise and recreation as well as sections on British culture, what the locals already know, and getting around London. He is the author of several screenplays, and teaches screenwriting at NYU in New York City, where he now resides.

Tony Heiberg wrote the entertainment chapter. He is a freelance writer and has worked as a critic and journalist for a number of magazines on both sides of the Atlantic. He is now working on a novel.

Tracy Thompkins updated the nightclub profiles after extensive research during a semester at Regents College in London. She is an indefatigable and fearless traveler who hopes to go into travel writing after graduation from the University of New Hampshire.

Acknowledgments

First and foremost I want to thank Tom and Nora Logan without whom nothing, least of all this book, would be possible.

And to Bob Sehlinger and Molly Merkle of Menasha Ridge Press, thanks for a wonderful assignment. I want to also thank Gabriela Oates for all her work in this second edition, which was hugely improved by the excellent editing skills of Carolyn Carroll.

Many heartfelt thanks to the legions of anonymous curators, cab drivers, London Transport people, London Tourist Board employees (especially Rosemary Beazley), shopkeepers, waiters, concierges, hotel managers, bellhops, B&B owners, and people on the street, who generously gave me tips, information, guided tours, and unfailingly pointed me in the right direction.

I am grateful to all the family and friends who stayed at our house and regaled me with tales from the tourist trail, as well as forced me out onto it. They are too numerous to mention, but they know who they are, and they know they are welcome back anytime.

My deepest thanks to the people who made the first edition possible: Andy Craft, Tony Heiberg, Atalanta Knatchbull, Denise Knestaut, and Rusty Egan; and to the contributors to the second edition, Delilah Durrant, Tracy Thompkins, and of course Richard Erlich, the restaurant critic.

I also appreciated the letters and evaluations I received from so many readers, the kind and the critical. Your suggestions and your generosity in taking the time to write made me grateful that I got the chance to update the book, to make right some wrongs, and to learn from your own London experiences.

—Lesley Logan

London Zones

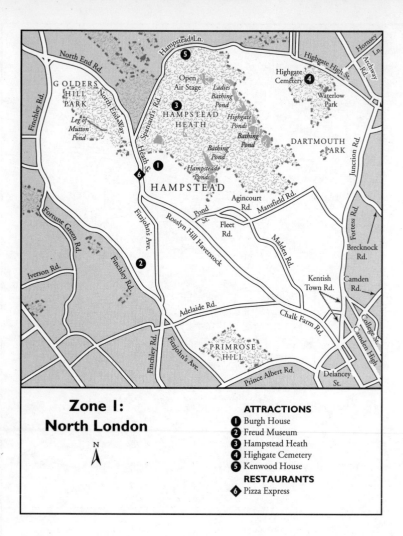

Zone 1:
North London

N

ATTRACTIONS
1. Burgh House
2. Freud Museum
3. Hampstead Heath
4. Highgate Cemetery
5. Kenwood House

RESTAURANTS
6. Pizza Express

Zone 2: Bloomsbury & Holborn

N

ACCOMMODATIONS
1. Grange White Hall Hotel
2. Hotel Russel
3. The Montague on the Gardens
4. Morgan Hotel
5. Ruskin Hotel
6. St, Margaret's Hotel

ATTRACTIONS
7. British Museum
8. Dickens House
9. Dr. Johnson's House
10. Sir John Soane's Museum

ATTRACTIONS
11. Somerset House

RESTAURANTS
12. Admiralty
   (in Somerset House)
13. Alfred
14. Bank
15. North Sea Fish
   Restaurant
16. Wagamama

ACCOMMO-
DATIONS
1 Great Eastern Hotel
2 The Rookery

ATTRACTIONS
3 Bank of England Museum
4 Bethnal Museum of Childhood
5 Guildhall
6 Millennium Bridge
7 The Monument
8 Museum of London
9 Old Bailey
10 St. Bartholomew-the-Great
11 St. Paul's Cathedral
12 Tower Bridge
13 Tower of London

RESTAURANTS
14 Arkansas Café
15 Café Spice Namaste
16 Corney & Barrow
17 1 Lombard Street
18 Moro
19 Pret à Manger
20 St. John's

NIGHT CLUBS
21 Turnmills

Zone 3:
The City
& Barbican
Zone 4:
East End

N

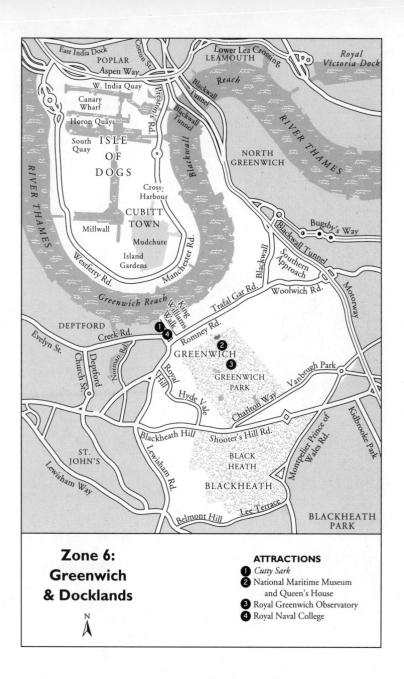

Zone 6:
Greenwich
& Docklands

N

ATTRACTIONS

1 *Cutty Sark*
2 National Maritime Museum and Queen's House
3 Royal Greenwich Observatory
4 Royal Naval College

Zone 5:
South London

ACCOMMODATIONS
1. London Marriott Hotel,
   County Hall

ATTRACTIONS
2. The British Airways London Eye
3. Clink Exhibition
4. Design Museum
5. The Globe Theatre
6. *HMS Belfast*
7. Imperial War Museum
8. Lambeth Palace
9. London Aquarium
10. London Dungeon

ATTRACTIONS
11. Millennium Bridge
12. Old Operating Theatre,
    Museum, and Herb Garrett
13. Southwark Cathedral
14. Tate Gallery of Modern Art
15. Tower Bridge

RESTAURANTS
16. Blue Print Café
17. Cantina Vinopolis
18. Livebait

NIGHTCLUBS
19. The Fridge
20. Ministry of Sound

Zone 7:
Soho & the West End

ACCOMMODATIONS
1. Covent Garden Hotel
2. The Charlotte Street Hotel
3. The Fielding Hotel
4. The Hampshire Radisson Edwardian
5. Hazlitt's
6. The Pastoria Edwardian Radisson
7. Sanderson
8. The Savoy

ATTRACTIONS
9. London Transport Museum
10. National Gallery
11. National Portrait Gallery
12. St. Martin-in-the-Fields

RESTAURANTS
13. Belgo
14. Corney & Barrow
15. fish!
16. Chez Gerard
17. Chuen Cheng Ku
18. The Ivy
19. Joe Allen
20. Richard Corrigan at Lindsay House

RESTAURANTS
21. Livebait
22. Mash
23. Mr. Kong
24. Pollo
25. Prospect Grill
26. Rules
27. Spiga
28. Stanley's
29. Teatro
30. Veeraswamy
31. Wagamama

NIGHT CLUBS
32. Brown's
33. Cafe De Paris
34. Emporium
35. Heaven
36. Hippodrome
37. Noise Bar
38. Pizza Express
39. Rock Garden
40. Ronnie Scott's
41. Venom Zoo Bar

Zone 8:
Mayfair &
Piccadilly

N

ACCOMMODATIONS
1 Brown's Hotel
2 Claridges
3 The Connaught
4 The Dorchester
5 Flemings
6 The Four Seasons
7 Grosvenor House
8 Hilton Mews
9 Holiday Inn Mayfair
10 London Hilton
11 The Metropolitan
12 Millennium Hotel Mayfair
13 The Ritz

ATTRACTIONS
14 American Embassy
15 Apsley House

ATTRACTIONS
16 Royal Academy of
    Arts

RESTAURANTS
17 Connaught
    Restaurant
18 Le Gavroche
19 Nobu
20 Rasa
21 Tamarind

NIGHTCLUBS
22 Dover Street
    Restaurant
    & Bar
23 Hanover Grand

Zone 9: Victoria & Westminster

N

ACCOMMODATIONS
1. The Cherry Court Hotel
2. Dukes Hotel
3. Goring Hotel
4. Quality Hotel
5. Thistle Hotel Victoria

ATTRACTIONS
6. Buckingham Palace
7. The Cabinet War Rooms
8. Green Park
9. Guards Museum

ATTRACTIONS
10. Houses of Parliament and Big Ben
11. Queen's Gallery
12. Royal Mews
13. St. James's Park
14. Tate Britain
15. Westminster Abbey

RESTAURANTS
16. Al Duca
17. Le Caprice
18. Matsuri
19. Quaglino's

**Zone 10:
Knightsbridge
& Belgravia**

N

ACCOMMODATIONS
1. The Basil Street Hotel
2. The Berkeley
3. The Cadogan Hotel
4. The Claverley
5. The Franklin
6. The Hyde Park Hotel
7. L'Hotel
8. The Lanesborough
9. Mandarin Oriental Hotel
10. Parkes Hotel

ATTRACTIONS
11. Hyde Park
12. The Wellington Arch

RESTAURANTS
13. Boisdale Restaurant and Bar
14. Fifth Floor
15. Pizza on the Park

Zone 11: Chelsea & South Kensington

ACCOMMODATIONS

1. Blakes
2. The Cliveden Town House
3. 11 Cadogan Gardens
4. Five Sumner Place Hotel
5. The Gainsborough
6. The Gallery
7. The Gore
8. Jury's
9. The Milestone Hotel
10. Number Sixteen
11. The Pelham
12. The Rembrandt Hotel

ATTRACTIONS

13. Carlyle's Museum
14. Natural History Museum
15. Science Museum
16. Victoria and Albert Museum

RESTAURANTS

17. Bibendum
18. Cactus Blue
19. Cambio Detercio
20. Wôdka

NIGHTCLUBS

21. Embargo
22. Crazy Larry's
23. 606

Zone 12:
West London

N

ACCOMMODATIONS
1. Riverside Hotel
ATTRACTIONS
2. Chiswick House
3. Hogarth's House
4. Kew Gardens
5. Richmond Park
NIGHTCLUBS
6. Bull's Head

Zone 13: Kensington, Holland Park, Notting Hill

ACCOMMODATIONS
1 Abbey Court
2 Comfort Inn Notting Hill
3 Halcyon Hotel
4 Miller's Residence
5 Pembridge Court Hotel
6 The Portobello Hotel
7 Thistle Hotel
  Kensington Palace

ATTRACTIONS
8 Albert Memorial
9 Holland Park
10 Kensington Palace
11 Kensington Gardens
12 Leighton House
13 Linley Sambourne House

RESTAURANTS
14 Clarke's
15 Zaika

Zone 14:
Bayswater, Marylebone, Little Venice & St. John's Wood

N

ACCOMMODATIONS
1. The Columbia Hotel
2. Dorset Square Hotel
3. Durrants
4. The Edward Lear Hotel
5. The Landmark
6. Thistle Hotel Hyde Park

ATTRACTIONS
7. Madame Tussaud's Waxworks/ London Planetarium
8. Pollock's Toy Museum
9. Sherlock Holmes Museum
10. Wallace Collection

RESTAURANTS
1. Ibla
2. L'odeon
3. Orrey
4. Pied a' Terre
5. Royal China
6. Silks & Spice

Zone 15:
Regent's Park & Camden Town

N

ATTRACTIONS
1 British Library at St. Pancras
2 London Zoo
3 Regent's Park

RESTAURANTS
4 Hearstone
5 Mango Room

NIGHTCLUBS
6 Jazz Cafe
7 Bagley's

London Parks

N

1. Green Park
2. Hampstead Heath
3. Highgate Cemetery
4. Holland Park
5. Hyde Park
6. Kensington Gardens
7. Kew Gardens
8. Regent's Park
9. Richmond Park
10. St. James's Park

Introduction

London Calling

Let's just get it out of the way, shall we? Dr. Samuel Johnson's quote about his beloved city is as famous as Big Ben: "When a man is tired of London, he is tired of Life, for there is in London all that Life can afford." Only in London could the words of an eighteenth-century writer be put to such persistent, modern public-relations use; it is exactly this easy—some might say surreal—conversation between past and present that makes London so appealing to its visitors and residents alike.

London is a historical free-for-all where, against the gorgeous Georgian facade of the Royal Academy, you'll find a series of seriously modern sculptures; where horse-drawn carriages and soldiers on horseback in full regalia barely merit a passing glance from Londoners in their cars; where the Liberty department store on the eighteenth-century Nash-designed Regent Street is housed in a Tudor building straight out of a fairy tale. This wonderful palimpsest of centuries—the layering of post–World War II London over Edwardian elegance, on top of Victorian glory, over eighteenth-century exuberance, under which the medieval and even the Roman city can be appreciated—is, especially to the American eye, a miracle of conservation and civic pride. But if London was only the sum of its past, it might not be the contemporary scene of a constantly evolving culture of theater, arts, and music, not to mention the birthplace of cutting-edge clothing designers, rock and rollers, and night-clubbers.

In 1978, Bette Midler said, "When it's three o'clock in New York, it's still 1938 in London." Today, this remark might be received with some puzzlement, except perhaps by those who expect stores to be open on Sunday and remain open past six and who believe that the London Underground trains (the subway system in London we commonly refer to as the tube or, more formally, the underground) ought to run after midnight. Despite its high prices, London attracts over 25 million visitors a year, swelling its permanent population of 7 million. This is not to say it's a nirvana for visitors—London is no quaint theme park. This city takes a bit of work, and visitors may struggle to reconcile the picture of London carried in their minds against the sometimes dirty, indifferent, and confusing modern reality of the place. But the payoff for a little footwork is huge.

London can be many cities to many people. Contrast Dr. Johnson's hymns of worship ("The happiness of London is not to be conceived but by those who have been in it") with Percy Bysshe Shelley's assessment of early nineteenth-century London: "Hell is a city much like London—a populous and smoky city." People may have a wide range of feelings about London, but indifference is usually not one of them. It's rare for an English speaker to come here without a mental trunk full of preconceptions. Those of us of a certain age had an intimate acquaintance with the bells of St. Clements, London Bridge, and the Drury Lane home of the muffin man before we could even read. When we could read, we absorbed the London of Charles Dickens, who captured the nineteenth-century city in all its degradation and beauty, who spent hours each night exploring his city on foot, and who left his unforgettable impressions on the pages of his novels and in the psyches of his readers. London has appeared as a character in so much English literature and so many films that it is a place we carry in our collective consciousness like a dream.

Waking up to London is another story. To arrive here for the first time is to suddenly confront the fantasy with the fact. The most outstanding fact about London is its sprawling geography—there is nothing so neat as a "downtown" of London. It isn't so much one big city as a series of interconnected villages on a human-size scale, liberally dotted with breathing spaces of greenery. London can take a lifetime to explore fully, and a tourist with only a week to cover the major sights will find it impossible to take it all in. The best approach to London is to decide where your interests lie; you will soon discover that there are few interests known to humanity that London cannot entertain.

We want you to make the best of this best-of-all-possible cities. We want you to not waste one minute getting lost on the tube or taking a taxi if walking would be quicker. We don't want you to get such a bad case of museum legs that you can't make it to the theater that night, and we definitely don't want you to spend your hard-earned money buying anything that's cheaper back home. London is a great place for visitors—tourism is its second largest industry—and we love the fact that we North Americans can, for the most part, communicate with the locals without needing a course from Berlitz. We hope to identify and address any difficulties you might have in visiting London, so that you can pursue whatever course of entertainment you desire, efficiently and happily. And there's so much to be done. . . .

London has the best museums in the world, the famous as well as some lesser-known ones. There are miles of parks, offering some of the most beautiful natural scenery to be found in any metropolis. Part of London's charm lies in the sudden deluges from leaden skies that will just as quickly be sliced open with swords of sunlight. There are also the people of London, who speak in a rich concoction of accents, in over 200 languages, and represent multiple classes, nationalities, and political views. No matter what moves you—theater, architecture, sports, antiques, markets, designer clothing, contemporary art and old masters, heart-stopping cathedrals, Internet cafes, palaces, poetry readings, elegant casinos, lunatic nightclubs, pubs, bungee jumping, horticulture, witchcraft, fencing, pigeons, boating—there truly is, as the good doctor pointed out almost three centuries ago, "in London all that Life can afford."

About This Guide

Why Unofficial?

Most London travel guides follow the usual tracks of the typical tourist, automatically sending everyone to the well-known sights without offering any information about how to do this painlessly; recommending restaurants and hotels indiscriminately; and failing to recognize the limits of human endurance in sight-seeing. This guide is different: we understand that in a huge city like London it is essential for one to discriminate, make plans, whittle the town down to size, and be just a little bit flexible when hours-long lines appear out of nowhere or when the clouds burst and you've forgotten your umbrella.

We'll tell you what we think of certain tourist traps, what the real story is on the famous restaurants and hotels, what the options are if you want to stay off the beaten track, or how to spend a little less money on one thing so you can spend more on another. We'll complain about rip-offs, we'll advise you on bargains, and we'll steer you out of the madness of the crowds for a break now and then. We also hope to give you the kind of information that will make you love London all the more—some of the endearing eccentricities that make you realize you're definitely not in Kansas anymore.

London is such a complex and sprawling city, so full of fantastic anecdote and incident, that it's hard to edit out the trivia—it's all great stuff, and the more tales you hear, the more you want to know. London is all about history—every building and monument, every alley and lane has a story that has seeped through the mists of time and simply must be passed on.

The longer you stay here, the larger London becomes in some ways. Each door that opens reveals ten windows through which to gaze. In the old days a visit to London was a rite of passage for the upper classes of North America, and they used to spend six months at it. You probably haven't got that luxury (unless you're here as an exchange student), so you have to be very efficient and organized if you want to make the most of your time. The majority of overseas visitors stay only for about five to ten days. How much can you squeeze into that time? How much do you want to see? What are your priorities, and how can they best be served? Like any worthwhile undertaking, some preparation and strategy is needed to make London reveal its charms to you. We have done the footwork: We've checked out the hotels to find the best deals and the most interesting buildings; Richard Erlich, who has been reviewing the restaurants for years, will give you the benefit of his experience; and we've got the low-down on the nightlife from those who have crawled through their fair share of clubs. If a museum is dull, or there's a two-hour wait for an attraction that just isn't worth it, we'll tell you why—and we hope in the process to make your visit more fun, efficient, and economical.

We've tried in this book to anticipate the special needs of older people, families with young children, families with teenagers, solo travelers, people with physical challenges, and those who have a particular passion for literature, sport, architecture, shopping, painting, antiques, or whatever.

London has hundreds of attractions, and we've tried to sort them based upon which are first rate, which are intended for those with special interests, and which are hype jobs. Obviously, even if you visit London dozens of times, you won't be able to see all that we describe to you, and by then you'll have discovered some of your own favorite haunts. But we want you to always have the options of exploring more and more of this endlessly interesting city, and we want to give you the best tips for doing so. We take things easy, the way we think you'll want to, but we don't forgive exploitation or stupidity. If it isn't fun, if it isn't informative, if it isn't a reasonable deal, if there's a better alternative, we want you to know. We hope to keep the quality of your visit high and the irritation quotient low.

We've covered attractions in these various ways because we want to make sure you can pick out the ones you'd enjoy most. For those of you who don't wish to do it all yourselves, we've listed a number of good commercial and customized tours on pages 156–164 in Part Six, "Sight-Seeing and Tours."

Even keeping in mind that your time will be filled, we have included a list of opportunities for exercise. Travel can be pretty hard on the body—airplane stiffness, walking around galleries and streets—and it's wise to get some endorphins going at some point in your visit. Also, London has so many great restaurants and opportunities to try new foods that you may well need a little calorie-corrective run or swim, unless you want to take home more than photos and souvenirs (try a few days of cream teas and you'll see what we mean).

Please do remember that prices and admission hours change constantly; we have listed the most up-to-date information we can get, but it never hurts to double-check times in particular (if prices of attractions change, it is generally not by much). Remember, this is one of the busiest tourist towns in the world, so make your reservations early and reconfirm at least once.

About Unofficial Guides

Readers care about authors' opinions. The authors, after all, are supposed to know what they are talking about. This, coupled with the fact that the traveler wants quick answers (as opposed to endless alternatives), dictates that travel authors should be explicit, prescriptive, and above all, direct. The authors of the *Unofficial Guide* try to do just that. We spell out alternatives and recommend specific courses of action. We simplify complicated destinations and attractions to allow the traveler to feel in control in the most unfamiliar environments. Our objective is not to give the most information or all the information, but the most accessible, useful information. Of course, in a city like London, there are many hotels, restaurants, and attractions that are so closely woven into the fabric of the city that, to omit them from our guide because we can't recommend them, would be a disservice to our readers. We have included all the famous haunts, giving our opinion and experience of them, in the hopes that you will approach (or avoid) these institutions armed with the necessary intelligence.

An *Unofficial Guide* is a critical reference work; we focus on a travel destination that appears to be especially complex. Our authors and researchers are completely independent from the attractions, restaurants, and hotels we describe. The *Unofficial Guide to London* is designed for individuals and families traveling for fun as well as for business, and it will be especially helpful to those hopping "across the pond" for the first time. The guide is directed at value-conscious, consumer-oriented adults who seek a cost-effective but not Spartan travel style.

SPECIAL FEATURES

Vital information about traveling abroad.

Friendly introductions to London's "villages."

Listings that are keyed to your interests, so you can pick and choose.

Advice to sightseers on how to avoid the worst crowds; advice to business travelers on how to avoid traffic and excessive costs.

Recommendations for lesser-known sights that are off the well-beaten tourist path but no less worthwhile.

A zone system and maps to make it easy to find places you want to go and to avoid other places.

A hotel section that helps you narrow down your choices quickly, according to your needs and preferences.

A table of contents and detailed index to help you find things fast.

WHAT YOU WON'T GET

Long, useless lists where everything looks the same.

Information that gets you to your destination at the worst possible time.

Information without advice on how to use it.

How This Guide Was Researched and Written

In preparing this work, we took nothing for granted. Each hotel, restaurant, shop, and attraction was visited by trained observers who conducted detailed evaluations and rated each according to formal criteria. Team members conducted interviews with tourists of all ages to determine what they enjoyed most and least during their London visit.

Though our observers are independent and impartial, they are otherwise "ordinary" travelers. Like you, they visited London as tourists or business travelers, noting their satisfaction or dissatisfaction.

The primary difference between the average tourist and the trained evaluator is the evaluator's skills in organization, preparation, and observation. A trained evaluator is responsible for more than just observing and cataloging. Observer teams use detailed checklists to analyze hotel rooms, restaurants, nightclubs, and attractions. Finally, evaluator ratings and observations are integrated with tourist reactions and the opinions of patrons for a comprehensive quality profile of each feature and service.

In compiling this guide, we recognize that a tourist's age, background, and interests will strongly influence his or her taste in London's wide array of attractions and will account for a preference for one sight or museum over another. Our sole objective is to provide the reader with sufficient description, critical evaluation, and pertinent data to make knowledgeable decisions according to individual tastes.

Letters, Comments, and Questions from Readers

We expect to learn from our mistakes, as well as from the input of our readers, and to improve with each new book and edition. Many of those who use the *Unofficial Guides* write to us asking questions, making comments, or sharing their own discoveries and lessons learned in London. We appreciate all such input, both positive and critical, and encourage our readers to continue writing. Readers' comments and observations will be frequently incorporated in revised editions of the *Unofficial Guide* and will contribute immeasurably to its improvement.

How to Write the Author

Lesley Logan
The Unofficial Guide to London
P.O. Box 43673
Birmingham, AL 35243

When you write, be sure to put your return address on your letter as well as on the envelope—sometimes envelopes and letters get separated. Remember, our work takes us out of the office for long periods of time, so forgive us if our response is delayed.

How Information Is Organized: By Subject and by Geographic Zones

To give you fast access to information about the best of London, we've organized material in several formats.

Hotels

There are many hotels in London that are small, quirky, and unique. Even the world-class, well-known, and very expensive hotels can vary dramatically in room size and amenities, and a hotel priced somewhere in the middle of the price range can have under one charming roof and at a similar price both closet-size attic rooms and magnificent salons with French windows. We have tried to stick to the hotels that are more reliable and consistent in their accommodations, and we have attempted to summarize this somewhat unwieldy and problematic subject in ratings and rankings that allow you to quickly focus your decision-making process. We concentrate on the specific variables that differentiate one hotel from another: location, size, room quality, services, amenities, and cost.

Entertainment and Nightlife

Visitors frequently try several different clubs or nightspots during their stay in London. Since clubs, like restaurants, are usually selected rather spontaneously after arriving, we believe that detailed descriptions are warranted. The best nightspots in London are profiled in Part Nine, "Entertainment and Nightlife." Be warned, though, that the popularity and character of clubs can change, even disappear overnight. We've tried to select places that have withstood the tests of time and fluctuations of fashion.

Restaurants

We provide plenty of detail when it comes to restaurants. You will probably eat a dozen or more restaurant meals during your stay, and not even you can predict what you might be in the mood for on Saturday night. You can browse through our detailed profiles of the best restaurants in London before dining out.

Once you've decided where you're going, getting there becomes the issue. To help you do that, we have divided London into geographic zones, which we briefly describe below to give you an idea of what they're about. These zones are unrelated to and should not be confused with the zones laid out by the London's public transportation system for purposes of assigning travelling cost—the London Transport zones 1 and 2 are probably the ones you will be travelling in, and they are the same price and the minimum price of a bus or tube ticket.

The post codes that appear at the end of an address are for the purpose of delivering mail and are known to the citizens as shorthand for a certain area. Everyone knows that SW1 is royal borough of Westminster and includes the neighborhoods of Victoria, Pimlico, and parts of Knightsbridge and Belgravia. Chelsea and Kensington are in the SW3 and SW7 codes. Neighborhoods to the north are known by their "N" prefix followed by a number. They represent compass directions (N, S, W, E) that radiate generally from central London (C), with the lowest numbers being in the center of town, roughly to the east of Hyde Park. The higher the number, the farther from the center you will be.

But, to get back to the zones as determined by this guide: we have made what seemed to us to be natural divisions between areas or neighborhoods, and have numbered them to make it easier for you to get a handle on the far-flung environs of London. These divisions are germane only to this book, and again, have nothing to do with the London Transport zones.

All profiles of hotels, restaurants, attractions, and nightspots include zone numbers. If you are staying in Knightsbridge, for example, and are interested in a place to eat within walking distance, look at the profiles for restaurants in zone 10.

Zone 1: North London—Hampstead, Highgate

This is an almost suburban area, which can seem to be in the heart of the country when you're standing in Hampstead Heath looking out at a castle-like mansion on a hill, surrounded by old trees and wild grass. Hampstead Heath is approximately 800 acres of natural beauty, with a bucolic bounty not often found within miles of a large city. Hampstead has always been a salubrious place: during the Black Death of the early 1200s and again during the Great Plague of 1665–66, people fled to Hampstead. By the eighteenth century, Hampstead had become a fashionable resort for Londoners seeking fresh air and healthy spring water. The nineteenth century saw an influx of artists, writers, and intellectuals, a community still found here. There are views from Highgate and Hampstead across the whole of London which, along with the charm of the high street, make this a satisfying destination for the discerning tourist. Kenwood House is a stately home on the heath that is well worth a visit.

Zone 2: Bloomsbury and Holborn

Bloomsbury is dominated by the British Museum and the University of London, as well as by many hospitals and institutes of learning. In Holborn, one finds many traces of old London: Dickens's House, Coram's Fields, Dr. Johnson's House, the Silver Vaults, and more. There are a number of reasonably priced lodgings here, within walking distance of the West End—a good thing for the club crawlers, as many buses and all trains stop running shortly after midnight. There's also a lot of literary history here: the famous Bloomsbury Group of the early 1900s—a tightly related gang of writers and artists that included Virginia Woolf and Lytton Strachey—will always be associated with this area, and this is reflected in the content of numerous blue plaques on various buildings.

Zone 3: The City, Clerkenwell, and Barbican

This is the oldest part of London, where you will find the magnificent St. Paul's Cathedral, the occasional whispers of a medieval past, and some remnants of the town the occupying ancient Romans called Londinium—things that managed to survive the devastating Great Fire of 1666 and the Blitz of World War II. This is also where most of the financial business of London is conducted. The area pretty much dies at night and on weekends, but during the day you'll find many good restaurants here. The Bank of England Museum and the Lloyd's of London building by Richard Rogers are two other attractions. There are some amusing architectural visions here, such as the grasshopper on the top of the Stock Exchange. The old markets—Smithfield's, Billingsgate, and Leadenhall—are fun to check out.

Zone 4: East End—Spitalfields, White Chapel, Bethnal Green

Besides the Tower of London, zone 4 offers markets, Victorian architecture, art galleries and churches, and cockney English. The once-thriving Jewish center of London used to be here, and you can still go to the schwitzes, the old-style men's steam baths, or get a great piece of smoked fish and latkes from the oldest Jewish deli in London. The East End is, like so much of this crushingly expensive city, experiencing a bit of gentrification, as the prices of real estate in Central London push people ever further afield. New luxury apartments, artsy nightspots, galleries, and even the Prince of Wales's School of Architecture now share the streets where Jack the Ripper stalked his prey and Sweeny Todd made mincemeat of his customers. Here, too, you can get boats to Greenwich, see some of the old Roman wall around London, and visit Tower Bridge.

Zone 5: South London: South Bank, Lambeth, Brixton

Zone 5 encompasses the great renaissance of the South Bank—the London Aquarium, the Marriott Hotel, the National Theatre, the Hayward Gallery, the magnificent new British Airways London Eye—as well as the ancient palace of Lambeth, where the archbishop of Canterbury lives; Waterloo Station, from which the Eurostar leaves; and the Old Vic Theatre. There's great nightlife in Brixton, with lots of reggae venues, thanks to its large Caribbean contingent. From the South Bank you get the very best views of the halls of Westminster and Big Ben, and in the summer along the promenade you will find outdoor cafes where you can lounge and watch the river run.

Zone 6: Greenwich and Docklands

Greenwich, where the time of the day is calculated as Greenwich Mean Time, has a lot for the scientifically as well as historically inclined visitor. There is the Old Royal Observatory, the National Maritime Museum, the Royal Naval College, Indigo Jones Queen's House, and two old tea clippers. One of every visitor's favorite photo ops in Greenwich is the spot from which the world's longitude, known as the Prime Meridien, is measured. The great thing about Greenwich is that all its attractions are within walking distance of each other, including the street market that's open on the weekend. You could easily spend a full day seeing Greenwich. The Docklands are less appealing, featuring mainly Canary Wharf, a high-rise office complex, and the currently empty shell of the Millennium Dome.

Zone 7: Soho and the West End

This is where the nightlife and the theater district are located. Charing Cross bookshops, St. Martin-in-the-Fields, Trafalgar Square, rowdy Leicester Square, Chinatown, the National Gallery, and pubs, pubs, pubs are in this zone. Carnaby Street and Neal's Yard are the alternative lifestyle, clothing, and health-therapies areas, and Covent Garden has absolutely everything for everybody. There's also the London Transport Museum, the Trocadero, the Rock Circus, and the Theatre Museum. You might want to stay in a hotel around here, but it can get loud at night, with drunks roaring up and down side streets and tourists as far as the eye can see. Of course, that may be part of the appeal.

Zone 8: Mayfair and Piccadilly

This is a very high-class area, in which you can find the most expensive shops in the world—from the designers on New and Old Bond Streets, to the bespoke trade in St. James, to the White House linen shop, where you can spend thousands on bedclothes. There is every imaginable hotel here, except for inexpensive ones—the Atheneum, Park Lane, Ritz, Brown's, Dorchester, Metropolitan, Claridges . . . the list is impressive. Hatchard's, the oldest bookstore in London, is on Piccadilly, as are Fortnum and Mason's, the Burlington Arcade, and the wonderful Royal Academy, whose exhibits are always top notch. Here is Shepherds' Market, which in the 1600s was the site of the riotous saturnalia known as the May Fair and a place for the entertainers of the day—jugglers, fire eaters, boxers, prostitutes—to parade their talents. Today, Shepherds' Market is a mere shadow of its former self, but interesting nonetheless.

Zone 9: Victoria and Westminster

This zone encompasses the halls of government and power in London: Whitehall, Westminster Abbey, Parliament, and Buckingham Palace. There are plenty of hotels to go along with the preponderance of tourist attractions. Due to the heavy concentration of World War II bombing in this area, there are patches of ugliness here and there where rebuilding went on without much attention to architectural coherence. Much of Westminster simply closes down on the weekend—not the attractions but the eateries, which cater mainly to the business crowd. Pimlico, to the south, has lots of cheap hotels and bedsits, but may not be the greatest place to be late at night. This zone runs from the seedy to the sublime. There is the most magnificent vista here—the fairy-tale view from Buckingham Palace across St. James's Park toward Westminster Abbey will have you reaching for your camera.

Zone 10: Knightsbridge and Belgravia

This zone is the stronghold of the very wealthy—expatriate entrepreneurs, British aristocrats, movie stars, rock-and-roll gods, and sultans coexist peacefully in the splendor of Georgian townhouses or in deceptively simple mews houses within walking distance of Hyde Park, Harrods, and Harvey Nichols. Knightsbridge is mainly about shopping: Sloane Street, Walton Street, and Beauchamp Place have all the trendiest designer shops; the auction house Bonhams is in Knightsbridge Village, as is an assortment of secondhand designer-clothes shops. Knightsbridge is famous for having the most consonants in a row in any English word. Belgravia has less to talk about, as it is an enclave of ambassadors and billionaires, with enormous attached mansions, some of which are five houses strung together as one, as in the humble home of the sultan of Brunei. The zone is a very convenient to stay in, if you can afford it. You can walk to Oxford Street; the Victoria and Albert Museum; the Natural History Museum; Hyde, Green, and St. James's Parks; and Piccadilly. Also, from Hyde Park Corner there are buses that go everywhere.

Zone 11: Chelsea and South Kensington

South Kensington is known as Albertopolis and Museumland because of the many cultural institutions Prince Albert founded here, including the Victoria & Albert and the Natural History Museums, Royal Albert Hall, the Royal Art College, Imperial College, and numerous other learned societies. You can now see the Albert Memorial in all its restored glory; its gold magnificence was covered in black for close to a century. South Kensington is also known as Little France, thanks to the Lycee Français and the Institute Français in the middle of town. There are lots of great patisseries, a few good restaurants, and plenty of fine hotels. Chelsea is to the south and is home to the famous King's Road—the once-swinging home to 1960s hipsters, 1970s punks, and later to 1980s yuppies and 1990s just-plain-rich folk. In the neighborhoods off King's Road, there are a multitude of blue plaques identifying the many writers and artists who once called Chelsea home: Oscar Wilde, George Eliot, Thomas Carlyle, Dante Gabriel Rossetti, James Whistler . . . the list goes on. Chelsea is very beautiful and a very smart area in which to live—and the property prices reflect this.

Zone 12: West London—Hammersmith, Chiswick, Richmond, Kew

These are primarily residential areas outside of central London, with only a couple of tourist attractions. Chiswick has Hogarth's House, Chiswick House, and a few good restaurants; Richmond has the huge Park and Wimbledon Common; Hammersmith has its beautiful old bridge that one can walk across, a theater, Olympia Arena, some old pubs, and new strip clubs. Kew is, of course, the home of the gorgeous and world-famous Kew Gardens, and nearby is historic Syon House on whose grounds will be found the London Butterfly House and an aquatic feature. Hampton Court, the great Tudor palace on the Thames, is in this zone too.

Zone 13: Kensington, Holland Park, Notting Hill

As a result of King William and Queen Mary moving their royal residence to the then far-flung country village of Kensington in 1689, lots of grand houses were built in this area. As rich attracts rich, the neighborhoods to the west and north, especially in Holland Park, developed into very exclusive places to live. Kensington High Street is a big bustling shopping street, with a huge range of clothing for young and old alike, and Kensington

Church Street is lined with interesting, although expensive, antique shops. Notting Hill used to be a big Jamaican enclave, but was soon attracting the idle trust-fund kids who were dubbed "trustafarians." It is a very happening place as its ever-increasing rents attest. This is where the famous Portobello Market is, which is worth a look on Saturday as long as you're not prone to agoraphobia. Attractions: Kensington Palace and Gardens, Leighton House, Holland Park, and the Kensington Church Street antiques-store mecca.

Zone 14: Bayswater, Marylebone, Little Venice, St. John's Wood

At the north border of Hyde Park, Bayswater and Marylebone have an enormous Arab population and a lot of great Middle Eastern restaurants. Here you'll find the Wallace Collection, Whiteley's Shopping Mall, Queensway Skating Rink and Bowling Alley, Regent's Canal Waterbus, Sherlock Holmes Museum, Madame Tussaud's, and two horseback-riding stables that take customers for trots around Hyde Park. There are tons of cheap hotels here, some downright dismal, some of relatively good value. Paddington Station is the terminus for the train from Heathrow, as well as for trains that serve the West Country and South Wales. There's a bit of a sleaze factor, with hooker hotels in the vicinity. Farther north is Little Venice, which has a canal running through it with boats that can be taken on Regent's Canal and the Grand Union Canal. St. John's Wood is the home of the American School, where a lot of the expats send their kids. The main attraction is the Abbey Road zebra crossing, where tourists annoy the locals by taking pictures of themselves re-creating the Beatles' famous album cover.

Zone 15: Regent's Park and Camden Town

Regent's Park houses the London Zoo, the London Central Mosque, Regent's Open Air Theatre, and affords some of the most beautiful eighteenth-century vistas in London. Designed in concert with King George IV, who was regent at the time, this area is the crowning achievement of architect John Nash. Camden Town, to the northwest, is a bustling market town, and rivals Portobello Road for good buys and cool stuff. There's a great antiques market and lots of hip clothing and knickknacks, plus plenty of body piercing and tattoos on display. It's a must-go for teenagers. Primrose Hill is another sylvan glade in this zone and is one of the best places to watch the Guy Fawkes' Day fireworks.

Part One

An Overview of London

London offers something for every mood, desire, and interest, and there are so many ways to appreciate it. Music, sports, architecture, theater, fashion, antiques, gardens, nightlife . . . London is an amazing place today, but it takes on even more interesting dimensions when you know what it was yesterday. A bit of the history of this town on the Thames is just as useful for the discerning visitor as a street map. So, here we go.

The Long Life of an Ancient City

London's history, perhaps because the city is situated on the banks of a wide river cutting through a large island, is initially one of invasion and conquest. Because of England's system of monarchy, her later history is one of bloody factionalism and revolving persecutions. As the empire began to take shape, the blood was shed on foreign soil, because the idea of England's sovereignty was propped up by the exploitation of foreign continents and by the misery of the impoverished workers in London. But throughout all of it, the history of the city of London has been the history of commerce: this port city has beckoned to artisans and sailors, farmers, prostitutes, and wheelers and dealers of all shades of corruption for two millennia. London shows no signs of flagging in its appeal as we head into the third millenium.

Some of the highlights from London's past can be found in the Museum of London, where you can wander from the prehistoric banks of the Thames all the way through to the Millennium Dome, seeing the everyday sights of London's long life that you won't find anywhere else, such as the underground heating system of Roman Londinium or an Anderson Shelter from the days of the Blitz. The museum's overall style is nostalgic and cheerful, although you do get to look into a cell of Newgate Gaol. It's a great experience for the young and the old, the well-informed and the merely curious.

When Rome Ruled Londinium

Julius Caesar's famous remark about how Britons were simply not good slave material was sour grapes: in 55 and 56 B.C., he tried to subdue England twice and failed both times. In A.D. 43, the Romans again sent an army to conquer the island. This time they built a bridge over the Thames at the narrowest crossing, near the present London Bridge. Soon, this Roman fort called Londinium grew into a thriving port of commerce, as luxury goods from all over the Roman Empire arrived and were exchanged for corn, iron, and—Julius Caesar notwithstanding—slaves. Roman historian Tacitus wrote that Londinium was "famed for commerce and crowded with merchants," a description that would remain accurate for the next 2,000 years (and will continue to do so, one assumes). Roadways, the most ubiquitous and long-lasting feature of Roman rule, soon headed in every direction from this trading post and were well traveled by Romans and Britons in search of adventure and wealth. After a period of Pax Romana (peace imposed by ancient Rome on its dominions), the Roman rule became increasingly unbearable to the local tribes. Queen Boudicca of the Iceni tribe led a violent revolt, invading Londinium, massacring everyone in sight, and burning the camp to the ground. The revolution was short lived, however; Londinium was rebuilt with a huge wall around it, encompassing what is presently the City and Barbican area. A piece of the wall is preserved near the Museum of London.

In 410, the sun was setting on the Roman empire and the troops were withdrawn, leaving the sprouts of the newly adopted Christian faith behind. London then went into a decline; when new invaders arrived, they superstitiously stayed away from the Roman ruins, which were soon buried, not to be rediscovered until after the Blitz of World War II.

The Saxon's Lundenwic

After the Saxons came over the North Sea in about 450 to settle in southeast England, London slowly began its rise from the Roman ashes to again become a trading post, called Lundenwic. King Ethlebert, after presiding over a pagan society, became a Christian convert, and the first cathedral of St. Paul was built. The Saxon kings spent most of the next five centuries fighting Viking invaders and fortifying their kingdom, whose capital was at Winchester. London has King Alfred to thank for rebuilding it after Danish invaders left it in ruins, as well as for lighting a few other candles in those dark ages. The tenth century saw a new prosperity as neighborhoods and parishes were formed on the banks of the Thames River. In the eleventh century, the Danes finally won the day, and England was forced to accept the Danish King Canute as its leader. He put London on the map as the capital of the kingdom, and by 1042, when Edward the Confessor took the scepter, London was poised on the brink of a great architectural leap forward. Westminster Abbey and the Palace at Westminster gave the raucous commercial port a dignity that was soon complemented by the construction of the White Tower, the tallest building at the Tower of London.

William the Conqueror

In 1066, at the Battle of Hastings, a Norman army led by William conquered the Saxon armies, and with that victory spelled a new dawn for London. William decided to have his coronation in Westminster Abbey, a tradition since that time. He saw that London was perfectly placed to be a rich capital, and located the impressive stronghold of the White Tower on the Thames to show the inhabitants of this headstrong city just who was in charge. However, he was also a smart politician and granted freedoms to the Saxon-dominated church and the local governors that ensured a pleasant and profitable back-scratching for all concerned. London grew rich under the watchful eye of the monarchs, who knew the key to their power lay in the wealth and acquiescence of London's merchants and churchmen. In 1180, William Fitzstephen, in the preface to his *Life of Thomas à Becket*, sang high praises of London: "It is blessed by a wholesome climate . . . in the strength of its fortifications, in the nature of its site, the repute of its citizens, the honour of its matrons; happy in its sports, prolific in noble men. . . . I can think of no other city with customs more admirable. . . . The only plagues of London are the immoderate drinking of fools and the frequency of fires." True, but he forgot that other plague of London: the plague.

A Vibrant Medieval Port

Medieval London was a crazy conglomeration of streets, alleys, markets, outdoor brothels, bear-baiting pits, pubs, and theaters. The vibrancy of the streets was matched in energy by the jostling for power among the court, the burgesses, and the church. In 1215, the Magna Carta, which attempted to limit the excesses and power of the king and establish personal rights and political freedom for the nobility, was signed by King John, who was forced to do so by rebellious barons and the newly created lord mayor of London. Soon Parliament and the House of Commons were created, and England became a place of liberty and justice for at least a few more than before. Though the Magna Carta was designed to free the aristocracy from the despotism of a monarch, it contained the fateful word *freemen* and so signaled at least theoretical rights for the common people.

The port was thriving, with houses and warehouses lining the river banks, and the power of the guilds and merchants grew apace. The position of London as a window on the world, crowded with thousands of people living in appalling sanitary conditions, led to the first outbreak of plague. The Black Death of 1348 came across from the European continent, which was reeling from the disease. Nearly half of London's population succumbed to the plague, which was carried by rats that multiplied in the filthy streets and fetid sewers. The general unrest and loss of labor led to the ill-advised poll tax imposed in 1381 by a financially strapped court—a shilling a person, regardless of income or situation. The Peasant's Revolt, led by Jack Straw and Wat Tyler, put every future monarch on notice that Londoners had a breaking point that should be avoided. After a riotous spree of looting, burning, and murder, the rebels were overcome, and order was restored by a young King Richard II, but the point was taken—and the poll tax was quietly dropped.

A new intellectual age dawned around this time. In the 1390s, Geoffrey Chaucer wrote *The Canterbury Tales,* and in 1476 William Caxton set up his printing press at Westminster. The numerous and wealthy monasteries became centers for teaching and learning, and literacy began creeping into the middle and upper classes, setting the scene for the Renaissance culture of the Tudor era.

Tudor London

The War of the Roses between the fractious factions of the House of Plantagenet—York and Lancaster—provided William Shakespeare with a superabundance of material for his tragedies.

The bloody dynastic feud for the throne had relatively little effect on the daily lives of Londoners scrambling for a living, but when Richard III allegedly smothered the two young princes, the rightful heirs to the throne, in the Tower of London, the citizenry grew restless; few regretted the end of Richard's reign. Next came the Tudor dynasty, whose heirs were at least as ruthless when it came to insulting relatives as any of the previous Plantagenets had been.

Henry VIII married his brother's widow, Catherine of Aragon, to keep the peace with Spain. After 20 years of marriage and one daughter, Mary, Henry fell in love with Anne Boleyn and decided he had to marry again in order to have a male heir. He cast off his wife, alienating the Catholic Church in Rome, which refused to grant him an annulment. Not one to take no for an answer, and a man who willingly threw out baby *and* bath with the bathwater, Henry reformed the church in England, styling himself as its supreme ruler. Then he went on a serial marital spree that left in its wake a total of six wives; as the nursery rhyme goes, "two beheaded, two divorced, one died, and one survived." The most radical expression of this religious overhaul was in the dissolution of the monasteries, in which Henry took for the Crown all the property of the Catholic cathedrals, churches, priories, convents, and monasteries in England. He destroyed huge numbers of beautiful gothic and medieval buildings, redistributing the land among the new, loyal-to-Henry aristocracy, creating new streets, houses, and courtyards where there had once been wealthy Catholic establishments. Resistant nuns and clergy were hung, drawn, and quartered; the army of crippled, diseased, and homeless who had been supported by the charity of the churches were thrown upon their own resources, and the streets of London resounded with the cries of their misery.

After Henry VIII died, syphilitic and obese, the six-year reign of the child-king Edward didn't amount to much more than a vicious power struggle among his courtiers and further religious persecutions. When Bloody Mary, Henry's first daughter, became queen a bit after Edward's early death, she put her half-sister, Elizabeth, in the Tower of London, and it was the turn of the Protestants to have their property seized and be hung or burnt alive. The daily spectacle of burning heretics at the marketplace of Smithfields finally disgusted even the Londoners accustomed to gruesome public punishments. Another turn of the dynasty, Elizabeth returned England to its Protestant base, forestalling any Catholic overthrow by having her cousin, Mary Queen of Scots, executed at the Tower. (The Tower of London is probably as haunted a place as you can find in ghost-ridden London. Heads rolled like billiard balls there, innocent souls were racked and tortured regularly, and their tormented specters are well known to the people who remain there past nightfall, such as the governor of the Tower and his family and others who work and live on the property.)

The Elizabethan Flowering of London

What were the good citizens of London doing while all the royal kin-killing kerfuffle and musical thrones were being played out? Well, while the aristocrats built over-the-top estates from the remains of the monasteries, and Hyde Park became a happy hunting ground for King Henry, the ordinary Londoner was going about the usual: earning and eating, fornicating and frolicking, marrying and burying. In 1586, in London arrived William Shakespeare, joining Ben Jonson, Christopher Marlowe, John Donne, and others of the day's glitterati in the boom years of English letters, helping record the uproar that was London. The city now had a population of 200,000 people, up from 50,000 in the 1300s, and more arrived every day. The great era of exploration was under way as the English plied the oceans in search of riches, returning with sugar, spice, coffee, and tobacco. Sir Thomas Gresham started the Royal Exchange from its humble beginnings as a coffee house and made London the world's most important financial center, a position it maintained into the early twentieth century.

Although Queen Elizabeth could be as dangerous a friend (and cousin) as she was a foe, she was devoted to the welfare of her kingdom and understood that her greatest power lay in the love her subjects had for her—she had an instinctive gift for public relations. Perhaps the greatest gift she gave the nation was her much vaunted virginity: by not marrying a foreign prince, she kept England solidly English for 45 prosperous years. By the end of her long reign, the memories of those ugly battles of succession had faded.

Roundheads and Restoration

The Gunpowder Plot—in which a group of Catholic conspirators, including Guy Fawkes, were thwarted in their plan to blow up King James, his ministers, and Parliament at the Palace of Westminster—rather appropriately opened London's apocalyptic seventeenth century. King James died in 1625, leaving on the throne a somewhat backwards son, Charles I.

Although at this time London was the wealthiest city in the world, Charles I simply could not let well enough alone. Insisting on the divine right of kings, a philosophy that was anathema to the Parliament and businessmen of London, he started a civil war. The monarchist Cavaliers were defeated by the Puritan Roundheads, and Charles I was beheaded outside his beloved Banqueting Hall, designed by Inigo Jones. (The king's last walk is still commemorated on the last Sunday in January.) Although the majority of London had been on the side of the Commonwealth, 18 years of dour Puritan reign under Oliver Cromwell's rule, during which all fun was canceled, left the city gasping for a breath of fresh air. The diarist John Evelyn wrote at Cromwell's death that "it was the joyfullest funeral I ever saw, for there were none that cried but dogs." In 1661, London warmly welcomed the exiled Charles II back from France, "shouting with inexpressible joy" and watching undismayed when Charles ordered the exhumation of the three-year-old corpses of Cromwell and two cronies for the dubious purpose of hanging and beheading them publicly for the murder of his father. Perhaps the citizens thought it fitting punishment for closing the theaters, brothels, and gambling houses.

1660s: Plague and Fire

Charles II barely had time to adjust his crown when disaster struck. In early 1665, the first cases of a second major round of the bubonic plague were seen in London. Samuel Pepys, the great diarist, first heard of the outbreak in April, writing, "Great fear of the sickness here in the city, it being said that two or three houses are already shut up. God preserve us." The hot summer saw the outbreak burst into an epidemic, with affected houses painted with red crosses and shut up with a guard outside—people trapped inside died either of the plague or starvation. By September, red crosses bloomed everywhere, and the rattle of the death cart was heard in the streets with its mournful accompaniment, "Bring out your dead!", a wretched parody of the cries of the apple or mussel sellers that had been silenced by the calamity. On September 7, John Evelyn wrote, "I went all along the city and suburbs from Kent Street to St. James's, a dismal passage and dangerous, to see so many coffins exposed in the streets thin of people, the shops shut up and all mournful silence, as not knowing whose turn might be next."

It was not humanity's finest hour: the stricken were prevented from leaving their homes, or if they had escaped London, from traveling on roads. They were often pelted with rocks and dung at the outskirts of villages. Con artists and quacks sold phony cures, and the rich and powerful jumped ship like the rats who were carrying the plague. The problem was that no one had figured out that it was the rats'—or, more accurately, the fleas' on the rats—fault. Mistaking the disease as airborne, someone decided that the very cats and dogs who could have helped control the rats had to be destroyed and, in killing 60,000 animals, certainly added to the disaster. The horror and pain of the disease was unspeakable, dispatching an estimated 100,000 by the time this epidemic began to abate, around Christmas 1665. In February the king returned to London to survey—in safety, he thought—the melancholy scene of a decimated London still smelling of rotted flesh. But the rough hand of fate hadn't finished with London yet.

On September 2, 1666, a baker's oven in Pudding Lane was left unbanked. Its sparks, teased out of the chimney by a stiff wind, fired like tinder the dry wood of summer-baked houses and ignited the city in a matter of hours. Pepys was called by a servant to look at it at three in the morning, and, being used to little local fires in the cramped wooden alleys and byways of London, he "thought it to be on the back side of Mark Lane at the furthest . . . I thought it far enough off, and so went back to bed."

The lord mayor also brushed the fire off, saying "a woman might piss it out," and no measures were taken to control the conflagration until it was too late. Amazingly, only a handful of people lost their lives, one of them a servant in the house of the baker where the fire had started. John Evelyn describes a ghastly picture of the event two days after it started: "The burning still rages, and it was now gotten as far as the Inner Temple; all Fleet Street, the Old Bailey, Ludgate Hill, Warwick Lane, Newgate, Paul's Chain, Watling Street, now flaming, and most of it reduced to ashes; the stones of St. Paul's flew like grenados, the melting lead running down the streets in a stream, and the very pavements glowing with fiery redness, so as no horse nor man was able to tread on them, and the demolition had stopped all the passages, so that no help could be applied."

King Charles finally stepped in and did what the lord mayor should have done sooner: his navy blew up the houses in the way of the fire, creating a break in its path. After four grim days, the driving wind died down and the fire finally ended. In its wake lay an unrecognizable London, suffering untold losses in its architecture, treasures, books, and art. In all, 436 acres of London had been consumed by the fire: 13,200 houses, 87 parish houses and many of their churches, 44 merchants' halls, the Royal Exchange, the magnificent medieval Guildhall, and St. Paul's Cathedral. It was, if nothing else, an opportunity to rebuild the city along straight and reasonable lines, obliterating the medieval maze of streets that had contributed to the tragedy.

But this was not to be. Although both John Evelyn and the young Christopher Wren submitted designs for a new London with wide thoroughfares and sensible squares and circuses, the urgent need for housing and the legal problems of ownership of land assured that the rebuilding followed the original "plan" of medieval London somewhat faithfully. The main differences were that the lanes were widened to a mandatory 14 feet, and the buildings were made of stone. This was Wren's great opportunity, as he rebuilt 51 of the ruined churches, including St. Paul's Cathedral. Despite the loss of many of those edifices during World War II, Wren's name will forever be associated with the glory of that age, as London rose like a phoenix from the ashes of the fire into the magnificence of the eighteenth century.

Georgian London

To most London connoisseurs, the 1700s remain the very apex of the city's greatness: in architecture, literature, theater, painting, sculpture, in the building of stately homes and parks, in philosophy and sciences, there can be no other century to rival the verve and creativity of the eighteenth. The names of the artists, thinkers, and artisans of the day have come to define their disciplines: William Hogarth, Sir Joshua Reynolds, Thomas Gainsborough (painting); Jonathan Swift, Henry Fielding, Oliver Goldsmith (literature); David Garrick (theater); Alexander Pope (poetry); John Nash, Robert Adams (architecture); Edward Gibbon (history); John Gay (opera); David Hume (philosophy); Captain James Cook (exploration); Adam Smith (economics); James Watt (technology); and the naturalized British subject, composer George Frederic Handel. Of course, you can hardly mention London and the eighteenth century in the same breath without a bow to the looming figure of the formidable writer and lexicographer Dr. Samuel Johnson and his biographer and friend, James Boswell. There are countless other figures who made major breakthroughs in technology, medicine, and science in this robust century. There was something in the air it would seem, and not just the stench of the tanneries, slaughterhouses, and privies. In the 100-year span of this period, London grew from 650,000 souls to close to a million. The small villages north and west of the city were embraced by London's expansion; near the bucolic hamlet of Knightsbridge, a country house was bought and grandly rebuilt by the duke of Buckingham, later to go to King George III as a private royal residence.

The 12-year reign of Queen Anne left her name to a wildflower and a style of furniture. In 1714 came the Hanover succession from Germany. Georges I through IV presided over the acquisition of imperial lands from Canada to Australia and the ignominious loss of the wealthy American colonies to the war of independence. They saw the rise of a new technology that revolutionized the cotton and wool trades of England. They watched as the Bastille was stormed, igniting the French Revolution, and managed to keep their crowns on while across the channel others were losing their heads. They continued to prefer the German language while ruling an English-speaking kingdom. Due to this oddity, the position of prime minister came to be; thanks to the madness of King George and the dissolute lifestyle of the prince regent, the policy-making powers of the monarch were carefully whittled away by an increasingly powerful Parliament.

The expansion and progress of London were attended by an increase in crime, corruption, drinking, and poverty. Dr. Johnson, famed for his remark that "when a man is tired of London, he's tired of life," wrote a poem about London that exposes this dark underbelly:

> *Here malice, rapine, accident, conspire,*
> *And now a rabble rages, now a fire;*
> *Their ambush here relentless ruffians lay,*
> *And here the fell attorney prowls for prey;*
> *Here falling houses thunder on your head,*
> *And here a female atheist talks you dead....*
> *Prepare for death if here at night you roam,*
> *And sign your will before you sup from home....*

Tired of life, indeed!

There was an increasing polarization—due to the incipient Industrial Revolution—of London's society into owners and workers, rich and poor. The coarseness and insensitivity to the less fortunate on the part of the wealthy was truly shocking. Their entertainment included outings to the insane asylums for a laugh and attendance at public executions. There was one law for the rich and one for the poor; the criminals who weren't executed for the slightest offense were made to endure a grueling and often fatal passage to the new penal colony in Australia. It was only by the most repressive of measures that the revolution in France did not spread to London's gates, especially after the Gordon Riots of 1780, in which the Newgate Gaol was stormed and 300 were left dead. There were a few reformers and progressive thinkers, most memorably Jonathan Swift, who with his "Modest Proposal" of solving the problem of the Irish poor by feeding their babies to the rich, refined a tradition of savage English satire and social commentary that found many talented exponents in the Victorian century.

Victorian London

Queen Victoria's reign started in 1837, after the unlamented last gasp of Georgian rule by the grotesque George IV. He may have been the patron of John Nash, who developed Regent's Park and filled the city with white stucco-covered houses, but other than that, George IV didn't do much for London, although the extravagances and vices of his court certainly helped fill the coffers of money-lenders, gambling dens, and whore-houses. Princess Victoria was a woman of only 18 years when she became queen and gave her name to an age of change and reaction, reform and wretchedness, empire and exploitation.

There is another name so completely identified with nineteenth-century London that it has become an adjective describing it: Charles Dickens. He is never far from the hearts and minds of the London dweller; his face appears—appropriately for one who wrote so much about money's awful power—on the £10 note. It is the London of Dickens we tend to think of when we envision the nineteenth century: poor Bob Cratchit freezing in Scrooge's office; the convict Magwitch and Pip fleeing on the Thames under cover of a pea-soup fog; Oliver Twist asking for more food in the orphanage. Dickens was an insomniac who walked the streets of London for hours every night, and in his travels he picked up the sounds and secrets of the city. He is as much the voice of nineteenth-century London as Pepys and John Evelyn were of the seventeenth. Through his deeply compassionate reporting and fiction, Dickens opened up the eyes of the middle class to the misery of the poor. He helped steer England toward a more humane course as reformers worked to abolish the slave trade, put limits on child labor, allow women to keep their own property, extend voting rights, and open the first state schools.

The Industrial Revolution didn't so much flower as detonate in the nineteenth century; its effects were not entirely salutary. The gulf widened between rich and poor, the landscape and atmosphere were degraded, and as people in the country lost their self-sustainability, they trickled into a city already bursting at the seams with immigrants from the far reaches of the empire. But with all that cheap labor available, London grew at an amazing rate. New houses were built in every direction, with formerly quiet outlying villages becoming part of London's urban scene. The first underground trains began operation, sewers were built, transatlantic cable laid, the first police force was established, train tracks originating in London crisscrossed the country, omnibuses were pulled through the streets by huge work horses, streets were gas lit, and roads were laid all over the city. Museums, monuments, learned societies, and public libraries flourished. The Great Exhibition of 1851, organized by Victoria's husband, Prince Albert, showed the world that London was a city of cosmopolitan suaveness and culture, firmly looking to the future.

That Karl Marx wrote *Das Capital* while living in this two-faced city, has a certain poetic logic. The terrible contrast between the shiny new city, with its shops and theaters, hotels and townhouses, and the unmitigated squalor of the East End slums in many ways defined the Victorian Age. It's interesting to see how rosy with nostalgia that era has come to be: look at the industry that has sprung up around all things Victorian in the last 20 years. It couldn't have been all that much fun to be alive then: the sexual hypocrisy, claustrophobic class system, sexism, racism, xenophobia, and social Darwinism must have been about as easy to deal with as a night out with Jack the Ripper. Yet it was a time in which enormous changes took place, a time in which terrible injustices were at last redressed, and a time of unforgettable literature and indelible heroes. After all, any age that could produce Florence Nightingale, Oscar Wilde, Lewis Carroll, and Mary Shelley's *Frankenstein* can't be all bad.

World War I

Queen Victoria made a perfect exit in January 1901, keeping her era clearly defined by century. And now the twentieth century dawned with poor old Bertie, prince of Wales, at last out from under his mother's long shadow to lend his own name of King Edward to a new age. It was a short reign—only a decade, a mere fraction of his mother's 64 years on the throne—but it was distinctive enough to earn the title of the Edwardian Age—England's last age to be described in terms of the monarch. It was a clear cusp between the centuries, a time of accelerated progress. Motor cars became common, corsets came off, women demonstrated for the vote and smoked in public, and people started to challenge a number of tired Victorian verities. As a well-known sensualist of the time, King Edward helped usher in a more permissive era in which free love, divorce, and bohemian living arrangements were practiced without the terror of ostracism from an uptight moral majority. The famous free-thinking Bloomsbury Group formed around this time, during which artists and writers who lived in the then shabby-genteel neighborhood of the British Museum redefined not only their artistic disciplines but also their relationships. Virginia Woolf's famous quote, "In or about December 1910, human character changed," underscores the leap made in thought and behavior by this new generation.

In 1914, London and the British empire enjoyed the zenith of their world power. The British pound sterling was as safe as gold and was the currency of international commerce all over the globe. There was peace and prosperity. Social activists were kept busy working to get the vote for women, get children out of the factory and into a classroom, and force legislation that would make the government responsible for its neediest citizens. But the shadow of the German zeppelins loomed above London. Despite the efforts of pacifists like George Bernard Shaw, England was plunged into the ghastly war fought across the English Channel that came close to wiping out an entire generation of young Englishmen. When it was over in 1918, the whole social order changed. It was a completely different London, filled with emancipated working women and powered by electricity.

The Long Weekend: 1918–1939

There is a sense, as there is of America of the 1920s, that this period between the two World Wars was a last gasp of glamour for London. There is something to that, despite the ugly rumblings from the black-shirted British fascists led by Nazi-sympathizer Sir Oswald Mosley; despite the economic depression that left millions unemployed; and despite the terrible losses of life, limb, and hope during World War I. It may be that we view this interlude with an acute awareness of how much was soon to be buried under the Blitz, which makes the frivolity of that time seem all the more poignant.

People embraced the work of humorist P. G. Wodehouse, which helped them shake off the blues of the war and depression. To this day, the country still loves Wodehouse's version of London between the wars: gin-soaked parties with bright young things, dim right honorables, creaking lords and terrifying aunts, the Drones Club, and of course the unflappable Jeeves and his young master Bertie Wooster. They inhabit a hilarious fictional world that reveals what made London laugh between cataclysms. Noel Coward, Cecil Beaton, Virginia Woolf, George Orwell, Nancy Mitford, W. H. Auden, and T. S. Eliot are a few of the artists whose work also captures the feeling of the time and still resonates for us.

London gave Hollywood a run for its money, making movies with such luminaries as Sir Laurence Olivier, Peggy Ashcroft, Charles Laughton, and Alfred Hitchcock. Agatha Christie and Dorothy Sayers fed the increasing demand for murder mysteries. The West End was alive with plays, from melodramas to social realism. But nothing cooked up in the imagination could even come close to the real-life drama, to the big story of 1936: the abdication of King Edward VIII for the woman he loved, the American divorcée Mrs. Wallis Simpson. Although the event was billed as a grave constitutional crisis, it was clear that the monarch of England was becoming increasingly irrelevant to the citizenry, except as gossip and news-reel fodder. The citizens were mainly concerned with their own lives as they joined trade unions, built suburban communities, and tried to figure the map of the underground. In 1931, this tangled web was simplified into the sleek, art-deco design we know and love, and the population of 8 million began using it to escape the brown-fogged city to ever-more distant reaches of residential London.

Meanwhile, across the English Channel, Europe was increasingly threatened by Adolf Hitler, dismissed in the early days by most intelligent Londoners as a twisted clown and admired by a shameful number of hate-filled fascists and dim-witted minor nobility known as Right Honourables. They would all come to despise his name, as his Luftwaffe rained destruction on London, and Europe's fleeing Jews came to town with stories of concentration camps and genocide.

The Blitz: "Our Finest Hour"

World War I, the "war to end all wars," couldn't live up to that promise for long; only two decades after the armistice was signed, London was once again anxiously watching the skies over Whitehall, though this time it wasn't the lumbering zeppelins but the significantly more deadly Messerschmitts, Stukas, and the unpiloted "doodle-bugs" that spelled disaster. The attack started in earnest on a sunny day on September 7, 1940, when hundreds of fighter planes and bombers buzzed up the Thames and destroyed docks, gas works, and power stations. The Luftwaffe went on to bomb London nightly for 76 consecutive nights, dropping over 27,000 high explosives and thousands more incendiaries. The Blitz was on. Children were hurriedly sent to the countryside or to America, but the royal family made a point of staying in town, even after nine bombs dropped on Buckingham Palace. People sheltered in the tube stations in staggeringly large numbers, sleeping on the ground or in bunk beds placed on the tracks and platforms. Above ground, civilians coped with bombed-out streets, nightly fires, disrupted railways, power and water failures, the destruction of their homes, and, most terribly, the deaths of their friends, neighbors, and families. Novelist Nancy Mitford described the scene vividly in a letter to a friend:

> I find my nerves are standing up to the thing better now—I don't tremble quite all the time as I did.... NOBODY can have the slightest idea of what it is like until they've experienced it. As for the screaming bombs, they simply make your flesh creep but the whole thing is so fearful that they are actually only a slight added horror. The great fires everywhere, the awful din which never stops, and wave after wave after wave of aeroplanes, ambulances tearing up the street and the horrible unnatural blaze of lights from search-lights, etc.—all has to be experienced to be understood. Then in the morning the damage—people ring one another up to tell one how their houses are completely non-existent.... People are beyond praise, everyone is red eyed and exhausted but you never hear a word of complaint or down-heartedness. It is most reassuring.

(Selina Hastings, Nancy Mitford [London: Hamish Hamilton, 1985], p. 134.)

The bombardment put to the test the famous English stiff upper lip, and London's amazing rise to the challenge earned the admiration of the rest of the country and the world. Prime Minister Winston Churchill was the voice of the people during those dark days, author of such unforgettable war cries as "we shall defend our island, whatever the cost may be, we shall fight on the beaches, we shall fight on the landing grounds, we shall fight in the fields and in the streets, we shall fight in the hills; we shall never surrender," and "Let us therefore brace ourselves to our duties, and so bear ourselves that, if the British Empire and its Commonwealth last for a thousand years, men will still say, 'This was their finest hour.'"

And so it was. Despite the thousands killed, the millions wounded and made homeless, the destruction of hundreds of thousands of dwelling places and buildings, and the nearly total destruction of the city and the East End, London carried on. The people lived in corrugated steel caves called Anderson shelters (to be replaced later by the heavier Morrison shelters) buried three feet under ground. The homeless were sheltered by hotels—when the East End was first bombed, a huge crowd marched to the Savoy and demanded to be admitted, which they were—as well as by the not-completely-invulnerable tube stations. Brigades of men and women pulled all-night duties to put fires out in likely targets such as Westminster Abbey and St. Paul's Cathedral, saving some of the precious treasures of London's past. When the war finally ended, it could be well said of the Blitzed Londoners that, again in the words of Churchill, "their will was resolute and remorseless, and as it proved, unconquerable."

Sunset of the Empire

In 1948, England lost the jewel of her colonial crown when India became independent, and over the next decade it continued to lose colonies around the world, as well as much of the shipping and manufacturing business that made her rich. The 1950s were spent cleaning up the wreckage of the Blitz and continuing to live under strict food rationing. There was a grayness in the city; grim gaps of bomb sites yawned among the old Victorian buildings that were still black with coal grime and sagging under the weight of the years. People abandoned the city for the suburbs, whose spread was contained by the public lands of the Green Belt on the outer perimeters of London. Yet London was buoyant; the welfare state of the Labour government helped people rebuild their lives and gave them a sense of security unknown up to that time. In 1946, Heathrow Airport was opened, followed by Gatwick Airport three years later; the city was quickly rebuilt with modern glass-and-steel towers (Samuel Johnson and Charles Dickens would weep with confusion if they time-traveled back to their old haunts); and domestic labor-saving devices were new, plentiful, and affordable.

The most influential of these was certainly the television, on which people watched the colorful coronation of Queen Elizabeth II in 1953 from the comfort of their own armchairs. The prime minister, Harold Macmillan, said in 1959, "Most of our people never had it so good."

The Festival of Britain celebrated the centennial of Prince Albert's Great Exhibition, and it was on the site of it that the South Bank Arts Centre came to be. The fog lifted, thanks to antipollution measures, and the future looked as bright as the sky on a clear day. A new age was indeed coming, and it was a doozy. After the war, a quarter of the map of the world had been colored with empire pink; by the mid-1960s, England had lost almost all of her colonial possessions.

The Swinging Sixties and Punk Seventies

Whatever England may have lost in her empire, London certainly tried to make up for by becoming ground zero of the 1960s' "youth quake." The quintessential 1960s figures of the Beatles and James Bond joined the thinner ones of Twiggy and Julie Christie in making all things British very hip. England was swinging like a pendulum, and London, as always, was the epicenter of the groove. Movies such as *A Hard Day's Night, Blow Up, To Sir with Love,* and *A Man for All Seasons* were worldwide hits. The comedy of Spike Milligan gave way to Monty Python. Michael Caine, Vanessa and Lynn Redgrave, Oliver Reed, and Terrence Stamp were among the many English stars who could pull off a Hollywood blockbuster as well as do Pinter in the West End. Peter Sellers's Inspector Clouseau made him a superstar—a word and concept born in the bright light of the 1960s. Fashion designers of Carnaby Street and the King's Road started the miniskirt and bell-bottom trends, and fashion photographers like David Bailey became as famous as their subjects. The Rolling Stones, The Kinks, Cream, The Yardbirds, Marianne Faithfull, Led Zeppelin, The Who . . . London's bands in the 1960s were a veritable Debrett's Peerage of rock and roll. Twentysomething rock stars and their birds got their clothes at Granny Takes a Trip and Biba, drove around in Bentleys, and bought stately old piles in the country from hard-up toffs. *Hair* was performed in the West End; the Rolling Stones put on a free concert in Hyde Park, home to political demonstrations and love-ins. Drugs, sex, and rock and roll became a way of life for the new generation.

No one did sex, drugs, and rock and roll better than the glam rockers and punks of the 1970s. Green mohawk hairdos, safety pins piercing cheeks, very high platform shoes, and in-your-face attitudes were the usual for the King's Road, where designer Vivian Westwood and Malcolm McLaren (later manager of The Sex Pistols) had a punk-rock clothing shop—still there with the fast backward-moving clock outside—under a series of interesting names ("Sex" was one, and "Too Fast to Live, Too Young to Die" another). Feminism had many local, brilliant exponents, with Angela Carter writing in south London and Aussie expat Germaine Greer lecturing around the city. The literature of the day was pretty dark; Martin Amis's "Dead Babies" was a savage and chilling portrait of young people in 1970s London that opened the door to many imitators. "A Clockwork Orange," filmed by Stanley Kubrick in 1972 from the novel by Anthony Burgess, was a surreal prediction of a London gone viciously mad in the not-too-distant future. The Sex Pistols recorded a little ditty called "God F— the Queen," and that forecast must have seemed to have come quite true to the older generation. Squatters took over entire buildings that were earmarked for renovation; value-added tax was introduced; and a Women's Year Rally coincided with the election of Margaret Thatcher as leader of the Conservative Party. By the time Sid Vicious of The Sex Pistols had (allegedly) stabbed his girlfriend and then overdosed himself in New York City, people were exhausted and disillusioned with the 1970s, and it seemed as if it might be time to get on to more upbeat pastimes—like making money, that old-time London passion.

The Thatcher Years

When Margaret Thatcher was made prime minister in 1979, she announced the somewhat astonishing goal of returning to Victorian values. She axed 40,000 civil-service jobs, wrested control of London Transport away from the Greater London Council (GLC), and sold it to private investors. The gap between rich and poor became wider, as a very Victorian economic and social Darwinism—the survival of the fittest and fattest cats—took shape. After fighting constantly with the Labour-based GLC over social services and privatization, in 1986 she abolished the GLC altogether. People in the City were suddenly making gobs of dough (as they were on Wall Street across the pond), property prices were sky high, and the materialistic yuppie came to define the era in both England and the United States.

London in the 1980s also saw race riots in Brixton, the first cases of AIDS, strikes by tube and steel workers, and a ban on smoking on the London Underground after a fire at King's Cross killed 31 people. Homelessness rose most disturbingly, as Thatcher dismantled the socialist safety net, and the real-estate boom took its toll on government housing. In 1989, Thatcher closed out her decade nicely by resigning, and John Major took over as another Conservative prime minister.

Cool Britannia: The 1990s and Beyond

The 1990s started with the historical joining of the French and English sides of the new tunnel beneath the English Channel, linking Paris and

London with a three-hour train ride. The local fears that hordes of foreigners would breach London by rail never quite materialized, although the train surely had a part to play in the huge upsurge of tourism in the 1990s.

In 1992, the queen suffered her famous "annus horribilis" (you've got to love a queen who thinks everyone still understands Latin). A fire at Windsor Castle caused extensive damage, two of her sons were going through horrendously public marital scandals, and she started paying taxes for the first time in her life. Not one to leave books unbalanced—this is a woman who lived through the Blitz and food rationing—the queen decided to pay for the repair of Windsor Castle by opening Buckingham Palace to the public for two months a year. They're now raking in so much money that there's enough left over to upgrade the Queen's Gallery, which will let us see even more of the royal treasures. This tends to keep everyone but the most die-hard antimonarchists quiet.

The 1990s saw *Big Issue* launched, the magazine that helps the homeless earn money and tries to keep a conscience alive in the city. The 1990s also saw the premier of the runaway television hit, *Absolutely Fabulous,* which neatly and hilariously skewered the hypocrisies of the day. The two royal divorces, between Charles and Diana and Andy and Sarah (Fergie), as well as the mad-cow disease that rocked the British beef industry, helped to keep the media eye on London. By the time the Britpop explosion signaled the start of "Cool Britannia," everyone in the world knew that London was again the place to be. The Spice Girls, Oasis, All Saints, and Robbie Williams put British music back at the top of the charts. London Fashion Week became one of the hottest tickets in Europe, rivaling even Milan and Paris as the event in which to showcase new collections.

In May 1997, Tony Blair of the Labour Party was voted in as prime minister, signaling an end to the Conservative Party's 18-year run. Blair ran on a platform of finding the "third way" between the policies of Tory and Labour, and he has succeeded in annoying both parties. The same year also saw the tragedy of Princess Diana's death in a car crash in Paris, and the resulting week of completely un-British mourning: a spasm of national grief that had Buckingham Palace doing backflips to appease the people who found fault with how the royal family was responding. People stood in line for days to sign the condolence book at St. James Palace, while a sea of flowers numbering in the millions were left at the gates of Kensington Palace. It was a London no one had ever seen before and will likely never see again. London has recovered enough to have dislodged plans to build a memorial garden to Diana in Kensington Gardens, and the anniversaries of her death have passed quietly enough.

Next up for London was the opening of the Millennium Dome, the much maligned and hyped exhibition to celebrate the turning of the century and the next millennium. To the bitter delight of its critics, the exhibition failed to draw the crowds anticipated, and plans on what to do with the hulking thing are still up in the air.

Another millenium damp squib was the Sir Charles Foster designed footbridge over the Thames, connecting the Globe Theater and St. Paul's Cathedral. While it beautifully fulfilled its design as a "blade of light" across the Thames, on the opening day it shook so dangerously that it had to be closed for a rethink, with everyone involved blaming each other for the humiliating foul up.

What is a roaring success, however, is the British Airways London Eye, the elegant ferris wheel that now looms over the Thames with surprising grace, adding to the grandeur of views of Parliament Square and beyond.

A more mixed blessing to London has been the election of its first mayor, former Greater London Council–head Ken Livingstone. The man has his work cut out for him, and he is trying to cut through all the bureaucracy and Tory-antagonism to make London a better place to live in. His top priorities include upgrading the tube, and we wish him good speed and good luck. At the time of publication, however, the tube continues to groan and shudder under its commuter weight, strikes bring the city to a standstill regularly, automobile traffic is horrendous, and the streets after midnight are rife with muggers and drunken louts. It's a big city with big problems, along with its huge delights. But no matter what the century, London will *always* remain a fascinating, fast-paced, infuriating, and fun-filled tourist destination of choice. So come on over; you're gonna love it here.

British Culture: Queues, the Weather, and a Stiff Upper Lip

A Foreign Tribe

The most wonderful thing about coming to London is the opportunity for English-speaking transatlantics to learn more about a foreign culture than could be possible in any European city with a language barrier. That is not to say that there won't be communication problems, but at least you'll know the words, if not the meaning behind them. The great misunderstandings are not in language but in nuance. This is a society born in the oblique and the tacit, with an intrinsic orderliness based on the old class system. You'll never understand it, so just be polite and go along with the program. They're not going to change a hair for you.

George Bernard Shaw said that it is impossible for one Englishman to open his mouth without inviting the disdain of another. When the British meet each other for the first time, they know instantly from each other's accent how they may feel toward their new acquaintance: superior (relief) or inferior (depressed). These days some people would very much like to believe that this is no longer true; whether it is still reality is open to argument. It is certain, however, that, as a foreigner, you will never have to go through the process of having your class and social status sized up, judgements made, and conclusions drawn. You will likely be treated as an unknown, perhaps a novelty, and if you are American, with a curious combination of envy, contempt, and admiring amusement.

The primary exposure most Brits have to Americans is via Hollywood, and the Brits may check you out to see if the stereotype matches up with the real thing. You, of course, are free to do likewise. But you will probably not find Mary Poppins, Bertie Wooster, Jeeves, James Bond, Miss Marple, or Austin Powers. You will find that they Are Not Amused by any attempts to claim some kind of special kinship with them—this is essentially an island culture, insulated for centuries against all comers, and still in some ways quite impenetrable by outsiders. This gives Brits their strength, eccentricity, and quiet assumption of superiority. The wonderful thing about us transatlantics is how we buy into this assumption in an automatic, reflexive way. Americans, it has been observed, can go weak before an English accent—and it doesn't even have to be a "posh" one, because we've somehow trained ourselves to think of the English as indeed superior in intelligence and experience. It could be thought of as the Masterpiece Theatre complex, except that it existed long before television. Americans visiting London have admitted that they start to feel ashamed of their accents and slightly contemptuous when they hear other Americans speaking. Don't fall into that trap—we're just different, like apples and oranges, or as the British say, chalk and cheese.

Get in Line: The English Art of Queuing

All the rumors are true: the British queue for everything. Even soccer hooligans queue for tickets and beer. To jump the queue is the height of bad manners, and to do so is to invite certain tut-tutting, muttered comments, and possibly even an open challenge. In fact, it is such a violent breach of etiquette that it is about the only time the British will break another taboo, the one that prohibits raising one's voice in public (markets, pubs, and soccer stadiums notwithstanding). Raising one's voice attracts attention and may possibly give someone *the wrong idea,* whatever that is. However you may be tempted, do *not* jump the queue.

Also, always stand to the right when riding on escalators—the locals, even if they have no intention of passing you, hate it when tourists stand two abreast and clog up the path.

Weather Reports

The old saw about how everyone talks about the weather but no one does anything about it is not entirely true in London. The passion that the British have for talking about the weather amounts nearly to an interactive hobby. They will even go so far as to discuss it vigorously with complete strangers. Part of the reason may be the basically mild but changeable weather. London often goes through four seasons in one day (except in the winter, when cold, gray, and damp are the standards). The casting of aspersions on the abilities of the forecasters is a tried-and-true ice breaker and will pave the way for inquiries from the Brits about the extreme and interesting weather (tornadoes, blizzards, hurricanes, and so on) of America. As everyone must know by now, the famous London fogs of the past were a result of the coal burned in London, and a bona fide "pea-souper" hasn't been sighted since the early 1960s, after the Clean Air Act of 1956 put a stop to industrial pollution. The idea that it does rain constantly in London is also a myth, although there isn't one Londoner who doesn't own at least one umbrella (called a brolly), nor will you find too many tourists who haven't been forced to buy a rain poncho or umbrella on short notice.

At Your Service, Sort of

A recent study concluded that the British complain more about poor service than the residents of any other country. However, it also concluded that this is because they have more to complain about. They have only recently realized that it's okay to enjoy good food; the deprivations and sacrifices of the postwar years have cast a long shadow. The old-fashioned British Rail sandwich (inedible, of dubious content, and possibly poisonous) is, mercifully, a thing of the past. There's good fast food all over London now, and extra-virgin olive oil is no longer considered a foreign delicacy. However, they will not put iced water and a basket of bread on the table as a matter of course (worse, they may charge you a pound). They will not rush to take your order or bring you your bill. They will not take kindly to complaint—it's not so much that the customer is always wrong, but that the customer overestimates his or her importance. They subscribe to a theory of blame and will deluge the dissatisfied with unwanted information about *why* the food took so long to arrive or *how* the trains got to be so late. What they will *not* do is say, "I'm sorry, let me fix that for you right away." Don't take it personally. It's a British thing.

The Great British Reserve

This is alive and well, stiffening the upper lip and continuing to define "Englishness." You will see it manifested in the advertising, where wit and word play take precedence over volume, sloganeering, and repetition. It is apparent in the weather forecasts ("Today will be rather damp, with a possibility of patchy fog and maybe a spot of drizzle in between clear intervals") and on the tube at rush hour, where instead of mouthing off at an annoying commuter who refuses to move down in the carriage, passengers will mutter "excuse me's," issue irritated coughs, and initiate great flappings of newspapers. All pass for expressions of anger and frustration. This quietude can be almost soothing to an American accustomed to the chattering hordes of compatriots asking personal questions and offering the usual too much information, but it can take a bit of getting used to at first and might leave the visitor feeling a little out in the cold.

However, this reserve is not to be taken for granted. Road rage is a big problem in traffic-choked London, but luckily the gun laws are stringent enough that it results in shouting matches and fisticuffs rather than more serious consequences. There is nothing quite so terrifying as standing on the terraces at a soccer game, trapped among 10,000 grown men singing with one voice, "You're shite and you know you are!" Not for them the cozy familiarity of the seventh-inning stretches and the lilting tones of "Take Me Out to the Ballgame."

A similar contradiction to the stereotype is found during the prime minister's question period in the House of Commons. This has to be seen to be believed. Barely veiled or even naked insults are hurled by members of Parliament at one another, while howls of derision and guffaws of braying laughter render the institution more like a high-school classroom whose teacher has stepped out than a hallowed hall of government. There is something rather invigorating about this cacophony, and it gives you an idea of the healthy self-regard in which the English hold themselves. The great paradox is that they yield to no one, except for the monarch.

To Do or Not to Do: That Is the Culture

There was an article in *The Spectator* magazine a few years ago about how the staff would try to think up the worst possible advice to put in a tourist guide to London. They came up with, among others, "Introduce yourself and shake hands all around in your train compartment," and, "Try out the famous echo in the British Library Reading Room." As funny as we find this concept, we will resist temptation and will give you the following dos and don'ts guaranteed to be 100% valid.

- Don't call people by their first names unless expressly asked to do so—it is considered normal not to use names when addressing people.

- Don't expect people to introduce you to others. One can spend an entire evening with a group of people who neither introduce themselves nor their friends to you.

- Don't try to intervene in soccer arguments—it's a very serious subject, one no outsider can comprehend properly. Remember at games that the hooligans mean business.

- Don't take it personally when people act as if you're not there, correct your pronunciation, look at you as if you're daft when asking directions to "Lye-cester Square," act slightly exasperated by your inability to read a complex map of London, or try to run you down in the street. You'll get a lot of this—get used to it.

- Don't brag about how much sunlight you get at home; this will not endear you to anyone.

- Don't tell anyone that their accent is "cute." It is you who have the accent, and it is not considered remotely cute by the British.

- Don't gloat about the American Revolution. Again, not cute.

- Do watch out for queues and take your place in them.

- Do be courteous; be very courteous—it's much more appreciated than friendliness.

- Do remember that this is a country of rules, rules, rules—and they aren't just making them up as they go along, though it sometimes seems they are.

- Do be patient in restaurants and stores; use your vacation as an opportunity to slow down and practice your manners.

- Do learn to enjoy being called "love" and "darling" and "sweetheart" by certain strangers.

- Do prepare for your visit by reading as much as you can on London; try to listen more than you speak. This is a very interesting place, and the people are fascinating. Make the most of your visit.

DIVIDED BY A COMMON LANGUAGE: A BRITISH/ENGLISH GLOSSARY

Thanks to the broadcasting of television shows and films (in London, films are viewed at the cinema, as opposed to movies or flicks viewed at the theater), the British are more hip to our lingo than they may let on. But if your exposure to Brit-speak has been limited to watching some shows on PBS or A&E, you may need a bit of a leg up. We have provided a short glossary of some words you may not have caught on *Prime Suspect* or *Pride and Prejudice.*

American	English
At the airport	
bill	bank note
wallet	billfold/purse
telephone booth	telephone box/kiosk
On the road	
baby carriage/stroller	pram/buggy
back-up lights	reversing lights
dead-end road	cul-de-sac
delivery truck	van
divided highway	dual carriageway
detour	diversion
gas	petrol
hood (car)	bonnet
license plate	number plate
minivans	people carriers
sedan car	saloon car
subway	underground or tube
overpass	flyover
one-way ticket	single journey
pull-off	lay-by
round-trip ticket	return ticket
station wagon	estate car
truck	lorry
trunk	boot
underpass (pedestrian, under streets)	subway
windshield	windscreen
At the hotel:	
antenna	aerial
apartment hotel	service flats
apartment building	block of flats, mansion flats
baby crib	cot
baggage room	left-luggage office
bathe (verb)	bath (bathing—short "a" sound)

DIVIDED BY A COMMON LANGUAGE: A BRITISH/ENGLISH GLOSSARY

American	English
On the road (continued)	
bathrobe	dressing gown
cot	extra bed or camp bed
call (on the telephone)	ring
call collect	reverse charges
closet	cupboard/wardrobe
comforter/quilt	eiderdown/duvet
connect (on the telephone)	put through
elevator	lift
first floor	ground floor
second floor	first floor
long-distance call	trunk call
make a reservation	book
milk in coffee/tea or not	white or black
outlet/socket	power point
rent	let
vacuum	Hoover
washcloth	face flannel
In a restaurant or food store	
buffet	sideboard
broiled	grilled
bun (hamburger)	bap
can (of food)	tin
candy	sweets
check	bill
cookie	biscuit
cotton candy	candy floss
cracker	savoury biscuit
dessert	pudding
diaper	nappy
downtown	town center/high street
druggist/drugstore	chemist/chemist's shop
eggplant	aubergine
eraser	rubber
French fries	chips
hamburger meat	mince
hardware store	ironmonger
lima bean	broad bean
molasses	black treacle
potato chips	crisps

DIVIDED BY A COMMON LANGUAGE: A BRITISH/ENGLISH GLOSSARY

American	English
In a restaurant or food store *(continued)*	
pit	stone
popsicle	ice lolly
raisin	sultana
smoked herring	kipper
zucchini	courgette
At the theatre	
aisle	gangway
balcony	gallery/upper circle
intermission	interval
mezzanine/loge	dress circle
movie theater	cinema
movie	film
In the markets and on the high street	
cigarettes	fags
liquor store	off license
news stand	newsagent
notions	haberdashery
panties	knickers
panty hose	tights
raincoat	macintosh (or mac)/kagool
rest room	public convenience/loo/ w.c./lavatory
sneakers	trainers or plimsolls
scotch tape	cellotape
shorts (underwear)	pants
sweater	jumper
undershirt	vest
vest	waistcoat
In sickness and in health	
acetaminophen (Tylenol)	paracetamol
emergency room	casualty
Band-Aids	plasters
funny bone	crazy bone
pimples	spots
rubbing alcohol	surgical spirit

Part Two

Planning Your Visit
to London

Airline Deals

British Airways (1-800-AIRWAYS, www.britishairways.com) and Virgin Atlantic Airways (1-800-862-8621, www.virgin.com) are the two largest transatlantic carriers in and out of London and are certainly the ones to check with first to get a baseline on a fare. They often engage in price wars, which means the other airlines will lower their prices too, or at least match the lowest rate.

Other airlines that fly from the United States to London are American (1-800-433-7300, www.aa.com); Delta (1-800-241-4141, www.delta.com); Northwest (1-800-447-4747, www.nwa.com); TWA (now partners with American) (1-800-892-4141, www.twa.com), and United (1-800-241-6522, www.united.com). They all fly into either Heathrow or Gatwick, and while I personally prefer Heathrow—it offers more options for getting into London—Gatwick is a perfectly fine airport.

Flight consolidators are a good way to shop for the best deal, but be sure that the one you use books foreign travel. Consolidators buy up blocks of unsold seats from airlines and resell them to you. Some consolidators deal primarily with domestic tickets, and while they may get you a ticket to London, it might be the same price as the published fare from an airline, and more restrictions may apply. The internet has made it so easy to shop for fares, but in these days of crumbling dot-com companies, you want to be aware of the here-today-gone-tomorrow qualities of the web. So far, the following discount and flight consolidator businesses are doing well, but I am including a large number just in case you strike out with any of them. Some of the so-called discount websites are actually owned by various airlines and offer no discount at all, and some are merely agencies to sell tickets. Before you go searching the Internet, do call a couple of the big airlines to get an idea of what prices are available directly from them.

- *www.airconsolidator.net* discounted tickets for flights originating in the U.S.

- *www.airdiscounters.com* airfares from the U.S. to most major cities worldwide

- *www.bestfares.com* big database; lots of vacation options (cars, hotel rooms, packages)

- *www.blueskytravelinc.com* an airfare consolidator with discounted tickets to Europe

- *www.cheapflights.com* discounted flights from travel agents in the U.K.

- *www.cheaptickets.com*

- *www.discountairbrokers.com* international travel discounts

- *www.1800airfare.com* airfares for American, Delta, United, Northwest, and Continental

- *www.expedia.com* well-established travel website; always check prices against the airlines' websites before booking

- *www.flightdiscount.com* discounted airfares for any destination

- *www.flights4less.co.uk* U.K.-based cheap flights

- *www.goodfare.com* international travel discounts, including consolidator fares

- *www.Orbitz.com* good place to browse (thousands of fares); not always best prices

- *www.ticketplanet.com* international travel discounts

If you prefer the telephone contact, call (800) FLY-4-LESS or (800) FLY-CHEAP; or contact Council Travel at (800) 226-8624 (www.council-travel.com). You will also see ads for flight consolidators in the travel section of most Sunday-newspaper editions.

Winter is London's off-season, and that's when some hotels offer impressive air-and-land packages, which are discussed on page 61 in Part Three, "Hotels."

Quick Check

Travel Insurance Your own insurance company may offer some form of travel insurance, so check first with them before buying any additional coverage. You can purchase insurance for cancelled travel, lost luggage, and medical emergencies through Travel Guard International at (800) 826-1300, www.travel-guard.com; or Travel International, Inc. at (800) 243-3174, www.travelinsured.com.

Luggage Every airline has different rules, so call ahead to find out number of bags that can be checked, maximum weight, and size and weight of carry-ons. Virgin is very strict about carry-on luggage and will make you check even a backpack if it is too heavy. This also depends on the class in which you are traveling—if it's economy, don't try to bring all your luggage on board with you; it may not get by check-in, and if the flight is full, you will be depriving others of their fair share of space.

With the more stringent security enforced for carry-on luggage, you must be careful to put the following items in your check-in luggage: scissors, nail files, nail clippers, pen-knives, razors or razor blades, or any other sharp object that could conceivably be used as a weapon.

Valuables   Be sure to bring valuables, such as cameras, laptops, jewelry, money, and anything particularly fragile or precious, including medication, on the plane with you. They may be able to send a man to the moon, but they can't always match up the luggage with the flight.

Medications   You may want to bring an extra supply of any medicine you are taking, as well as a spare pair of eyeglasses. If you do lose your medication, it will help to know its generic name in order to get a new prescription. Prescriptions from a foreign doctor will usually be honored in England, so you might ask your doctor for a backup before you go. Wear a Medic Alert tag if you have a serious health condition.

Personal Electronics   Your laptop will most likely be fitted with a built-in electrical transformer, and all you'll need to do is buy a plug adapter. In London, the most common electrical plug is the three-prong type, which is not the same as in the rest of Europe (where two round plugs are used). Radio Shack or Brookstone have foreign-plug adapter packages that cover pretty much any type of plug. Forget about hairdryers, electric tooth-brushes, and other personal electronics; you will blow them up if you plug a 110 volt into the British 220 volt system without running it through a heavy and clumsy currency converter. Your cell phone, unless it is one of the very expensive world-wide-use models, will not work in England. Many hotels have cell phones to rent, and you can pick up a pay-as-you-go U.K. cell phone for about $100 or even less.

Car Rental   It's not a bad idea to reserve a rental car before you go to London; you can often get a better price from the States. You should call your hotel and ask if there is a nearby rental place, so you don't have to cross the entire city to pick the car up and drop it off.

Brit Rail   If you are going to travel around rural England by train, you can purchase a Brit Rail Pass before you leave and save a bundle. Call (888) BRITRAIL in the U.S. or (800) 555-BRIT in Canada, or order the pass through www.raileurope.com. You can also order Travel Cards for the tubes and buses at that website, but there's no financial incentive, only convenience. You can get Travel Cards also when you get to London, at any tube station or London Tourist Office.

Money   There are ATMs with Cirrus, MAC, and credit-card account systems all over London. This is your best bet for getting the best rate. Remember, you can't access your credit-card funds from an ATM without a

PIN number, so make sure you have one before you go. If you don't have a credit card or ATM card, be sure to ask for traveller's checks in pounds only.

The Weather

Average Temperatures and Rainfall in London (Daytime):

Month	Temperature (°F/C)	Rainfall (inches)
January	40/4	2.1
February	40/4	1.6
March	44/7	1.5
April	49/9	1.5
May	55/13	1.8
June	61/16	1.8
July	64/18	2.2
August	64/18	2.3
September	59/15	1.9
October	52/11	2.2
November	46/8	2.5
December	42/6	1.9

London measures its mild weather in degrees Celsius (Centigrade) rather than Fahrenheit, so you might want to memorize a few conversions. You can check out the weather from the United States before you go. Call (900) WEATHER and dial the first four letters of your destination city (LOND), and you'll get a recording of current temperatures, current weather conditions, and the forecast for the next few days. If you're online, go to the Weather Channel website at www.weather.com or check CNN weather at www.cnn.com. You can also access local newspapers at www.sunday-times.co.uk, www.guardian.co.uk, or www.telegraph.co.uk for weather info.

A wonderful new website, www.livesights.com (click Thames cam) will not only give you the weather but a realtime picture of the Thames!

Convert temperatures (approximately) from Celsius to Fahrenheit by doubling Celsius and adding 30. Here are some more exact numbers:

–3°C = 26.7°F	15° = 59.0°
–1° = 30.2°	20° = 68.0°
0° = 32.0° (temperature of freezing)	25° = 77.0°
1° = 33.8°	30° = 86.0°
5° = 41.0°	37°= 98.6° (normal human-body
10° = 50.0°	temperature)

What to Bring

What to bring on your trip to London depends on the weather, which we've mapped out seasonally, but there are a few things that you might appreciate having handy at all times of the year:

- this book
- small map of Central London and a portable street atlas, a small pocket-sized book that has exhaustive maps on all of London, which even the natives can't do without; *London A to Z, Collins* or *Nicholsons London Street Atlas* are all equally good
- £50 to £100 (use your ATM bank card to stock up when you get here; it's the best way to avoid money-changing commissions)
- money belt
- good backpack or shoulder bag
- small, collapsible umbrella
- folding rain poncho
- currency converter
- portable electrical transformer from American 110V to British 220V, if you bring your own hair dryer or electric toothbrush (check amps to make sure it can handle your appliances—hair dryers are notorious for blowing out transformers)
- camera and lots of extra film (like everything else, film is expensive here)
- sugar substitute (it's not as readily available in restaurants as it is in the United States)
- favorite snacks (American snacks and candy are not always easy to find and often can't be found anywhere)
- books on London that relate to your interests
- good walking shoes
- passport-size photos for travel card

Clothing

London is a city where people dress with a degree of decorum—at least they do in Central London, where you'll probably be spending most of your time. This neatness is something of a tradition and may have to do with the fact that the majority of schools, private and public, have uniforms. If you happen to come across a wedding, you'll see how seriously Londoners take their clothing—formal suits and amazing hats are de rigueur at most British nuptials, even at civil ceremonies at town hall. Harrods, which has a ridiculously high opinion of itself, actually has a dress code, as does the Ritz Hotel (no blue or black jeans at the Ritz; no cut-offs or offensive-wear; at Harrods it's completely and mysteriously up to their discretion). Generally speaking, globalization has ensured that the Western countries of the world all dress pretty much the same way, and except for very fancy and/or uptight places, there is no need to change the way you dress normally. Theaters are no longer a place that require formality, but I would urge you to dress in layers as it can get quite warm in the middle of a sold-out play.

Bring one or two good comfortable outfits for stepping out to restaurants; smart casual is always safe. This is not Paris, where urban chic is the style on the street and the average American suburbanite can feel hopelessly dowdy. London is more about being presentable than being fashionable. In the same way, the British tend to consume their meals in restaurants and not on the street; they tend to leave the workout clothes at the gym and dress more properly in public. Of course, in the tourist areas that you may frequent, everyone will be dressed for comfort, so don't sweat the skirts and stockings, ties and jackets.

When to Go

The best time to go to London is whenever it's possible for you. If you want more than anything to see this remarkable city but can't afford the high-season airfare, then by all means go in the winter, when the fares drop by as much as 75%—if you book sufficiently in advance and look around for the good deals. Other considerations might include what special events you're eager to see—perhaps Wimbledon or the Chelsea Flower Show—or which attractions you're most interested in. Some of your choices—stately homes, for example—may be closed for the winter. Although the winter is dark and dreary, it's free of the swarms of tourists that you find in the summer. Let's take it season by season:

Summer For many of us, summer is the *only* option because of our children's summer vacation and the slowdown in our work lives. Summer in London, though unpredictable, is often quite gorgeous. Henry James was probably thinking of England, his adopted home, when he declared the two most beautiful words in the English language to be "summer afternoon." One thing these summer afternoons can't promise, though, is heat—three consecutive days of 75° and sun is considered a heat wave. However, the global-warming trend is upsetting London's traditional brisk summer, and 1999 saw record-breaking heat that upset many tourists, as air conditioning is relatively rare in shops, restaurants, and many hotels and it's nonexistent in buses and trains. But don't take the warming trend as a given—the summer of 2000 was wet and chilly, confounding the meteorologists, although the following summer was more or less perfect, with lots of sunny days and cool nights. At night the temperature of even a hot day will drop, and, generally speaking, a fan will suffice to cool a hotel room.

During each season in London, you should plan your clothing in layers, as the weather can change dramatically in one day. *Don't* pack only shorts and T-shirts, which you may not even get a chance to wear. Be sure to bring socks, a sweater or two, trousers ("pants" here are underpants, also known as knickers), a light jacket, and a rain poncho. The most crucial piece of clothing is a good pair of walking shoes, whichever shoes you personally find most comfortable, be they sneakers or sandals.

In the summer you can count on all the museums and attractions being very crowded. Busloads of tourists are constantly bearing down on the most popular attractions, and the decent hotels are often completely booked by April or May. Unless the global economy goes completely into the toilet (or the "loo" as it's called here), a summer visit to London can require nerves of steel and the planning capabilities of Winston Churchill.

On the plus side, summer in London means that the parks are at their most fragrant and riotously floral and that all the stately homes and palaces are open (many have an April–October season); buskers (street performers) are everywhere on the streets; there are carnivals, street fairs, and more out-door dining than makes sense in a country with such a variable weather. Private garden squares are open to the public on one Sunday in June. The Royal Parks have green-and-white-striped lawn chairs ready for hire, and stables lay on extra horses for rides in the parks. The locals take off on hol-iday, so the streets are relatively free to accommodate the stampedes of tourists. I repeat: *always* book your hotel well in advance for summer visits.

Fall   I much prefer the autumn to the summer in London for many reasons, the most important being that the hordes of tourists almost clear out. Also, since even in summer London's weather may tend toward the fall-like, it is reassuring to have the weather match the calendar. Because of London's mild climate, many flowers in the parks last all the way into November, and to see their radiance blending with the hues of the changing leaves is wonderful. The sunny days are mood lifting and the briskness in the air invigorating. The main thing to remember is that most of the stately homes and palaces close October 30, so come before then if these sights are on the top of your list. (Buckingham Palace closes at the end of September or in the first week of October.) November can get as cold as 45°F, but not much below that. Bring gloves and a hat for the windy days. The days get shorter and shorter.

Winter   There is a beautiful old English folk song heard at Christmas and called "In the Bleak Midwinter" ("ground as hard as iron, water like a stone"), which plays in many Londoners' minds as they wake up to the dark-ness that returns around 4 p.m. The ancient trees in the parks have shed their leaves, standing like skeletons against a leaden sky. I personally don't mind the bleakness much, as it doesn't include temperatures below freezing very often and because the museums are so warm and inviting in the winter. The airline deals are fantastic, the hotels are cheaper, there aren't tourists everywhere (just busloads of uniformed school children flooding the museums), and your choice of plays at the half-price ticket booths expands considerably. All in all, it's an economical time to make a cultural holiday. No one does Christmas quite like the English. They aren't constrained by Thanksgiving a month earlier and start their decorating and selling in the first couple of weeks of November. There are the Oxford Street and Regent Street Christmas lighting ceremonies, and there's a Santa Parade when Santa arrives at Harrods the first week of November. (The decorations of Oxford and Regent Streets are getting tackier and more commercial every year—go to Marylebone High Street, Bond Street, or St. Christopher's Place for the more appealing Christmas lights.) There are scores of wonderful Christmas concerts at churches and cathedrals—check Time Out or What's On for where and when. What you won't find much of is snow, which may be a relief for some of you Northerners. But there is plenty of rain, and it's the cold kind. The best news is that after December 21, the days start getting longer.

Spring   Spring starts early in London. Carpets of crocuses cover Hyde Park as early as February, with daffodils not far behind. It's a fine time to visit; the stately homes reopen at the end of March or April, and the parks and gardens come into bloom. The weather is still quite brisk, though. Early May can be downright nippy, even though the cafes start putting tables on the street around then. London starts coming back to its outdoor life, with the London Marathon, boat races on the Thames, and the Chelsea Flower Show. The weather can be fantastic, with not as much rain as in winter, but it's the foolish optimist who ventures out without an umbrella.

Gathering Information

Lucky for you, the British Tourist Authority is ready to help with your vacation. They have the following offices in the United States and a central toll-free number for information: (800) GO-TO-BRITAIN. (In London the number is (0208) 846-9000.) They have brochures, maps, and a booklet that they will be happy to give you. Make a point of calling, writing, or going in for these goodies.

In Chicago: no phone calls; write or walk in at 625 N. Michigan Avenue, Suite 1510, Chicago, IL 60611.

In New York: (212) 986-2200 or (800) 462-2748; 555 5th Avenue, 7th Floor, New York, NY 10176. There is a bookstore next door to the office, which has many London-related items of interest.

In Australia: (02) 267-4555 or fax (02) 267-4442; University Centre, 8th Floor, 210 Clarence Street, Sydney NSW 2000.

In Canada: (800) 847-4885; 111 Avenue Road, Suite 450, Toronto, Ontario M5R 3J8.

In New Zealand: (09) 303-1446 or fax (09) 377-6965; Dilworth Building, Suite 305, Queen and Customs Streets, Auckland 1.

Websites

There are so many websites coming and going about London, it's hard to keep up with them. They are always being improved, sometimes removed, and the addresses may change, but the following websites should be able to provide you with enough links to keep you glued to your computer for weeks:

- www.londontouristboard.com   up-to-the-minute info on events, hotels, restaurants, sight-seeing, exhibits, and more

- www.LiveSights.com   real-time views of the Thames' various vistas, via Thames Cam!, plus weather

- www.royal.gov.uk   info on royal palaces, castles, and museums, other links

- www.westminster.gov.uk   links to London sites

- www.cityoflondon.gov.uk   city government site

- www.london.gov.uk   another government site

- www.24hourmuseum.org.uk   info on museums, plus many London- and art-related links.

- www.timeout.com   *Time Out* magazine, the city's best source for events, online

- www.Londonnet.co.uk   magazine guide to events, plus articles

- www.guardianunlimited.co.uk   *The Guardian* and *The Observer* newspapers online

- www.thisislondon.co.uk   events listings and local news from the *Evening Standard*

Special Considerations

Passport, Visas, and Customs

If you're American, Canadian, or from New Zealand, all you need to enter England is a valid passport. If you have one, be sure to check the expiration date at least a month before going. Americans can find passport information, including downloadable forms, at the Department of State Bureau of Consular Affairs website, http://travel.state.gov.passport_services.html. Alternatively, call the National Passport Information Center at (900) 225-5674. You don't need a visa for a vacation; you will be allowed in for up to 90 days. Make a copy of the information page of your passport and keep it in your luggage in order to expedite replacement in case your passport gets lost or stolen.

What You May and May Not Bring into the United Kingdom

You can bring in, duty-free, a carton of cigarettes, a few bottles of wine, perfume, toilet water, and other items, up to a value of £136 (about $225). You may not bring in controlled drugs (any medication you have should be in its original bottle with your name on it), firearms and/or ammunition, plants and vegetables, fresh meats, or any kind of animals. See page 48 for more details about customs.

Electricity

The electricity supply is 220 volts AC, which will blow out any American 110-V appliance you may have. Electric lamps are the only items that don't require a transformer. Check to be sure your laptop computer has a built-in transformer; it's a pretty standard feature. Razors, hair dryers, boom boxes, cell-phone rechargers—all will need to be plugged into a transformer. Leave them at home is my advice. Since the British outlets are made for large three-prong plugs, you will also need to get an adapter, available at any iron mongers (hardware store), chemists (drug store), supermarket, or gadget store. *Don't plug anything in until you've checked the voltage on the transformer!* It should be set to "Input AC 110 volt, output AC 220 volt." You'll know by the pop, flash, and smoke if you got it wrong.

Pounds, Pence, and Traveler's Checks

The British are going slowly into this European Union business, taking a wait-and-see attitude toward the Euro Unit. At this writing, they are still using pounds (£), and the pound converts to about 1.5 dollars. Check any major newspaper's business section for current exchange rates, or go to www.travlang.com or www.x-rates.com. The pound is a unit divided into 100 pence, abbreviated "p." One p is called a penny. Gone are the days of the shilling, the tuppence, and the farthing; what we lose in quaintness we make up for in manageability.

There are no longer any £1 notes. There are red 50s, purple 20s, brown 10s, and green 5s. Coins are divided into £2, £1, 50p, 20p, 10p, 5p, 2p, and 1p. It's a worrisome sign of inflation that the government intends to introduce a £5 coin soon, which will no doubt add to the already considerable weight of a pocketful of British change. Coins cannot be changed into foreign cash, so spend them while you're in London; better still, donate them on your way home to the brilliant UNICEF Change Collection scheme that most airlines sponsor.

Go to your bank before you leave and buy about £100 worth of British pound sterling notes so you will have plenty on hand to pay for transportation from the airport and maybe even that first meal. Request 20s, as 50s can sometimes be hard to break.

See Part Four, "Arriving and Getting Oriented," for details on ATMs, changing money, and using your credit cards.

Value Added Tax (VAT)

VAT is one of the great frustrations of shopping in London. It is a 17.5% tax slapped on everything from hotel rooms to lipstick; the only exceptions are food, children's clothing, and books, yet these are still very expensive. There are ways to get this tax refunded, which we'll tell you about in Part Ten, "Shopping in London." Almost everything has the VAT added into the sticker price, except for merchandise sold in some small shops, as well as various services. Check before you book a hotel as to whether the quoted price includes VAT. It can make a huge difference in your bill, obviously.

Embassies and High Commissions

United States

The American Embassy is housed in Mayfair at 24 Grosvenor Square, London, W1A1AE; (0207) 499-9000 (zone 8; tube: Bond Street). This is where you will go if your passport gets lost or stolen or if you have some emergency. The embassy's website is at www.usembassy.org.uk. The hours are 8:30 a.m.–5:30 p.m. Passports are handled from Monday to Friday, 8:30–11a.m.; and Monday, Wednesday, and Friday, 2–4 p.m. The Passport Office is on 55 Upper Brook Street, around the corner from the main entrance (tube: Marble Arch or Bond Street).

Canada

The high commission is at MacDonald House, 38 Grosvenor Square, W1; (0207) 258-6600 (zone 8; tube: Bond Street). It is open Monday to Friday, 8–11 a.m.

Australia

The High Commission is at Australia House, Strand, WC2; (0207) 379-4334 (zone 7; tube: Charing Cross) and is open Monday to Friday, 10 a.m.–4 p.m.

New Zealand

The High Commission is at New Zealand House, 80 Haymarket at Pall Mall, SW1; (0207) 930-8422 (zone 7; tube: Charing Cross). It's open Monday to Friday, 9 a.m.–5 p.m.

Ireland

The Irish Embassy is at 17 Grosvenor Place, SW1; (0207) 235-2171 (zone 10; tube: Hyde Park Corner). Hours are Monday to Friday, 10 a.m.– 4 p.m.

Traveling with Children

In planning your vacation, remember that children get jet lag, too, and plan your first day so you all can recover from it. We have a rating system in our attraction profiles that attempts to gauge suitability for children and adults of various ages, but bear in mind that all children have different interests and differing levels of tolerance for museums and attractions. See Part Seven, "Children's London."

Disabled Access in London

London may be more wheelchair- and disabled-access ready than many cities in Europe, but it still has some insurmountable problems in many of its attractions. In America one can count on wheelchair access and disabled rest rooms in public buildings; in London you need to call ahead or use any of the following excellent references:

- *Access in London.* This is the best book on the subject, researched by disabled people and updated regularly. It is published by the Access Project and is available at various bookstores and in the London Museum Giftshop; you can also call or write to order it: Access Project, 39 Bradley Gardens, London, W13 8HE; (0208) 858-2375; www.artsline.org.uk. You can also try www.amazon.com or another online bookstore to get hold of it.

- *Access to the Underground,* a brochure published by London Transport, is available at tube stations or by writing the London Transport Unit for Disabled Visitors, 172 Buckingham Palace Road, London, SW1 9TN.

- *Information for Wheelchair Users Visiting London* is a pamphlet that you can find in any tourist office in London.

- *Artsline* will give information on access to galleries and museums. Call (0207) 388-2227.

- *Holiday Care Service* offers advice on disabled-friendly lodging; call (0129) 377-4535 or visit www.holidaycare.org.uk.

- *Tripscope* gives advice and information on transport for the elderly and disabled throughout the United Kingdom and London. Call (0208) 994-9294 or visit www.justmobility.co.uk/tripscope.

- *Can Be Done* is a tour operator specializing in London holidays and tours for disabled people: call (0208) 907-2400 or visit www.canbedone.co.uk.

Easing Jet Lag

Jet lag is a very real problem as any long-distance traveler can tell you. The number of time zones passed through is directly proportional to how much jet lag you'll suffer; visitors from Lost Angeles will feel worse than the New Yorkers. The common wisdom is that you will have roughly one day of symptoms for each hour of time difference. Though some people don't experience jet lag at all (or so they say), most of us do to varying degrees. The symptoms include fatigue, muscle aches, and headaches, changes in appetite, sleep disturbances, irritability, forgetfulness, confusion, and dizziness. Of course, these symptoms could also describe middle age, but jet lag is much more pronounced. There are a number of confusing remedies— eating a certain kind and amount of food on either end of your trip, taking homeopathic remedies every hour on the plane, digesting a number of vitamins, and so on. For me, and I learned this through many painful flights between Hong Kong and New York, the best remedy is to try to reset your internal clock as soon as possible. The main thing to remember on the plane is to drink lots and lots of water, but *no* alcohol, and eat sparingly. Sleeping on the plane is not always an option, but do try. When you arrive, change your watch immediately and try to forget what time it is "for you." Your time is the time of wherever you are, and you've got to get on it as soon as possible. The best way to reset your clock is to get as much sunlight as possible—not always easy in London. I advise my friends to use their first day to take an open-top bus tour, not just for the great introductory overview of the city but also for the generous helping of sunlight you get. Exercise is also advised; a walk in the park helps stretch muscles that are achy from hours of immobilization on a plane.

One jet-lag solution is the hormone melatonin. It is a controversial supplement, and the strict scientific rules for its use are so complicated that only a trip of 12 time zones could really merit trying to follow them. Melatonin cannot be bought in England, but it is easily found in the United States in health-food stores, vitamin shops, and pharmacies. It is often used as a sleep aid, which can be helpful in the first few days of your trip, when your body clock tells you it's 7 p.m. but it's really after midnight and you have a full day of sight-seeing planned for the next day. Take two to three milligrams for sleep—more than that will leave you groggy in the morning. As with any drug, check with your physician before taking it.

Health

You may want to take out medical insurance before you leave—you won't be covered by the National Health Service, unless you're an EU citizen. You may be eligible for free emergency care, but anything else, including follow-up or specialist services, will be paid for out of your pocket. Check your existing policies to see if they cover medical services abroad. If they don't, call Mutual of Omaha at (800) 228-9792 or Healthcare Abroad at (800) 237-6615. Both companies offer good coverage at a good price.

Pharmacies are open 24 hours and on Sundays on a rotating basis. Call your front desk or the local police station for a list. Bliss Chemist, 5 Marble Arch, W1, is open until midnight every day; phone (0207) 723-6116. Zafash Pharmacy, 233-235 Old Brompton Road, SW5, is open 24 hours a day; phone (0207) 373-2798.

Dentist   For dental problems, call the Dental Emergency Care Service 24 hours a day at (0207) 937-3951. They will give you the name of the nearest dental clinic.

Doctors   The better hotels will have their own doctor on call. If not, contact Doctor's Call at (0700) 037-2255. There's a private clinic in the famous Harley Street (number 117A) where you can seek medical help; call Medical Express at (0207) 499-1991. It's open 9 a.m.–6 p.m. Monday through Friday, 9:30 a.m.–2:30 p.m. on Saturday, and closed Sunday.

In England the emergency room is called the Casualty Department. Call 999 or 112 for an ambulance. You'll be taken to the nearest hospital, or, if your symptoms are not life threatening, you'll be advised which is the closest hospital to you.

We really don't think you'll get sick—London has good water and food. But you had better watch out for the cars. You will automatically look in the wrong direction when crossing the street, which is why you'll see directions ("Look Left") written on the street. Also keep a beady eye out for bicyclists and motorcyclists; they drive like maniacs here.

Self Help

If you're looking for 12-step meetings, there are plenty in London. Call for times and places.

- Alcoholics Anonymous, (0207) 833-0022; www.alcoholics-anonymous.org.uk
- Narcotics Anonymous, (0207) 730-0009; www.ukna.org
- Overeaters Anonymous, (0142) 698-4674

Calendar of Special Events

London has a huge number of traditional and modern events each month, so many that we had to try to narrow them down to the most interesting and important. When you arrive in London, pick up a *Time Out* magazine for the full selection, dates, and times, or if you're the kind of person who likes to plan ahead, go to www.timeout.com, ww.visitbritain.com, or to the London Tourist Board's website at www.Londontown.com.

January

London Parade   January 1. A big, brash spectacle with giant balloons, marching bands, clowns, vintage cars, and more, much in the style of the big Fifth Avenue parades in the United States. Starting at Parliament Square at noon, the parade follows Whitehall, Trafalgar Square, Lower Regent, and Piccadilly, ending up at Berkeley Square at 3 p.m. Lots of spillover fun can be had in Hyde Park later that day. (tube: for start of parade, Westminster, zone 9; for middle, Charing Cross, zone 7; for end, Green Park, zone 8)

Charles I Commemoration   Last Sunday of January. The English Civil War Society, dressed in authentic seventeenth-century uniforms complete with arms, follows the route King Charles I took on January 30, 1649, before he lost his head. They march from St. James's Park at 11:30 a.m., down the mall, through the Horse Guards, to the Banqueting House. It's an amazing sight. (zone 9; tube: St. James's Park)

London International Boat Show   The biggest boat show in all of Europe, it takes place in mid-January and lasts about ten days. A must for even the most casual water bug. For information, call (0178) 447-222, or go to www.bigblue.org.uk. (zone 11; tube: Earl's Court)

February

Chinese New Year Celebrations   Chinese New Year changes every year, but is always in either late January or early February. The celebration is usually on the first Sunday after the first day of the new year. London's Chinatown is located in Soho, around Garrard Street. It comes alive with bright decorations, red streamers, and the Lion Dance. Great food is everywhere. Call the Hong Kong government office at (0207) 499-9821. (zone 7; tube: Picadilly Circus)

Great Spitalfields Pancake Race   Shrove Tuesday (changes yearly; check calendar—it can also fall in early March). Starts at noon at the Old Spitalfields Market. Here's fun: teams of people running around Spitalfields flipping pancakes as they go. Why not? If you want to join in, call a few days before—(0207) 375-0441. (zone 3; tube: Liverpool Street)

March

Ideal Home Exhibition   Mid-March through April, Earl's Court Exhibition Centre 5. Enormous display of every possible gadget, knickknack, or consumer item one could attach to or use in a home. For information, call (0207) 244-0371. (zone 11; tube: Earl's Court)

Head of the River Boat Race   End of March (usually the Saturday before the Oxford vs. Cambridge Boat Race). Starting at Mortlake and ending at Putney, this is a smaller affair than the mighty Oxford and Cambridge race, but no less interesting to observe from the banks of the Thames. The Surrey Bank above Chiswick Bridge is a good viewing station, or you can park yourself in any of the riverside pubs along the way. Call (0193) 222-0401 for date and starting time. (west of zone 12; BritRail: Mortlake for start; tube: Hammersmith for mid-point, Putney Bridge for finish).

Oxford vs. Cambridge Boat Race   This takes place on a Saturday in late March or early April and is considered the big magilla, held since 1829. Teams of eight battle the current, rowing 6.8 kilometers upriver from Putney to Mortlake. Be prepared for crowds on the bridges, banks, and riverside pubs. Call (0207) 379-3234 for information. (west of zone 12; tube: Putney Bridge for start, Hammersmith for mid-point; BritRail: Mortlake for finish)

April

Gun Salute to Mark the Queen's Birthday   April 21 features a 41-gun Royal Salute to Queen Elizabeth II, fired at noon by the King's Troop Royal House Artillery in Hyde Park, opposite Dorchester Hotel, then a 62-gun fiesta at the Tower of London at 1 p.m. Take your pick or enjoy both. Bring earplugs. If the date falls on a Sunday, the event will take place on the Monday that follows. (zones 10 and 3; tube: Marble Arch for Hyde Park, Tower Hill for Tower of London)

London Harness Horse Parade   Easter Monday, Battersea Park. This competition of magnificent "working" horses drawing carriages and carts make the parade a treat unlike any. Battersea Park is a beautiful place in which to enjoy it. For information, phone (0173) 323-4451 or visit www.eastofengland.org.uk. (zone 11; tube: Sloane Square, then bus to Battersea)

London Marathon   Occurs on a Sunday in mid-April, starting at Greenwich Park and ending at Buckingham Palace. On average, 35,000 competitors participate, so if you want in, you'd better apply early. Entries close in October. Call (0207) 620-4117 or check www.londonmarathon.co.uk. (zones 7 and 6; BritRail: Blackheath or Greenwich for start; tube: Charing Cross for finish)

May

Chelsea Flower Show   Runs for two weeks in May at the Chelsea Royal Hospital. This is the *ne plus ultra* of London's spring affairs, so you'd better get tickets in advance and prepare to be jostled. Go early in the morning to see the amazing flora and fauna and garden accoutrements, the great passion of even the city-dwelling English. Call Ticketmaster at (0207) 344-4343; for more information, call (0207) 630-7422 (zone 11; tube: Sloane Square)

May Fair and Puppet Festival   Second Sunday at St. Paul's Church Garden and Covent Garden. A procession, a service at St. Paul's, and then hours of Punch-and-Judy shows amount to family fun. Call Alternative Arts at (0207) 375-0441 for information. (zone 7; tube: Covent Garden)

Royal Windsor Horse Show   Mid-May, Home Park, Windsor Castle. A wonderful day out for everyone, equestrians or not. Besides the jumping and showing competitions, there are amazing Pony Club games, booths galore, and a few carnival rides, all conducted under the impressive, hulking shadow of Windsor Castle. For information, call (0207) 341-9341 or visit www.olympia-show-jumping.co.uk. (outside zones; BritRail: Windsor)

June

Beating Retreat Household Division   Early June, Buckingham Palace. This is a floodlit nighttime spectacle of all the queen's horses and all the queen's men. Tickets available from March; book early. Call the Household Division at (0207) 839-5323.

Trooping the Colour   Early June, Horse Guards Parade, Whitehall. Yes, the lucky queen gets two birthdays: one in April when she was actually born, and an official one in June, when the weather is better for her to inspect her troops, which parade before her. There is a procession to Buckingham Palace, where the air force flies overhead and a gun salute is fired. Tickets are awarded by ballot; call (0207) 414-2479 for details. Check in Hyde Park during the preceding Saturdays—you may catch a rehearsal. (zone 9; tube: Westminster)

Kenwood Lakeside Concerts   These are held at the beautiful Kenwood House grounds, every Saturday night until September in Hampstead Heath. A 50-year-old tradition, these open-air classical concerts also feature laser shows, fireworks displays, and the Heath at sundown—enchanting. For info call (0208) 233-5892. (zone 1; tube: Archway, Golders Green, or Highgate, then bus 210)

Royal Academy Summer Exhibition   From early June to mid-August at the Royal Academy in Piccadilly. For over 200 years, the Royal Academy of Art has been showing the work of contemporary artists in its summer exhibitions, many of which have caused scandals in their day. You can browse or buy. Call (0207) 300-8000. (zone 8; tube: Green Park or Picadilly Circus)

Royal Ascot   Mid-June, Ascot Racecourse, Berkshire. Made famous to Americans by the scene in the movie *My Fair Lady*, Ascot brings out all of social London. It's almost more entertaining to dish the outfits and hats than to watch the races. For information call (0134) 462-2211. (outside zones; BritRail: Ascot)

Wimbledon Lawn Tennis Championships   Late June to early July, Wimbledon, Southwest London. This is where all true tennis fans want to be, and everyone else loves the strawberries and cream. Tickets are hard to come by, so make plans in advance if possible. Tickets for Centre and Number One

Courts are awarded by ballot. Call (0208) 946-2244 for information. (zone 12; tube: Wimbledon)

July

BBC Henry Wood Promenade Concerts (the Proms)   Mid-July through September, Royal Albert Hall, Kensington Gore. Known affectionately as the "Proms," these eight weeks of a variety of orchestral concerts, from classical to contemporary, can be seen for a small fee (standing) or for significantly more (sitting). The last night is the big extravaganza. Call to get a copy of the BBC Proms Guide—(0191) 222-0381. For more information, call (0207) 765-5575. (zone 13; tube: South Kensington or Gloucester Road)

August

Opening of Buckingham Palace   Early August through October. While the queen's away, the tourists will play. Lines and lines of camera-laden hoi polloi wait to take the grand tour through Queen Elizabeth's townhouse while she summers in Scotland. Tickets can be ordered in advance by calling (0207) 321-2233 or bought at the ticket booth in Green Park. For recorded info, call (0207) 799-2331, or visit www.royalresidences.com. (zone 9; tube: Green Park or St. James)

Notting Hill Carnival   End of August, Ladbroke Grove and Portobello Road. It's the biggest street fair in all of Europe, held on a rather slim street, so be ready to stand shoulder to shoulder to enjoy the Caribbean flavor of steel bands and wild partying. Call (0208) 964-0544 for exact date. (zone 13; tube: Notting Hill)

September

Great River Race   Mid-September, starting on the Thames at Richmond. You have never seen such a collection of boats. Over 200 traditional crafts—including such diverse specimens as whalers, Viking longboats, Chinese dragon boats, and canoes—race from Ham House in Richmond at 10:30 a.m., finishing at Island Gardens, across from Greenwich Pier about three hours later. Call (0208) 398-9057. (zones 12 and 5; tube: Richmond for start; Docklands Light Rail: Island Gardens for finish)

Horse of the Year Show   End of September, Wembley Arena, Wembley. In a country that takes its horses seriously, this event features the finest creatures and most gifted riders. It doesn't get any better than this. Get your tickets early from the Wembley Arena Box Office at (0208) 900-1234. (outside zones; tube: Wembley Park)

Open House London   Mid-September. Finally, a chance to get in to look inside (for free!) more than 500 amazing houses and buildings usually off-limits to the likes of us commoners. Call (0900) 160-0061 for information or visit www.londonopenhouse.org.

October

Costermongers Pearly Harvest Festival   First Sunday in October, St. Martin-in-the Fields, Trafalgar Square. An old cockney tradition celebrating the apple ("coster") harvest that starts with a service at the church and displays a Pearly King or Queen decked out in a costume bombarded with white buttons. Musical merry-makers everywhere. Service starts at 3 p.m. Call (0207) 930-0089 for details. (zone 7; tube: Charing Cross)

Trafalgar Day Parade   Third Sunday in October, Trafalgar Square. Big traditional, military-style parade commemorating Lord Nelson's sea victory at the Battle of Trafalgar in 1805. Marching bands, Sea Cadets. Call (0207) 928-8978. (zone 7; tube: Charing Cross)

November

Bonfire Night and Guy Fawkes' Day Firework Displays   November 5, all over London. Guy Fawkes was the Catholic conspirator who gave his name to history to commemorate the narrowly averted Gunpowder Plot to blow up King James I and Parliament. To find out the best displays and the best places to see them, consult *Time Out,* call the London Tourist Board at (0207) 971-0026, or check their website at www.londontown.com.

London to Brighton Veteran Car Run   First Sunday of November. Come to Hyde Park to see the array of vintage cars that will drive to Brighton. Call (0175) 368-1736 for time and exact place. (zone 10; tube: Hyde Park Corner)

Lord Mayor's Show   Mid-November. This is an event that goes back 700 years, which is old even by England's standards. The lord mayor rides through the city in a let-them-eat-cake-type gilded carriage (which can be seen at the Museum of London during the rest of the year), followed by a retinue of floats, bands, and military marchers. Call for details at (0207) 606-3030. (zone 3; tube: Mansion House)

Remembrance Day   November 11. At the 11th hour on the 11th day of the 11th month, all of England falls silent in remembrance of those who died in the two World Wars. Red poppies are bought and worn by an enormous number of Londoners to show respect for the soldiers who gave their lives for England. On the nearest Sunday to the 11th, there is a service for the war dead at the Cenotaph in Whitehall. (zone 9; tube: Whitehall)

December

Christmas Lights and Tree   Late November and December, central London. Various Christmas lighting ceremonies take place on Regent, Oxford, Bond, and Jermyn Streets, among others. These often involve some flavor-of-the-month celebs. Check *Time Out.* The real fun is the tree-lighting ceremony in Trafalgar Square, which is followed by caroling around the tree each evening, between 4 and 10 p.m. Consult the London Tourist Board at www.londontown.com, or try www.timeout.com.

Olympia International Show Jumping Champions   Mid-December, Grand Hall, Olympia. This is a fun-filled exhibition, rivaling even the Wembley Show for sheer excitement. Lots of trade booths provide plenty of Christmas-shopping opportunities for horse lovers. Call the box office for tickets at (0207) 373-3113. (zone 13; tube: Olympia)

Part Three

Hotels

Selecting Accommodations

Your accommodations can make or break a vacation or business trip. Traveling is stressful, touring around London is certainly tiring, and nothing takes the edge off like sinking into a warm, comfortable, hospitable room—that doesn't cost an arm and a leg—after a long day.

London hotels, like everything else here, are expensive. The standards for hotels are different than those for hotels in the United States: when you're paying enough, you can safely assume a variety of goods and services, such as bellhops, concierge, 24-hour room service, a health club, king-size beds, air conditioning, full business facilities, minibar, cable TV, and so on. Because many hotels in America are part of a chain, they tend to have standardized properties with predictable amenities. Not so in London. You can go from crash pads to castles in one neighborhood, even on the same street, maybe even in the same hotel. In a typical townhouse-conversion hotel, you can have a room on the first floor with a balcony and French windows looking onto a garden square, and for the same price get a room on the top floor with small windows, a slanted ceiling, and a view of the brown-bricked backs of white-fronted houses. Even the chains that do operate here can have wildly varying properties with unvarying prices.

What to Expect

Here are some important facts to remember and resign yourself to regarding London hotels:

1. Expect small rooms. A single room usually means a very small room, with a single full-size bed.

2. Certain amenities are not a given. Air conditioning is not always available, neither are minibars, safes, cable TV, health facilities, or even private bathrooms. We have

listed some of the amenities, but call or check websites to be sure of what is offered.

3. If the price is really low, say £30 a night, the likelihood is high that the hotel is going to be pretty funky, and you'll be sharing a bathroom. Budget hotels can be abysmal. I have included a couple of places costing £50 that I have checked out and that are clean and reasonably bearable.

4. When you're looking for a discount, you're better off calling a hotel directly and making a deal with the reservations managers than booking through a travel agent.

5. Take advantage of the weekend break rates at the five-star hotels, and spend the weekdays at a moderately priced one.

6. Don't expect the level of service you would get in a moderate-to-expensive hotel in the United States in comparable London hotels. It's pretty much only the five-star hotels here that have the customer-is-always-right-what-can-I-do-for-you-right-away-sir-yes-ma'am kind of service.

7. Always check to see if breakfast is included in your price. Also, it's very important to know if service and the 17.5% Value Added Tax (VAT) are also included in the price. These two add-ons can amount to a considerable addition to your bill.

Best of Britain

The hotels listed here are those that I think are very English, with the best kind of British atmosphere and charm. It seems a shame to come to London and not get to enjoy traditional English style. I've included a few plain, chain-like, moderate hotels, but I have concentrated on the ones that don't remind me of America. There are so many hotels in London with pleasing sitting rooms that have gas fires, antiques, and deep sofas, and that serve an authentic cream tea and massive English breakfast—they simply must be experienced to get the full flavor of London. Of course, some of the standard chain hotels might well have features that make the most sense for you, such as wheelchair access, fitness club, frequent-flier-mile tie-ins, good incentive packages, and the price and location you prefer. I have my own preferences as to neighborhoods, but they may not be yours.

Neighborhoods for Hotels

There are a number of excellent neighborhoods to stay in. Here are my favorite:

Zone 11 South Kensington: an easy walk to Hyde Park and Kensington Gardens, three museums, Harrods, Albert Hall, Christies' Auction House, and Chelsea; three tube lines, many buses; lots of French bakeries, restaurants for every budget; and a small-town feeling in the big city. Downside: a bit expensive for smallish quarters (although that could be said of most hotels in London).

Zone 8 Mayfair and Piccadilly, where you'll find Hyde Park, Green Park, St. James's Park, Bond Street shopping, art galleries everywhere, the Royal Academy, an easy walk to the West End, and good transportation. Downside: extravagantly expensive—look for deals at the (few) moderately priced choices.

Zone 7 Soho and the West End: theaters, restaurants, National Gallery, Covent Garden, bookstores on Charing Cross, better people-watching and nightlife than anywhere else. Downside: noise and fumes, and a bit dicey at night. When the bars close, the drunks and louts come out.

Zone 2 Bloomsbury: convenient to the British Museum, bookstores, the West End and Soho as well as Lincoln's Inn and the City. Downside: a little desolate here and there at night.

Zone 1 Hampstead: enjoy fresh air, the Heath, the feeling of country. Downside: need to commute to everything on the Northern line.

Cheap but Not Always Cheerful Hotel Neighborhoods

- Bayswater
- Earl's Court
- Victoria

Out There

There's something to be said for staying well out of central London, but not all of it is good. The public transportation can be dreadful and downright unapproachable at rush hours. Many of the outer areas of London do not offer a wide choice of amenities like restaurants, convenience stores, and entertainment. There are also parts of outer London that are aesthetically unpleasing, downright grotty, or dully suburban. Whatever hotels you may find may be less expensive, but will rarely—with some exceptions in Richmond and in Hampstead—offer the standard of service that the central London hotels will.

Having said that, there *are* good bed-and-breakfast deals in areas that are far from the sound and fury and pollution of London and are served by tube and rail services, which can get you into the middle of town in 30–40 minutes or less. People can get more house for their money out there, and so you may find a bed-and-breakfast with a garden, your own private entrance, perhaps a basement apartment or your own floor, cleanish air, and blessed quiet. The innkeepers probably will leave you quite alone, as personal reserve is still one of the great British traditions.

Call for Deals

Almost every hotel in London, except for the already cut-rate ones, will have some kind of saver scheme, be it a weekend reduction, a package that includes breakfast and a free night, price reductions during the seasonal (January and August) sales held in London's big shops, a summer season, a low season, a Christmas season, a corporate rate, a half-price scheme, a no-reason lowered rate, and so on. They want you to come to London, and they want you to stay in their hotel. There is also the possibility of a last-minute room, in which a hotel with an empty room will agree to a huge reduction just to fill it. This requires flexibility but it can spell big savings.

Rule Number One in making any of these deals is to talk to the reception manager—she or he is the only person who can agree to making deals. Chat with the manager and see what can be arranged—service is their business, and they do aim to please. But remember that some hotels don't need to make deals—check out the listings and see how many rooms a hotel has. Chances are that the more rooms there are, the more rooms will be empty. Often, the rooms that remain empty are the junior, executive, or superior suites. To get one of those for the price of a standard double is a worthy coup, and you will be very happy in such a room, especially in the grand hotels.

Bed-and-Breakfasts

Bed-and-breakfasts are big in Britain, and in London there are some drop-dead gorgeous homes that are open to you through agencies—you won't believe your luck. The price, with a few exceptions, includes breakfast and is per person per night. There is often a minimum stay required. You may be asked to pay a booking fee and to place a deposit in sterling or credit card.

Some Excellent Companies

The Bulldog Club   (Phone (0207) 371-3202; fax (0207) 371-2015; www. bulldogclub.com. In the U.S., call (877) 727-3004; in Australia, call (612) 9960-5812). Only the crème de la crème of houses are included in this exclusive group. There are about 30 properties available, and the criteria are that the guests have a reasonably separate area from the host family's quarters, the inn is within a five-minute walk to public transportation, there are amenities such as tea and coffeemaking facilities and bathrobes, and that the inn be in a very fine and beautifully decorated house. Prices range from £105 for two people to £85 for a single. You pay a fee of £25 to join the "club" for a three-year membership, which is the best money you'll spend in London.

Uptown Reservations   (Phone (0207) 351-3444; fax (0207) 351-9383; or visit www.uptownres.co.uk.) This is another very high-tone agency, with fine houses of high standard in good central neighborhoods as well as in outer London's leafy zones. Singles are a mere £65 a night, double or twin is £85, family room is £110.

London Homestead Services   (Phone (0208) 949-4455; fax (0208) 549-5492; or visit www.lhslondon.com.) This service has about 200 homes in the London area, many of which are pretty far out of central London, where you can get a double room for as little as £16. Naturally, rooms cost more in central London.

London First Choice Apartments (Phone (0208) 990-9033; fax (0208) 754-1200; or visit www.lfca.co.uk.) LFCA has a large assortment of hotels, serviced and nonserviced apartments, and bed-and-breakfasts. See the website for more information. Prices vary according to neighborhood and type of accomodation, from £89 for a studio in Earl's Court, to £646 for a 3-bedroom apartment in Mayfair.

Serviced and Self-Serviced Apartments

A serviced apartment can be a good alternative to a hotel room, with commensurate prices and much more room—to be able to close a door on your traveling companion(s) once in a while can be a great luxury. The best ones will offer everything a hotel does; some even provide meals. You may get a 24-hour concierge, cable TV, laundry, and daily maid service; you may even get a washer/dryer in the apartment, secretarial services, membership to a health club, a fully equipped kitchen, and more. When you factor in the costs of eating all your meals in restaurants, a hotel costs considerably more than its nightly rate. An apartment can save you wads of dosh, as they say here, by allowing you to make some of your meals yourself.

Manors & Co. (Phone (800) 454-4385 in the U.S. or (0207) 486-5982 in London; fax (0207) 486-6770; or visit www.manors.co.uk.) Manors & Co. offer a selection of high-end apartments in good neighborhoods, from studios to five-bedroom pads. Luxurious 1-bedrooms start at £140; 3-bedrooms/2-bathrooms at £310 per night.

Home From Home (Phone (0207) 584-8914; fax (0207) 823-8433; or visit www.homefromhome.co.uk.) With over 200 properties in London, Home From Home can be dialed from America toll free at (800) 748-9783 for a brochure, but its website suffices to show you what gorgeous houses and decent prices they offer: a 1 bedroom starts at only £575 per week!

London's Luxury Hotels

The various star ratings given by Michelin have placed the five-star hotel firmly at the top of the heap. In the *Unofficial Guide to London,* we have our own star-rating system, ranging from five to one, five being the best. When we give a hotel a five-star rating, it is only in the relative context of the hotels covered in this book, and doesn't reflect the standard five-star rating of hugely expensive, world-class luxury hotels that we have listed below.

The reason these luxury hotels are listed separately is that some of them are classic London establishments, such as the Ritz or Claridges, and no book on London would be complete without them. But if you can afford the $500+ a night that these hotels charge, you really don't need guidance from me. You will know that an expensive luxury hotel in London will have all the amenities and services found in the great hotels all around the world.

However, a word of caution about the following hotels: the styles vary to a large degree, from the stark minimalism of the Hempel to the Georgian excesses of the Lanesborough or the art deco insouciance of Claridges. They will also vary in size. Views are never a given, even when you're paying $600 a night; and business amenities are not always part of the package. So, buyer beware: if you are splurging on a luxury hotel, question the reservations clerk closely as to what is offered, and make a point of requesting a good view, a spacious room, and a good location on your floor. In the converted-townhouse variety of hotel, the first floor (first above the ground floor, that is) rooms in the front will have the balconies and the French windows, and the top floors may have tiny windows and angled ceilings.

The majority of the following hotels are in the Mayfair and Piccadilly areas of Zone 8. In the hotel-profile listing, you will find somewhat more moderately priced establishments in this zone (except for the extended profile on Brown's), but the fact is that this is a very expensive hotel neighborhood, frequented by movie stars on studio tabs and assorted millionaires with expense accounts.

You can, however, call any of the following hotels and look into a discount. There are a number of possibilties: low-season rates, applicable in January and February; summer discounts; weekend break rates; upgrading to a bigger room; paying for your room in advance in dollars; executive discounts; and frequent-flier tie ins. Call directly and talk to the reservations manager to work out a deal—many of the good hotels have toll-free numbers in the United States. A few of these luxury hotels are owned by chain groups, such as Savoy, Forte, Intercontinental, and Hilton. Chains may offer any number of promotional deals, from holiday discounts to packages that include meals. Some of these otherwise astronomically priced hotels have single rooms at surprisingly good rates—the room may be small, but you'll have the best of comfort and service you can imagine. Many will upgrade you to a junior suite if there's one available. Remember that no hotel likes an empty room. All the prices quoted below are for standard double rooms and I have calculated and included the 17.5% VAT, which adds up to a sizable dollop on top of a sizable basic rack rate—the more expensive hotels just don't have the nerve to include it in quoted prices. Some think the best way to experience these hotels is to have tea or a meal in one, and save your money on a less pricey pad.

The Berkeley   Right off Knightsbridge by Hyde Park Corner, this hotel has a magnificent spa, two excellent restaurants (La Tante Claire and Vong), and well-appointed, spacious rooms. There are 157 rooms, starting at £440 (zone 10, Wilton Place, SW1; phone (0207) 235-6000; fax (0207) 235-4330; www.savoy-group.com; tube: Knightsbridge).

Blakes   Completely gorgeous hotel in South Kensington, catering to rock stars, models, actors, and so on. Although less expensive than the others in this class, you can still fracture your credit card between the tariff and the very fine restaurant, also called Blakes. The rooms are exuberantly and individually decorated in styles ranging from expensive bordello to country squire to Raj's field tent. Good value for a five-star hotel, even though some of the rooms are smallish. There are 51 rooms, starting at £282 (zone 11, 33 Roland Gardens, SW7; phone (0207) 370-6701; fax (0207) 373-0442; www.blakeshotel.com; tube: South Kensington).

Brown's Hotel   Victorian gentlemen's club atmosphere and beautiful antique furnishings; there's nothing showy or over the top about this place except for its prices. Some of the rooms can be surprisingly small, although cozy, and there is no air conditioning. They serve an excellent afternoon tea in one of the three lovely sitting rooms. There are 118 rooms, starting at £360. See profile for more information (zone 8, 30–34 Albemarle Street, W1; phone (0207) 493-6020; fax (0207) 493-9381; www.brownshotel. co.uk; tube: Green Park).

Claridges   Bold decor evokes Jazz Age glamour and royal luxury. People of serious substance stay here. Fantastic, albeit expensive tea in impressive surroundings, with a likely chance to see a society wedding. There are 203 rooms, quite deluxe, starting at £435 (zone 8; Brook Street, W1; phone (0207) 629-8860; fax (0207) 499-2210; www.savoy-group.com; tube: Bond Street).

The Connaught   Grand country house is the style here, and perfect service the watchwords. It's been around since 1897; Chalres DeGaulle made it his wartime headquarters, and Cecil Beaton and David Niven called it home. It attracts so many regulars that it's almost a club; make reservations well in advance of your visit. There are 90 rooms, starting at £475 (zone 8; 16 Carlos Place, W1; phone (0207) 499-7070; fax (0207) 495-3262; www.savoy-group.com; tube: Bond Street).

The Dorchester   One of London's grandest establishments, this hotel is right across from Hyde Park and walking distance to some of the toniest shops in London. Restaurants and the health club are of the highest standards, as are the rooms and the decor. You can see where your money is going at this hotel. There are 244 rooms, starting at £346 (zone 8; 53 Park Lane, W1; phone (0207) 629-8888; fax (0207) 409-0114; www.dorchesterhotel.com; tube: Marble Arch).

The Four Seasons   Owned by the Four Seasons Group, this hotel often offers promotional packages. The decor is opulent without being ostentatious; they provide excellent service and food. There are 220 rooms, starting at £358 (zone 8; Hamilton Place in Park Lane, W1; phone (0207) 499-0888; fax (0207) 493-6629; www.fourseasons.com; tube: Hyde Park Corner).

Grosvenor House   Old and fabulous, this hotel houses the splendid restaurant Nico at 90, among other fine eateries. It's a bit formal, but very luxurious, and is owned by the Meridien group. There are 586 rooms, starting at £400 (zone 8; Park Lane, W1; phone (0207) 499-6363; fax (0207) 493-3341; www.lemeridien-grosvenorhouse.com; tube: Hyde Park Corner).

The Halcyon Hotel   What a charmer this one is, in this fashionable neighborhood, a stone's throw from Richard Branson's huge pied à terre. Exquisitely decorated and well sited for a stroll in Holland Park, this 43-room hotel attracts the rich and famous in droves. Double rooms start at £325 (zone 13; 81 Holland Park, W11; phone (0207) 727-7288; fax (0207) 229-8516; www.thehalcyon.com; tube: Holland Park).

The Landmark   Tucked between Oxford and Baker streets, The Landmark gives good value for money because it's out of the Mayfair-Piccadilly high-rent district. There's an impressive atrium in which to eat, a fitness center and pool, and good-sized rooms. Modern refurbishment in an old building. All 298 rooms are double and start at £390 (zone 14; 222 Marylebone Road, NW1; phone (0207) 631-8000; fax (0207) 631-8033; www.landmarklondon.co.uk; tube: Marylebone).

The Lanesborough   You'd never guess to look at the elaborately Georgian interior that gurneys used to be rolled around these floors instead of room-service carts. This former hospital is now a formal hotel, full of charm and mahogany-paneled splendor, with an Asian theme–decor restaurant of high quality. There's a butler call button in all the rooms; need I say more? There are 95 rooms, starting at £435 for a standard double (zone 10; Hyde Park Corner, SW1; phone (0207) 259-5599; fax (0207) 259-5606; www.lanesborough.com; tube: Hyde Park Corner).

London Hilton   The place where Elizabeth Taylor reportedly spent more than one of her wedding nights, the London Hilton has successfully made the transition from the James Bond era to today with all five stars firmly intact. It isn't a picturesque building on the outside, but it does have the greatest views of Hyde Park available and good-sized rooms. If you want to check the view but not pay the £382 for a room, stop in for a drink on the twenty-eighth-floor restaurant. Half of the 449 rooms overlook the park. If you want to be near the Hilton, try the Hilton Mews around back, a slightly less expensive but charming alternative. (Zone 8; 22 Park Lane, W1; phone (0207) 493-8000; fax (0207) 208-4140; www.hilton.com; tube: Green Park.)

Mandarin Oriental Hotel   A grand old hotel in the most marvelous location. There are only suites facing north on Hyde Park; the hotel also faces Knightsbridge, one of the noisiest streets. There is a newly renovated restaurant on the first floor—much too modern for this elegant Edwardian building, but with a good view into the park. There are 200 rooms; doubles start at £440 (zone 10; 66 Knightsbridge, SW1; phone (0207) 235-2000; fax (0207) 201-3633; www.mandarinoriental.com; tube: Knightsbridge).

The Metropolitan   This is where the renowned Met Club is housed, a private club that was at the top of the social ladder when it opened in 1997, and is still formidable. Guests at The Metropolitan can get in, a big plus for young social types. It has a state-of-the-art gym. Its sister hotels, The Halkin in Belgravia (5 Halkin Street in Belgravia; (0207) 333-1000; 41 rooms from £334) and Myhotel in Bloomsbury (11–13 Bayley Street, Bedford Square; phone (0207) 667-6000; 76 rooms from £346) are also shrines to cool beige, beech, and blank walls. There 155 rooms, from £315 (zone 8; Old Park Lane, W1; phone (0207) 447-1000; fax (0207) 447-1100; www.metropolitan.co.uk; tube: Hyde Park Corner).

The Ritz   What can you say about a synonym for luxury and extravagance? Before you think it's just plain out of the question, call and see what kind of deals they may have. They have a lot of rooms to fill. If all you want is tea, call well in advance of your trip to make a reservation—weekends can be booked as much as a month ahead. The decor is Versailles on Piccadilly, and the comfort is sumptuousness itself. The rooms facing Green Park are the best, sharing the view with such worthy mansions as Spencer House. Individually decorated rooms, 131 in all, start at £405 and go up, up, up (zone 8; 150 Piccadilly, W1; phone (0207) 493-8181; fax (0207) 493-2687; www.theritzlondon.com; tube: Green Park).

Sanderson   This hotel is the latest, hippest addition to the Ian Schrager chain, favored by rich, high-profile media personalities, whose personal needs may be inferred by the excessive luxury offered here: 450-thread count cotton, three two-lined phones in each room, a yoga studio and two-story holistic bathhouse, a private fitness area in each room, the list goes on and on (I was most struck by the children's play area—most luxury hotels hope that children will stay home). The decor is quirky, dreamy, Dali-esque, with eclectic furnishings in an array of colors and periods. Swathes of white muslin shrouding mirrors, lights, and doorways add mystique. The rooms are stark, yet chic, with chrome and white furnishings. All this makes up for the fact that Sanderson in a charmless 1960s block building.

Hang out in the state-of-the-art gym or the bar long enough and you are guaranteed a close encounter with the likes of Madonna or Brad Pitt. There are 150 rooms, ranging from £346 upwards. Its sister hotel, St. Martin's Lane, is equally chic, hip, and trendy, but the attitude of the employee who answered when we called to arrange to see the hotel was so appallingly rude, that I will do no more for that hotel than give you the website and let you make up you own mind. (Zone 7; 50 Berners Street, W1; phone (0207) 300-9500; fax (0207) 300-1401; www.ianschragerhotels.com; tube: Oxford Circus or Tottenham Court.)

The Savoy I don't think the Savoy has changed much since it was Frank Sinatra's favorite hotel in foggy London town. It is still a gorgeous place: like Claridges, it maintains the decor of its salad days, and its service is impeccable. It's located right in the thick of things, perfect for theatergoers. Rooms, 161 in all, start at £405; £1,200 will get you a one-bedroom suite. The only rooms overlooking the Thames are junior suites plus. I believe Frank took the penthouse suite. (Zone 7; 1 Savoy Hill, Strand, WC2; phone (0207) 836-4343; fax (0207) 240-6040; www.savoy-group.co.uk; tube: Charing Cross.)

Hotel Ratings

Overall Ratings We have distinguished properties according to relative quality, tastefulness, state of repair, cleanliness, and size of standard rooms, grouping them into classifications denoted by stars. Overall star ratings in this guide apply to London properties only and do not correspond to ratings awarded by the British Tourism Board, automobile clubs, or other travel critics. Overall ratings are presented to show the difference we perceive between one property and another. They are assigned without regard to location or to whether a property has restaurants, recreational facilities, entertainment, or other extras.

★★★★★	Superior	Tasteful and luxurious by any standard
★★★★	Extremely Nice	Above average in appointments and design; very comfortable
★★★	Nice	Average but quite comfortable
★★	Adequate	Plain but meets all essential needs
★	Budget	Spartan, not aesthetically pleasing, but clean

Quality Ratings In addition to overall ratings (which delineate broad categories), we also employ quality ratings. They apply to room quality only and describe the property's standard accommodations. In addition to standard accommodations, many hotels offer luxury rooms and special suites that are not rated in this guide. Our rating scale is ★–★★★★★, with ★★★★★ as the best possible rating and ★ as the worst.

Value Ratings We also provide a value rating to give you some sense of the quality of a room in relation to its cost. As before, the ratings are based on the quality of room for the money and do not take into account location, services, or amenities.

Our scale is as follows:

★★★★★	An exceptional bargain
★★★★	A good deal
★★★	Fairly priced (you get exactly what you pay for)
★★	Somewhat overpriced
★	Significantly overpriced

A ★★½ room at £100 may have the same value rating as a ★★★★ room at £180, but that does not mean that the rooms will be of comparable quality. Regardless of whether it's a good deal or not, a ★★½ room is still a ★★½ room.

For each hotel we also provide the London geographic zone where the property is located.

How the Hotels Compare

What follows is a table that contains the hotels we have researched and profiled organized by overall rating. To find a particular hotel listed in this table, look through the alphabetical section of profiles later in the chapter.

If you use subsequent editions of this guide, you will notice that many of the ratings and rankings change. In addition to the inclusion of new properties, these changes also reflect guest-room renovations or improved maintenance and housekeeping. A failure to properly maintain guest rooms or a lapse in housekeeping standards can affect negatively the ratings.

Finally, before you begin to shop for a hotel, take a hard look at this letter we received from a couple in Hot Springs, Arkansas:

> We cancelled our room reservations to follow the advice in your book [and reserved a hotel room highly ranked by the Unofficial Guide].We wanted inexpensive, but clean and cheerful.We got inexpensive, but [also] dirty, grim, and depressing. I really felt disappointed in your advice and the room. It was the pits.That was the one real piece of informaton I needed from your book! The room spoiled the holiday for me aside from our touring.

Needless to say, this letter was as unsettling to us as the bad room was to our reader. Our integrity as travel journalists, after all, is based on the quality of the information we provide our readers. Even with the best of intentions and the most conscientious research, however, we cannot inspect every room in every hotel. What we do, in statistical terms, is take a sample: we check out several rooms selected at random in each hotel and base our ratings and rankings on those rooms. The inspections are conducted anonymously and without the knowledge of the management. Although unusual, it is certainly possible that the rooms we randomly inspect are not representative of the majority of rooms at a particular hotel. This is particularly true in the smaller London hotels that offer such a variety of room sizes and styles.

Another possibility is that the rooms we inspect in a given hotel are representative, but that by bad luck a reader is assigned a room that is inferior. When we rechecked the hotel our reader disliked, we discovered our rating was correctly representative, but that he and his wife had unfortunately been assigned to one of a small number of threadbare rooms scheduled for renovation.

The key to avoiding disappointment is to snoop around in advance. We recommend that you ask for a photo of a hotel's standard guest room before you book, or at least get a copy of the hotel's promotional brochure.

HOW THE HOTELS COMPARE				
Hotel	Overall Quality	Room Quality	Value	Zone
The Charlotte Street Hotel	★★★★★	★★★★	★★★★	7
Great Eastern Hotel	★★★★★	★★★★★	★★★★	3
The Cliveden Town House	★★★★★	★★★★½	★★★	11
Dukes Hotel	★★★★★	★★★★½	★★★★	9
Goring Hotel	★★★★★	★★★★½	★★★★	9
Brown's Hotel	★★★★★	★★★★	★★★	8
L'Hotel	★★★★★	★★★★	★★★★★	10
11 Cadogan Gardens	★★★★★	★★★★	★★★	11
Thistle Hotel Victoria	★★★★★	★★★★	★★★★★	9
The Basil Street Hotel	★★★★½	★★★★½	★★★★★	10
London Marriot Hotel at County Hall	★★★★½	★★★★½	★★★	5
The Milestone Hotel	★★★★½	★★★★	★★★	11
Covent Garden Hotel	★★★★	★★★★½	★★★★	7
Dorset Square Hotel	★★★★	★★★★½	★★★★★	14
The Gore	★★★★	★★★★½	★★★★	11
The Pelham	★★★★	★★★★½	★★★★	11
The Rookery	★★★★	★★★★½	★★★	3
The Hampshire Edwardian Radisson	★★★★	★★★★	★★	7

HOW THE HOTELS COMPARE (continued)

Hotel	Overall Quality	Room Quality	Value	Zone
Hilton Mews	★★★★	★★★★	★★★	8
Millenium Hotel Mayfair	★★★★	★★★★	★★★	8
The Cadogan Hotel	★★★★	★★★½	★★★	10
The Franklin Hotel	★★★★	★★★½	★★★★	10
The Montague on the Gardens	★★★★	★★★½	★★★	2
Thistle Hotel Hyde Park	★★★★	★★★½	★★★★★	14
Hazlitt's Hotel	★★★½	★★★★	★★★★	7
Parkes Hotel	★★★½	★★★★	★★★★	10
The Claverley	★★★½	★★★½	★★★★★	10
Abbey Court	★★★	★★★★	★★★★★	13
Miller's Residence	★★★	★★★★	★★★★	13
Number Sixteen	★★★	★★★★	★★★★★	11
Pembridge Court Hotel	★★★	★★★★	★★★★★	13
Durrants	★★★	★★★½	★★★★★	14
Flemings	★★★	★★★½	★★★★	8
The Gallery Hotel	★★★	★★★½	★★★★	11
Grange White Hall Hotel	★★★	★★★½	★★★★	2
Jury's	★★★	★★★½	★★★	11
The Portobello Hotel	★★★	★★★½	★★★	13
The Rembrandt Hotel	★★★	★★★½	★★★★	11
Thistle Hotel Kensington Palace	★★★	★★★½	★★★★★	13
The Gainsborough	★★★	★★★	★★★★	11
Hotel Russell	★★★	★★★	★★★★	2
The Columbia Hotel	★★	★★★½	★★★★★	14
Holiday Inn Mayfair	★★	★★★½	★★★	8
Morgan Hotel	★★	★★★½	★★★★★	2
Quality Hotel	★★	★★★½	★★★★★	9
Five Sumner Place Hotel	★★	★★★	★★★★★	11
The Pastoria Radisson Edwardian	★★	★★★	★★	7
Riverside Hotel	★★	★★★	★★★★★	12
The Edward Lear Hotel	★	★★★½	★★★★★	14
The Fielding Hotel	★	★★★	★★★	7
Comfort Inn Notting Hill	★	★★½	★★★★★	13
Ruskin Hotel	★	★★½	★★★★★	2
St. Margaret's Hotel	★	★★½	★★★★★	2
The Cherry Court Hotel	★	★★	★★★★	9

HOTELS BY ZONE

Zone 2: Bloomsbury and Holborn

Hotel Russell

Morgan Hotel

St. Margaret's Hotel

The Montague on the Gardens

Ruskin Hotel

Grange White Hall Hotel

Zone 3: The City, Clerkenwell, and Barbican

Great Eastern Hotel

The Rookery

Zone 5: South London—South Bank, Lambeth, Brixton

London Marriott Hotel, County Hall

Zone 7: Soho and the West End

Covent Garden Hotel

Hazlitt's Hotel

The Pastoria Radisson Edwardian

The Fielding Hotel

The Hampshire Edwardian Radisson

The Charlotte Street Hotel

Zone 8: Mayfair and Piccadilly

Brown's Hotel

The Connaught

The Four Seasons

Grosvenor House

Holiday Inn Mayfair

The Metropolitan

The Ritz

Claridges

The Dorchester

Flemings

Hilton Mews

London Hilton

Millennium Hotel Mayfair

Zone 9: Victoria and Westminster

The Cherry Court Hotel

Goring Hotel

Thistle Hotel Victoria

Dukes Hotel

Quality Hotel

Zone 10: Knightsbridge and Belgravia

The Basil Street Hotel

The Cadogan Hotel

The Franklin Hotel

The Lanesborough

Parkes Hotel

The Berkely

The Claverley

L'Hotel

Mandarin Oriental Hotel

Zone 11: Chelsea and South Kensington

Blakes

11 Cadogan Gardens

The Gainsborough

The Gore

The Milestone Hotel

The Pelham

The Cliveden Town House

Five Sumner Place Hotel

The Gallery

Jury's

Number Sixteen

The Rembrandt Hotel

Zone 12: West London: Hammersmith, Chiswick, Richmond, and Kew

Riverside Hotel

HOTELS BY ZONE (continued)

Zone 13: Kensington, Holland Park, Notting Hill

Abbey Court	Comfort Inn Notting Hill
The Halcyon Hotel	Miller's Residence
Pembridge Court Hotel	The Portobello Hotel
Thistle Hotel Kensington Palace	

Zone 14: Bayswater, Marylebone, Little Venice, St. John's Wood

The Columbia Hotel	Dorset Square Hotel
Durrants	The Edward Lear Hotel
The Landmark	Thistle Hotel Hyde Park

Hotel Profiles

All prices include the 17.5% Value Added Tax (VAT) and refer to the starting price for standard single and standard double room. Prices for deluxe, executive, triple-occupancy, family rooms, and suites and rooms with special features (such as four-poster bed, fireplace, balcony, etc.) will be significantly higher. See websites for all prices as well as promotional deals.

ABBEY COURT   *£105–£155*

OVERALL ★★★ | QUALITY ★★★★ | VALUE ★★★★★ | ZONE 13

20 Pembridge Gardens, W4; (0207) 221-7518; fax (0207) 792-0858; abbey@telinco.co.uk; www.abbeycourthotel.co.uk

Abbey Court is a lovely old Victorian house in a white-stucco-front neighborhood quite close to Portobello Road. It's a real beauty, and very well priced, too. It's quite popular with antiques dealers, not only because they can walk to Kensington Church Street and all the other antiques warrens along Portobello, but also because it has plenty of really fine old furniture, art, and decorations to admire. It's comfortable and homey, as well as elegant and serene—almost like visiting a rich aunt's house who has very good taste. There are plenty of good old books, some first editions, which you can (carefully) borrow to read. Downstairs there's a small conservatory where breakfast is served (continental breakfast is included), and an honor bar is set out all day. A tiny little patio off the conservatory has a small pool with goldfish. Newspapers are ordered for you free, and there are plenty of English magazines in each room. You can get a reduction for stays longer than a week. Except for the fact that there's no elevator, this is truly a four-star townhouse hotel at three-star prices.

SETTINGS & FACILITIES

Location Notting Hill Gate. **Nearest Tube Station** Notting Hill Gate. **Quietness Rating** A in back, B in front (quiet street). **Dining** Small breakfast room. **Amenities** Newspapers, bathrobes, biscuits, and bottled water; associated with nearby health club; breakfast included, honor bar. **Services** Receptionist does work of concierge; 24-hour room service, bellhop, laundry.

ACCOMMODATIONS

Rooms 22. **All Rooms** Telephone, TV, hair dryer, iron, bathrobe, heated towel racks, Jacuzzi baths. **Some Rooms** Four-poster beds. **Bed & Bath** Italian marble bathrooms with tubs that have Jacuzzi jets, shower, and heated towel racks. The beds are excellent, some old brass bedsteads. **Favorites** The four-poster rooms are the biggest and the nicest. **Comfort & Decor** The decor is quite fine, with lovely antiques and prints all around, fantastic mirrors, and nice wallpaper. It's a pleasure to see how well appointed it is, and for me, that spells comfort. However, there is no elevator for the five floors, but the stairway is beautiful.

PAYMENT, RESERVATIONS, & RESTRICTIONS

Deposit Credit card; 48-hour cancellation policy. **Credit Cards** All major. **Check-In/Out** 1 p.m./11:30 a.m. **Pets** Not allowed. **Elevator** No. **Children** Yes. **Disabled access** No lift.

THE BASIL STREET HOTEL   £150–£225

OVERALL ★★★★½ | QUALITY ★★★★½ | VALUE ★★★★★ | ZONE 10

Basil Street, Knightsbridge, SW3; (0207) 581-3311, in U.S. (800) 448-8355; fax (0207) 581-3693; The Basil@aol.com; www.thebasil.com

For over 85 years, The Basil Street Hotel has been attracting loyal customers with its homey (a very extraordinary home) comfort and elegance. It's the kind of hotel you want to hang around in; there are a few common sitting areas that are so comfortable, so pleasing to the eye, and so well appointed that you may not be tempted outside to nearby Harrods, Hyde Park, the museums of South Kensington, Harvey Nichols, or the designer boutiques of Sloane Street. This is not an ostentatious hotel by any means, but if you look at the art on the wall—check out the paintings on glass on the way to the dining room—or the furniture, the carpets, and the bric-a-brac, you may imagine yourself in a very fine stately home or a museum. A country-house feeling is maintained even against all the noise and hubbub on the streets outside. There are sitting alcoves, looking out over the roofs of Knightsbridge, that have desks supplied with writing paper, evoking a gentler time before e-mail. It's a feminine place in many ways, but it is in no way frilly; compared to some of the ye-olde-English-country-house imitation decor in so many hotels in London, it's positively restrained—probably because it's the real thing. It offers some of the best value for the money you will find in this part of town, if not in all of central London.

SETTINGS & FACILITIES

Location Knightsbridge. **Nearest Tube Station** Knightsbridge. **Quietness Rating** C on lower floors, B+ on higher floors. **Dining** Dining room was given award by the British Automobile Association. It's a very lovely, traditional sort of dining room, with live classical music most nights. There's also a warm and comfy sitting room for excellent afternoon teas. **Amenities** Women's Club (The Parrot Club) into which men only can go if accompanied by a woman, and which provide office services for businesswomen; ironing rooms on each floor; parking spaces available at a reasonable charge; smoking and nonsmoking rooms. **Services** Concierge, bellhop, laundry.

ACCOMMODATIONS

Rooms 93. **All Rooms** Cable TV, hair dryer, bathtubs, writing desk, comfortable sitting chair. **Some Rooms** Air conditioning, bay windows, glass-fronted cabinets. **Bed & Bath** Bathrooms range from irreproachable to irresistable: some simply enormous, some paneled in pine wainscoting. Beds are quite comfortable. **Favorites** Singles are among the largest in London. Beautiful bay windows in some rooms. You can't go too wrong at the Basil, whatever room you get. **Comfort & Decor** Exquisite antiques and a huge collection of mezzotints, fine carpets, superior furniture, and really good pieces of porcelain and lamps. High ceilings, good closet space. Functional and roomy layout in all rooms (by London standards, anyway.)

PAYMENT, RESERVATIONS, & RESTRICTIONS

Deposit Credit card; 24-hour cancellation policy. **Credit Cards** All major. **Check-In/Out** mid-day/noon. **Pets** Not allowed. **Elevator** Yes. **Children** Yes. **Disabled access** Limited.

BROWN'S HOTEL   £320–£360

OVERALL ★★★★★ | QUALITY ★★★★ | VALUE ★★★ | ZONE 8

30–34 Albemarle Street, W1; (0207) 493-6020; fax (0207) 493-9381;
brownshotel@brownshotel.com; www.brownshotel.com

This five-star hotel has something of a reputation among Americans as *the* English Hotel to stay in, and I am including it in the profiles because so many people want to stay here. It is normal to see at least one celebrity during a typical stay: I've seen Johnny Depp and Annie Leibovitz. The service is excellent and good-natured in that arch English way, and the food, though sky-high in price, is simple and good. Especially at teatime: The afternoon cream tea is excellent, and the ambience of the sitting room is great. The history of the place is pretty remarkable: Alexander Graham Bell made the first telephone call in Britain from here, Rudyard Kipling wrote from here, and Theodore Roosevelt got married while a guest at Brown's. Lord Byron's valet, James Brown, started the hotel in 1837, with funds apparently acquired through his wife's connection as maid to Lady Byron. His wife, Sarah, and he had learned a thing or two from living in the "mad, bad, and dangerous to know" lordship's household, and the hotel was a success from the start.

After the Browns sold it in 1859, the next owner made it the first hotel in London to have an elevator, telephone, and electricity. It grew from 1 town house to 11, which is why you'll find the configurations of the rooms so completely unpredictable. Brown's is all about service: With 118 rooms, it has 160 in staff. Yes, the prices are very steep, so be sure to talk to reception about deals. The location is excellent, by the way.

SETTINGS & FACILITIES

Location Mayfair. **Nearest Tube Station** Green Park. **Quietness Rating** A. **Dining** Fine dining (and expensive, too) at award-winning 1837 Restaurant features English fare, with the greatest wine list in London. Breakfast in dining room, and afternoon teas in The Drawing Room. St. Georges' Bar for drinks and cigars. **Amenities** Fitness room, afternoon teas, business center. **Services** Concierge, 24-hour room service and valet, laundry, business support.

ACCOMMODATIONS

Rooms 118. **All Rooms** Minibars, multiline phones, voice mail, sitting area, writing desks, cable TV, air conditioning. **Some Rooms** Sitting areas with sofa, working fireplaces, four-poster beds, French doors. **Bed & Bath** Superior. Heated towel racks, Moulton Brown toiletries, bathrobe, and slippers. Queen- or king-size beds. **Favorites** Mayfair and Royal suites. First-floor rooms are the best, with high ceilings and big windows. Avoid the rooms at the top—they are low-ceilinged, and some of the junior suites are small. **Comfort & Decor** You will find the comfort factor high, although some of the rooms are not as large as one would expect, and some are downright cramped. The decor is English country-house traditional, very comfy and unpretentious, with some fine pieces of furniture, carvings, and art here and there. Carved fireplace in the reception, paneling, cut glass, and the stained-glass windows in the stairwells and elsewhere are all exquisite.

PAYMENT, RESERVATIONS, & RESTRICTIONS

Deposit Credit card; 24-hour cancellation policy. **Credit Cards** All major. **Check-In/Out** 2 p.m./noon. **Pets** Not allowed. **Elevator** Yes. **Children** Yes. **Disabled access** Yes, though limited.

THE CADOGAN HOTEL £225–£285

OVERALL ★★★★ | QUALITY ★★★½ | VALUE ★★★ | ZONE 10

75 Sloane Street, SW1; (0207) 235-7141; fax (0207) 245-0994; www.cadogan.com

This is the hotel at which Oscar Wilde was arrested. Its other famous association is with Lillie Langtry, the actress more well known these days for her long-term affair with the prince of Wales (later King Edward) than her career, which was impressive. The two of them represent a time and place in Victorian London that the Cadogan Hotel has tried to evoke in its decor and atmosphere. It is impossible not to feel some connection with that time when you walk in the door and see the leaded windows, the William Morris–style wallpaper, and the stately and elegant drawing room that sports a notice asking people to leave their mobile phones and laptop computers outside. Terribly civilized. The restaurant is quite grand looking and is reputed to have an excellent menu. There are tons of great restaurants within walking distance of the hotel. The rooms aren't breathtaking, but they're attractive, each individually decorated, with some enjoying a fair amount of space and views of the greenery of Cadogan Place across the street. Hotel guests have access to these widely coveted gardens that have a tennis court, also at guests' disposal.

SETTINGS & FACILITIES

Location Knightsbridge. **Nearest Tube Station** Knightsbridge or Sloane Square. **Quietness Rating** A in the interior, B/C on Sloane and Pont Streets side. **Dining** Restaurant has two rosettes from the Automobile Association. **Amenities** Drawing room and a bar with leaded windows, health-club affiliation, access to gardens and tennis. **Services** Concierge, 24-hour room service, bellhop, laundry.

ACCOMMODATIONS

Rooms 65. **All Rooms** Telephone, voice mail, satellite TV, air conditioning, hair dryer, iron, writing desk. **Some Rooms** Sitting rooms, two bathrooms, view of gardens. **Bed & Bath** High standard of both. **Favorites** The large studio in the front with two bathrooms is lovely, as are some of the luxury doubles. Try the Oscar Wilde Room. **Comfort & Decor** Beautiful William Morris wallpaper and wood paneling in halls. All rooms are individually decorated, nice, and comfortable.

PAYMENT, RESERVATIONS, & RESTRICTIONS

Deposit Credit card. **Credit Cards** All major, though they prefer to not take AMEX. **Check-In/Out** noon/noon. **Pets** Small dogs allowed. **Elevator** Yes. **Children** Yes. **Disabled access** Yes, though there are limits on wheelchair access.

THE CHERRY COURT HOTEL £30–£48

OVERALL ★ | QUALITY ★★ | VALUE ★★★★ | ZONE 9

23 Hugh Street, SW1; (0207) 828-2840; fax (0207) 828-0393; info@cherrycourthotel.co.uk; www.cherrycourthotel.co.uk

The Cherry Court Hotel has the cheeriest exterior of all the many budget/ backpacker hotels and hostels in this neighborhood. There are flowers in the window sills, and a wooden sign has been carefully hung. The best features of the hotel (it's really more of a rooming house, minus a dining room), besides the price and the ensuite toilets and showers, are the friendliness and good will of the owners, the Patels. They've been here for 17 years and are committed to constant improvements, one of which includes turning the back patio into a rose garden and making a small breakfast room that opens onto it. The rooms are small and utilitarian, some are a bit sadsack, but to the traveler on a serious budget they offer a clean place to sleep and a private toilet.

SETTINGS & FACILITIES

Location Victoria. **Nearest Tube Station** Victoria. **Quietness Rating** A. **Dining** No. **Amenities** Fruit basket and cereal bar for breakfast, though that may be upgraded in the future. **Services** Helpful management, daily cleaning.

ACCOMMODATIONS

Rooms 11. **All Rooms** Telephone, five-channel TV. **Bed & Bath** Small beds and bathrooms, which are showers and toilet in a small closet, but are clean and adequate. **Favorites** Rooms in the back. **Comfort & Decor** This is a backpacker's rooming house. The rooms are small, the beds are serviceable. The decor has been upgraded recently, and there are nice blue carpets and wallpapers in the hallways, which are fresh and clean.

PAYMENT, RESERVATIONS, & RESTRICTIONS

Deposit Credit card. **Credit Cards** All major. **Check-In/Out** 1 p.m./11 a.m. **Pets** Not allowed. **Elevator** No. **Children** Yes. **Disabled access** Two rooms on ground floor, but you must get up the three steps from the sidewalk to the hotel.

THE CHARLOTTE STREET HOTEL   £175–£525

OVERALL ★★★★ | QUALITY ★★★★ | VALUE ★★★★ | ZONE 7

Charlotte Street, W1; (0207) 806-2000; fax (0207) 806-2002;
reservations@charlottestreet-hotel.co.uk; www.charlottestreethotel.com

The Charlotte Street Hotel is a small luxurious hotel located in an area known to locals as Fitzrovia, or alternatively, North Soho. The area is the epicenter of media activity and includes production houses, TV stations, and advertising agencies and as a result is both trendy and busy, with plenty of restaurants and bars all up and down Charlotte Street. The hotel has been decorated and furnished in a fresh, modern English style, including lots of wood paneling, wooden floors, plump soft furnishings, and leather chairs. The large lobby area leads into an "Oscar" bar and restaurant that serves modern European cuisine. The bar is very popular with the local media lushes. The drawing room and library just off the restaurant area are for guest use only and are the ideal sports in which to don a smoking jacket, grab a stiff brandy, and puff on a large cigar in front of the open fireplace, while pondering on the original Bloomsbury-set artwork hanging on the walls. The bedrooms are individually decorated, with traditional British features such as floral curtains and floral wallpaper that somehow manage to avoid looking hideously chintzy. The designer, Kit Kemp, is renown for her trademark mannequin dummies that stand sentry style in every room (a quirky, superfluous detail, yet good for draping your jacket on). If it's within your budget, try staying in a loft suite; these have stairs leading to the bedroom area on a mezzanine level and are more like a doll's house than a hotel room. Although more useful for those attending a corporate event or for a local film director, another cool feature is the state-of-the-art screening room. The gym is tiny but better than nothing.

SETTINGS & FACILITIES

Location Soho (North). **Nearest Tube Station** Tottenham Court Road/Goodge Street. **Quietness Rating** All windows double glazed. **Dining** "Oscar" restaurant serving modern European food; open Monday–Saturday and Sunday for breakfast only. **Amenities** Reastaurant, lounge areas, 24-hour gym, 2 meeting rooms, 1 screening room (67-seater mini cinema). **Services** Concierge, 24-hour room service, same-day laundry service, bellhop.

ACCOMMODATIONS

Rooms 52. **All Rooms** Air conditioning, ensuite bathrooms, 2-line telephone with voice mail, cable TV, VCR and DVD, mini TV in bathroom, mini bar, safe, movies to rent, CD player, hair dryer, writing desk. Fax machine, mobile phone, laptops available on request. **Some Rooms** Walk-in shower and bidets. The more deluxe rooms have bigger (king-sized) beds, some four-poster. **Bed & Bath** Bathrooms are in solid granite and oak, with a shower, plus a mini TV. Regular rooms have queen-sized beds which can be split into twins. **Favorites** Room 108, one of the loft suites, is very popular, as are the penthouse suites, which offer good views. **Comfort & Decor** The rooms all have a homey feel, and the soft furnishings are very comfortable.

PAYMENT, RESERVATIONS, & RESTRICTIONS

Deposit Credit card; 24-hour cancellation policy. **Credit Cards** All major, except DC. **Check-In/Out** 1 p.m./11 a.m. **Pets** Not allowed. **Elevator** Yes. **Children** Yes. **Disabled access** Good general access (2 modified rooms).

THE CLAVERLEY   £85–£120

OVERALL ★★★½ | QUALITY ★★★½ | VALUE ★★★★★ | ZONE 10

13–14 Beaufort Gardens, SW3; (0207) 589-8541, in U.S. (800) 747-0398; fax (0207) 823-3410; www.claverleyhotel.co.uk78

This inn is an award winner for Best Bed-and-Breakfast Hotel in Central and Greater London. It is clean, well decorated, has a charming breakfast room much larger than what most competitors offer, and has a selection of rooms that range from serviceable to lovely. The single rooms all have large three-quarter beds. Smoking is allowed only in the sitting room downstairs, not in the rooms. The breakfast is big and hearty, the location is perfect, and the service is friendly and unstuffy, but completely professional. Harrods is around the corner, South Kensington museums and restaurants a four-minute walk away, and Hyde Park can be accessed in minutes. The traditional English style of decor, the sunlight in the front rooms, and the relatively reasonable price will delight the discerning tourist.

SETTINGS & FACILITIES

Location Knightsbridge. **Nearest Tube Station** Knightsbridge. **Quietness Rating** A. **Dining** Breakfast in room or in breakfast room. **Amenities** Sitting room with carved fireplace and complimentary papers and magazines; breakfast room with waiter service and full English breakfast included in price; airport transfer and taxis. **Services** Concierge, bellhop, laundry, faxing.

ACCOMMODATIONS

Rooms 29. **All Rooms** Cable TV, hair dryers. **Some Rooms** Four-poster bed, balcony, pull-out sofa, writing desk, sitting area, walk-in closet. **Bed & Bath** Beds are new. Bathtubs in 85% of rooms; the rest have shower stalls. All the bathrooms have been recently renovated and are in pristine condition. **Favorites** Number 12 is the best junior suite, with balcony, French windows, and awesome four-poster bed. Junior suite number 33 has a walk-in closet. Single number 35, in the rear of the building, is pretty good, too, with a large bed and a charm not defeated by the view of the backs of houses. **Comfort & Decor** Individually decorated, each room is attractive and clean and some are downright luxurious. The hotel has a great collection of portraits and drawings on the walls, and curtains in the magnificent English style.

PAYMENT, RESERVATIONS, & RESTRICTIONS

Deposit Credit card; 48-hour cancellation policy. **Credit Cards** All major. **Check-In/Out** 1 p.m./11:30 a.m. **Pets** Not allowed. **Elevator** Yes. **Children** Yes. **Disabled access** No wheelchair access.

THE CLIVEDEN TOWN HOUSE   £155–£400

OVERALL ★★★★★ | QUALITY ★★★★½ | VALUE ★★★ | ZONE 11

26 Cadogan Gardens, SW3; (0207) 730-6466; fax (0207) 730-0236;
stephen.colley@clivedentownhouse.co.uk; www.clivedentownhouse.co.uk

As you might expect from the sister town house of the world-famous Cliveden, former country house of the Astors, the Cliveden Town House is quite grand. However, it isn't pretentious and feels like a really beautiful home. The rooms are not numbered but named after theatrical legends—Laurence Olivier, Edmund Kean, Edith Evans, George and Ira Gershwin, the Redgraves, Noël Coward, and so on. The lovely drawing room has a welcoming, comfortable atmosphere and opens onto a nice-sized garden square that makes a wonderful place to sit in good weather. As you walk in the door, there are two urns on either side, each filled with apples, only the first of many appealing touches in this hotel town house. The rooms all have Cliveden teddy bears on the beds. There are gas fires in all but the single rooms. A self-service tea is set out each day at 4 p.m., and a complimentary bottle of champagne is uncorked at 6 p.m. The toiletries are made by Penhaligons for Cliveden, one of the little features that help justify the price. You should ask about deals; they are extremely accommodating here. The single rooms are okay, but if you can afford it, step up to a double—even the standard doubles are quite big and have fireplace and sofa. You're within a short walk of Sloane Square and Knightsbridge, but you'd swear you were in the country when you're in a room with a garden view.

SETTINGS & FACILITIES

Location Knightsbridge/Chelsea. **Nearest Tube Station** Knightsbridge or Sloane Square. **Quietness Rating** A. **Dining** Dinner on request, but it's not a dining room with waiters hovering. Breakfast room is delightful and bright. **Amenities** Private dining room, drawing room, smoking room, afternoon tea, honor bar, breakfast room, garden. **Services** Concierge, complimentary chauffeur service into city each weekday, 24-hour room service, laundry, baby-sitting.

ACCOMMODATIONS

Rooms 35. **All Rooms** Telephone, voice mail, fax and modem line, air conditioning, satellite TV, VCR, stereo CD. **Some Rooms** View onto gardens, fireplace. **Bed & Bath** Mattresses made specifically for Cliveden; baths are superior as would be expected. **Favorites** Any of the deluxe junior suites overlooking gardens; the doubles are quite fine, too. **Comfort & Decor** Highest standard of comfort, the decor is elegance itself, light but sumptuous.

PAYMENT, RESERVATIONS, & RESTRICTIONS

Deposit Credit card. **Credit Cards** All major. **Check-In/Out** 2 p.m./11 a.m. **Pets** Dogs allowed on certain conditions. **Elevator** Yes. **Children** Yes. **Disabled access** No, too many stairs.

THE COLUMBIA HOTEL £60–£116

OVERALL ★★ | QUALITY ★★★½ | VALUE ★★★★★ | ZONE 14

95–99 Lancaster Gate, W2; (0207) 402-0021; fax (0207) 706-4691; www.columbiahotel.co.uk

This is probably one of the best deals in the area—there may be cheaper rooms to be had, but not with the amenities and friendliness of the Columbia. It looks out on Hyde Park and is well located for buses and the tube. The rooms are plain hotel style, but they're clean and some are fairly roomy. The hotel is comprised of five Victorian houses strung together, so as with all such buildings, there will be great disparity among the size and shapes of the rooms. Unfortunately, the first floor, with its elegant high ceilings and huge windows, is mostly conference rooms, but there are many park-view rooms on the remaining floors. The only problem is that it's noisier on the park. This is a good budget hotel and one that can accommodate families, pets, and even automobiles (parking on a first-come, first-served basis). Queensway, a few minutes' walk away, has lots of great restaurants (not to mention a skating ring and bowling alley). The staff is friendly and helpful.

SETTINGS & FACILITIES

Location Lancaster Gate (Bayswater). **Nearest Tube Station** Lancaster Gate. **Quietness Rating** C in front, A in back. **Dining** Breakfast and dinner. **Amenities** Dining room, bar. **Services** 24-hour reception desk, laundry.

ACCOMMODATIONS

Rooms 100. **All Rooms** Shower and toilet, telephone, BBC TV, hair dryer. **Some Rooms** View over park, connecting rooms, four beds in one room. **Bed & Bath** Clean and satisfactory, mostly showers. **Favorites** Big rooms. **Comfort & Decor** Very plain and simple.

PAYMENT, RESERVATIONS, & RESTRICTIONS

Deposit Credit card; 24-hour cancellation policy. **Credit Cards** All major, except DC. **Check-In/Out** 2 p.m./11:30 a.m. **Pets** Allowed. **Elevator** Two. **Children** Yes. **Disabled access** One disabled room, and a bedroom for deaf or hearing disabled.

COMFORT INN NOTTING HILL   £82–£100

OVERALL ★ | QUALITY ★★½ | VALUE ★★★★★ | ZONE 13

6–14 Pembridge Gardens, Kensington, W2; (0207) 221-3433; fax (0207) 229-4808; hillgate@lth-hotels.com; www.londonhotels.net

Here's a good budget hotel within a short walk of Portobello Road and Kensington Church Street—perfect for antiques hunters who want to spend all their money on treasures instead of hotels. It's also a short walk to Kensington Gardens and Hyde Park, and the tube is very near. The hotel is comprised of three buildings put together and is on a very nice street off the busy Notting Hill Gate; apparently there's not too much noise from it. It's undistinguished aesthetically, but clean and serviceable, with a couple of nice touches, like the huge crystal chandelier. There are two video games and a chocolate vending machine in the honesty bar/lounge, which, along with the breakfast room, has piped-in pop music. Continental breakfast is included in the price. The breakfast room is a good size and pleasant enough. Good value for money here.

SETTINGS & FACILITIES

Location Notting Hill Gate. **Nearest Tube Station** Notting Hill Gate. **Quietness Rating** A in back, B in front. **Dining** Breakfast room, honor bar. **Amenities** Breakfast included, satellite TV in bar, video games. **Services** Reception acts as concierge, laundry.

ACCOMMODATIONS

Rooms 66. **All Rooms** Ensuite shower/tub and toilet, telephone, five-channel TV, hair dryer. **Bed & Bath** Utilitarian, clean, and serviceable. **Favorites** Take the double or twin room if you're alone, take the twin if you're with a spouse (double beds are small). **Comfort & Decor** Serviceable comfort, plain and forgettable decor. Like a college dorm.

PAYMENT, RESERVATIONS, & RESTRICTIONS

Deposit Credit card; 48-hour cancellation policy; two-night minimum stay is required on weekends. **Credit Cards** All major. **Check-In/Out** 1 p.m./10:30 a.m. **Pets** Not allowed. **Elevator** Two. **Children** Yes. **Disabled access** Steps outside, small lifts.

COVENT GARDEN HOTEL   £205–£350

OVERALL ★★★★ | QUALITY ★★★★½ | VALUE ★★★★ | ZONE 7

10 Monmouth Street, WC2; (0207) 806-1000; fax (0207) 806-1100;
covent@firmdale.com; www.firmdale.com

Another hit by the Firmdale Group, which also owns the Pelham Hotel, the Charlotte Street Hotel, and the Dorset Square Hotel. The Covent Garden is more spacious than the Pelham and offers more square footage, both in the size of the beds and the size of the rooms and hallways. Amenities such as cell phones and VCRs are offered. There is a fitness room, which has recently been upgraded, with treatment rooms for massages and the like added. The brasserie has been enlarged, and a 56-seat cinema offering first-run films has been installed (not quite necessary, when you're so close to the West End cinemas). But the outstanding thing about this hotel is the decor—it is the most delightful place imaginable, where the decoration is just plain appealing, not trying to be traditionally English or stylishly modern. It's just a place where all the possessions and talents of the designer come together effortlessly and pleasingly. It is a superb location: Monmouth Street, on which the hotel is situated, is a relatively quiet street in Seven Dials, but is within skipping distance of Soho, Covent Garden, Bloomsbury, and the theaters of the West End. No wonder so many movie stars call this hotel home. Of course, they can afford it.

SETTINGS & FACILITIES

Location Covent Garden. **Nearest Tube Station** Covent Garden. **Quietness Rating** A, but perhaps C on weekend nights. **Dining** Brasserie Max is a modern-style dining room with good food. **Amenities** Two drawing rooms, one very large, with working fireplaces; restaurant; honor bar with snacks; personal safe; cell phone for rent at £10 a day; workout room; 56-seat cinema. **Services** Concierge, 24-hour room service, valet, bellhop, laundry.

ACCOMMODATIONS

Rooms 50. **All Rooms** U.S.-size queen and king beds (even in singles), air conditioning, telephones with extra line, modem with U.S.-style socket, voice mail, cable TV, VCR and movies to watch, CD player and CDs to borrow, cell phone for rent, writing desk, bathtubs, umbrella. **Some Rooms** Ornamental fireplace, four-poster bed, sofa and sitting area, roof terrace. **Bed & Bath** Bathrooms are splendid, all gray marble and perfection. The beds are huge, outfitted in 100% cotton sheets and covered with the most beautiful duvets and pillows. **Favorites** Number 304 is a deluxe double with a blue theme, gorgeous four-poster bed, and an ornamental fireplace with two big chairs in front of it. The terrace suite is preferred by the many movie stars who stay here; it has its own little patio overlooking the roofs of the West End, a library, a sofa, and a sweetly appointed queen-size bed. The walls have been painstakingly painted with a sponge effect in red... stunning (as are all the rooms, really). **Comfort & Decor** All of your possible needs will be accounted for. The decor is sublime—Tim and Kit Kemp are geniuses at interior decoration, neatly blending traditional antiques with their own brand of quirky great taste, creating an atmosphere of delight.

PAYMENT, RESERVATIONS, & RESTRICTIONS

Deposit Credit card; 24-hour cancellation policy. **Credit Cards** All major. **Check-In/Out** 1 p.m./11 a.m. **Pets** Not allowed. **Elevator** Two. **Children** Yes. **Disabled access** Yes, big elevators and wide hallways.

DORSET SQUARE HOTEL	£115–£165

OVERALL ★★★★ | QUALITY ★★★★½ | VALUE ★★★★★ | ZONE 14

39 Dorset Square, Marylebone, NW1; (0207) 723-7874; fax (0207) 724-3328; dorset@firmdale.com; www.firmdale.com

Once again, the Firmdale Group has created a home away from home in this excellent hotel that looks out on two acres of gardens, seemingly far from the bustle of nearby Baker Street and Marylebone Road. It's within walking distance of Regent's Park and Oxford Street. The rooms are all beautifully decorated, and the luxury of the common areas is perfect. All the possible amenities of a good hotel are here, with the Potting Shed Restaurant and Bar providing fine meals and wines, 24-hour room service, and business support facilities. Each room is individually decorated and is of a decent size, with some magnificent four-poster rooms with garden views. The staff is extremely attentive and can organize anything you need, but most interestingly, you can hire a chauffeur-driven Bentley for business or pleasure. Check out the Firmdale website to see all their properties. Ask about weekend payment and other promotions.

SETTINGS & FACILITIES

Location Marylebone. **Nearest Tube Station** Baker Street. **Quietness Rating** A in garden rooms, B in front. **Dining** Potting Shed Restaurant serves excellent food and wines. **Amenities** Potting Shed Restaurant and Bar, business support, chauffeured Bentley available. **Services** Concierge, 24-hour room service, valet, bellhop, laundry.

ACCOMMODATIONS

Rooms 50. **All Rooms** U.S.-size queen and king beds (even in singles), air conditioning, telephones with extra line, modem with U.S.-style socket, voice mail, cable TV, VCR on request, cell phone for rent, fabulous antiques and art. **Some Rooms** Four-poster, fireplace, sitting room, garden view. **Bed & Bath** Superb. **Favorites** Any of the rooms looking out on the garden, but especially number 202, which has a sitting room and fireplace. **Comfort & Decor** Top of the line, as is usual in the Firmdale establishments. The decor is delightful.

PAYMENT, RESERVATIONS, & RESTRICTIONS

Deposit Credit card. **Credit Cards** All major. **Check-In/Out** 1 p.m./noon. **Pets** Not allowed. **Elevator** Yes. **Children** Yes. **Disabled access** Limited.

DUKES HOTEL £230–£265

OVERALL ★★★★★ | QUALITY ★★★★½ | VALUE ★★★★ | ZONE 9

35 St. James Place, SW1; (0207) 491-4840, in U.S. (800) 381-4702; fax (0207) 493-1264; dukeshotel@compuserve.com; www.dukeshotel.co.uk

Behind a charming courtyard, in one of the most appealing areas of central London is the extremely deluxe Dukes Hotel. Outside this Edwardian building remain gas lamps lit by hand every night. Inside, you'll find a sumptuous hotel with penthouses that promises the highest standards in service and accommodation. It's expensive and caters to the kind of clientele who likes its cognac to be 100-years old and doesn't flinch at outrageous prices for it. It's an intimate, clubby kind of place, but not stuffy or intimidating. The location is great: right by St. James's Park and Piccadilly; you couldn't ask for a more central yet quiet spot to enjoy London. And if you're feeling particularly flush, check out Penthouse One, with the views of all the glory that is London.

SETTINGS & FACILITIES

Location St. James. **Nearest Tube Station** Green Park. **Quietness Rating** A. **Dining** Private dining room can be booked. **Amenities** Bar with exceptional cognacs and wines; health club with massage and personal trainer available. **Services** Concierge, butler, valet, secretarial services, 16-hour room service.

ACCOMMODATIONS

Rooms 89. **All Rooms** Telephone, satellite TV, air conditioning, private bar, writing desks. **Some Rooms** Oversize (7'x7') "Emperor" bed; sitting rooms; views of Big Ben, Westminster Abbey, parks, and Parliament; exceptionally large (penthouse is 700 square feet). **Bed & Bath** Magnificent marble bathrooms with bathrobes and beds that you'd be proud to call your own. **Favorites** The penthouses are more like flats, absolutely huge and unimaginably luxurious, but even the standard doubles and the deluxe singles are very big for London (190 and 140 square feet, respectively). You can't go too wrong in any of the rooms here. **Comfort & Decor** Highest standards of comfort and completely pleasing decor—not overdone, just serene and elegant.

PAYMENT, RESERVATIONS, & RESTRICTIONS

Deposit Credit card. **Credit Cards** All major. **Check-In/Out** 2 p.m./noon. **Pets** Not allowed. **Elevator** Yes. **Children** No children under age five. **Disabled access** Limited.

DURRANTS   £110–£165

OVERALL ★★★ | QUALITY ★★★½ | VALUE ★★★★★ | ZONE 14

George Street, W1; (0207) 935-8131; fax (0207) 487-3510;
www.durrantshotel.co.uk

A hotel that has been run by the same family since 1921, Durrants has a
lot going for it, not least of all its proximity to the Wallace Collection and
Regent's Park. But mainly, it's a hotel that gives very good value for the
money. The prices quoted are inclusive of VAT, and the cost of £130 for a
double room is quite good. The rooms are more spacious than comparably
priced places and they certainly are more lovely, furnished with genuine
antique pieces, as well as bright soft furnishings. The atmosphere in the
hotel is that of a leather-chaired gentleman's club with oil paintings and
gas fires. There's a tiny bar called The Pump Room, where women used to
not be allowed, which gave license for the hotel to feature paintings of
nudes on the walls. Breakfast (an expensive breakfast) is served by waiters
in a very charming breakfast room, and the restaurant on the other side of
the lobby is of a good quality. The hotel is a great location for shopping on
Oxford and Bond Streets, going to Regent's or Hyde Park and running in
and out of the free Wallace Collection any time of the day.

SETTINGS & FACILITIES

Location Marylebone. **Nearest Tube Station** Bond Street. **Quietness Rating** A.
Dining The restaurant has the best booths in the world and decent food besides.
Amenities Pump Room, lounges with fireplaces, bar downstairs. **Services**
Concierge, 24-hour room service, bellhop, laundry, airport transfer, baby-sitting.

ACCOMMODATIONS

Rooms 92. **All Rooms** Telephone, TV, hair dryer, iron, writing desks. **Some Rooms**
Minibars, sitting chairs. **Bed & Bath** New mattresses in all rooms, newly remodeled
bathrooms that are nice and relatively spacious. **Favorites** Suite number 305 is a
two-room pleasure: the sitting room has lots of conversation areas and is beautifully
decorated with old portraits. **Comfort & Decor** Top notch; the antiques warm up
the cleanliness of the hotel decor. There's an effortlessness that is very appealing, and
the comfort is part of this.

PAYMENT, RESERVATIONS, & RESTRICTIONS

Deposit Credit card; must cancel by noon on the day before arrival hour. **Credit
Cards** All major, except dc. **Check-In/Out** 2 p.m./noon. **Pets** Not allowed. **Elevator** Two. **Children** Yes; baby-sitting and cribs can be arranged. **Disabled access**
One room with wheelchair access and porters to help; call ahead.

THE EDWARD LEAR HOTEL   £49–£93

OVERALL ★ | QUALITY ★★★½ | VALUE ★★★★★ | ZONE 14

28/30 Seymour Street, W1; (0207) 402-5401; fax (0207) 706-3766;
edwardlear@aol.com; www.edlear.com

The Edward Lear Hotel is a simple place, and the price is right. The hotel offers many more amenities than comparative hotels, such as telephone and satellite TV. It's clean, well run, and provides a good breakfast in its price. Only 100 yards from Oxford Street and within a short walk of Hyde Park, the Edward Lear Hotel is popular among budget travelers. The decoration includes cheerful and charming drawings and limericks by the famous Victorian artist and poet Edward Lear, who once lived here. The exterior has greenery spilling from every window which lends a nice homey touch.

SETTINGS & FACILITIES

Location Marble Arch. **Nearest Tube Station** Marble Arch. **Quietness Rating** B in back, C in front. **Dining** Breakfast room. **Amenities** Full English breakfast, two lounges. **Services** Breakfast.

ACCOMMODATIONS

Rooms 30. **All Rooms** Telephone, satellite TV, radio, tea and coffee. **Some Rooms** Shower/toilet. **Bed & Bath** Rooms without toilets and showers ensuite do have them nearby and they are clean; beds are satisfactory. **Favorites** Rooms in back, triples with shower/toilet. **Comfort & Decor** Plain, cheerful, clean, and decorated with Edward Lear's marvelous drawings and nonsense poems and limericks. Smallish rooms.

PAYMENT, RESERVATIONS, & RESTRICTIONS

Deposit Credit card; 24-hour cancellation policy. **Credit Cards** VISA, MC. **Check-In/Out** 1 p.m./11 a.m. **Pets** Not allowed. **Elevator** No. **Children** Yes. **Disabled access** No.

11 CADOGAN GARDENS   £165–£240

OVERALL ★★★★★ | QUALITY ★★★★ | VALUE ★★★ | ZONE 11

11 Cadogan Gardens; (0207) 730-7000; fax (0207) 730-5217;
www.numbereleven.co.uk

This is a perfectly delightful hotel tucked away behind Sloane Street in the expanses of red-bricked Victorian town houses. It was built in the 1860s, has been a hotel for 40 years, and has a certain quiet, non-hotel charm. The building has held on to all of its oak-paneled walls, which are perfectly set off by the William Morris–style wallpaper. The antiques are of high quality, and the walls are filled with fascinating portraits of people from the past few centuries—worthies on every wall. The drawing room has a genuine clubby atmosphere, and one could get extremely comfortable sitting before the fireplace with a book. Number 11 is popular for its brand of discreet, efficient service. The hotel has a rare feature for this type of hotel: a decent gym room in the lower ground floor, with a couple of Stairmasters, a treadmill, two bikes, and a whole lot of weight equipment. All the rooms are different—in size, in decor, in views. The hotel is so impressive overall that any room will no doubt suit you just fine. Breakfast is not included in the price of the room and is quite expensive, but you are very near many cafés in Chelsea.

SETTINGS & FACILITIES

Location Knightsbridge/Chelsea. **Nearest Tube Station** Sloane Square. **Quietness Rating** A. **Dining** A dining room serves breakfast, lunch, and dinner. **Amenities** Drawing room, exercise room, aromatherapy, massage. **Services** Concierge, 24-hour room service, bellhop, laundry.

ACCOMMODATIONS

Rooms 62. **All Rooms** Telephone, satellite TV, safe, hair dryer, excellent antiques. **Some Rooms** Writing desk, views, air conditioning. **Bed & Bath** Bathrooms are marble and provide Moulton Brown toiletries; beds are comfortable; many single rooms have double beds. **Favorites** The ones in front with the view of the garden are nice, but the best is definitely the biggest suite in the hotel, which is more like a stately flat, with high ceilings, four-poster bed, limited kitchenette, big windows, and plenty of room for a family of four. **Comfort & Decor** Exquisite decor suggesting a graceful bygone age; extremely comfortable.

PAYMENT, RESERVATIONS, & RESTRICTIONS

Deposit Credit card. **Credit Cards** All major. **Check-In/Out** 1 p.m/noon. **Pets** Not allowed. **Elevator** Yes. **Children** Yes. **Disabled access** Will accommodate.

THE FIELDING HOTEL £76–£100

OVERALL ★ | QUALITY ★★★ | VALUE ★★★ | ZONE 7

4 Broad Court at Bow Street, WC2; (0207) 836-8305; fax (0207) 497-0064; www.the-fielding-hotel.co.uk

The Fielding is like a college dormitory: completely utilitarian and inoffensive. It even manages a small amount of charm; certainly the exterior is pretty with the ivy-covered leaded windows. The fact that the hotel sits on a pedestrian court with nineteenth-century lamps in the shadow of the Royal Opera House renders it extremely attractive. It's all cheap pine and hard beds, but you don't share bathrooms, and everything is as clean and simple as you could ask for at the price. The superior double rooms in front are a bit nicer than the double suite, which actually costs more. The Fielding is around the corner from Covent Garden and is within walking distance of the City, the British Museum, the Thames, and Piccadilly. It's a good location at a very low price.

SETTINGS & FACILITIES

Location Covent Garden. **Nearest Tube Station** Covent Garden. **Quietness Rating** A. **Dining** Breakfast room. **Amenities** Breakfast at a very low price, honor bar. **Services** Helpful reception desk.

ACCOMMODATIONS

Rooms 24. **All Rooms** Telephone, five-channel TV with remote control, toilet. **Some Rooms** Sitting area, writing desk. **Bed & Bath** Hard beds, clean bathrooms with showers only. **Favorites** Superior doubles in the front of the building have the most space and light. **Comfort & Decor** Somewhere between utilitarian and spartan, with an unfortunate shade of orange paint in the halls and stairways.

PAYMENT, RESERVATIONS, & RESTRICTIONS

Deposit One night's rate; 72-hour cancellation policy. **Credit Cards** All major. **Check-In/Out** noon/11:30 a.m. **Pets** Not allowed. **Elevator** No. **Children** No children under age 12. **Disabled access** No.

FIVE SUMNER PLACE HOTEL   *£100–£152*

OVERALL ★★ | QUALITY ★★★ | VALUE ★★★★★ | ZONE 11

5 Sumner Place, South Kensington, SW7; (0207) 584-7586; fax (0207) 823-9962; no.5@dial.pipex.com; www.sumnerplace.com

Five Sumner Place has those most formidable of qualities: good value and good location. It is on the small side, as one would expect from a Victorian town house, but it makes much of its size, and the prices are good for the neighborhood. It was twice awarded the British Tourist Association Best Small Hotel prize and would probably have won it more often, except they stopped giving out these awards. The place is modest but comfortable and extremely clean and well kept. A couple of good rooms at the front have a scenic Mary Poppins–type view of a white row of town houses. Breakfast is served in the conservatory, which doubles as a sitting area at other times. The owners made a conscious decision to forego cable TV, the thinking being that, as the place is so intimate, it wouldn't do to have some jet-lagged wide-eyed traveler staying up till 3 a.m. watching CNN or MTV at high volumes. There are a lot of repeat customers, so book well ahead. You may get a 10% discount during January and February.

SETTINGS & FACILITIES

Location South Kensington. **Nearest Tube Station** South Kensington. **Quietness Rating** A. **Dining** Breakfast; tons of restaurants and a 24-hour grocery nearby. **Amenities** Daily newspapers, magazines, conservatory. **Services** Concierge services, laundry, bellhop, tea and coffee.

ACCOMMODATIONS

Rooms 13. **All Rooms** Telephone, TV, radio. **Some Rooms** Refrigerator. **Bed & Bath** Very good bed and showers, some baths. **Favorites** Numbers 4 and 6 have balconies. Number 5 is a surprisingly spacious-feeling single. **Comfort & Decor** It's not luxury, but it's not spartan either; in some rooms the decor is very comely, and in all rooms, clean and fresh. Some of the original moldings from 1848 have been beautifully preserved.

PAYMENT, RESERVATIONS, & RESTRICTIONS

Deposit Credit card; 14-day cancellation policy. **Credit Cards** All major, except DC. **Check-In/Out** 11 a.m. **Pets** Not allowed. **Elevator** Yes. **Children** No children under age 6. **Disabled access** Two ground-floor rooms; no wheelchair access.

FLEMINGS £195–£230

OVERALL ★★★ | QUALITY ★★★½ | VALUE ★★★★ | ZONE 8

10 Half Moon Street, W1; (0207) 493-2088; fax (0207) 499-1817;
reservations@flemings-mayfair.co.uk; www.flemingsmayfair.co.uk

Flemings is seven old houses strung together, with the result that the rooms are of all different shapes and sizes, mostly of the smaller variety. It's a friendly place, with a very homey atmosphere. The junior suites are nice, as are the common sitting areas. The decoration is an interesting pastiche of periods, a kind of art deco meets Victorian, which is more attractive than it sounds. The hotel has a restaurant and a bar downstairs, and the rooms are equipped with all the amenities you could want (except for a minibar). However, the rooms and the beds are small, which prevents Flemings from being really good value for the money.

SETTINGS & FACILITIES

Location Mayfair. **Nearest Tube Station** Green Park. **Quietness Rating** A in back, B in front (double-glazed windows). **Dining** Flemings Restaurant serves European food with a good wine selection; the Claridge Bar is downstairs, and tea is served in the lounges. **Amenities** Restaurant, bar, modem connections for British and American plugs, bathrobes. **Services** Concierge, 24-hour room service, bellhop, laundry.

ACCOMMODATIONS

Rooms 121; apartments available as well as rooms. **All Rooms** Telephone, satellite TV, air conditioning, hair dryer, iron, tea and coffee, in-house movies, writing desk. **Some Rooms** Four-poster bed. **Bed & Bath** Bathrooms are made of marble and are nicely appointed; beds are on the small side—ask for a twin put together for a king. Doubles are good only for one or two very thin and short people. **Favorites** The junior suites. **Comfort & Decor** Victorian paneled wood, art deco cast-iron sculptures, nice art on the walls, great smell in the hotel. Small rooms, but very comfortable, and the owners aim to please.

PAYMENT, RESERVATIONS, & RESTRICTIONS

Deposit Credit card; must cancel on day of arrival by 4 p.m. **Credit Cards** All major. **Check-In/Out** 2 p.m./noon. **Pets** Not allowed. **Elevator** Yes. **Children** Yes. **Disabled access** Limited, but possible.

THE FRANKLIN HOTEL   £188–£225

OVERALL ★★★★ | QUALITY ★★★½ | VALUE ★★★★ | ZONE 10

28 Egerton Gardens, Knightsbridge, SW3; (0207) 584-5533, in U.S. (800) 473-9487; fax (0207) 584-5449, in U.S. (800) 473-9489; www.franklinhotel.co.uk

The Franklin Hotel is a small, elegant hotel situated on (and with access to) Egerton Gardens, which is a beautiful expanse of greenery wild with bright blooms in the spring. The hotel's almost sylvan peace is uncompromised by the fact that the bustling Brompton Road lies mere steps away. The magnificent Brompton Oratory, a Catholic Church, is a neighbor, and you can visit the nearby Victoria & Albert Museum a few times a day. The atmosphere is serene, with antique furniture and art decorating the sitting rooms. The two sitting rooms look onto the garden, and a fire is kept blazing while you read the complimentary newspapers. The hotel has a clean Georgian feel to it, and though the rooms may be on the small side, they are perfectly appointed. Check the website for special offers.

SETTINGS & FACILITIES

Location Border of Knightsbridge and South Kensington. **Nearest Tube Station** South Kensington. **Quietness Rating** A in garden-facing rooms, B in front rooms. **Dining** Breakfast only. **Amenities** Honor bar in separate leather-chaired room, access to gardens, breakfast in breakfast room or bedroom, nonsmoking rooms, small computer room for use of guests. **Services** Concierge, 24-hour room service, butler, valet.

ACCOMMODATIONS

Rooms 50. **All Rooms** Direct-dial phones, modem lines, optional fax, cable TV, minibar, hair dryer, iron, heated towel racks. **Some Rooms** Garden view and entrance, four-poster, sitting area, two TVs, bay window. **Bed & Bath** Good beds; all baths are marble and include power showers. **Favorites** There are two rooms that are split level and spacious, number 24 and number 26. Number 1 has the entrance to the gardens and a four-poster. Number 5 has a long view of the gardens; number 19 is just about two rooms, with a wall dividing the bedroom and the sitting room. **Comfort & Decor** Excellent decor, very pleasing to the eye; very comfortable.

PAYMENT, RESERVATIONS, & RESTRICTIONS

Deposit Credit card; 48-hour cancellation policy. **Credit Cards** All major. **Check-In/Out** Whenever possible/noon. **Pets** Not allowed. **Elevator** Yes. **Children** Yes. **Disabled access** Steps in front, but help can be arranged.

THE GAINSBOROUGH   £79–£141

OVERALL ★★★ | QUALITY ★★★ | VALUE ★★★★ | ZONE 11

7–11 Queensberry Place, SW7; (0207) 957-0000, in U.S. (800) 270-9206; fax (0207) 957-0001; gainsborough@eeh.co.uk; www.eeh.co.uk

This is very similar to its sister hotel across the street, The Gallery, except that it's slightly less expensive, which makes for a very good value. There are no large sitting rooms, but the hotel is extremely serviceable and well decorated. It has been redone recently, and the smallish rooms are comfortable and tasteful. You can feel quite at home here without spending all your money on lodging—not an easy feat in London. The staff is helpful and friendly. There is a hearty breakfast included in the price, set out each day in the bright room off the lobby that becomes a tea room/bar in the afternoon. Walk out of the hotel and you'll see the magnificent Natural History Museum—one of three museums on your doorstep. This is a very good location.

SETTINGS & FACILITIES
Location South Kensington. **Nearest Tube Station** South Kensington. **Quietness Rating** A in back, C in front and on lower floors. **Dining** Breakfast room and snack/sandwich room service. **Amenities** Breakfast room and bar, fax in lobby, discount at two fitness clubs nearby. **Services** Concierge, room service, laundry, breakfast, bellhop.

ACCOMMODATIONS
Rooms 49. **All Rooms** Telephone, cable TV, tea and coffee, safe, hair dryer, iron. **Some Rooms** French windows, balcony, bigger TVs, air conditioning. **Bed & Bath** Beds are a bit hard. Singles all have shower stalls in the bathrooms, and doubles have shower/tub combinations. Very nicely decorated bathrooms. **Favorites** Number 112 has a balcony and French windows and seems a little bigger than the others. **Comfort & Decor** Rooms are small, but everything is clean and nicely presented. The decor is subdued, individual in each room, but homey.

PAYMENT, RESERVATIONS, & RESTRICTIONS
Deposit Credit card; 24-hour cancellation policy. **Credit Cards** All major. **Check-In/Out** 1 p.m./noon. **Pets** Not allowed. **Elevator** Yes. **Children** Yes. **Disabled access** Wheelchair access planned, call ahead.

THE GALLERY HOTEL   £140–£155

OVERALL ★★★ | QUALITY ★★★½ | VALUE ★★★★ | ZONE 11

8–10 Queensberry Place, SW7; (0207) 915-0000, in U.S. (800) 270-9206; fax (0207) 915-4400; gallery@eeh.co.uk; www.eeh.co.uk

This is a good hotel in the heart of South Kensington, with the imposing Natural History Museum at the end of the street, the tube a two-minute walk away, and Kensington Gardens/Hyde Park a five-minute walk away. The rooms are not big, except for the totally fabulous suite, number 502 (a mere £235), which has a private garden terrace! There is a very good breakfast room (breakfast is included) with a well-stocked buffet. Upstairs you'll find a pleasant sitting room with a bar and a chess board. Newly refurbished, the decor is attractive; everything shines and sparkles, especially the mahogany-and-marble bathrooms. Check website for deals.

SETTINGS & FACILITIES

Location South Kensington. **Nearest Tube Station** South Kensington. **Quietness Rating** A in back, C in front. **Dining** Breakfast room; room service of sandwiches and snacks. **Amenities** Minibars, cable TV, iron, tea and coffee, safes, writing desk, fitness club nearby, music in bar on occasion, fax in lobby. **Services** Concierge, 24-hour room service.

ACCOMMODATIONS

Rooms 36. **All Rooms** Cable TV, hair dryer, safe. **Some Rooms** Air conditioning, fax, couches, Jacuzzi. **Bed & Bath** Excellent on both counts. Baths in doubles and suites, shower stalls in singles. **Favorites** Number 502 is a penthouse suite with a huge bed, a private garden terrace, a dining table, two couches, and three phone lines. **Comfort & Decor** Care has been taken to ensure all comforts, and the decor is individual and restful, a bit on the plain side, but clean and pleasing to the eye.

PAYMENT, RESERVATIONS, & RESTRICTIONS

Deposit Credit card; 24-hour cancellation policy. **Credit Cards** All major. **Check-In/Out** 1 p.m./noon. **Pets** Not allowed. **Elevator** Yes. **Children** Yes. **Disabled access** No wheelchair access.

THE GORE   £141–£182

OVERALL ★★★★ | QUALITY ★★★★½ | VALUE ★★★★ | ZONE 11

189 Queen's Gate, SW7; (0207) 584-6601; fax (0207) 589-8127; www.gorehotel.com

I raved so much about this hotel in our first edition that visitors to the Gore were dissapointed and unimpressed. There were complaints by three readers that The Gore did not live up to my description, so I shall tone it down a bit. The Gore was the brainstorm of two antiques dealers who had started their hotel career with the wonderful Hazlitt's in Soho. They bought this fine old mansion on Queen's Gate, steps from Kensington Garden, in which to hang 4,500 prints and paintings and house their fabulous collection of antiques. The Tudor Room could be part of a National Trust property, and its sixteenth-century bed could easily find a home in a museum. Even the single rooms are extraordinary, with beds from the nineteenth century, each one distinct and delightful. The bathrooms are good, with attention paid to details. There is a restaurant, Bistrot 190, that serves excellent food and good breakfasts and is bright and cheerful. On the lower ground floor is the more formal and pricey restaurant known simply as 190. The Gore has two sister hotels—Hazlitt's in Soho and The Rookery in the City. The Gore's location is superb, right on the park, minutes from South Kensington, the Albert Hall, and Kensington High Street. A word of caution: the beds are genuine Victorian antiques, and some of the larger guests have a problem with the size. If you are extremely tall or particularly overweight, the beds may pose a problem to you. Talk to the concierge about your needs.

SETTINGS & FACILITIES

Location South Kensington/Kensington border. **Nearest Tube Station** Gloucester Road. **Quietness Rating** A in back and top floors, B in lower front floors. **Dining** Two restaurants: Bistrot 190 and Restaurant 190. The first is informal but with an excellent menu, and the second is more formal and expensive. Both are excellent restaurants. **Amenities** Use of two nearby fitness centers. **Services** Concierge, 24-hour room service, bellhops, laundry.

ACCOMMODATIONS

Rooms 48. **All Rooms** Minibars, limited cable TV, antiques and art, genuine Victorian beds, fans, writing desks. **Some Rooms** Stained-glass windows, French doors and balconies, sitting area, fireplace. **Bed & Bath** The beds may be too small for some people used to king-size modern hotel beds. Try the twin bedded rooms if you can't fit into a double with your partner. The bathrooms are amazing: many of them have the old-fashioned loo chair around the toilet—a genuine "throne." In one of the suites, there is a shower head as big as a dinner plate. **Favorites** The Tudor is astonishing: a Victorian re-creation of an Elizabethan gallery, complete with huge stone fireplace (using gas) and stained glass of the queen herself. Carved lintels of heads and gargoyles are not for the faint of heart. Miss Ada's room (number 207) has a lovely Victorian theme and the aforementioned enormous shower head. It's masculine and mahogany, with a very good double bed and a bust of Queen Victoria at the foot of it. In the Venus Room, a very feminine and well named room, you can sleep in an antique rococo bed once owned by Judy Garland. The Dame Nelly suite is wonderful, and as for singles, number 108 has an ornate bed and airy atmosphere. **Comfort & Decor** There is a sense of perfect comfort throughout the hotel, and the decor is endlessly fascinating, although a minimalist would run screaming from its portals. There is something everywhere to look at and love.

PAYMENT, RESERVATIONS, & RESTRICTIONS

Deposit Credit card; 48-hour cancellation policy. **Credit Cards** All major. **Check-In/Out** 1 p.m./11:30 a.m. **Pets** Not allowed, exceptions made for guide dogs and perhaps well-behaved lap dogs. **Elevator** Yes. **Children** Yes. **Disabled access** Wheelchair access is planned.

GORING HOTEL £217–£265

OVERALL ★★★★★ | QUALITY ★★★★½ | VALUE ★★★★ | ZONE 9

Beeston Place, SW1; (0207) 396-9000; fax (0207) 834-4393; reception@goringho-tel.co.uk; www.goringhotel.co.uk

The Goring is a lovely hotel, pure elegance and comfort a few steps from Victoria Station and within easy reach of the wonders of Westminster Abbey and Buckingham Palace. It has the great benefit of being on a tiny street where most of the traffic belongs to the hotel; in the back there's a lawn that is a real oasis of peace, even though you can only look at it. Sometimes that's enough, especially when St. James's Park is so nearby. The hotel is justifiably proud of having remained in the same family since 1911, and it does indeed call to mind a fine country club of the early 1900s. It doesn't have any Victorian frippery, just a cool Edwardian elegance and comfort, from the bright yellow and marble of the beautiful lobby to the lounge tables that look like they've seen quite a few bridge games in their day. There's a finely carved fireplace and a wall of windows through which you can view the garden, and drinks and light food are served there all day. The dining room is of a high quality, as are the rooms themselves. Strangely but appealingly, there are adorable stuffed sheep in the rooms, which also have lovely furniture and excellent bathrooms outfitted with Penhaligon's toiletries. The Goring plays to a lot of repeat customers—generations of them—and it's easy to see why. Special weekend payment are available.

SETTINGS & FACILITIES

Location Victoria. **Nearest Tube Station** Victoria. **Quietness Rating** A/B (double-glazed windows). **Dining** Beautiful dining room, plus garden bar and drawing room for teas and light meals. **Amenities** Dining room, a very attractive and capacious drawing room and bar, a splendid expanse of lawn out back to admire, complimentary membership in nearby health club. **Services** Concierge, 24-hour room service, bellhop, laundry.

ACCOMMODATIONS

Rooms 75. **All Rooms** Individual temperature control (including air conditioning), telephone, cable TV, hair dryer, writing desk. **Some Rooms** Balcony overlooking garden, fax. **Bed & Bath** Beautiful wood-and-marble bathrooms and good-sized beds in all the rooms. **Favorites** There are a few rooms with balconies that overlook the garden. These are fantastic and quite a rarity in London (or in any big city for that matter). **Comfort & Decor** The decor is extremely well done, suggesting a quite pleasing Georgian elegance and cheerfulness. All the common areas and the individual rooms are bright and warmly welcoming.

PAYMENT, RESERVATIONS, & RESTRICTIONS

Deposit Credit card. **Credit Cards** All major. **Check-In/Out** Noon. **Pets** Dogs and birds not allowed (since 1911, when, judging from the posted restriction, apparently many people traveled with birds in hand). **Elevator** Yes. **Children** Yes. **Disabled access** Yes.

GRANGE WHITE HALL HOTEL £175–£190

OVERALL ★★★ | QUALITY ★★★½ | VALUE ★★★★ | ZONE 2

2–5 Montague Street, WC1; (0207) 580-2224; fax (0207) 580-5554; www.grangehotels.co.uk

This is a pleasant and well appointed hotel literally in the shadow of the British Museum (which just doesn't look quite as magnificent from the back—the bricks have not been stuccoed over), with an exquisite and large garden. There's a glassed-in (air-conditioned) conservatory in the garden that can be used for afternoon teas or private functions. The rooms are as small as most London hotel rooms, but if you require space, ask for the lower ground (basement) rooms—some have more space for the same price as an upstairs room. The ambience is pleasing, and although all the furniture is reproduction, the decor still has a certain cleanliness and orderliness that is attractive. There are some really lovely touches, such as the elaborate molding in every room that has been painstakingly painted, the stencils on the walls, the glass and brass elevator, and the sumptuous curtains. There are a number of money-saving schemes—one of which is to book through the hotel's website, though you can also call and negotiate a deal.

SETTINGS & FACILITIES

Location Bloomsbury. **Nearest Tube Station** Russell Square. **Quietness Rating** A on garden in back, B+ in front (double glazing helps). **Dining** Breakfast, lunch, and dinner in the gorgeous English Garden Restaurant; The Museum Wine Bar is attached to the hotel, but with a separate entrance. **Amenities** Garden, minibar, TV with BBC and Sky News, in-house movies, buffet breakfast, smoking and nonsmoking rooms, daily newspaper. **Services** Concierge, 24-hour room service, bellhop, laundry, fitness center two-minutes' walk away.

ACCOMMODATIONS

Rooms 50. **All Rooms** Telephone, TV, minibar, iron, tea and coffee, hair dryer, writing desk, computer modem. **Some Rooms** Four-poster beds, balcony, garden view, French doors, sofa bed. **Bed & Bath** Bathrooms are in perfect condition; beds are okay and some are wonderful, such as the four-posters. **Favorites** Number 109 has four-poster bed and a balcony on the garden; number 106 has a sofa bed and also a balcony on the garden. All the rooms on the first floor have high ceilings and French doors. **Comfort & Decor** Decor is quite rich and handsome, and there is a surprising amount of light for a period conversion building. Care has clearly been taken to make this hotel visually gratifying, although it lacks a certain authenticity (not a lot of real antiques). It is comfortable enough, even though rooms are of the usual small-ish variety.

PAYMENT, RESERVATIONS, & RESTRICTIONS

Deposit Credit card; 24-hour cancellation policy. **Credit Cards** All major. **Check-In/Out** 2 p.m./11 a.m. **Pets** Not allowed. **Elevator** Yes. **Children** Yes. **Disabled access** Limited.

GREAT EASTERN HOTEL   £225–£260

OVERALL ★★★★★ | QUALITY ★★★★★ | VALUE ★★★★ | ZONE 3

Liverpool Street, EC2M 7QN; (0207) 618-5000; fax (0207) 618-5000; www.great-eastern-hotel.co.uk

The Great Eastern Hotel is one of the best—one of the only—full-service, fabulous hotels in the Square Mile, as the financial center of the City is known. This is a great boon to business travelers, and for those who want to stay further east than the usual pleasure visitor does, it's a fine hotel indeed. Liverpool Street Underground and Trail Station, a major hub of London travel (with a direct train to Stansted Airport), is adjacent to the hotel, and while the neighborhood is not as charming as many others in London, there is the growing trendiness of nearby Hoxton Square and Spitalfields. The Great Eastern was one of the grand old Victorian train-station hotels, built in 1884 and expanded in 1901. Recently, it was closed for three years for a massive renovation, and all the millions spent really show. Luckily, many of the fine Victorian period elements were left in place, the best being the magnificent stained-glass dome in the restaurant Aurora. The hotel has everything a traveler could want, including 24-hour massages and a special jet-lag treatment. (It's not cheap, I hardly need add.) There are more restaurants than you will know what to do with. There is also a guide to the hotel that gives you two maps and plenty of up-to-date local information. Beware of the suggestions to go to any of Sir Terence Conran's (the hotel's co-owner) many restaurants or to buy his book on London—it's clearly a bit of in-house publicity. The health club is top of the line.

SETTINGS & FACILITIES

Location Liverpool Street, by the City and the East End. **Nearest Tube Station** Liverpool Street or Bishopgate. **Quietness Rating** C. **Dining** Huge selection: Myabi for Japanese, the Fishmarket for guess what, the George for Ye Olde England pub-style food, Aurora for fancy European dining under an amazing stained-glass dome, and Terminus for a modern room with a menu that could be described as upscale dinner. You'll never go hungry, day or night. Prices are high. **Amenities** Aromatherapy in-room amenities, business center, health club with treatment facilities; see below for what's included in each room. **Services** Concierge, room service, same-day laundry, mobile-phone rental, shoe-shine, shops, valet parking.

ACCOMMODATIONS

Rooms 267, including 21 suites. **All Rooms** Ergonomically designed workstation with two-line telephones, fax, modem, ISDN, voice mail, and all the usual amenities such as cable TV, hair dryer, minibar, safe, CD player, DVD player, and DVD library. **Some Rooms** Fireplaces, high ceilings, big windows; others are more of a modern loft effect. **Bed & Bath** Splendid, with Frette sheets and the latest bathroom fittings. **Favorites** The rooms on the lower floors of the east block are best because they have more Victorian features; the higher floors are more modern. **Comfort & Decor** As you'd expect from furniture magnate Terence Conran, the decor is modern, solid, and comfy, with clean lines and relaxing colors.

PAYMENT, RESERVATIONS, & RESTRICTIONS

Deposit Credit card. **Credit Cards** All major. **Check-In/Out** 2 p.m./noon. **Pets** Not allowed. **Elevator** Yes. **Children** Yes. **Disabled access** Yes.

THE HAMPSHIRE EDWARDIAN RADISSON   £169–£259

OVERALL ★★★★ | QUALITY ★★★★ | VALUE ★★ | ZONE 7

Leicester Square, WC2; (0207) 839-9399, in U.S. (800) 333-3333; fax (0207) 930-8122; www.radissonedwardian.com

Housed in a magnificent building right on Leicester Square behind the half-price theater-ticket booth, The Hampshire is a five-star hotel run by the Radisson Group. It has all the amenities you'd expect from a five-star inn, though, as with so many of London's hotels, not quite as much space as you would want in some of the standard rooms. The rooms are well appointed and there's a kind of Asian theme to the decor—check out the grandfather clock in the lobby. The lobby is gorgeous, with walnut paneling everywhere, offering a quiet sitting place far from the madding crowds of Leicester Square, yet with them still in view. There's a bar attached, a restaurant, and Oscar's Wine Bar with seating right on the square from which you can watch the milling crowds. There's a fitness room with two treadmills, a bike, and a stepper. The four-poster bedrooms are beautiful, and all the junior suites are of reasonable size. Telephones are everywhere, and you'll find plenty of closet space. Some of the rooms have views over Trafalgar Square and Leicester Square. Leicester Square isn't for everyone; it's noisy and people packed, and the sleaze factor can be high. Ask about the theater packages and other Radisson-related deals. There are so many variables in price at the Radisson hotels, I hesitated to even list the costs. Call or visit the website to see what a wide array of payment they have.

SETTINGS & FACILITIES

Location Leicester Square. **Nearest Tube Station** Leicester Square. **Quietness Rating** Triple glazing in all the windows on the Leicester Square side makes those desirable rooms quiet, but beware of the Carnival Fair that comes to the square occasionally—you may want to be in the back. **Dining** Apex Bar and Restaurant and Oscar's Wine Bar, both for good food and ambience. **Amenities** Room safes, small fitness room, bathrobes, telephones in bathrooms, fully air-conditioned. **Services** Concierge, 24-hour room service, bellhop, laundry, business support.

ACCOMMODATIONS

Rooms 124. **All Rooms** Minibar, telephones with modem lines, satellite TV, in-house movies, hair dryer, bathrobe, tea and coffee, iron, writing desk. **Some Rooms** Four-posters, views, floor-to-ceiling windows. **Bed & Bath** High quality. **Favorites** Number 705 is a four-poster suite with a view over Trafalgar. Any of the junior suites is great. **Comfort & Decor** Five-star-hotel-style comforts and interesting decor, mixing eighteenth-century reproductions with Asian artwork. Nice, soft furnishings.

PAYMENT, RESERVATIONS, & RESTRICTIONS

Deposit Credit card; 24-hour cancellation policy. **Credit Cards** All major. **Check-In/Out** 2 p.m./11 a.m. **Pets** Not allowed. **Elevator** Yes. **Children** Yes. **Disabled access** Yes.

HAZLITT'S HOTEL   £182–£230

OVERALL ★★★½ | QUALITY ★★★★ | VALUE ★★★★ | ZONE 7

6 Frith Street, Soho Square, W1; (0207) 434-1771; fax (0207) 439-1524; reservations@Hazlitts.co.uk; www.hazlittshotel.com

Hazlitt's Hotel was the first establishment of the creators of The Gore and The Rookery. Hazlitt's, which happens to be author Bill Bryson's favorite home away from home, is a perfect evocation of another time, with handsome antiques and decor in the Georgian style. For those allergic to Victoriana, Hazlitt's is the perfect alternative to The Gore, and it is in the heart of Soho, where sleepy London tends to stay awake. It is a simple hotel, without an elevator and with only a tiny sitting room for communal amenities. Staying here is more like staying at a particularly well-appointed rooming house from days gone by. The house was built in 1718, and the floors sag and droop as you would too, if you'd been trod on for close to 300 years. The rooms are luxuriously comfortable, with beautiful antique bedsteads and cotton sheets. Busts sculpted by one of the owner's relatives grace many of the bathrooms and rooms, and genuine antique prints adorn the walls. The period verisimilitude is strict, and the house of a writer like William Hazlitt in that period would not have been overdone. And Hazlitt's does draw the writers like honey draws flies. In the newly expanded and upgraded sitting room is a bookcase with signed copies of books written by guests, and it's an impressive collection: Seamus Heaney, Ted Hughes, Vikram Seth, Jostein Gaardner, Susan Sontag, Dava Sobel, and scores of others. Of course, the brilliant Bill Bryson's books are there; in his *Notes from a Small Island,* he sent the phones ringing off the hook with his mention of his favorite hotel in London. Hazlitt's attracts a loyalty—or eccentricity—hardly ever met: one of the regulars paid for double glazing to be put on the windows of his favorite room. This is not to say that you will like Hazlitt's; it's for a particular type of person, one who likes the noise and action of the present-day West End as much as the atmosphere of long-ago Soho. Book way, way in advance.

SETTINGS & FACILITIES

Location Soho. **Nearest Tube Station** Tottenham Court. **Quietness Rating** C/D in front during weekend nights, A/B in back at all times. **Dining** No. **Amenities** Writing desks and modems, cotton sheets, continental breakfast at extra charge. **Services** Receptionist, bellhop, laundry, 24-hour room service.

ACCOMMODATIONS

Rooms 23. **All Rooms** Telephone, satellite TV, bathtub, antiques, writing desk. **Some Rooms** Ornamental fireplace, four-posters, high ceilings. **Bed & Bath** Superb on both counts. Victorian tubs; one bathroom has a dinner-plate–size Victorian shower head. Beds are comfortable, big, and cotton sheeted. **Favorites** The suite on the ground floor, the double-glazed Jonathan Swift room, and a small room in the back are best. Really, there are no rooms here that aren't charming and inviting; the high ceilings are on the first and second floors. **Comfort & Decor** Top-notch comfort (unless you require an elevator), and the decor is superb, pleasing to the eye and soul.

PAYMENT, RESERVATIONS, & RESTRICTIONS

Deposit Credit card; 48-hour cancellation policy. **Credit Cards** All major. **Check-In/Out** 2 p.m./noon. **Pets** Not allowed. **Elevator** No. **Children** Yes. **Disabled access** No.

HILTON MEWS   £193–£217

OVERALL ★★★★ | QUALITY ★★★★ | VALUE ★★★ | ZONE 8

2 Stanhope Row, Park Lane, W1; (0207) 493-7222, in U.S. (800) 774-1500; fax (0207) 629-9423; www.hilton.com

This is not a moderately priced hotel exactly, but it is less than the big Hilton and it's right around the back from it. The neighborhood is extremely posh, and the hotel itself is very attractive and beautifully appointed. There are 72 rooms with all the amenities you could possibly want, and you are welcome to use all the facilities at the big Hilton: beauty salon, fitness center, treatment rooms, business support. And of course, Hyde Park and Piccadilly, with all their various delights, are nearby.

SETTINGS & FACILITIES

Location Mayfair. **Nearest Tube Station** Green Park. **Quietness Rating** A. **Dining** Small, 32-seat restaurant and lounge for tea and drinks. **Amenities** All the facilities at the big Hilton (fitness, beauty, hair stylist, restaurants) are at your disposal.

Services Concierge, 24-hour room service, bellhop, laundry, rental computers and printers, business support.

ACCOMMODATIONS

Rooms 72. **All Rooms** Two-line telephone, modem, voice mail, cable TV, in-house movies, air conditioning, iron, hair dryer, tea and coffee. **Some Rooms** Mayfair Suite has lounge and private entrance. **Bed & Bath** Top notch. **Favorites** The more expensive doubles are quite nice. **Comfort & Decor** Upscale hotel style, with more than a touch of jolly olde England and all the comforts of a Hilton.

PAYMENT, RESERVATIONS, & RESTRICTIONS

Deposit Credit card; must cancel by 4 p.m. on day of arrival. **Credit Cards** All major. **Check-In/Out** 2 p.m./noon. **Pets** Not allowed. **Elevator** Yes. **Children** Yes. **Disabled access** No, stairs in lobby.

HOLIDAY INN MAYFAIR   £200–£300

OVERALL ★★ | QUALITY ★★★½ | VALUE ★★★ | ZONE 8

3 Berkeley Street, W1; (0207) 493-8282; fax (0207) 629-2827;
mayfair.holiday-inn.com

In the United States, the name Holiday Inn has the connotation of a budget-to-moderate kind of a place, which is why I had to gasp when I saw a Holiday Inn rack rate of £250! But hang on, that's not what you'll end up paying if you are smart and join the Priority Club or take advantage of any of the many packages and deals available here and on the website. They don't even have a tariff card to give out (nor will you get very far with them on the phone unless you have definate dates in mind), because there are so many possible combinations of discounts and promos. The neighborhood is fabulous, and the rooms have pretty much everything you want. Okay, the place is not dripping with traditional charm, but it's attractive and well decorated with nice pictures and furniture. If you want to stay in the beautiful Mayfair, give the hotel a call or go to their website to see if you can get a good rate.

SETTINGS & FACILITIES

Location Mayfair. **Nearest Tube Station** Green Park. **Quietness Rating** A in back, B in front (double-glazed windows). **Dining** Nightingale's Restaurant serves international cuisine. **Amenities** Bar, very small fitness room. **Services** Concierge, 24-hour room service, bellhop, laundry.

ACCOMMODATIONS

Rooms 184. **All Rooms** Telephone, modem lines and Internet access, cable TV, mini-bar, air conditioning, hair dryer, iron, tea and coffee, in-house movies, writing desk. **Some Rooms** Suites have two rooms, two bathrooms, two TVs. **Bed & Bath** Bathrooms are fine; beds are comfortable. **Favorites** The suites and executive rooms, which have the most space. **Comfort & Decor** Hotel style, but not at all drab; major refurbishment has been ongoing and plans are that it will continue.

PAYMENT, RESERVATIONS, & RESTRICTIONS

Deposit Credit card; must cancel by 6 p.m. on the day of arrival. **Credit Cards** All major. **Check-In/Out** 2 p.m./1 p.m. **Pets** Not allowed. **Elevator** Yes. **Children** Yes. **Disabled access** Two disabled rooms available.

HOTEL RUSSELL   £178–£198

OVERALL ★★★ | QUALITY ★★★ | VALUE ★★★★ | ZONE 2

Russell Square, WC1; (0207) 837-6470; fax (0207) 837-2857; www.principalhotels.co.uk

This is a grand old edifice looking out on Russell Square, a stone's throw from the underground Piccadilly line, which, along with the A2 Heathrow Express that leaves from across the street, makes this hotel a good Heathrow-airport connection. It's got a lot of space, unlike so many hotels in London, plus all the services one expects from a four-star hotel. The decor is a bit tired, but it's perfectly suitable. The hotel attracts a business crowd due to its conference facilities, and so is accustomed to demanding customers. As part of the Forte Group, it knows how to cater to the international traveler. The restaurants are good and quite convenient, and it's close to the West End, the City, and of course, the British Museum. It's a magnificent building to look at—one of the great Victorian hotel palaces.

SETTINGS & FACILITIES

Location Bloomsbury. **Nearest Tube Station** Russell Square. **Quietness Rating** C in front (double glazing), A in back. **Dining** Fitzroy's Doll Bar-Restaurant serves European and British food; Virginia Woolf's Brasserie serves burgers, pastas, and so on. The King's Bar and Lounge has a club atmosphere (fireplace, red leather) and drinks. **Amenities** Full business support, executive floor with lounge and continental breakfast. Guest-relations manager maintains database with guest history—your preferences and needs—to help with repeat visits. **Services** Concierge, 24-hour room service, bellhop, laundry, conference ready.

ACCOMMODATIONS

Rooms 329. **All Rooms** Telephone, cable TV, hair dryer, iron, tea and coffee. **Some Rooms** Minibar, writing desk, bathrobes, balcony. **Bed & Bath** Perfectly serviceable; some bathrooms are quite big. **Favorites** Number 347 is a suite with a sitting room and French doors in both rooms looking out onto Russell Square. Ask about the French-window rooms. **Comfort & Decor** It's your basic hotel style, but with old-fashioned huge hallways, high ceilings, and big rooms. The common areas are appealing, with a beautiful Victorian lobby that has a lovely grand staircase.

PAYMENT, RESERVATIONS, & RESTRICTIONS

Deposit Credit card; must cancel before 2 p.m. on day of arrival. **Credit Cards** All major. **Check-In/Out** 2 p.m./noon. **Pets** Not allowed. **Elevator** Three. **Children** Yes. **Disabled access** As a Grade II building, they can't alter structure for built-in ramps, but management can help a lot.

JURY'S   £190–£210

OVERALL ★★★ | QUALITY ★★★½ | VALUE ★★★ | ZONE 11

109–113 Queen's Gate, South Kensington, SW7; (0207) 589-6300; fax (0207) 581-1492; www.jurysdoyle.com

The best things about Jury's are the location and the lobby. The rooms run a fairly wide gamut from much too small and dull to rather grand, with French windows looking out on the white stucco town houses of Queen's Gate. This hotel provides an airport shuttle bus for a fee, a nonsmoking floor, and a great reading room with a fireplace. All the restaurants, shops, and public transportation of South Kensington are at its doorstep, as are Hyde Park and the museums. This is a large enough corporation that it offers deals; call to ask about them, and definitely get an upgrade, because I saw a couple of so-called doubles that were very small.

SETTINGS & FACILITIES

Location South Kensington. **Nearest Tube Station** South Kensington. **Quietness Rating** B. **Dining** Copplestone's Restaurant; Kavanaugh's Irish Pub. **Amenities** Elegant lobby and reading room for tea and drinks. **Services** 24-hour room service, business services, same-day laundry.

ACCOMMODATIONS

Rooms 156. **All Rooms** Satellite TV, tea/coffee-making facilities, iron. **Some Rooms** Minibars and modems in suites only. **Bed & Bath** Clean, if boring. **Favorites** Executive suite looking out on Queensgate and Manson Place. **Comfort & Decor** Comfortable, if small; decor is standard, dull hotel-chain style.

PAYMENT, RESERVATIONS, & RESTRICTIONS

Deposit Credit card; 24-hour cancellation policy. **Credit Cards** All major. **Check-In/Out** 2 p.m./11 a.m. **Pets** Not allowed. **Elevator** Yes. **Children** Yes. **Disabled access** Yes.

L'HOTEL   £159–£182

OVERALL ★★★★★ | QUALITY ★★★★ | VALUE ★★★★★ | ZONE 10

28 Basil Street, SW3; (0207) 589-6286, in U.S. (800) 926-3199; fax (0207) 823-7826; www.Lhotel.co.uk

This is essentially a bed-and-breakfast owned by the neighboring Capitol Hotel, and it only has 12 rooms. Speak up early if you want to book here—it's very popular among the cognoscente. The hotel is located 50 meters from Harrods and 250 from Hyde Park, with Sloane Street right down the way. The rooms are all quiet and simple, in a French country style that may come as a relief to those who find the English traditional too floral. Pine furniture and neutral colors accented by elegant artwork and bibelots make it restful and aesthetic experience. The staff is friendly and helpful—reception will act as concierge and help out wherever needed. Best of all, there are three rooms and one suite that come with gas fireplaces, and these are the rooms that need booking well ahead. The price, for the area and the quality, is good. All the rooms are double, with no extra charge for the second person.

SETTINGS & FACILITIES

Location Knightsbridge. **Nearest Tube Station** Knightsbridge. **Quietness Rating** A (double glazing throughout). **Dining** Le Metro is a wine bar that serves breakfast, lunch, and dinner with cool modern style. **Amenities** Continental breakfast is included in price and can be served in room; fax and iron on request. **Services** Concierge, breakfast room service only, laundry.

ACCOMMODATIONS

Rooms 12. **All Rooms** Minibar, telephone, cable TV, in-house movies, hair dryer, tea and coffee, writing desk, ceiling fan. **Some Rooms** Fireplace. **Bed & Bath** 100% Egyptian cotton Fretta sheets and perfect bathrooms. **Favorites** Number 302, a room with a fireplace, and the suite. **Comfort & Decor** Dedicated to comfort and simplicity of decor. A good feeling pervades.

PAYMENT, RESERVATIONS, & RESTRICTIONS

Deposit Credit card; 72-hour cancellation policy. **Credit Cards** All major. **Check-In/Out** 1 p.m./noon. **Pets** Not allowed. **Elevator** Yes. **Children** Yes. **Disabled access** One ground-floor room.

LONDON MARRIOT HOTEL AT COUNTY HALL £310–£340

OVERALL ★★★★½ | QUALITY ★★★★½ | VALUE ★★★ | ZONE 5

County Hall, SE1; (0207) 928-5200; in U.S. (800) 228-9290; fax (0207) 928-5300; www.marriotthotels.com

This hotel has the largest rooms of any Marriott in London, and it has all the amenities you'd expect from the chain, but with one major difference: it's located in the old County Hall building right on the Thames and has spectacular, postcard-perfect views of Parliament, Big Ben, the London Eye, and the tower of Westminster Abbey. You may feel a bit cut off from a sense of a neighborhood; Waterloo Station is in the rear, and across the bridge is Westminster, which tends to roll up the sidewalks at night and on weekends, but it doesn't matter, as the South Bank has plenty to look at and the stroll along the river path is wonderful. The hotel has a 25-meter pool(!) and an excellent gym for which, unfortunately, you have to pay £25 per day or £45 per week to use; beauty and health treatments are available. There are some delightful eating and lounging areas, which you should visit even if you don't stay here—the view is magnificent, especially at night. The library has been preserved from when it was part of the County Hall, and the books are all the original volumes. There are wood-paneled walls everywhere and all kinds of interesting architectural features in this historical, listed building. And the beds are huge. Ask for deals and promotions, as the price is steep.

SETTINGS & FACILITIES

Location South Bank. **Nearest Tube Station** Westminster or Waterloo. **Quietness Rating** A. **Dining** County Hall Restaurant has English cuisine and an oyster-and-seafood bar, plus great views of the Thames—be sure to make reservations. Library Lounge has tea and snacks. There is also Leaders Cocktail Bar. **Amenities** Restaurant, lounge, bar, views of Parliament and Big Ben, health club with pool, disabled rooms, valet parking at good payment for London. **Services** Concierge, 24-hour room service, valet parking, bellhop, laundry.

ACCOMMODATIONS

Rooms 195. **All Rooms** Telephones, voice mail, cable TV, air conditioning, minibar, hair dryer, tea and coffee, iron, personal safes. **Some Rooms** Separate sitting rooms, views of river. **Bed & Bath** Excellent bathrooms; beds are queen or king sized. **Favorites** Rooms with a river view are superior. **Comfort & Decor** Comfort is high, decor is high-standard hotel type, with some unfortunate choices in fabrics.

PAYMENT, RESERVATIONS, & RESTRICTIONS

Deposit Credit card; must cancel by 4 p.m. on day of arrival. **Credit Cards** All major. **Check-In/Out** 2:30 p.m./noon. **Pets** Not allowed. **Elevator** Yes. **Children** Yes. **Disabled access** Six disabled rooms of a very high standard.

THE MILESTONE HOTEL   £295–£340

OVERALL ★★★★½ | QUALITY ★★★★ | VALUE ★★★ | ZONE 11

1 Kensington Court, W8; (0207) 917-1000; fax (0207) 917-1010; www.themilestone.com

The Milestone is a relatively new purchase by an owner determined to offer the best in services to international travelers and businesspeople. It is beautifully decorated, especially the common areas, and although all the rooms may not suit all tastes, they are all carefully and imaginatively put together, with lovely antiques and fine furnishings. Comfort and convenience are of an unusually high standard here, and the location is wonderful for park lovers: it is directly across the street from Kensington Gardens. Some of the rooms have excellent views of the palace. There is a room especially designed for disabled guests. The hotel offers the very latest in business-support systems, not to mention a snooker table that turns into a conference table. The lounge is a fine place to hang out, and there's a bar that has a leathery pub atmosphere.

SETTINGS & FACILITIES

Location Kensington. **Nearest Tube Station** High Street Kensington. **Quietness Rating** A in back, B in front (double glazing on all but corner room, 102, which has leaded windows protected by landmark status). **Dining** Chenistons Restaurant. **Amenities** Sleeping sound machines on request, sitting room, bar, breakfast room, health club. **Services** Concierge, 24-hour room service, business support.

ACCOMMODATIONS

Rooms 57. **All Rooms** Telephone, voice mail, cable TV, air conditioning, minibar, modem station, in-house movies, CD player, U.K./U.S. video player. **Some Rooms** Video-conferencing cables, pop-up TVs, electronic blinds, Jacuzzi, fireplace, four-posters, fax machine. **Bed & Bath** Excellent, the highest quality. **Favorites** Number 509 has bay windows and a park view; number 106 has the most panoramic view of Kensington Gardens. Number 102 suite has two fireplaces, red velvet sofas, crystal chandeliers, leaded-glass windows, the works. **Comfort & Decor** Very beautifully decorated by owner and extremely comfortable in all ways.

PAYMENT, RESERVATIONS, & RESTRICTIONS

Deposit Credit card; 24-hour cancellation policy. **Credit Cards** All major. **Check-In/Out** 2 p.m./noon. **Pets** Not allowed. **Elevator** Yes. **Children** Yes. **Disabled access** Specially designed disabled room and entrance.

MILLENNIUM HOTEL MAYFAIR   £205–£300

OVERALL ★★★★ | QUALITY ★★★★ | VALUE ★★★ | ZONE 8

Grosvenor Square, W1; (0207) 629-9400; fax (0207) 629-7736; sales.britannia@mill-co.com; www.mill-cop.com

The 319-room Millennium Britannia Mayfair faces Grosvenor Square, a most peaceful and dignified old part of London, with the glaring exception of the modern American embassy at one end. It's a perfect hotel for people who have a problem with noise. Piccadilly, Park Lane, or Oxford Street are all within a few blocks. The neighborhood is full of magnificent buildings from all different periods, and walking around is a delight. The hotel has most of the amenities of a four-star, deluxe hotel and is associated with a Japanese restaurant next door. The fitness room is no more than a couple of bikes, a treadmill, a stepper, and some weight machines, but for London that's not bad. The rooms are all a good size, and the decor is pleasing if unadventuresome. There are various promotions that you should certainly investigate, as the rack rate is high, though perfectly in keeping with the posh neighborhood. The hotel has been refurbished extensively since 1996 and it looks quite fresh. There's an executive lounge that businesspeople will find attractive.

SETTINGS & FACILITIES

Location Mayfair. **Nearest Tube Station** Green Park or Bond Street. **Quietness Rating** A. **Dining** Restaurant, Shogun Japanese Restaurant, two bars. **Amenities** 24-hour fitness room, business center, 24-hour valet, free modem access in rooms, reduced rate at National Car Park. **Services** Concierge, 24-hour room service and valet, bellhop, laundry.

ACCOMMODATIONS

Rooms 319. **All Rooms** Telephones with free modem access, cable TV, in-house movies, air conditioning and individual climate control, minibar, writing desk. **Some Rooms** Tea and coffee, iron, fax, safe. **Bed & Bath** Marble baths with phone in them, good-sized beds. **Favorites** The Millennium Rooms are the best size before you get into suites; those rooms overlooking the Square are nice. **Comfort & Decor** Decor is uninspired, but of a good hotel standard.

PAYMENT, RESERVATIONS, & RESTRICTIONS

Deposit Credit card; must cancel by 2 p.m. on day of arrival. **Credit Cards** All major. **Check-In/Out** 2 p.m./noon. **Pets** Not allowed. **Elevator** Three. **Children** Yes. **Disabled access** Yes, but limited.

MILLER'S RESIDENCE   £188

OVERALL ★★★ | QUALITY ★★★★ | VALUE ★★★★ | ZONE 13

111A Westbourne Grove, W2 (entrance on southeast side of Hereford Road); (0207) 243-1024; fax (0207) 243-1064; www.millersuk.com

Miller's Residence is becoming one of London's worst-kept secrets; it opened in 1997 and has been quietly drawing strength from the numbers of people who love it and keep going back and the newspaper and magazine writers who keep writing about it. Martin Miller, of *Miller's Antique Guide,* and Kay Raveden have created an eccentric and beautiful "rooming house" in Notting Hill Gate, filled to bursting in the common areas with sublime antiques (there's a covered sedan chair in the front hall and an old sled on the wall, to name only two of the first things to hit your eyes). The drawing room is wonderful, with a fireplace that is stunningly well carved, and still more antiques. The Millers have clearly spent years successfully scavenging in markets like Portobello and Bermondsey and at many a country auction. The seven rooms are all named after English Romantic poets and have lines from the poems of these masters on the back of each door. The Coleridge room has an old model of the HMS *Bounty,* and the "Rime of the Ancient Mariner" is quoted on the door. Guests who book long stays will get a discount. Book well in advance. The house is on a busy stretch of Westbourne Grove, not a tremendously charming neighborhood, but there are lots of restaurants, and Planet Organic down the street has a great juice bar.

SETTINGS & FACILITIES

Location Notting Hill Gate. **Nearest Tube Station** Bayswater. **Quietness Rating** B/C. **Dining** Breakfast only. **Amenities** Amazing drawing room with coffee and tea and a fireplace, all lit up with candles at night, and another lounge, equally pleasant. **Services** Reception acts as concierge, limited room service (from local restaurants), laundry.

ACCOMMODATIONS

Rooms 6; 2 apartments. **All Rooms** Telephone, voice mail, satellite TV, wonderful antiques. **Some Rooms** Four-poster, even more wonderful antiques. **Bed & Bath** Beds are of good quality, and the bathrooms are of a high standard. **Favorites** All rooms are different and very cool. Try the red Coleridge Room or the lighter Tennyson Room. **Comfort & Decor** Comfort is fine, except for the lack of a lift and the possibility of a hot day or two without air conditioning. The decor has to be seen to be believed. The Millers have spent their time amassing the most amazing antiques and they have spread them wildly and well all over this wonderful rooming house.

PAYMENT, RESERVATIONS, & RESTRICTIONS

Deposit Credit card; must cancel within seven days of arrival. **Credit Cards** All major. **Check-In/Out** 2 p.m./11 a.m. **Pets** Not allowed. **Elevator** No. **Children** Yes. **Disabled access** No.

THE MONTAGUE ON THE GARDENS   £192–£224

OVERALL ★★★★ | QUALITY ★★★½ | VALUE ★★★ | ZONE 2

15 Montague Street, Bloomsbury, WC1; (0207) 637-1001, in U.S. (800) 424-2862; fax (0207) 637-2516; www.redcarnationhotels.com

A deluxe hotel, The Montague on the Gardens is part of the Red Carnation Group, which also owns the Milestone in Kensington. It features the same type of sumptuous interior design that uses fabric as wallpaper and cleverly combines fine antiques with bold patterns and pleasing colors. It provides all the services one would expect of a deluxe hotel and then some. There's a garden in the back that you can enjoy while sitting on the patio off the Terrace Bar, and the restaurant is of very good quality at reasonable (for London) payment. It's also across the street from the British Museum, and within walking distance from the West End. The delightful decor of the rooms can't conceal the small size of most, but it does tend to divert one's attention from it. The Montague is made from eight Grade II town houses strung together, so the rooms are all of different sizes and shapes. Some of the suites are comprised of three different levels, which might be good if you have a need for privacy from your roommate, but it has less floor space than you might have if it were all on one floor. There are a couple of deluxe kings that are spacious (numbers 319 and 317). Ask about promotional deals. It's a bit pricey for the neighborhood—unless you simply *have* to be near the West End or the British Museum and want a full-service hotel.

SETTINGS & FACILITIES

Location Bloomsbury. **Nearest Tube Station** Russell Square. **Quietness Rating** A in garden rooms, B on street. **Dining** Blue Door Bistro is a three-star restaurant serving breakfast, lunch, and dinner, with a very pleasing and elegant interior. **Amenities** Smoking and nonsmoking rooms, bar, restaurant with piano music, bathrobes, in-room express checkout via TV system, executive room with business-related amenities, mobile phones for rental, fax machines on request, healthy guest rooms featuring a Nordic exercise bike. **Services** Concierge, 24-hour room service, bell-hop, laundry, business support.

ACCOMMODATIONS

Rooms 104. **All Rooms** Telephone, voice mail, cable TV, in-house movies, air conditioning, hair dryer, writing desk, iron, tea and coffee. **Some Rooms** Minibars, fax lines, CD players and CD selection. **Bed & Bath** Beautiful beds, most with elaborate canopies and handsome duvets and curtains. The bathrooms are first rate. **Favorites** Number 219, The Duchesse, is a fine suite that has a sky painted on the ceiling. **Comfort & Decor** They aim to please here, so the comfort factor—even adjusting for the size of the rooms—is particularly high. The decor is quite impressive, if a bit over the top in places.

PAYMENT, RESERVATIONS, & RESTRICTIONS

Deposit Credit card; 24-hour cancellation policy. **Credit Cards** All major. **Check-In/Out** 2 p.m./noon. **Pets** Large pets not allowed (small pets conditional). **Elevator** Yes. **Children** Yes. **Disabled access** Ramps for main stairs, and the people here are very helpful, but since it's a Grade II listed building, they can't create total wheelchair access.

MORGAN HOTEL   £59–£85

OVERALL ★★ | QUALITY ★★★½ | VALUE ★★★★★ | ZONE 2

24 Bloomsbury Street, WC1; (0207) 636-3735; fax (0207) 636-3045

Make your reservation well in advance (months) to get a room at this extremely popular family-run bed-and-breakfast/budget hotel. Practically on the doorstep of the British Museum and within walking distance of the West End, this is the place discerning cheapskates love to go. It's an easy, informal sort of a place, run by a family who seem to do absolutely everything themselves, and pretty nicely, too. The breakfast room is the jewel here: it's done up in booths and decorated with an extraordinary collection of English ceramics, some very interesting pieces. Clearly, someone here has the taste to make a budget place look inviting and interesting, or maybe it's because they got started on decorating the place when they opened it over 20 years ago, back when you could still get a deal on Portobello Road. All the rooms have a private shower and toilet.

SETTINGS & FACILITIES

Location Bloomsbury. **Nearest Tube Station** Tottenham Court. **Quietness Rating** A in back, B+ in front (double-glazed windows). **Dining** Breakfast, which is included in price. **Amenities** Breakfast in delightful dining room. **Services** Bellhop.

ACCOMMODATIONS

Rooms 21 hotel rooms and 4 flats. **All Rooms** Telephone, TV (BBC and CNN), hair dryer. **Some Rooms** Tea and coffee, air conditioning, writing desk, bath, TV and VCR in apartments. **Bed & Bath** Highest cleanliness and comfort. **Favorites** Number 1 is a good size, with lots of drawers. Room B is a favorite; and Flat 1 is a nice apartment, with eat-in kitchen, pleasant decoration, and good space. **Comfort & Decor** The decor is superior to most of the local B&Bs in this price range, with really interesting pictures on the walls and a fine collection of English porcelain. The family is well versed in making visitors comfortable.

PAYMENT, RESERVATIONS, & RESTRICTIONS

Deposit Credit card; 72-hour cancellation policy. **Credit Cards** Most major. **Check-In/Out** Noon/10:30 a.m. **Pets** Not allowed. **Elevator** No. **Children** Yes. **Disabled access** No elevator.

NUMBER SIXTEEN   £115–£170

OVERALL ★★★ | QUALITY ★★★★ | VALUE ★★★★★ | ZONE 11

16 Sumner Place, South Kensington, SW7; (0207) 589-5232, in U.S. (800) 592-5387; fax (0207) 584-8615; www.numbersixteenhotel.co.uk

As of press time, this town-house hotel had been bought by the Firmdale Group (which owns the Pelham, Dorset Square, Covent Garden, and other hotels) and at some point will be closed for six months of renovation. Check www.firmdale.com to stay abreast of this development. My guess is that the prices will go way up, but so will the style and comfort. As it stands now, Number Sixteen is an exceptional place, and everybody knows it, so you'd better look sharp if you want to book a room. It's modestly displayed, with no waving banners or lights outside. Number Sixteen is more like a big bed-and-breakfast than a hotel; it has the feel of a warm home, thanks to the pretty decor and the kind staff. And the location is primo. Four Victorian town houses were connected to make Number Sixteen, stringing together enough room in the back to create a sweet little garden with a fountain; there is a conservatory from which to enjoy the view in the winter. The ground-floor rooms look out to the garden, which manages to dispel the molelike feeling of being in the lower ground. The rooms are all decorated differently, and instead of numbers have names: Terrace, Olive, Berry, Studio, and so forth. They are all attractive, not grand or showy, just comfy English in style. The downstairs drawing rooms are appealing; the library and sitting room feature an honor bar, and then there's the aforementioned conservatory. Ask about deals; they sometimes have a winter discount.

SETTINGS & FACILITIES

Location South Kensington. **Nearest Tube Station** South Kensington. **Quietness Rating** A/B. **Dining** Breakfast; scores of restaurants nearby. **Amenities** Breakfast is included in price; you choose what you want and where you want to eat it, or it will be brought to your room as a matter of course; access to health club nearby. **Services** Concierge, laundry.

ACCOMMODATIONS

Rooms 42. **All Rooms** Telephone, minibar, room safe, BBC TV, hair dryer. **Some Rooms** Balcony, French doors. **Bed & Bath** Beds are comfortable; some bathrooms have shower stalls only; all have bathrobe and basket of Moulton Brown toiletries. **Favorites** Terrace, Fawn, and Berry. **Comfort & Decor** The decor is very Edwardian, not trendy or spiffy, but relaxing and charming. A very comfortable place to hang your hat. Singles are small.

PAYMENT, RESERVATIONS, & RESTRICTIONS

Deposit Credit card; 48-hour cancellation policy. **Credit Cards** All major. **Check-In/Out** 3 p.m./11am. **Pets** Not allowed. **Elevator** Yes. **Children** Yes. **Disabled access** Four ground-floor rooms, three stairs outside.

PARKES HOTEL   £176–£205

OVERALL ★★★½ | QUALITY ★★★★ | VALUE ★★★★ | ZONE 10

41 Beaufort Gardens; (0207) 581-9944; fax (0207) 581-1999; www.parkeshotel.com

You'll find pristine English elegance at this hotel, a mere stone's throw from Harrods on a tree-lined, dead-end street off the busy Brompton Road. It's not at all stuffy, but it does seem to have high standards for decor and service. There are plenty of maids and bellhops, and very friendly they are, too. There is no restaurant, but there is a breakfast room with a full English breakfast for £5, and you can get room service. But the best thing is that all the rooms have kitchens, so you can feast from Harrods Food Halls without any difficulty. Parkes doesn't offer any deals, and it stays solidly booked.

SETTINGS & FACILITIES

Location Knightsbridge. **Nearest Tube Station** Knightsbridge. **Quietness Rating** A. **Dining** Breakfast room. **Amenities** Sitting room, complimentary newspaper, kitchens. **Services** Concierge, room service, bellhops, laundry, chauffeur service and airport transfer.

ACCOMMODATIONS

Rooms 33. **All Rooms** Kitchen, cable TV and in-house movies, tea and coffee, hair dryer, iron, minibar, double bed, iron, safe, bath. **Some Rooms** Fax, writing desk, sitting area, chandeliers, fireplaces (electric). **Bed & Bath** Excellent. **Favorites** Number 32 is a front-facing junior suite, and number 37 is a fine one-bedroom suite with huge crystal chandeliers, high ceilings, and French windows in the bedroom and the sitting room. They are switching some things around, making smaller suites out of the three-bedroom ones, so the room numbers may change. The doubles are a bit small, but the junior suites are a good size. **Comfort & Decor** Pains have been taken to make the rooms comfortable, and the decor is well composed and pleasant.

PAYMENT, RESERVATIONS, & RESTRICTIONS

Deposit Credit card; 48-hour cancellation policy. **Credit Cards** All major. **Check-In/Out** 2 p.m./noon. **Pets** Allowed by arrangement. **Elevator** Yes. **Children** Yes. **Disabled access** No wheelchair access, lots of stairs and small hallways.

THE PASTORIA RADISSON EDWARDIAN £175–£200.

OVERALL ★★ | QUALITY ★★★ | VALUE ★★ | ZONE 7

These Radisson hotels are just a bit too standardized for my taste, however, they offer many deals, frequent-flier tie ins, and all the services and amenities that Radisson Hotels offer all over the world. You will know what to expect with them, which for many people is important when traveling abroad. This hotel serves a large American clientele, and in response to the overwhelming demand, is now installing air conditioning in every room. The visitors at this hotel can use the fitness room at the Hampshire across the street. The rooms are very small, and the singles in back are awful; but certainly every basic need is attended to in the rooms. The location is great for action seekers; it's right on Leicester Square, which is host to hordes of people all weekend—buskers, tourists, criminals, drunks, you name it. You'll either love or hate staying on the Square; noise-phobics need not apply. Of the six floors, you'll find the high front rooms are the most quiet and bright. There's a small restaurant attached called Flicks Brasserie.

SETTINGS & FACILITIES

Location Leicester Square. **Nearest Tube Station** Leicester Square. **Quietness Rating** C in front, low-floor rooms, A in back (double glazing throughout). **Dining** Flicks Brasserie serves burgers, salads, and pasta. **Amenities** Small sitting area, in-house movies. **Services** Concierge, 24-hour room service, bellhop, laundry.

ACCOMMODATIONS

Rooms 58. **All Rooms** Telephone, satellite TV, in-house movies, writing desk, tea and coffee. **Some Rooms** iron, chairs. **Bed & Bath** Standard and clean. **Favorites** The singles are not great, very small and cramped, so for the extra money get a double. **Comfort & Decor** As you'd expect: inoffensive decor, good beds, and reasonable comfort in small rooms.

PAYMENT, RESERVATIONS, & RESTRICTIONS

Deposit Credit card; 72-hour cancellation policy. **Credit Cards** All major. **Check-In/Out** 2 p.m./11 a.m. **Pets** Not allowed. **Elevator** Yes. **Children** Yes. **Disabled access** Very limited, with small elevator and narrow hallways. 3 St. Martin's Street, Leicester Square, WC2; (0207) 930-8641, in U.S. (800) 333-3333; fax (0207) 925-0551, www.radissonedwardian.com

THE PELHAM   £177–£211

OVERALL ★★★★ | QUALITY ★★★★½ | VALUE ★★★★ | ZONE 11

15 Cromwell Place, SW7; (0207) 589-8288, in U.S. (800) 553-6674; fax (0207) 584-8444; pelham@firmdale.com; www.firmdale.com

The Pelham Hotel is a beautiful hotel and the price is relatively reasonable. Each room is unique and exquisitely decorated by the deft hand of the owner, and the hotel's size (46 bedrooms and suites) guarantees the guest the most punctilious and personal service. The atmosphere is that of a luxurious town house, with all the amenities you could desire. There are two sitting rooms with fireplaces, mahogany paneling, artfully arranged flowers, stunning furniture, and deep, comfy chairs and sofas. The views in the front are of the town of South Kensington, and there's not much to look at out of the rear windows except for the French Lycee playground. The location is excellent, with the museums of South Kensington just steps away, three tube lines across the street, buses that stop in front of the hotel, and the shops of Knightsbridge within a five-minute walk. The staff is friendly, helpful, and knowledgeable. They can get you anything you need at any time—baby-sitter, massage therapist, tickets, tours, airport transfer. Call about the special deals they offer. Breakfast is included with some rooms.

SETTINGS & FACILITIES

Location South Kensington. **Nearest Tube Station** South Kensington. **Quietness Rating** A in rear, C in front (the front has double glazing twice). **Dining** Kemp's Restaurant has an excellent menu that changes every few weeks. The room is quite comfortable and as beautiful as you'd expect from this exquisite hotel. **Amenities** Sitting rooms with fireplaces, champagne and hors d'oeuvres on Wednesdays, honor bar and coffee and tea in back sitting room. **Services** 24-hour room service, concierge, laundry, anything you can think of.

ACCOMMODATIONS

Rooms 46. **All Rooms** Satellite TV, two telephones, mobile phone, voice mail, mini-bar, sitting area. **Some Rooms** Video, sofa, balcony, four-poster. **Bed & Bath** Twin, double, king (which can be turned into twin) are all very comfortable; all private bathrooms, big tubs, good showers, granite and mahogany decor. **Favorites** Number 101: front-facing luxury double, with French doors leading to balcony; number 204 is a deluxe double, pleasingly decorated; number 409 is a luxury double; number 406, a new deluxe, has walk-in wardrobes, two sinks in bathroom, and shower cubicle as well as tub; rooms 405 and 305 are also new and distinguished. **Comfort & Decor** The comfort factor is what we'd all like to achieve in our own homes, and the decor is like stepping into the pages of *Architectural Digest*.

PAYMENT, RESERVATIONS, & RESTRICTIONS

Deposit Credit card; 48-hour cancellation policy. **Credit Cards** All major, except DC. **Check-In/Out** 1 p.m./noon. **Pets** Not allowed. **Elevator** Yes. **Children** Yes. **Disabled access** Yes, except stairs into hotel must be negotiated with assistance.

PEMBRIDGE COURT HOTEL   £125–£160

OVERALL ★★★ | QUALITY ★★★★ | VALUE ★★★★★ | ZONE 13

34 Pembridge Gardens; (0207) 229-9977, in U.S. (800) 709-9882; fax (0207) 727-4982; www.pemct.co.uk

This is an excellent town-house hotel within perfect reach of Portobello Road, a very happening part of town. You only need slip out the back of the house and through an alley and you're there. The atmosphere of this Victorian house is bright and friendly, with the resident cats adding a lovely homey touch. They roam freely, and if they take a liking to you, may hang out in your room with you. The rooms are of a decent size—some bigger than others—and decorated in ingenious ways: antique gloves, dresses, belts, fans, and other accessories are beautifully framed and hung all around. There's a very pleasant sitting room with a library and fireplace, and downstairs you'll find a wonderful bar/restaurant called Caps that used to be open to the public until the success of the hotel made the owners decide to keep it as a private place for guests only. The bar will stay open as long as you need, though they try to close it at 11 p.m. or midnight. A full English breakfast is included in the price. There's nothing precious or pretentious about this place; it's just good value and good vibrations in a beautiful setting.

SETTINGS & FACILITIES

Location Notting Hill Gate. **Nearest Tube Station** Notting Hill Gate. **Quietness Rating** A. **Dining** The Caps Restaurant has a limited but fine menu. **Amenities** Full English breakfast included, sitting room, arrangements with nearby health club, fax on request. **Services** 24-hour room service, limited menu, bellhop, laundry.

ACCOMMODATIONS

Rooms 20. **All Rooms** Telephone, satellite TV, writing desk, iron. **Some Rooms** Air conditioning. **Bed & Bath** Bathtubs in all but four rooms (which have showers), some four-poster beds. **Favorites** They're all different, but they're all good. If you want a lot of space, look for the ground-floor room, or any of the suites. The rooms at front have marvelous large windows. **Comfort & Decor** Very comfortable, and the decor is charming.

PAYMENT, RESERVATIONS, & RESTRICTIONS
Deposit Credit card; 48-hour cancellation policy. **Credit Cards** All major. **Check-In/Out** 2 p.m./noon. **Pets** Dogs allowed as long as you don't leave them cooped up in the room. **Elevator** Yes. **Children** Yes. **Disabled access** Steps in front.

THE PORTOBELLO HOTEL £150–£195

OVERALL ★★★ | QUALITY ★★★½ | VALUE ★★★ | ZONE 13

22 Stanley Gardens, W11; (0207) 727-2777; fax (0207) 792-9641;
www.portobello-hotel.co.uk

This is a trendy place with corporate accounts held by a number of modeling, music, and film agencies. It's in an old Victorian terrace house, and the rooms are each completely different from one another, and admirably so. The rooms in the rear look out over a communal garden into which you may not go, but which provides a sublime view. The Portobello has a lot of charm, with whimsical and traditional decor blending nicely. There's a sitting room that looks out over the garden and a small breakfast room on the ground floor. Continental breakfast is included in the price and is sent to your room. The ambience is pleasant, especially if you get one of the larger rooms, but the singles are cell-like, despite the gracious decor, and there is no space to do anything other than sleep. The most imposing room, number 16, features a big round bed and a balcony on the garden, with an antique copper bathtub right in the room; it's great for romance. Number 13 has a huge, high four-poster bed that requires a footstool to mount. Book ahead, for these rooms are coveted by all who've been here. It's within walking distance of Portobello Road, which makes it a good hotel for committed Portobello and Kensington Church Street shoppers, but it's not terribly well situated for general sightseeing due to its distance from public transportation.

SETTINGS & FACILITIES
Location Notting Hill Gate. **Nearest Tube Station** Notting Hill Gate. **Quietness Rating** A. **Dining** Very small breakfast room. **Amenities** Tiny basement restaurant with a few tables for breakfast and lunch; drawing room with fireplace and view of garden; health-club facilities are a four-minute walk away; computer in most rooms. **Services** Concierge, 8 a.m.–4 p.m. room service, continental breakfast sent to room, laundry.

ACCOMMODATIONS
Rooms 24. **All Rooms** Telephone, satellite TV. **Some Rooms** Balcony, couches, minibar, air conditioning, four-poster. **Bed & Bath** Beds are divinely comfy; baths range from a huge clawfoot tub to tiny shower stalls, but all are clean and user

friendly. **Favorites** Of course number 16, with the balcony overlooking the garden and the big round bed, is everyone's favorite. I also like the Asian-style number 46, also with a garden view. The single number 38 is very small, but has a good feeling to it. The first-floor rooms with the large French windows are spaciousness and fine. **Comfort & Decor** The decoration here is extraordinary and includes a range of furnishings, from traditional English antiques to exotic Asian and Middle Eastern treasures. Comfort is as high a priority as style.

PAYMENT, RESERVATIONS, & RESTRICTIONS

Deposit Credit card; 48-hour cancellation policy. **Credit Cards** All major. **Check-In/Out** After noon/noon. **Pets** Not allowed for a long stay. **Elevator** Yes, but only to third floor. **Children** Yes. **Disabled access** No.

QUALITY HOTEL   £109–£120

OVERALL ★★ | QUALITY ★★★½ | VALUE ★★★★★ | ZONE 9

82–83 Eccleston Square, SW1; (0207) 834-8042; fax (0207) 630-8942; admin@gb614.u-net.com; www.choicehotelseurope.com

This is a very good deal. The hotel is standard, without any charisma or glamour, but the rooms are tidy and reasonably sized. There is a small restaurant and a self-service coffee area. It's the kind of place that has an automatic shoe shiner near the public telephones, a video slot machine in the bar, and a condom dispenser in the ladies room. But it's also the kind of place that has a marble-floored lobby, with plants in the windows. There's a fax/Internet laptop in the lobby for your use, a sitting area, and a bar that opens at 5 p.m. Apparently, guests can get a key to Eccleston Square, a charming garden with benches and flora across the street. You can also walk to many of the great sights of London, such as Westminster Abbey and Buckingham Palace. There are many promotional deals offered in conjunction with the Choice Hotels Europe Group, which has over 3,000 hotels worldwide.

SETTINGS & FACILITIES

Location Victoria. **Nearest Tube Station** Victoria. **Quietness Rating** A/B. **Dining** Connaught's Brasserie serves delicious breakfast, lunch, and dinner. **Amenities** Dining room, bar, airport transfer, key to private gardens across the street. **Services** Reception functions as concierge, limited room service, bellhop, laundry.

ACCOMMODATIONS

Rooms 107. **All Rooms** Telephone, satellite TV, ceiling fans, iron, tea and coffee, writing desk. **Some Rooms** Minibar, teletext TV; some triples have two rooms. **Bed & Bath** Standard hotel style. **Favorites** Go for a premier double or triple. **Comfort & Decor** Standard hotel style, inoffensive and restful.

PAYMENT, RESERVATIONS, & RESTRICTIONS

Deposit Credit card. **Credit Cards** All major. **Check-In/Out** 2 p.m./noon. **Pets** Small pets allowed conditionally. **Elevator** Yes. **Children** Yes. **Disabled access** Steps outside, but people to help.

THE REMBRANDT HOTEL   £175–£200

OVERALL ★★★ | QUALITY ★★★½ | VALUE ★★★★ | ZONE 11

11 Thurloe Place; (0207) 589-8100; fax (0207) 225-3476; rembrandt@sarova.co.uk; www.sarova.co.uk

The three main reasons to stay at the Rembrandt are location, location, location. It's across the street from the Victoria and Albert and a hop, skip, and jump from the Science Museum, the Natural History Museum, and Harrods. It is also a four-minutes' walk from the South Kensington Tube Station, where one can access the Piccadilly (which goes to Heathrow), Circle, and District lines. There are three useful buses within shouting distance, and taxis are a breeze to hail. The hotel has a pleasant feeling to it, with a big lobby that has a fireplace, bar service, and plenty of couches to go around. The staff is plentiful and courteous, if not overawed by one's personage (I once had a cleaning person vacuum around my feet as I sat in the lobby having tea with some friends). The rooms are nice enough and very clean, but without much character. Reservationists usually advise Americans to go for the double executive room since they're accustomed to lots of space. The Rembrandt attracts a lot of conferences and a business crowd, as well as tourists. Ask about upgrading rooms.

SETTINGS & FACILITIES

Location South Kensington, on the border of Knightsbridge. **Nearest Tube Station** South Kensington. **Quietness Rating** A at the rear and top floors; C/D front lower floors (double glazing is not 100% effective, but the traffic roar quiets down at night). **Dining** The Masters Restaurant serves traditional breakfast, lunch, and dinner. **Amenities** Lobby with bar and fireplace, big dining room and small conservatory, tour bus pick-up, health club with pool (£5 charge), conference rooms, professional business services. **Services** Concierge, 24-hour room service, bellhops, laundry, fax and Internet in lobby, baby-sitting.

ACCOMMODATIONS

Rooms 195; two floors nonsmoking. **All Rooms** Telephone, cable TV, in-house movies, minibar on request, tea and coffee, hair dryer, writing desk. **Some Rooms** Air conditioning, iron, bidets, sitting area. **Bed & Bath** Beds are so-so; bathrooms are clean and spacious by London standards. Jacuzzi on request for executive doubles. **Favorites** Executive-double front rooms on first floor facing Victoria and Albert Museum—you can admire the statues that you can't see from street level. The only drawbacks are daytime street noise and fumes. **Comfort & Decor** The lobby is appealing, with a fireplace and plenty of seating, as well as a bar, but the rooms are somewhat dull, if clean. The decor could be described as unimaginative but safe.

PAYMENT, RESERVATIONS, & RESTRICTIONS

Deposit Credit card; 48-hour cancellation policy. **Credit Cards** All major. **Check-In/Out** 2 p.m./noon; express check-out available. **Pets** Not allowed. **Elevator** Two. **Children** Yes. **Disabled access** Yes, but with three front stairs to be negotiated; doormen will gladly help.

RIVERSIDE HOTEL	£65–£90

OVERALL ★★ | QUALITY ★★★ | VALUE ★★★★★ | ZONE 12

23 Petersham Road, TW10; (0208) 940-1339; fax (0208) 948-0967;
riversidehotel@yahoo.com; www.smoothhound.co.uk/hotels/riverside

Richmond is a very beautiful town, and it would behoove anyone who wanted to see a bit of the lovelier nearby parts of the Thames to take a trip out there on the tube or by rail. If you wanted to be sure of comparatively clean air, you might even want to stay there. A five- to ten-minute walk from the tube along Richmond High Street is the Riverside Hotel, a Victorian building right smack dab on the Thames, with pretty views and easy access to all the shops and amenities of Richmond. Richmond has a lot to enjoy: a historic theater, an arts center, nearby golf course, swimming pools, tennis and squash courts, plenty of pubs and restaurants and shops, not to mention the huge park. The hotel is well priced and well located, and the owners are willing to help you find your way to and from central London. It's a homey place, and it's recently been refurbished and upgraded. Some of the rooms are smaller than others, as is the case with the old Victorian conversions, so discuss with the owners exactly what you need when booking. June and July are very busy times, so be sure to book well in advance. Full English breakfast is included. Ten percent discount applies for stays of over a week.

SETTINGS & FACILITIES

Location Richmond. **Nearest Tube Station** Richmond (or BritRail). **Quietness Rating** C in front (double-glazed windows), A in back. **Dining** Breakfast and dinner. **Amenities** Breakfast and dinner room, bar. **Services** Helpful reception, one-day laundry service.

ACCOMMODATIONS

Rooms 23. **All Rooms** Shower and toilet, telephone, satellite TV, hair dryer, tea and coffee. **Some Rooms** View over river, balcony, garden access, four-poster bed. **Bed**

& Bath Clean and satisfactory; about half have shower stalls only. **Favorites** Big rooms and balcony rooms with river view; the Riverside Room is the best. **Comfort & Decor** Eclectic decor; all rooms different, some very small.

PAYMENT, RESERVATIONS, & RESTRICTIONS

Deposit Credit card; 48-hour cancellation policy. **Credit Cards** All major, except DC. **Check-In/Out** 2 p.m./11 a.m. **Pets** Allowed by arrangement. **Elevator** No. **Children** Yes; younger than age 5 stay free. **Disabled access** No.

THE ROOKERY   £205–£240

OVERALL ★★★★ | QUALITY ★★★★½ | VALUE ★★★ | ZONE 3

Peter's Lane, Cowcross Street, EC1; (0207) 336-0931; fax (0207) 336-0931; reservations@rookery.co.uk; www.rookeryhotel.com

The Rookery is a charming hotel owned by the talented team of Peter McKay and Douglas Blain, who brought you The Gore and Hazlitt's. The hotel is in Clerkenwell, a short distance from the City, which makes it perfect for the businessperson. This is not the usual area where tourists stay, but it is definitely a viable choice, especially if you have an interest in the "real" historic London. Dr. Johnson would find himself completely lost in the postwar City of London, but you should be able to navigate from St. Paul's to the Old Bailey (both of which are visible from some of the hotel's windows). However, it is not only the neighborhood that lends appeal; the building itself is a conglomeration of amazingly restored eighteenth-century town houses that make for an intimate, delightful accomodation. All the modern conveniences are here, but they pale next to the glories of the past carefully culled from auction houses, flea markets, and antiques markets that litter the place. Like Hazlitt's, the exterior gives no hint of what wonders lie within: the old brick buildings are nondescript, located down a little lane and through an alley that cows used to cross making their fatal way to the Smithfield Meat Market. Look for lanterns and a discreet sign—no waving banners here. There are two common areas: a library and a conservatory that looks out onto a little garden. The rooms are of a decent size, and the bathrooms are unique. A great choice for the businessperson, the antiques freak, or one in search of a very good representation of old London. Sticking to the period theme, there is no elevator for the four floors.

SETTINGS & FACILITIES

Location Clerkenwell. **Nearest Tube Station** Farringdon. **Quietness Rating** A. **Dining** No. **Amenities** Conservatory, meeting rooms, personal safes in each room; you can take your breakfast in the lounge or in your room. **Services** Concierge, 18-hour room service, bellhop, laundry.

ACCOMMODATIONS

Rooms 33. **All Rooms** Telephones, statellite TV, fans on request, hair dryer, writing desk, personal safe. **Some Rooms** Views, four-poster. **Bed & Bath** Amazing. **Favorites** The Rook's Nest has a view of St. Paul's and the Old Bailey, and if you squint your eyes to remove the modern eyesores, you can really get the measure of Old London town. **Comfort & Decor** Of the highest quality on both scores, except for the lack of an elevator. The decor will make you drool.

PAYMENT, RESERVATIONS, & RESTRICTIONS

Deposit Credit card. **Credit Cards** All major. **Check-In/Out** 1:30 p.m./11:30 a.m. **Pets** Not allowed. **Elevator** No. **Children** Yes. **Disabled access** No.

RUSKIN HOTEL   £47–£85

OVERALL ★ | QUALITY ★★½ | VALUE ★★★★★ | ZONE 2

23–24 Montague Street, WC1; (0207) 636-7388; fax (0207) 323-1662

The Ruskin Hotel has been run by the same Spanish family for the past 22 years and it has very much the feel of an inexpensive hotel in Barcelona. It also has the loyalty of many customers who return again and again. Unlike many of the budget bed-and-breakfasts in London, the Ruskin has an elevator to all floors, accepts all major credit cards, and is clean and friendly. The owner is not interested in customers who want to argue about services and room size, but is happy to house the kind of sensible souls who welcome a square deal that's across the street from the British Museum (the rooms in front have a view of the museum's side). The sitting room has a beautiful painting from 1801 by John Ward, a painter for the Duke of Bedford, whose estate still owns all the land around here. The house is quite old, having started out as a private residence before it served as a warren of offices where Sir Arthur Conan Doyle was reputed to have worked on his Sherlock Holmes stories. For a no-frills B&B/budget hotel, the Ruskin is a good bet. The single rooms have no ensuite toilets; you will need to get a double for that.

SETTINGS & FACILITIES

Location Bloomsbury. **Nearest Tube Station** Russell Square. **Quietness Rating** A in back, B in front (double-glazed windows help). **Dining** Breakfast room. **Amenities** Breakfast included; generous portions served by waiters in a nice breakfast room. **Services** Se habla español; they can manage a few other languages as well.

ACCOMMODATIONS

Rooms 33; 6 with shower and toilet. **All Rooms** Telephones, hair dryer, tea and coffee. **Some Rooms** Garden view, bathroom. **Bed & Bath** Both communal and private bathrooms are in good shape; the beds are comfortable, though the doubles might be a squeeze for large Americans. **Favorites** Number 102 is a pleasant family room. **Comfort & Decor** The exuberance of the many plants and flowers on the outside may betray the utilitarian decor within: strip lights over beds, naughahyde, fake wood, and plastic furniture, plus pink walls that mimic but don't quite match the Mediterranean concept of pink walls. Sensitive souls might shrivel at the decor, frankly, but if you can close your eyes to it, you might find time to admire certain features like friezes and the sitting-room mural.

PAYMENT, RESERVATIONS, & RESTRICTIONS

Deposit One night nonrefundable, unless they can re-let room. **Credit Cards** All major. **Check-In/Out** 1 p.m./ 11:30 a.m. **Pets** Not allowed. **Elevator** Yes. **Children** Yes. **Disabled access** Yes.

ST. MARGARET'S HOTEL   £50–£95

OVERALL ★ | QUALITY ★★½ | VALUE ★★★★★ | ZONE 2

---

26 Bedford Place, Russell Square, WC1; (0207) 636-4277; fax (0207) 323-3066

This is aplace that you can't help but like, even if it has no frills. What it lacks in amenities and style, it more than makes up for in good intentions, friendliness, amazingly low prices, and a very fine dining room overlooking some lovely gardens. (You are welcome to enjoy the gardens at any time.) It has the feeling of a penzione, appropriately, as the owners are Italian. The senior Marazzis started it when they arrived in London after the war, and their son and his bride took it over. Mrs. Marazzi's daughter is now entering the family business, which makes it a real family affair and a labor of love. The place is informal but very clean, and although most of the single rooms don't have ensuite bathrooms, the shared conveniences are spotless. It's a big place and the management renovates rooms one after another, so there are always improvements being made. This is the kind of inexpensive hotel that people continue to come to time and time again for the friendliness, the British Museum around the corner, the relative spaciousness of the rooms, and the sensible cost. Be warned, though, that this is a low-cost, bed-and-breakfast-type hotel—if you're looking for elegance and three- or four-star service, you need to pay a lot more than they're charging. Also be warned that there are lots of stairs and no elevator.

SETTINGS & FACILITIES

Location Bloomsbury, off Russell Square. **Nearest Tube Station** Russell Square. **Quietness Rating** A. **Dining** A bright and very pleasant dining room overlooking gardens (for breakfast only, which is included in the price). **Amenities** Breakfast in dining room, tea and coffee served anytime, safe in office, fax available for use. **Services** 24-hour receptionist.

ACCOMMODATIONS

Rooms 64; 12 with ensuite bathrooms, more planned for future. No singles have toilets at present. **All Rooms** TV, phone. **Some Rooms** Ensuite bathrooms, hair dryers, French doors and high ceilings, view of gardens. **Bed & Bath** Beds are reasonably comfortable; baths are spotless in both communal and ensuite bathrooms.

Favorites Number 53 is a room that looks over the garden and features a glassed-in conservatory. Book this one well in advance, as it is the favorite of regulars. Number 40 is a fine family room with enough space for four to sleep comfortably, as is number 45. Rooms on the first floor all have high ceilings and long French windows. **Comfort & Decor** The decor is utilitarian, but would offend the very sensitive souls or those used to the Ritz. It feels like a place your sensible, thrifty grandma would put together for you.

PAYMENT, RESERVATIONS, & RESTRICTIONS

Deposit One night's charge, £6 administration fee for cancellation at any time. **Credit Cards** All major. **Check-In/Out** Check in whenever room is available; out at noon. **Pets** Not allowed. **Elevator** No. **Children** Yes. **Disabled access** There are two rooms on ground floor, but there are steps to reception. Not good for wheelchairs, as there are no porters.

THISTLE HOTEL HYDE PARK   £160–£180

OVERALL ★★★★ | QUALITY ★★★½ | VALUE ★★★★★ | ZONE 14

Lancaster Gate, W2; (0207) 262-2711; fax (0207) 262-2147;
hydepark@thistle.com; www.thistlehotels.com

If you really want to be on Hyde Park but don't want to shell out the kind of dough the luxury hotels on Park Lane charge, this is one of the many hotels along Bayswater that can solve your problem. As a Thistle hotel, it has all the amenities you can expect from a good hotel group: room service, a restaurant, newspaper at your door, packages and promotions, business facilities, minibars. What it doesn't have is loads of charm, but that may be made up for by its location and the possibility that you'll get a good deal. There's a good sitting room with leather chairs and a piano, and a conservatory that looks out across Bayswater to Kensington Gardens and Hyde Park. The traffic of Bayswater's four lanes can be stiff in the daytime, but it becomes relatively quiet at night—the higher the floor, the quieter the room and the more stunning the view.

SETTINGS & FACILITIES

Location Lancaster Gate (Bayswater Road). **Nearest Tube Station** Queensway. **Quietness Rating** A on high floors and in back; C on low floors and front. **Dining** The restaurant offers white-linen service (and prices). **Amenities** Restaurant, fax in reception, fitness center next door, piano in sitting room. **Services** Concierge, 24-hour room service, bellhop, laundry.

ACCOMMODATIONS

Rooms 54. **All Rooms** Telephone, minibar, cable TV, air conditioning, hair dryer, iron, safe. **Some Rooms** Balcony, park views, sitting area. **Bed & Bath** Good beds, perfect baths. **Favorites** Number 405 is a big room that gets lots of light, is very quiet, and has the most spectacular views over Kensington Gardens and Hyde Park. Any on the park are nice. **Comfort & Decor** Very comfortable; decor is of the upmarket hotel style.

PAYMENT, RESERVATIONS, & RESTRICTIONS

Deposit Credit card; must cancel by noon on day of arrival, except for group bookings. **Credit Cards** All major. **Check-In/Out** 2 p.m./noon. **Pets** Not allowed. **Elevator** Yes. **Children** Yes; near one of the playgrounds in Kensington Gardens. **Disabled access** Planning a wheelchair ramp.

THISTLE HOTEL KENSINGTON PALACE   £124–£160

OVERALL ★★★ | QUALITY ★★★½ | VALUE ★★★★★ | ZONE 13

DeVere Gardens, Kensington, W8 5AF; (0207) 937-8121; fax (0207) 937-2816; www.thistlehotels.com

Now that DeVere, the budget hotel across the street, is being gutted for a future fancy hotel, the Thistle Hotel Kensington Palace is the next best place. The prices (£124 for a standard room, £263 for a suite) are a good deal for the area and for what you get. Runners and park lovers will appreciate having Kensington Gardens and Hyde Park across the street, and shopaholics will love having the stores of Kensington High Street and the antiques of Kensington Church Street only steps away. Plenty of buses go by the hotel too. The restaurant isn't much to speak of, but Kensingon has tons of good restaurants all over. Ask about or check the websire for details and promotions.

SETTINGS & FACILITIES

Location Kensington, across from Kensington Gardens. **Nearest Tube Station** Kensington High Street. **Quietness Rating** C on park side, B in rear rooms. **Dining** Cafe/restaurant on the premises called Fox & Hendersons. **Amenities** The usual for a chain hotel, cable TV, telephone, tea and coffee facilities. **Services** Concierge, room service.

ACCOMMODATIONS

Rooms 285. **All Rooms** Cable, telephone, hair dryer, iron, coffee and tea in room. **Some Rooms** View of Kensington Palace and Gardens. **Bed & Bath** Rooms are a reasonable size, with American-sized beds; bathtubs in some, showers in others; clean and pleasant. **Favorites** Any of the rooms on the Kensington Gardens–side over the first floor are best. **Comfort & Decor** Comfort is of good standard, decor is nothing to write home about, but possesses a cheerful and tasteful uniformity.

PAYMENT, RESERVATIONS, & RESTRICTIONS

Deposit Major credit card. **Credit Cards** All major. **Check-In/Out** 2-3 p.m./11 a.m. **Pets** No. **Elevator** No. **Children** Under age 16 free. **Disabled access** Steps out front, doormen available to help.

THISTLE HOTEL VICTORIA   £205–£225

OVERALL ★★★★★ | QUALITY ★★★★ | VALUE ★★★★★ | ZONE 9

Buckingham Palace Road; (0207) 834-9494; fax (0207) 630-1978;
www.thistlehotels.com

This is one of those massive, grand Victorian hotels that makes your eyes
pop when you enter it, and by the time you reach the middle of the vast
dome with the huge chandelier swinging from it, you've unconsciously
straightened your posture. The hotel was built to accommodate the visitors
coming to see the Great Exhibition of 1851, and it was built to impress.
There are stained-glass windows, wrought-iron staircases, columns, marble
floors and walls, carved busts on the interior and exterior walls (the exterior
is in its own class altogether), potted plants, and huge windows. The whole
place underwent a £3-million, 8-month-long refurbishment in 1996, and it
shows. All the rooms are in excellent shape, the common areas are perfect,
and the Galleria, which rings the huge lobby one level up, is one of the
finest hotel sitting areas in London. It's a Thistle hotel, so it provides all the
services one can expect from a hotel group with global standards: modems,
fax on requests, cable TV, nonsmoking floors, complimentary newspapers,
business support, and so on. It's near Victoria, Westminster Abbey, and
Buckingham Palace—a central location that is also rather noisy during the
day. The rear rooms have unfortunate views over Victoria Station, but they
are very quiet. There are two sections: the "new" wing, built in the 1870s,
has more standard-size rooms, whereas the old wing was built at a time
when the guest would require a couple of rooms plus one for the maid or
valet, so there have been conversions there that have left the sizes of rooms
rather disparate. If you're visiting with a group or taking more than one
room, ask for the new wing so there are no disappointing comparisons. Ask
about the Leisure Breaks and Pound for Dollar promotions.

SETTINGS & FACILITIES

Location Victoria. **Nearest Tube Station** Victoria. **Quietness Rating** A in back, C
in front, D in lower floors with huge windows, but that doesn't stop people from
requesting these rooms again and again. **Dining** Very stately dining room, big enough
to seat the occupants of the whole hotel; Harvard Bar; Galleria and lounge for tea and
meals. **Amenities** The above, plus modems in some rooms, many different pillows
available, newspaper. **Services** Concierge, 24-hour room service, bellhop, laundry.

ACCOMMODATIONS

Rooms 364. All Rooms Telephone, cable TV, hair dryer, iron, tea and coffee, in-
house movies, writing desk. **Some Rooms** Minibar, modem, four-poster and half-

tester (half a four-poster, with canopy) beds, huge windows, and high ceilings. **Bed & Bath** 100% cotton sheets on the bed, and you can request pillows of all kinds. The bathrooms are perfect. **Favorites** The big rooms at the front in the old wing with the big windows—noisy, but gorgeous. **Comfort & Decor** High quality; all rooms individually decorated in nice colors and furniture.

PAYMENT, RESERVATIONS, & RESTRICTIONS

Deposit Credit card. **Credit Cards** All major. **Check-In/Out** 2 p.m./noon. **Pets** Dogs allowed conditionally. **Elevator** Yes. **Children** Yes. **Disabled access** No; many steps.

Part Four

Arriving and Getting Oriented

Entering the Country

After you land, try to make a speedy exit from the plane and walk quickly toward the immigration area, without looking like a pushy horror if possible (the English hate that). The walk from plane to immigration may be very long, so try to keep your carry-on luggage light and easy to handle. You should have been issued an arrival card on the plane; make sure it has been filled out, and stick it in your passport along with your customs form. Arrival cards must be completed by each passport holder in your family, but only one customs form per family is necessary.

IMMIGRATION

Keep your eyes on the signs and make sure you are heading for the right immigration line. If you have been traveling in first or business class, you can usually head straight for the Fast Track line and show your Fast Track Pass or boarding ticket. Fast Tracks often close at night—check with the flight attendnt so you don't get slowed down by a closed Fast Track. There are two other lines: one for EU passport holders and one for all other nationalities. Have your passport ready, as the line can move pretty swiftly. You may be asked pointed questions about what you're doing here and where you're staying. Answer honestly and solemnly; immigration is a serious business in this country with national health service and other quality-of-life attractions. Nationals from the United States, Canada, Australia, New Zealand, South Africa, Japan, or Switzerland can get in without a visa as long as they are on vacation. Anyone carrying another passport should check with the British consulate in their country.

Customs

Next, you will be sent into the luggage hall to collect your bags. Grab a free trolley, and after you have retrieved your luggage, follow signs for customs. The Goods to Declare exit is red, the Nothing to Declare exit is green, and the European Union exit (for anyone arriving from the continent) is blue. For our readers who may be traveling abroad for the first time, you'll decide which exit to use based upon what you have brought along with you that was purchased outside England.

The guidelines for what you can bring into England are divided into two categories: one for goods bought within the European Union, and the other for items purchased outside the EU. The likelihood that you will bring large jewels or luxury goods to London is remote, but you may want to save some money by bringing in your own instruments of vice. So, you may bring in, duty free:

- 200 cigarettes, 100 cigarillos, 50 cigars, or 250 grams of tobacco
- 2 liters of table wine and 1 liter of alcohol over 22% by volume (most spirits) and 2 liters of alcohol under 22% by volume (fortified or sparkling wine or liqueurs) *or* 2 more liters of table wine
- 50 milliliters of perfume
- Other goods up to a value of £145 (about $250)

You may not bring in controlled drugs (any medication you have should be in its original bottle with your name on it), firearms and/or ammunition, obscene material, threats to public health and the environment, plants and vegetables, fresh meats, or any kind of animals. There are strict quarantine laws here. These are in the process of being overturned by animal lovers who have organized a "passport for pets" scheme, which will replace the six-month law that has frustrated many animal owners for years.

If you have any questions about import and export issues, contact the Excise and Inland Customs Advice Centre (Her Majesty's Customs and Excise; (0845) 010-9000; www.hmce.gov.uk).

If you have to pay duty, you can pay in pounds sterling or by MasterCard or Visa. You have rights, which Her Majesty's customs officers are supposed to make perfectly clear to you, such as receiving help in repacking bags if they make you unpack them, the right to appeal on the spot to a senior officer against a proposed search, and claiming compensation if they have damaged any of your property. If you want to appeal a written tax or duty decision, let the officer know at the time. If you don't do so at the time, you must write to them within 45 days; they will give you a leaflet that explains how to appeal.

If you have any complaints about how you were treated, you can get seek assistance from the Adjudicator's Office (Haymarket House, 28 Haymarket, London, SW1 4SP; phone (0207) 930-2292; fax (0207) 930-2298).

The customs hall is often unstaffed, or there will be only one or two people there. Assuming you have nothing to declare, march quickly through the appropriate exit. There are large two-way mirrors in some of the airports here, and someone will definitely be looking through. If you are stopped—occasionally random checks are carried out—*never* make jokes about the contents of your bags. You are almost certain to be arrested, detained, and possibly deported. This is a nation that has had its share of terrorist bombings, and the officials are extremely and understandably jumpy. *Never* leave your bags unattended. They can and will be removed and destroyed quite swiftly.

Make sure you have some English pounds to pay for your transportation from the airport. Cash machines are found in all airports and train stations, and they will give you the best exchange rate. They are known as "cashpoints" here, and they abound in London. Most of them are on the Cirrus or MacPlus system and will take money straight from your checking account at home. If you only have a credit card, make sure before you leave that you have a four-digit PIN for use in the cashpoints. There are seldom letters on the machines, so memorize your PIN numerically.

Getting into London

Car Rentals

There are car rental counters at all the airports, with most of the major companies represented: Hertz, Avis, Europcar. You can rent a car when you arrive if necessary, but it's best to reserve ahead. You must be over age 23 and have a valid license from your country. You will need to use a parking lot in London, as there are only metered spots and restricted parking on the streets. For reservations, visit www.hertz.com, www.avis.com, or www.europcar.com.

From Gatwick Airport (phone (0870) 000-2468)

It's a long drive into London from Gatwick, with a good chance of plenty of traffic. A taxi to central London will cost as much as £65, and can take over an hour. By far the best way is the Gatwick Express (phone (0870) 530-1530), which leaves every 15 minutes and takes you right to Victoria Station in half an hour, where you can catch a taxi, tube, or bus to your final destination. Follow signs and take the escalator down to the platform. The Gatwick Express is clearly marked. You're encouraged to pay on board the train to avoid the long and pointless line at the airport ticket office. They take most credit cards and cash. The fare is £10.50 one way, £20 round trip, half price for children between the ages of 5 and 15; it's free for children under age 5.

Thameslink, another train line, also stops at Gatwick and is convenient if you're staying in north London, as it stops at King's Cross. These tickets must be purchased at the ticket office, and the trains don't run as frequently as the Gatwick Express.

From Heathrow Airport (phone (0870) 000-0123)

By Taxi   Heathrow has a number of excellent options for getting into London. The most expensive is the black-cab taxi, which can run from £40 for a no-traffic, west London drop off, to upward of £60 for a bad-traffic, central or north London destination. The best thing about the black cabs is that they are allowed to drive in the bus lanes, which saves time in rush hour. There are also car services known as "minicabs." They are normal-sized cars, but the name differentiates them from the black cabs. They don't run on a meter; they are slightly cheaper than the black cabs, but they can be unreliable. They will not know London as well as the black cabs, and they cannot drive in bus lanes. We have received enough complaints from our readers about minicabs—and indeed Londoners themselves tend to be wary of them—that my best advice is to take advantage of the safe and spacious black cabs, whose drivers have the "Knowledge" (a long and stringent study of London's roads) to get you anywhere you want to go. Driving time varies with traffic, but it will generally take between 45 minutes and an hour to most central London locations.

By Bus   The Airbus takes only slightly more time than a cab, but only costs £7 one way for an adult and £3.50 for children between ages 5 and 15 and students under age 26 with ID. It's free for children under age five. The A2 (they did away with the A1 recently) leaves from each terminal at half-hour intervals every day between 6 a.m. and 9 p.m. The bus is a double decker and a nice way to get your first look at the city. Depending on traffic, it can take between 50 to 90 minutes to get from Heathrow to central London.

The A2 runs north to east—stopping at the Kensington Hilton on Holland Park Avenue, Notting Hill Gate, Queensway, Paddington Station, Marble Arch—and ends up at Russell Square in Bloomsbury.

By Underground (Tube)   The Piccadilly line originates at Heathrow and is a fast and inexpensive way to get into the city, with convenient stops—Hammersmith, Earl's Court, South Kensington, Chelsea, Knightsbridge, Hyde Park Corner, Piccadilly, Leicester Square, Bloomsbury, King's Cross, Finsbury Park, and even beyond to the northern suburbs. This is a great option if you aren't carrying a lot of baggage and it's not rush hour. Be careful about the train—there are some trains from which you have to get out and change trains at Acton Town, which is a pain and can add a sizable chunk of time to your trip (on a good day, it should take about 45 minutes). Buy the correct ticket—you'll be going to Tube Zone One (not to be confused with this book's zones; it's an London Underground definition)—and hold onto it. You need it when you leave the tube station. If you have the wrong ticket, you can be fined £10 on the other end. You can take the tube into town and then hail a taxi on the street to get you to your hotel for a fraction of what a taxi would cost straight from the airport. Barring delays or train changes, it takes about an hour to get from Heathrow to Piccadilly Circus. The tube is the least expensive option and the best bet for large groups of travelers.

By Heathrow Express Train (phone (0845) 600-1515; www.baa. co.uk) Run and owned by British Airways, this train is the fastest way into London—at 100 miles an hour, it takes only 15 minutes, and it leaves every 15 minutes. The standard round-trip fare is £22, £12 one way from the ticket counter; round-trip fare is £24, £14 one way on the train. If you book on their website you will save a couple of quid. The first-class price of £40 round trip apparently makes it the most expensive public transport in the world per mile and minute traveled, even more than the Concord. There are plenty of taxis at Paddington, where you arrive; and returning to Heathrow is excellent, as you can check in right there and ride luggage free, with boarding pass in hand, to Heathrow. Paddington is in Zone 14, and its tube station connects with four tube trains, as well as overland trains that go west.

From Stansted Airport (phone (0870) 000-0303)

This is a relatively new airport and functions quite smoothly. As it's 35 miles outside of London, a taxi is prohibitively expensive; luckily, the Stansted Express train is reasonably priced (£10) and very fast: you'll arrive at Liverpool Street Station in 45 minutes. Just follow signs down one floor to the train platform and catch the train to Liverpool Street, which is a major rail hub and tube station. Journey time is 45 minutes, and the fare is £12 one way. Trains run every 30 minutes.

From Luton Airport (phone (0158) 240-5100)

Luton deals mostly with British charter flights or cut-rate budget airlines, so there seems to be no incentive for its employees to be efficient or pleasant. Getting into London from Luton by taxi can take up to 90 minutes in traffic and costs up to £60. It is, however, the best option for those in a hurry of with lots of baggage. Greenline Buses travel between Victoria Station in London and Luton for £7.50. Call (0870) 608-7261 for times.

From London City Airport (phone (0207) 646-0000)

This is the closest airport to central London, but it deals mostly with European short hops. It is a good, well-run airport, and the transportation is quite convenient: a black-taxi ride to London runs about £20; and buses leave every 20 minutes or so for Canary Wharf and Liverpool Street at a cost of only about £5.

By Eurostar (phone (0123) 361-7575 or website: www.eurostar.com

This high-speed train is a fast, though not necessarily cheap, way to get from the heart of Paris or Brussels to London's Waterloo Station. Prices are dependent on the day of the week and time of the day you travel, the length of your stay, and availability. If you book two weeks in advance, you can get a non-refundable, non-changeable ticket for £70 (first class £120). If you want to pop over for a one-night stand, it costs £300 for a fully refundable, fully negotiable ticket (first class £380). There is a youth fare for £75 for those under age 26. Eurostar offers as many as 20 different price categories, so do call to discuss. Waterloo Station is on the south side of the Thames across from Westminster and is served by the tube's Northern line, buses, and taxis (taxis are reasonably priced for a trip to central London). The great advantage of the Eurostar over the plane or ferry is that it is absolutely the fastest, most convenient way to get to and from the continent—three hours from London to the Gare du Nord in Paris. Don't forget your passport and to fill out an arrival card for immigration at Waterloo Station. The train travels at 185 miles per hour on French soil, but must slow down in England because the British didn't spring for the high-speed track. The plan is to lay the track down as soon as possible (we won't be holding our breath), at which point the train will operate from St. Pancras.

By Car from the Continent

Renting a car on the European continent to drive into Britain is expensive and a bit risky. There is compulsory insurance, and the European car will have the steering wheel on the "wrong" side of the car, which will make driving in England much more difficult. Driving in London is pretty hair raising, even for those who are used to driving on the left, so our advice is to drop your car off at the airport or in the suburbs and take public transportation into town. There are car-rental companies at all the major ports, most of which will allow you to drop off at other locations, though there may be a drop-off fee. It's important to buy a good road atlas of Great Britain if you plan to drive from any of the ports (Dover, Folkestone, Newhaven, Southampton, Harwich, or Ramsgate) into London. The signs are confusing at times, with more information on them than you may be able to take in at once, directing you off roundabouts. But this is the beauty of a roundabout: keep going around about it until you're sure what direction in which to go.

By *Ship from America*

If you're phobic about air travel, have plenty of time and money, or want to see what a transatlantic crossing is like, you can call Cunard at 800-CUNARD, or look for fares and schedules on www.cunard.com. A round-trip from New York to London starts at a thousand dollars. The crossing, on the *Queen Elizabeth 2,* takes six days. They also offer a one-way trip with a free economy air ticket for the return, starting at $1,500.

Getting Oriented in London

Post Codes

As we explained in the introduction, London is divided into post codes, which instantly identify an area to those in the know. You'll see the post code on maps, street signs, and addresses. This system is very helpful for the tourist, who may want to stay in the same post code as a particular museum, or for the business traveler who may want to be near the office. These are not arbitrary; they represent compass directions: W1 is west and WC is west central, just as E1 is east and EC is east central. The closer an area is to central London, the lower the code number—all "1s" abut central London. These post codes can encompass more than one "town" and vice versa; SW1 includes Victoria, Pimlico, and Westminster, and what we consider Chelsea can reach into districts SW3, SW7, and SW10. You'll quickly figure it out, and you'll have your own favorite post code before you know it.

Grasping London's Geography   The most important feature of London's geography is the rolling Thames River. It snakes through the city, bending around boroughs and post codes, and though it may not be the great and busy highway through London that it once was, it is still the major water artery. Starting in the east, the Thames is slowed down at the hairpin turn around the Isle of Dogs, with Greenwich on the south side of the river. Canary Wharf is on the Isle of Dogs, and at the next bend of the river is the East End. The river straightens out for the section that includes the Tower of London, Tower Bridge, and the City of London. To the south of this portion of the river is Southwark, turning into the South Bank to the west, with the Globe's thatched roof and the mighty London Eye ferris wheel visible. Continuing westward, the river slows down again for another curve; on this curve, along Victoria Embankment, you'll see the Temple, Cleopatra's Needle, Big Ben, the Houses of Parliament, and at Lambeth Bridge, on the opposite bank, is Lambeth Palace. Radiating north from this important stretch of the river is Soho, then Bloomsbury, and slightly northwest is Regent's Park. Come back down to the river and follow it past Westminster and Pimlico to Chelsea, where it will continue to flow west through Fulham, Hammersmith, and Chiswick, toward Richmond and Hampton Palace. North of Chelsea you'll find South Kensington, Hyde Park, Bayswater, and Marylebone, and run into Regent's Park again. North of that is Hampstead Heath.

Hyde Park is another landmark that helps visitors to get a handle on London's geography. The park is surrounded by central London; to the north is Bayswater, to the east lies Marble Arch and Mayfair, to the southeast are Belgravia and Knightsbridge, to the southwest is South Kensington, and to the west are Kensington and Holland Park.

London is a huge city, but it is divided into enough discrete areas that you can start to differentiate between parts of it rather easily, using the river and Hyde Park as baselines. Study the map of the whole city, see how the zones intersect; look at the tube map, bearing in mind that it's highly stylized, but it can help you get a grip on this vast metropolis. Look especially at the yellow Circle line, which circles around central London. The tube map was streamlined from a mess of meandering lines into what you see now. It works and it's readable, but it's not geographically exact. For instance, if you look at the tube map, the distance between Lancaster Gate to Paddington Station looks significant; in fact, it is only a three-minute walk. However, a walk from Marble Arch to Lancaster Gate looks pretty easy on the tube map, but it would take about 10 minutes. Use the street map to determine distance, not the tube map.

The *London A to Z Book,* pronounced "a to zed" by the British, is essential to you, as it is to any Londoner. There are other street atlases, by Collins and by Nicholson, which are also fine, but the *A to Z* is the most commonly used. It's not for tourists only—in fact, Londoners probably rely even more on these maps than tourists do, because they know how devilishly devious the streets here are. Not only are there streets of the exact name in different post codes but there are major arteries that change names as they wind through various areas. Thus the A4 from Heathrow becomes the Great West Road, then Talgarth Road, then Cromwell, Thurloe Place, Brompton Road, Knightsbridge, and Piccadilly, all without making a single turn.

Some of the major thoroughfares in London are of rather ancient vintage—old Roman commercial routes of strict design—and all the streets, mews, alleys, dead-ends, cul-de-sacs, terraces, and crescents that later made a mess of Rome's plans were often cowpaths, driveways, back passageways to a high street, or footpaths between neighborhoods and pubs. This city was never brought to heel by planners in the way New York and parts of Paris were, which is what makes it so much fun to explore. For seeing the best of London by foot, there is nothing better than to just get lost. Indeed, it is highly unlikely that you won't do so unintentionally at least once when you're here. But as long as you carry an *A to Z* book and persist in one direction or another, you are bound to eventually hit some major landmark . . . or a taxi.

In Covent Garden there's a fantastic shop called Stanford's (zone 7; 12–14 Long Acre; (0207) 836-1321; sales@stanfords.co.uk; www.stanfords.co.uk; tube: Covent Garden) that has every map known to London. Here you can find walking maps, cycling maps, backstreet maps for avoiding the large thoroughfares, and maps of the old city. For your purposes, it is best to get the big picture with a fold-out map that is relatively simple, listing the major attractions and streets, and keep the pocket street atlas for narrowing down your route.

Things the Locals Already Know

Getting the Low Down on What's Up

For the latest information on current plays, movies, art exhibits, clubs, fairs, museum tours, lectures, walking tours, or whatever, pick up a *Time Out* magazine. It's more thorough than its competitor, *What's On,* although *What's On* is a little simpler to read. On Thursday, the *Evening Standard* newspaper includes a magazine, *Hot Tickets,* which is the least expensive of the three and is quite comprehensive.

If you want to get a copy of *Time Out* before you leave, you could try emailing them at net@timeout.co.uk, or calling (0207) 813-6060 (distribution department). Check out their website at www.timeout.com. If you're in a big city, try a newsstand that carries foreign newspapers and magazines; they might carry the weekly London *Time Out.* If you're a confirmed London lover, and money is no object, you could order a yearly subscription at the cost of £200.

Tipping

In many restaurants, there is a service charge of between 12% and 15% added on; make sure you examine your menu and your bill to see if it has already been added. If service is not included, it will be mentioned in some obvious manner on the bill. Twelve to twenty percent is considered the normal range for tipping in restaurants.

Taxi drivers do appreciate a tip and in many cases really earn it by helping with bags, taking a smart route, and giving information. Anything from 50p to £1 is usual in short-haul trips, and after £10, a tip of 10% to 15% is fine. You won't be abused for giving a lousy tip, and you may be warmly thanked for a good one. Use your best judgment.

In the good hotels, just tip the staff in pounds the same way you would at home in dollars: £1 or £2 a bag for bellhops, a fiver for the maid. Remember that this city is very expensive, and while to you a pound is more than a dollar, here it can only buy about the same amount that a dollar can at home.

London's Media

Newspapers

London has a huge selection of newspapers, from the solemn to the sleazy. Make a point of reading at least a couple of them while you're here.

The Times   Now owned by media king Rupert Murdoch, it aspires to be a great newspaper, but falls short of the mark. It does have a big Sunday edition that has something for everyone.

The Independent   A decent broadsheet with some good writing and a very good Sunday edition.

The Observer   A Sunday-only paper with all the sections you'd expect; a fine read.

The Guardian   A well-written liberal newspaper.

The Daily Telegraph   Right-wing broadsheet with big Saturday and Sunday editions.

Financial Times   Printed on pink paper; a must for the businessperson.

International Herald Tribune   This is the fluff-free paper of choice for American expats—it features the best of the *Washington Post* and the *New York Times* and has no advertising. Great editorial section with weekly contributions from America's favorite columnists, and Doonesbury, too.

Evening Standard   Tabloid-sized afternoon newspaper; a little light on news, but featuring good local stories and entertainment listings.

Daily Mail   Usually manages to have a star, a royal, or a socialite on the cover. Fairly good money section. Relatively free of hard news.

Daily Express   Conservative middle-brow newspaper, not unlike the *Mail*.

The Sun   And now, the sleazy tabloids. This is the home of the infamous Page Three Girl, the gratuitous photo of a topless woman placed on the third page. Its content is similarly absurd. Read it and laugh.

There are the other tabloids that you may not want to be caught dead reading: *The Daily Star,* like the *Sun,* full of the important news of women's breasts, murder, and sex scandals; and the *Sport,* which doesn't even bother to pretend it's anything but a titillation rag.

Magazines

The Big Issue   You must buy this magazine. It provides the homeless with some income (feel free to give the vendor a tip when buying it) and it has some of the most interesting articles on London you can find. It's often guest edited by some literary or media worthy.

The Economist   Very serious and informative conservative mag on money and politics.

Harpers and Queen   Glossy magazine devoted to the rich, famous, and beautiful; a bit like the Tatler in its social diary, but with more beauty articles.

Hello!   Weekly rag that makes *People* look like *The New Yorker.* Lots of Hollywood celebs, minor royalty, gossip, puzzling media creations, and a weekly television and radio guide. Seems to be the family photo album for people like Sarah Ferguson and Posh Spice. *O.K.* is its closest competitor, and it's easy to get them mixed up; the same photos appear in both these weeklies.

The Literary Supplement   Like the *New York Times Review of Books,* this is a ripping good intellectual read, with articles and book reviews written by some of the brightest people in the world of letters. After you've read a few pieces you'll wonder how you've lived without it.

Private Eye   Funny political satire—it's the scourge of the establishment, any establishment. Might be a bit obscure for nonresidents, but worth a try.

Punch   Now owned by Mohammed Al Fayed, it's sold throughout Harrods and has certainly lost its punch. Don't bother, unless you happen across editions from the nineteenth century.

The Spectator   Entertaining, with intelligent wit; politically to the right.

Tatler   House (or castle) organ of aristocrats, social climbers, and wannabes. Features such edifying articles as guides to eligible rich bachelors and bachelorettes. Endless pages of photos of dull social gatherings of marquesses, dukes, and barons. Good info on how to spend all your money in one day.

Time Out   The most comprehensive weekly magazine on what's going on in London.

W. H. Smith, the bookstore chain, has an enormous range of magazines and newspapers from all over the world.

Television

TV in England is paid for by subscription to the tune of £109 a year. This means that there are no commercials on BBC 1 and BBC 2, except for BBC's own products. It's a lovely change of pace from American television.

BBC 1 is the weakest of the British TV stations, with lots of cheaply produced cooking shows, talk shows, and animal programs. BBC 2 used to be very stuffy, but now regards itself as quite hip. It produces some good drama, imports the occasional good movie, and has some good current-affairs shows. The independent station ITV is on channel 3 and currently produces the most expensive dramas seen on British TV. It's funded by commercials, which only appear (mercifully) every 15 minutes. Channel 4 is also a commercial station, but it's definitely the hippest. Conscientiously irreverent, and envelope pushing, it has an hour of news nightly at 7 p.m. There's a movie channel on 5.

Cable, which will be found in all the good hotels, provides Sky One, which has CNN, MTV, and plenty of movies and television programs from the United States. Do yourself a favor and watch some of the BBC—there are some truly wonderful shows on it, such as adaptions of Dickens or lesser recognized English authors.

Radio

The radio is mostly BBC, which has five national networks. The radio is in many ways quintessentially British: until the 1950s, BBC radio presenters were required to wear dinner jackets when reading the news. This British-ness is best heard on BBC Radio 3 and 4. Try to catch the shipping forecast at 6 p.m. daily on Radio 4. It is eccentric and incomprehensible to the lay person, and it articulates perfectly the voice of an old island culture.

The local listings in newspapers and magazines will tell you what is on when.

- **Radio 1** Pop music at 98.8 FM
- **Radio 2** Light entertainment at 89.2 FM
- **Radio 3** Classical music and related topics at 91.3 FM
- **Radio 4** To my mind, the best thing in British media. Like National Public Radio, but much more, with short stories, serials, dramatizations, interviews, quizzes, comedies, and plays. The hackles of every Radio 4 lover were raised recently when there were rumors of the Beeb's intention to "dumb down" the unusually intelligent programs to appeal to more people. No word on if this plot has been launched as of yet. Listen to it, and you decide.
- **Capital FM** Top-ten pop music on 95.8 FM and oldies on Capital Gold on 1548 kHz
- **Classic FM** More classical music on 100.9 FM (an English friend told me that no Brit will ever complain about classical music played at ear-deafening decibels)
- **Jazz FM** Great jazz and blues, at 102.2 FM
- **Newstalk** All news all the time, with phone-in commentary that can be quite interesting, at 97.3 FM

Telephones

Criminally, some pinheads at British Telecom (BT) decided to remove and sell off the majority of the red phone boxes that were such a pleasing and distinctive hallmark of London. They have been kept in many of the tourist areas, but mostly you'll see soulless and ugly glass boxes with tons of sex-trade advertising (it's the specific job of one person to remove these cards each week, but they go back up immediately). The public phone booths here take either coins or BT phone cards. Just to make things more confusing, there's a competitor, Mercury, which has its own phone booths and phone cards. Coins are your best bet, and you can make a very quick call for 10p. Some of the public phones in restaurants have a system in which you wait for the call to be answered before putting the money in—otherwise you lose it. Read the directions before using a pay phone.

The telephone jacks in England will not fit an American modem cord, so if you have your laptop and want to get online, ask the hotel for an adaptor or buy one at a department store (Harrods, John Lewis, Peter Jones, and so on carry them, as does Dixons).

International calls are made by dialing 00, then the country code, area code, and local number. To call through a long-distance service, dial their access lines and follow directions, using your credit-card number:

AT&T Direct (0800) 890-011   Australia (0800) 890-061
MCI World Com (0800) 890-222   New Zealand (0800) 890-064
                                                  Canada Direct (0800) 890-016

SOME IMPORTANT NUMBERS

- **00** International dialing code; that is, if calling outside England, dial 00 + 1 for U.S. and Canada, 61 for Australia, 64 for New Zealand
- **100** General operator
- **112** Emergency for police, fire, or ambulance
- **153** International-directory inquiries
- **155** International operator
- **192** U.K. directory inquiries
- **999** Emergency for police, fire, or ambulance

Public Toilets

London has earned the admiration of its tourists and the appreciation of its dwellers by its plentiful and clean public conveniences, also called WCs or loos. The secret may be that there's usually a small charge for their use, and people tend to be more respectful when they've invested some money. Twenty pence (hold onto those coins; they're very important) gets you 15 minutes in a free-standing cubicle, which is washed and sterilized automatically after each use. There always seems to be toilet paper in these loos as well as in the free lavatories found in the parks and in some tube stations and squares. Although we can't tell you it's okay to walk into a pub, hotel, or a restaurant and use the toilet if you aren't a customer, it is true that many people here aren't too uptight about that.

Mail

Get your stamps for postcards and letters from a news agent or a Mail Boxes shop. The post offices tend to be extremely crowded, as lots of people pay their bills there. If you want to get special-edition stamps, you will have to queue up at the post office. An overseas postcard stamp costs between 37p and 45p, and an overseas letter is 45p to 64p. Remember to put the air-mail sticker on your mail and don't forget to write "USA" or the name of the destination country at the bottom of the address. I once had a letter addressed to New York, New York, returned because I didn't write the country on it. Post offices are open Monday–Friday, 9 a.m.–5 p.m. and Saturday, 9 a.m.–12:30 p.m. (www.postoffice.co.uk).

Store Hours

This is where you get to really appreciate the American way: most retail shops here are on a rather old-fashioned schedule of 10 a.m.–6 p.m. and closed on Sundays. However, much to the dismay of the more traditional who deplore the Yankee incursions on their way of life (and to the delight of anyone with a 9-to-5 office job), stores are starting to open on Sundays. Some supermarkets and convenience stores are opening 24 hours a day, and even the great hold-outs—Harrods, John Lewis, and Peter Jones—are open later on Wednesdays and Thursdays. (Later only means until 7 or 8 p.m.) Call and check before you take off for any shop, especially on a Saturday, when strange hours such as 12–5 p.m. may be in effect.

Crime

There's a perception of London as one of the safest cities in the world, fostered by the fact that the bobbies (policemen) don't carry guns. Also, because of the strict gun laws in England, there just aren't the number of gunshot fatalities that plague the United States. Compared with other European cities, London is among the least violent, with one of the lowest homicide rates (2.1 homicides per 100,000 people in London; 18.1 in Moscow). Compared to New York City, London is practically peace loving—only 160 murders for the year from April 1997 to March 1998, compared to 462 in New York; 5,371 cases of grievous bodily harm in London, compared to 18,093 in New York. But women take note: there were 1,838 rapes in London, compared to 1,165 in New York. Robberies are also about the same in both cities. All these numbers have apparently continued to rise in the years since the statistics were taken.

There is definitely a disturbing trend on the streets of London toward the commission of crimes more violent than the usual purse snatchings. There have been a number of muggings involving knives and bodily harm. Shouting matches on the street are not an uncommon sight, and they frequently degenerate into fisticuffs. I lived in New York for many years, but I had to come to London to see grown men brawling in the street over a road incident. As in all cities, there's a lot of stress, and bad behavior often follows on its heels. Do keep a sharp eye out, and try to avoid areas with a high concentration of pubs (Leicester Square, Soho) late at night. If you take a night bus, sit downstairs; the rowdies congregate on the upper deck. I don't wish to frighten anyone, but we need to be realistic about life in the big city.

Here are some tips:

- Keep your pocketbook close at all times; sling it across your chest if possible, and don't leave it sitting unattended in public places.

- Don't put your wallet in a backpack unless it's in an inside, zipped pocket.

- Put your wallet in a front pocket.

- Use a money belt when carrying large sums.

- Don't hang around counting your money after using an ATM.

- Watch your belongings on the tube and on buses.

- Don't wear flashy jewelry or an expensive wristwatch.

- Avoid night buses after midnight; use a taxi or minicab instead. Women may be happier using one of the women's minicab companies that were formed after a spate of minicab-related rapes (Lady Cabs, phone (0207) 254-3501; or Lady Cars, phone (0208) 655-3959) or calling a black taxi (Dial a Cab, phone (0208) 253-5000; or Radio Taxis, phone (0207) 272-0272).

- Never allow yourself to be picked up by a minicab on the street.

- Leave your passport in a safe at the hotel and carry a photocopy of the information page.

- Ignore any implausible story you might hear on the street; this town is full of talented con artists.

- Stay out of the parks after dark.

- Late at night, travel in groups if possible.

- If you buy something at a very expensive store, don't parade around with the bag too long—get it back to your hotel or put the bag in a less ritzy one (there are jewelers on Bond Street who now offer a plain bag to their customers).

The emergency phone number is 999; *don't* use it unless it is truly an emergency. To report a crime, call directory assistance at 192 for the number of the nearest police station.

The Homeless and Beggars

The best way to help the homeless is to buy *The Big Issue* magazine, which is sold on the street by licensed vendors. Part of the money goes to the vendor, and you would be kind to also give the vendor a tip. They work hard in all weather for very little money. It's also an excellent magazine. There are an estimated 2,500 homeless persons on the streets of London, not so many compared to New York, but far too many in a modern society that purports to be committed to taking care of its own. I'm happy to give money to the people sitting on sleeping bags asking for spare change, especially when I consider the sums I spend just to get the basics in London, but many people are opposed to giving cash on various grounds. Giving a sandwich or some food is a good alternative.

Religion

Here are some phone numbers of various churches, synagogues, mosques, or meeting houses of the listed denominations to help you find a place to worship in your own way. If you're not picky, feel free to drop into any of the wonderful churches all over London for a bit of beauty and peace.

Anglican St. Paul's Cathedral, (0207) 236-4128, or Westminster Abbey,
   (0207) 222-7110 or (0207) 222-5897

Baptist (0208) 980-6818

Buddhist (0207) 834-5858

Catholic Brompton Oratory, (0207) 589-4811,
   or Westminster Cathedral, (0207) 798-9055

Evangelical (0207) 582-0228

Greek Orthodox (0207) 222-8010

Hindu (0208) 961-5031

Islamic (0207) 724-3363

Jewish Liberal Jewish Synagogue, (0207) 286-5181,
   or United Synagogue, (0208) 343-8989

Methodist (0207) 222-8010

Pentacostal (0207) 286-9261

Quaker (0207) 387-3601

Gay London

When Oscar Wilde was arrested at the Cadogan Hotel in the last days of the nineteenth century on charges of homosexuality, that afternoon's boat to Calais was so crowded with single gentlemen that it almost sank. The law banning homosexuality was often enforced more for political reasons than anything else, but it made being a homosexual in England fraught with real danger. And it was all the more peculiar because of the tacit acceptance of homosexual dalliances in the male segregated school system of the upper classes. Homosexuality was seen by many as an adolescent phase that one grew out of. In 1967 the outdated law was finally changed, and London can now boast the most happening gay scene in Europe. There are gay hotels, bookshops, health clubs, religious groups, bars, nightclubs, cafes, travel agencies, publications, and even a taxi company. The best neighborhoods are in Soho (Old Compton Street in particular) and Earl's Court. Clapham Common, Hampstead Heath, and the Brompton Cemetery are popular green spaces for hanging out and meeting people—and maybe doing a little cruising.

There is an excellent book by Graham Parker called *Gay London* (published by Metro Publications, P.O. Box 6336, London N1 6PY), which can be found in most bookstores and tourist centers. It lists and reviews every possible venue or service for the gay community in London. Unless you have an updated edition (first edition was in 1997), it might be wise to check club, pub, and other information against the more current weekly magazines.

Here are a few gay-friendly organizations and businesses you may want to seek out:

In the United States, call the **International Gay Travel Association,** in Florida at (305) 292-0217, or leave a message at (800) 448-8550, for information about gay-friendly tours and services. Pick up or call for a copy of *Out and About,* a magazine that offers reviews of the best hotels, clubs, gyms, and so on in the world; call (800) 929-2215.

London Lesbian and Gay Switchboard 24 hours a day, 365 days a year can be reached at (0207) 837-7324 or www.llgs.org.uk. They can offer help, information, or counsel on any issues related to being gay in London.

Philbeach Hotel is a reasonably priced and fun gay hotel where a cross-dressing party erupts once a week. It is located in zone 11, at 30–31 Philbeach Gardens, Earls Court, SW5 (phone (0207) 373-1244; www.phil beachhotel.freeserve.co.uk; tube: Earl's Court).

Number Seven is a Victorian townhouse in Brixton with eight suites ranging from £60 to 129 and located in zone 5, at 7 Josephine Avenue, SW2 (phone (0208) 674-1880; www.no7.com; tube: Brixton).

Gay's the Word is the first—and to date the only—specifically gay and lesbian bookshop in the United Kingdom and can be visited at 66 Marchmont Street, Bloomsbury, phone (0207) 278-7654.

The Clone Zone has two conveniently located shops, one at 64 Old Compton Street (phone (0207) 287-3530), and one at 266 Old Brompton Road (phone (0207) 373-0598) in Earl's Court. You'll find books, cards, magazines, sex toys, clothes, and—most importantly—people to answer questions you may have about what's up in London.

The **Sauna Bar** is a luxury spa for men in the heart of Soho, in zone 7, at 29 Endell Street (phone (0207) 836-2236; tube: Covent Garden).

You can check out the scene in *Time Out* or in any of these free mags distributed in London's clubs and pubs:

Boyz—phone (0207) 296-6110
QX (Queer Extra)—phone (0207) 379-8448 or www.qxmag.co.uk
GaytoZ—phone (0207) 793-7450 or freedom.co.uk/gaytoz

Lost/Stolen Credit Cards

Report missing credit cards to both the police and the 24-hour lost-or-stolen-card bureaus below:

American Express (0127) 369-6933
Diners Club (0800) 460-800
Mastercard/Eurocard (0800) 964-767
Switch (0113) 277-8899
Visa (0800) 895-082

Part Five

Getting around London

Public Transportation

The most important thing to take out with you in London is a good map and/or the *London A to Z* (called *A to Zed* here) pocket-sized book—the map for the overall big picture and the *A to Z* for the small streets. You won't regret the extra weight in your bag. Don't load yourself down with too much other stuff; you can always pick up water or snacks along the way. You will—one hopes—end up walking a fair amount, and huge backpacks are not conducive to fun. A camera is a must because you never know when you'll run into a horse-drawn carriage or a battery of the queen's guards outfitted as if waiting for the Battle of Waterloo. Strange details on buildings or gates will call out to be recorded, and you may never pass that way again. Bring extra film. Also, be sure to carry a few 20p coins for the public toilets.

London is a city that is trying to make its public transportation as attractive as possible in order to keep the cars off the road and reduce the woeful traffic jams. Though the transportation experts haven't been very successful—there are more cars on the road now than ever before, and the number keeps climbing—they do have some future plans to tax drivers, raise parking fees, and improve the public-transportation services with the revenue. Although the mayor claims public transportation is one of his top priorities, and has hired a New Yorker to overhaul the tube, it's still a mess. At present on the tube there are plenty of delays and interruptions of service, and on the weekends repairs are made, which causes whole lines to be shut down. Buses, when not stuck in traffic, have an infuriating habit of arriving at long last in packs. But having said that, as visitors, you will be more tolerant than regular commuters, and will be able to travel during off-peak times. Seven times out of ten, the tube will get you wherever you're going quickly and efficiently, and the double-decker buses are a fun way to see London. Just avoid public transport during rush hours, and resign yourself to taking a cab late at night.

For any questions you might have regarding London travel information, call London Transport at (0207) 222-1234. You can get information on any facet of travel, including how everything is running.

Travel Zones

London Transport has diveded London into six travel zones (which have nothing to do with the zones outlined in this book), with zone 1 in the middle of central London and the rest radiating outward in circles that end at zone 6 in the suburbs and at Heathrow in the west. Most of what you'll be doing in London will fall within zones 1 and 2. Bus and tube fares rise with zone numbers. For years, the transportation experts have discussed the possibility of simplifying fares by making one flat fee, but the size of London and the cost of gas unfortunately make such a master stroke impractical.

Travel Cards

The best deal for traveling on public transportation is the Travel Card, which gives you unlimited travel on the tube, buses, and most overland rail services in Greater London, including the Docklands Light Railway. The Travel Card will save you time and money. A one-day off-peak travel card for zones 1 and 2 (bought after 9:30 a.m.) costs only £4, whereas a round-trip tube ticket in the same zones costs £3.80. A weekend card is £6 for zones 1 and 2, and a weekly card costs £18.90 for zones 1 and 2—a very good deal if you're planning on being in London for a week. You'll need a passport-sized photo to get the weekly card. Most stations have photo machines for precisely this purpose.

The Family Travel Card is also a great deal: £2.60 per adult for zones 1 and 2 on a one-day card and 80p per child. The family must consist of at least one adult and one child between the ages of 5 and 15; they need not be related. Family cards are valid only after 9:30 a.m. Monday–Friday and all day on weekends. For tourists, alas, there are no senior or student discounts; you have to be a London resident. Travel Cards can be bought at tube stations and also at certain newsagents. Travel cards aren't valid on designated night buses or Airbuses. You can also use a tube ticket on a bus, providing your fare is equivalent.

Buses

There is no better view in the world than that of London from the top first-row seat of a double-decker bus. Many of the old buildings seem to have been designed expressly for the view from the top of the bus; the statues and gargoyles that decorate some of the fine architecture of the city are at eye level when you're riding up top. There are 17,000 bus stops all over London, so you should be able to get pretty close to whatever your destination may be. See pages 156–159 for some of the best London-viewing, double-decker public busses.

Types of Buses

- **Routemaster** This is the old-style double decker. You get on at the rear, take your seat, and wait for the conductor to come collect your fare. These are becoming more rare each year, so enjoy them while you can.

- **Double-decker front-entry buses** These are the newer buses, used solely by some routes and for all-night buses. You get on in front, pay the driver, and take your seat. Try to have change—the driver may not be able to break a bill, especially a 10 or 20. A Travel Card makes paying much less of a hassle.

- **Single-decker buses** These tend to be for shorter journeys through London. Same price as the others, less room inside. Pay upon entering or use Travel Card.

- **Night buses** Night buses tend to cost more than buses in the day; they follow the same routes, but run less often. They have an N before the route number, and run from around 11 p.m. to 6 a.m. They are the only all-night public transport, as the tube stops running around midnight. Most night busses have a stop at Trafalgar Square. It is advised that you not sit alone on the top of a night bus late at night; there are many drunks and more sinister types out then.

Here's how the buses go 'round and 'round:

Get on the Bus Most bus-stop shelters have a big map of London displaying the bus routes. There is also a list of the stops of each number bus on the route. Be careful that you're standing at the correct bus stop—on Oxford Street or Hyde Park Corner, for example, there are many buses and many stops. If your bus number is not written on the red-and-white sign, it won't stop there. The bus stop with a red symbol on a white background indicates a compulsory stop, and the signs with a white symbol on a red background are known as request stops. Supposedly, a bus will always stop at a compulsory stop, but don't believe it. When you see your bus, wave your hand to flag it down, or it may just sail sedately by (if it's full, it will definitely sail by, so don't take it personally). When preparing to get out, ring to stop the bus in advance of your stop. Ask for help if you're not sure where your stop is.

Paying Your Way The fares of the buses are determined by how far you travel, so you should know the name of your destination. The fares go up every year, but at time of publication, the fare for zone 1 was £1, for zones 2–4 was £1.20, etc. The Travel Card is the least expensive way to go. (I remind you: these London transport zones have nothing to do with the zones in this book.) Children under age 5 ride free; children ages 5–16 pay a child's fare of 40p in zones 1 and 2 until 10 p.m., after which they pay full fare. Fourteen- and fifteen-year-olds must carry child-rate photocards, and if your child looks borderline you may be hassled by some persnickety conductors. Photocards are available in any post office; take a passport-sized photo and proof of age.

The Tube

The first tube line ran in 1863 and carried 40,000 people the first day. It now carries millions of passengers a day; at rush hour it feels as if there are millions in your train car alone. Avoid it at peak time if possible.

It is the best possible way to get around London, even with the breakdowns and delays. The streets are just so choked that buses are too iffy when you need to get somewhere quickly. The tube's main failing is that it doesn't run 24 hours a day. The last trains leave central London around midnight and begin again around 5:30 a.m. You pay according to zones, as outlined in the buses section above, with zone 1 costing £1.50 and going up from there. Your best bet is the Travel Card as described above, or buying something called a Carnet, for which you receive ten zone-1 tickets for £11.50 (£5 for kids), a savings of £3.50. The ten tickets come in a handy holder with a tube map on it. *Beware:* if you are traveling with an invalid ticket (such as trying to leave a zone-3 station with a zone-1 ticket) you are liable to be fined £10 on the spot. You will certainly be asked to pay the difference. Look on one of the big maps posted near the vending machines and ticket windows—it will show you what stations fall in which zones.

Tickets Please   Buy a ticket for your trip at the ticket window or use one of two machines. There is a big machine, which has in alphabetical order all the possible stations you might go to. You pick your station and the type of ticket you want (adult single journey, child single, adult return, and so on), and the machine will tell you how much money to put in. The other machine is simpler, but assumes you know how much your ticket will cost and what travel zones you'll be in. You will most likely be buying the £1.50 ticket that works in zones 1 and 2.

Put the ticket in the front of the turnstile. It will come out the top of the turnstile. Don't lose it; put it in a convenient pocket because you will need to put it into another turnstile as you exit your destination. A lost ticket will cost you £10, so hold on to it.

Reading the Map   The tube map is an amazing feat of workmanship. Before it was standardized in 1931 by transport hero Harry Beck, it looked like an explosion in a string factory, with lines snaking all over central London. The map is not an accurate geographical representation of London, and much time and grief will be saved if you look at the *A to Z* first. Locate your destination and identify the color or pattern for each line. Look for the key to the lines at the right bottom of the map. There are 12 tube London lines; to change lines, you must find the station connecting the lines, which are indicated by white circles outlined in black. The conductor may tell you while you're on board which lines you can catch at the next station, but you're better off using your map and your head. If you get on a train and are totally confused, look at the map above the windows—it's a straight line of the stops on that particular train and is much easier to read than the big map.

Which Way?   Be aware of what direction you're traveling. Each platform has a sign indicating direction. See where you are on your map and figure out which direction you want to go in and go to the correct platform.

Check the front of the train for its destination! There are a few lines, you will see on the map, that split off into different directions. Look at the map to see where your line terminates, and make sure you get on the train with that name; the final stop is posted on the front of the train.

Tube Etiquette

Native travelers on the tube in London are usually very quiet, especially at rush hour. Tourists who converse in loud voices are looked at with some disapproval, as they are breaking a tacit taboo. Recent years have seen the rise of the weekend train buskers who do a song between stations and pass the hat before they move onto another car. They are tolerated by the day trippers, but would probably be strung up if they tried entertaining the daily commuters. Of course, the cell phone has made inroads on the traditional, paper-reading silence of the commuter hours, and off-peak is often a gab fest.

An important rule is to always stand to the right of the escalators to allow free passage to people who want to walk. Failure to observe this rule will always be met with an impatient reprimand. As in any big city, rush hour is a nightmare, and it is best to try to avoid the tube at this time.

You must never leave a bag unattended at a tube station. This is not so much an invitation to thieves (although it is certainly that) as it is an alarm to the commuters who will treat it as a possible explosive device. London has a history of terrorist bombings, and people tend to be cautious. You may notice that there are no trash cans on any London tube platform—trash cans are a good place to hide a bomb.

There is no smoking allowed on the tube platforms or trains.

Taxis

The famous black taxi cab of London is not always black now—many are besmirched by advertising painted all over the body, a disturbing sight indeed. This is also becoming common on buses. The taxis in London cruise the streets or line up in queues. If they are available, the yellow light atop the car will be on, and you may wave them down. You can usually get a taxi on the opposite side of the road to stop for you, so don't despair if none are going your way. They are famous for being able to make U-turns on a dime... or on a 5p piece. If there are zig-zagging lines running along the curb, the taxi cannot legally stop. Move to where those lines end to get picked up.

Seekers of the Knowledge   As much a part of the London scene as their automobiles, the taxi drivers are a respected part of the work force. They have remarkable powers of navigation, of which they are justifiably proud. They train for three to five years, memorizing every street and landmark in London. You'll sometimes see people on mopeds, with maps clipped to the handlebars, looking around and making notes. These are student cab drivers. They have to learn, by heart, 60,000 routes across and around London. During their exams they have to recite these "runs" to their examiner, citing traffic lights, one-way systems, roundabouts, and landmarks. During this recital, the examiner will do everything he can to distract the student, often playing a difficult customer, hurling insults, singing, or arguing. Those who pass this stringent test are said to have "the Knowledge."

How to Take a Taxi   It may be because of the respect to which drivers feel entitled that the preferred etiquette is that you do not enter the cab until you have told the driver, from the curb through the window, where you want to go. Do not ask if he knows the way; he's trained to know and what's more, he will not admit it if he doesn't (I say "he" because there are few women cab drivers at this time)—although to be fair, plenty of cabbies will gracefully turn to their oversized *A to Z*. When getting out of the cab, you are likewise expected to pay through the window, standing on the curb. This works to both your and the cabbie's advantage; you can get out and reach easily into your pocket or purse, and the driver doesn't have to turn around and reach through the partition. Smoking is prohibited in taxis, although if you see the driver light up, you can ask him if you might as well. Don't eat or drink in a taxi. Many cabbies own their cars—which cost upward of £26,000—and are fiercely protective of their well-being.

It is my sad duty to report that in recent years, some cab drivers, when hearing a foreign accent, will sometimes take a less than direct route to bump up the fare. These people are definitely the exception rather than the rule, and with the serpentine routes usually taken quite legitimately by a taxi, it's often hard to tell if they are playing games. Personally, American accent and all, I have never been run around like this—at least I don't think so. In his best-selling, hilarious book about England, *Notes from a Small Island,* Bill Bryson observes that, although London taxi drivers are absolutely the most excellent in the world, they do have a couple of idiosyncrasies. One is that they are incapable of driving for any distance in a straight line: "no matter where you are or what the driving conditions, every 200 feet a little bell goes off in their heads and they abruptly lunge down a side street." My own experience with London cabbies is that they are absolute geniuses at getting from point A to point B with the least amount of traffic and in the shortest amount of time. They know London better than anyone.

Worth Almost Every Pound I learn more about London and its roads when I take a cab, so much that I can justify the expense, which can be considerable. A short trip will cost about £5; a trip from central London to, say, Hampstead, will be about £20 plus. It's not a good idea to take a taxi in traffic; the tube is usually a better bet. But if you don't know where you're going and you're not in a hurry, it can be fun to jump in a taxi and watch London go by from the dark comfort of the cab's very civilized interior. Sometimes you can also get a great conversation out of the deal.

Some drivers, on hearing an American voice, will want to tell you about their experiences in the United States or give you a heads up as to what to expect in England. Cabbies are a talkative and opinionated lot, so much so that *Private Eye,* the satirical magazine, often runs op-ed pieces by "Lord Justice Cabdriver."

You can call a black taxi if you're staying in a place where they don't cruise regularly or if it's late at night. Some companies charge extra for booking over the phone or using a credit card—ask when you call.

Computer Cabs (0207) 286-0286	Data Cab (0208) 964-2123
Dial a Cab (0207) 253-5000	Radio Taxis (0207) 272-0272

Minicabs

Minicabs are a much less reliable option than the black cabs, but they are cheaper and come in very handy in many instances, such as when you find youself far from a tube stop in an outlying area or when you need to get back to your hotel very late at night and there's not a black cab in sight. There are plenty of reputable minicab companies, including some that have only women drivers. You can't hail a minicab on the street; in fact, *do not* get into one that stops and offers you a ride. It's not at all kosher; there are a lot of scams and dicey drivers out there. You must call to book a car; in that way you have some recourse should anything go wrong. Minicab drivers are not required to have "the Knowledge," which may be made abundantly clear by how lost they can get, but because there's a flat fee, there's at least no economical downside to this. Make sure you agree on a price when booking the cab, and confirm it with the driver when you get in. Tipping is normally between 10% and 15%. The cars are usually two-door compacts—nowhere near as roomy as the black cabs—so if you have four large or five regular people, get a black cab. Here are some good minicab companies:

A & A Chauffeurs Ltd. (0208) 958-3344   Addison Lee (0207) 387-8888
College Cars (0208) 955-6666   Greater London Hire Ltd. (0208) 444-2468
Pegasus (0207) 622-2222

In response to a number of rapes committed by minicab drivers a few years ago, some companies employ only women drivers. They are:

Lady Cabs (0207) 254-3501   My Fare Lady (0207) 379-9130
Lady Cars (0208) 655-3959

Motorcycle Taxis

Motorcycle taxis are a new travel twist, currently also enjoying success in Paris, another clogged European city. The bike will get you through the worst possible traffic in a very short time, and the helmets are equipped with microphones so you can tell the driver to slow down. Not for the faint of heart. Call Addison Lee Taxy-Bike (their motto: "Safe, Sedate, and You Won't Be Late") at (0207) 387-8888; or visit www.addisonlee.com.

Rail Services and Docklands Light Rail

Travel Cards can be used on some of the local commuter lines in London. The North London line is a good way to cross greater London as it cuts a swath from west (Richmond) to east (Woolwich); it stops at various tube stations along the way. It's above ground, which is a nice change of pace from the mole tunneling of the tube. Call (0345) 484-950 for all train inquiries.

If you are using British Rail to get out of London, ask about the discounts it offers. There are a number of discount cards, which you may not think apply to you, as they are good for a year, but the savings can be enormous. Ask at any major rail station or travel agency. You can apply for the discount at the same time you buy your tickets.

The Docklands Light Rail (phone (0207) 363-9700) is a relatively new wrinkle in East End public transportation. It is clean, quiet, has no conductor, and rides above the ground. It services the East End, Canary Wharf, Greenwich, the Cutty Sark, and ends in Lewisham. It is also becoming a tourist option, and special tickets that combine rail travel with riverboat trips, plus deals on certain attractions, such as the National Maritime Museum at Greenwich, are offered. These special trains leave from Tower Gateway and Bank every hour on the hour starting at 10 a.m., and you will hear interesting commentary from a guide as you ride.

Getting around on Your Own

Renting a Car and Driving in London

It's not a good idea to rent a car to drive around London. London is a confusing, frustrating, and dangerous place to drive, even for those who are already used to driving on the left. Although you need only present a valid driving license from any country or state to rent a car, traffic laws and driving customs are quite different from those of other countries. If you are driving out to the country and must rent a car, it might be best to take the tube out to Heathrow or Gatwick and rent a car from there to avoid the problems of central London's notorious traffic.

If you do find yourself driving in England, here's a tip: the best way to remember which side of the road you're supposed be on is to just keep yourself and your steering wheel (which is on the right side of the car, instead of the left) in the middle of the road, as you'll be accustomed to doing in the United States. As long as you remember to remain in the middle of the road, you'll be all right. And don't let the way the cars are parked throw you—you can park facing any old direction in England.

In London, the parking regulations are strict—look at lamp posts to find signs outlining them. You can't park on a double yellow line ever; your car will be clamped with a Denver boot or towed. If you're clamped, there will be a sticker telling you where to pay for its removal and the additional fine; if you're towed, call (0207) 747-7474 to find out where your car was taken.

There are resident permits for parking in most neighborhoods, and you cannot park in these areas except at night. Read the signs carefully. There are meters and Pay and Display spaces for visitors to use. Pay and Display works like this: park your car; find the ticket machine; pay the correct amount for the desired time; and display the ticket on your windshield or dashboard. There are a number of National Car Parks (signs say NCP) around central London: call (0207) 499-7050, or go to their website at www.ncp.co.uk for locations.

The central numbers for the big rental companies (cars will cost about £60 a day) are as follows:

Avis (0207) 917-6700; www.avis.co.uk

Europcar (0207) 387-2276; www.europcar.co.uk

Hertz (0870) 844-8844 or (0207) 730-8323; www.hertz.co.uk

Expect to pay about £40 to fill up the tank with gas.

Bicycling

As a way of getting around London, biking is just slightly suicidal. I have a bike, I use it to get to where I need to go, and I find it convenient and economical. However, it's more than the exercise that gets my heart rate up; it's the potent combo of fright and fury at the cavalier behavior of the motorists. It's pretty common for cyclists to get hit by cars while riding around London. This could really ruin your vacation. If you want to take advantage of the great parks and vehicle-free paths in London for fun, fine. Just look mighty sharp as you're riding through the strees, and wear a helmet. Call the London Cycling Campaign at (0207) 928-7220 for information about renting bikes, cycling routes, safety, and security.

Motorbike Hire

On the off chance that you might want to up the two-wheeling ante, you can rent a motorbike or moped at Scootabout, 1–3 Leeke Street, WC1; phone (0207) 833-4607. All you need is a foreign motorbike or British driving license . . . and nerves of steel.

Walking

Please do. You'll be surprised at how far you can go by foot—a lot faster at times than on the bus, and certainly more pleasantly than on the tube. You'll get to see small architectural curios, drop into inviting shops and restaurants, and find alleys and mews that you wouldn't see by cab. Keep your *A to Z* handy and get lost. You'll thank yourself for it.

Remember the maniac drivers, and be aware that your instincts when crossing the streets are all wrong. Take it slowly and *don't* try to outrun a walking light—the drivers will scare the devil out of you.

The zebra crossings, however, are where you get your own back—they belong to the pedestrian. When you see a flashing yellow light and a cross path marked with white stripes, you are in the right of way—cars *must* stop for you. There may be one or two foreigners who haven't quite got the hang of this system, so don't stride out without sensible caution.

Around big intersections such as Piccadilly Circus, Marble Arch, and Hyde Park Corner there are "subways," which are walkways beneath the street. They are well indicated with signposts, so you'll be able to know which way to go. Some are actually quite interesting—Hyde Park Corner has painted tiles giving you the goods on the duke of Wellington (whose house is right there) and the parks of London. Some of them use exit numbers and seem to go on forever. Avoid them late at night; some of the subways become little villages of sleeping homeless people.

Walking is the most interesting, healthy, revealing, ecologically sound, and inexpensive way to get around London, so bring the most comfortable shoes you have.

LOST AND FOUND

If you have left something in one of the above public conveyances, which is easily done when you're tired and jet lagged, take heart: you just might get it back. For insurance claims you must inform the police of your loss. Do not call the emergency number; find the nearest police station by dialing 192 information. Here are the numbers for lost property:

Buses (0207) 486-2496   Black taxis (0207) 833-0996
Train stations (railroad) (0207) 928-5151   Tube trains (0207) 486-2496

Part Six

Sight-Seeing and Tours

An Embarrassment of Riches

A trip to London surely must be on every dedicated traveler's wish list. For the indefatigable sightseer, there is an endless itinerary to follow. For one in need of a little R and R, there are theaters to enjoy and parks to kick back in. For the scholar, there is so much to learn, so much to swoon over. For more trendy types, there are clubs and shops that rival those in New York and Paris. There's so much to see and do in London that you must try to restrict yourself to only that which you find fascinating, or you'll find yourself very, very tired. There are the obvious tourist attractions—the Tower of London, the British Museum, Trafalgar Square—and then there are the other bits that make London so wonderful: the parks, the themed walking tours, the obscure collections, and the marketplaces. Only you can determine what is most interesting to you and your companions, but we can help you to make your decisions.

Dissension in the Ranks

In a place like London, with so many varied attractions, you can easily disagree with your traveling companions as to what are the most important sights. You may think that visiting the Globe Theatre without seeing a play is a yawn, and your spouse may be bored silly by the very idea of a design museum. There are two ways to go about solving these fundamental problems of taste, time, and touring. One is to compromise: you see one of mine, and I'll see one of yours. This at least addresses honestly the issue of not being keen on the attraction, instead of going along grudgingly and being clearly uninterested. The other is to split up and go your own way. This has the great advantage of making it less likely that you will grow tired of each other's company, and ensures a ready store of dinner conversation as you each recount your experiences.

Know Thy Limits

Everyone has a threshold at which sight-seeing moves from being a joy to a torture. Your feet hurt, the lines are too long, the weather is appalling, you're hungry. These thresholds vary from person to person, but for the disabled, the elderly, and the very young, the passage over it can be both uncomfortable as well as risky. There are a number of attractions in London in which you'll find no wheelchair access, or in which there are incredibly steep stairs, or where all the exhibits are too high for the young or a wheelchair user to see. You do not want to put yourself (or your companions if they are any of the above) in the position of finding out too late that the attraction just won't work. Although in our listings we try to tell you whether a place is disabled or child friendly, it is always a good idea to call first and find out for sure. There are improvements being made all the time in the interests of easier access at most attractions, museums, churches, and stately homes, so check ahead. Also, there are some places that call themselves disabled friendly, but in reality have a limit on the number of wheelchairs allowed in at a time. For children, you might want to find out if the museum you're visiting has any activities for kids. The Victoria and Albert and the British Museum are just two of the "grown-up" museums that are trying to keep the children entertained, but they do so only on weekends or school holidays (see Part Seven, "Children's London," for more specifics about touring the city with children).

Tourist Information Centers

The **London Tourist Board** has a many extremely well-stocked tourist centers as befits a city so supported by visitors. You can pick up an armful of pamphlets, brochures, maps, and fliers, and reserve tickets, tours, and hotel rooms. Before you arrive, visit their website at www.londontown.com. It's a magnificently useful and complete source. Center locations include:

Heathrow Airport Terminals 1, 2, 3. All open daily, 8:30 a.m.–6 p.m.

Liverpool Street Underground Station is in zone 3 and is open Tuesday–Saturday, 8:15 a.m.–6 p.m.; Sunday, 8:30 a.m.–5 p.m.; and Monday, 8:15 a.m.–7 p.m.

Selfridges (zone 14; 400 Oxford Street, W1; tube: Bond Street) is open Monday–Wednesday, Friday, and Saturday, 9:30 a.m.–7 p.m., and Sunday, 9:30 a.m.–8 p.m. The center is in the Basement Services Arcade.

Victoria Station, in zone 9, houses a center in its forecourt that is open from 8 a.m. to 7 p.m. Winter hours may be shorter.

Visitorcall will provide recorded details of events; phone (0183) 912-3456.

Touring

Jump on the Bus

The best thing to do on the first day in a city is to take advantage of a hop-on, hop-off bus tour. This gives you the lay of the land, and if the day is bright, the open top of a double-decker bus is the best place to get the sunlight that helps you get over jet lag. Three tour companies, as well as Harrods (see details below), provide such tours, with commentary; their prices and tour content are comparable. They all make stops at most of the major attractions/intersections, such as the Tower of London, Madame Tussaud's, Green Park, Hyde Park Corner, Harrods, in front of the Victoria & Albert Museum, and so on. You can pick up the buses at most any of the significant attractions; check with your hotel to determine the closest stop. Tickets can be bought on the bus or from the bus employees at some of the bus stops. It is crucial that you get on the bus as early as possible to avoid the crushing traffic jams that can make the tour a carbon monoxide-scented bummer. If you see traffic building up while you're touring, you can always hop off and continue your tour the next day or later in the afternoon, as the tour tickets are often good for 24 hours, which is great—you can break up the tour nicely. You can get your tickets online, although that seems rather extreme pre-planning to me, even if some companies will give you a £1 discount for online booking. Your move. Tour-bus options include:

Big Bus Company (phone (0208) 944-7810; www.bigbus.co.uk) has a Green Route (90 minutes) and a Blue Route (60 minutes), with live commentary. Buses run every 15 minutes or so. They will stop at 60 different points, including all the big attractions. Tickets, which cost £15 for adults and £6 for children ages 5–15, are good for 24 hours.

London Pride (phone (0207) 863-1122; www.londonpride.co.uk) has six different tours and routes, and you will have to change buses to get the full city tour. Buses run approximately every 10–30 minutes. The company offers a very good deal: for certain attractions you can buy your tickets on the bus (often at a small discount) and go straight to the ticket-holders' entrances of the attractions which in some cases can mean jumping fairly long queues. Both the Grand Tour (£13 for adults and £6 for children ages 5–15) and the Blue Tour offer eight language options and 100 hop-on, hop-off stops. Tickets are good for 24 hours.

The Original London Sightseeing Tour (phone (0208) 877-1722; www. theoriginaltour.com) offers tours in eight languages, fast-entry tickets, and four different touring options. It makes 80 stops and costs £12.50 for adults and £6 for children ages 5–15. Tickets are good for 24 hours.

Harrods (phone (0207) 225-6596) has a city tour that costs £20 and is more deluxe than those offered by the above buses. The luxury consists of a smooth double-decker bus on which there is a toilet, tea and cookies, and headphones with recorded commentary in different languages. However, you can't leave the bus to see the sights, and the 1 p.m. tour is guaranteed to be stuck in all kinds of horrendous traffic (take the morning one if possible). This is particularly abhorrent to children, who will fall asleep or get cranky. This tour is best for cold or rainy days, or for people who just want to sit and have a comfortable look at London. When you book your seats, try to get the top front row for the best view. Harrods also has a number of other tours—of Stratford, Windsor, and so on—which change by season and year. Harrods charges more than the other tour operators, but the advantage is that the bus leaves directly from Harrods and doesn't drive all over the city, picking up people before starting off.

On Your Own

You don't have to spend all that much to get a decent double-decker-bus ride. There is the famous **number 11** bus that takes you past many of the same sights the tourist buses pass, for a mere fraction of the cost. Pick it up at the King's Road at World's End or the Chelsea Town Hall stops, and you'll have a good look at that famous mod street, go through Victoria, past Westminster Abbey, Whitehall, Trafalgar Square, up the Strand to St. Paul's Cathedral, and finish in the East End at Liverpool Street. All this costs less than £2.

The **number 15** is also wonderful: I met a couple of elderly Londoner ladies on it once, and they told me they often get on it to take in the sights and visit with one another without having to spend money (British seniors, or old-age pensioners, as they're called, ride free). Pick up the 15 at Paddington and ride to Marble Arch, up Oxford Street, down Regent to Piccadilly Circus, down Haymarket to Trafalgar Square, up the Strand (which turns into Fleet Street), St. Paul's Cathedral, the Tower of London, and end up at Petticoat Lane (Middlesex Street), which has a market on Sunday mornings, as well as some stalls during the week.

The **number 14** goes from Tottenham Court Road (by the British Museum) over the Thames and west to Putney Heath, passing Piccadilly, Knightsbridge, the museums of South Kensington, and the antiques stores of Fulham.

Bus **number 24** will take you north, from Victoria Station all the way to Hampstead Heath and Highgate, from which you can get an amazing view of London.

To get a look at some of South London, take the **number 2** bus from either Marylebone Station, Marble Arch, or Hyde Park Corner and ride across the Thames through Brixton, up Tulse Hill to Crystal Palace Park, where you can get out and look at the prehistoric creatures imagined and modeled by the Victorians.

Get a bus map at any tourist center or hotel lobby and check out these routes and any others that look interesting to you. If, as you're traveling, you feel you are going too far afield, just get off and jump on a bus going in the opposite direction. All roads lead back to London.

Private Tours

The **Classic Coach Company** offers a small bus in a classic design with room for 11 passengers, who are given a 3-hour guided tour for £17 per seat, or you can hire the entire vehicle for £110 and up. The advantage to this coach tour is that, because it's smaller than the double deckers, it can take you into small streets and squares that you couldn't see on the other tours. And it's very cool looking, with plenty of windows to gape from. Tours go daily at 8:30 a.m., 10 a.m., and 1 p.m. Call (0208) 390-0888, 24 hours a day, or ask your hotel to book you a spot.

You can also hire a black cab to take you around London, creating your own tour, seeing only those sights that interest you most. Call **Black Taxi Tours of London** at (0207) 289-4371, fax (0207) 224-2833. A two-hour tour, day or night, will cost about £65, and you can have a maximum of five people. The great thing is that you can avoid traffic jams and get into the squares, mews, and back streets to which no tour bus can take you.

Seeing the Highlights

The double-decker-bus tours are designed for seeing the sights of London in a general way. They don't take into account how long you might want to linger at any museum or attraction, but they do give you the basics. You can see where everything is in relation to everything else, perhaps find out how long the lines are for certain attractions, figure out what can be done in a day or a week, and determine which areas seem most intriguing. Taking a general tour first thing will help you make plans for the days ahead more efficiently and specifically. You'll learn that you won't be able to do the Tower of London on the same day you take a walk in Hampstead Heath, which is so far away that it's off any standard London tour itinerary. Or you will note that a trip to the National Gallery can be combined with a visit to any or all of the following: the adjacent National Portrait Galley, St. Martin-in-the-Fields, Trafalgar Square, the Eros statue in Piccadilly Circus, and Madame Tussaud's Rock Circus.

Sight-Seeing Companies

There are a lot of tour companies in London doing very similar tours for roughly the same amount of money. You can find their brochures in any hotel lobby. A word of caution: they have many courtesy hotel pick-up points in London, which sounds very convenient—who doesn't want to fall out of their hotel room into a waiting coach at 8 a.m.? But yours may just be the first stop of 15, and if you get stuck in the normal London traffic, you can be on the bus for an hour before you actually get started on the tour. You'll probably find it less annoying to meet your bus at the final departure point. When you reserve your seat, find out where the bus will actually leave for the tour, then take the tube or a taxi to get there. The down side to this evasive action is that you may not get the seat you want on the bus. The best seats are clearly the top-floor front row.

The tour companies offer half-day, morning, night, full-day or two-day tours of London, plus tours to such places as Windsor and Leeds Castles, Eton, Hampton Court, Stonehenge, Bath, Stratford-upon-Avon, Oxford, Cambridge, Salisbury, Brighton, Dover, Canterbury, York, Chester, Warwick Castle, the Lake District, Scotland, and even Paris and Amsterdam. The price of the tour almost always includes entrance fees for the attractions and the cost of meals, and in the case of the overnight trips, the cost of accommodations.

Here are some of the tour companies; do take a look at their websites:

Astral Travels (phone (0700) 078-1016 or (0870) 902-0908; fax (0707) 071-2035; info@astraltravels.co.uk; www.AstralTravels.co.uk). Astral Travels courts small groups on mini-coach day tours and won the London Tourist Board Award for Best Sight-seeing Tours from London in 2000.

Evan Evans can be reached by phone (0208) 332-2222, fax (0208) 784-2835, or email: reservations@evanevans.co.uk. The website address is www.evanevans.co.uk.

Frames Rickards can be reached by phone at (0207) 837-3111 or (0207) 637-4171, or on the Internet at www.framesrickards.co.uk.

Golden Tours Deluxe Phone (800) 456-6303 in U.S. or (0171) 233-7030 in the U.K.; goldentours@aol.com; or www.goldentours.co.uk.

Visitors Sightseeing can be contacted by phone at (0207) 636-7175, by fax at (0207) 636-3310, or at www.visitorsightseeing.com.

For tours along the river, call **The Royal River Thames Passenger Boat Services** at (0207) 930-4097 or fax at (0207) 930-1616. For boat rides along the canals of Little Venice and Camden Lock, call **London Waterbus Company** at (0207) 482-2550, (0207) 482-2660, or visit their website at www.littlevenice.co.uk/waterbus.

Outside London

Although just getting a taste of London's richness can take all of even a long vacation, it may be a great change of pace to get out into the famous English countryside. The foot-and-mouth epidemic of the early part of 2001 was a terrible disaster, and some public foot paths may still remain closed to hikers. But a trip to the country can still be wonderful, even without rambling around the countryside. There are so many delightful medieval towns and inspiring cathedrals to see. The above tour companies conduct such trips conveniently and trouble free.

You may want to rent a car to do your sight-seeing, but sometimes it's just easier to let others do the driving. Astral Tours, especially, is a good option if you're not fond of big buses with lots of people. Taking a train will work for going to Bath, Oxford, Cambridge, or Stratford-upon-Avon, where you can get a hotel room and walk around town, but for trips to Stonehenge or to small medieval towns such as Laycock or Warwick Castle, you are better off going with a tour, in my opinion. Get any of the above companies' brochures and decide where you want to go. Ask how many people have already booked—perhaps you can find a day when it will only be a handful of people. Arrange to meet the tour bus at its last stop so you don't have to tack on too much sitting time while the bus picks people up.

Some Good Side Trips

Note: All the travel times given below are for British Rail train service.

Bath is about one-and-a-half hours from Paddington Station (170 miles) and is a gorgeous Georgian town with Roman relics, famous for its Sally Lunn cakes. Jane Austen once lived there.

Brighton One hour from Victoria station (53 miles), Brighton makes for jolly seaside and amusement-park fun, with its little shopping streets and alleys, the Brighton Pavilion, and the Oriental fantasy of George IV.

Cambridge One hour from King's Cross Station (85 miles), Cambridge is a quiet university town, with beautiful river views and significant buildings.

Canterbury is eighty minutes from Victoria Station (50 miles). The old pilgrimages used to come to the cathedral, in which St. Augustine converted King Ethelbert in 597, and Thomas à Becket was murdered.

Hatfield House Twenty minutes from King's Cross Station (20 miles), this is where Queen Elizabeth I spent her childhood.

Oxford One hour from Paddington station (56 miles), Oxford is the university city of "dreaming spires" and a good jumping-off place for the Cotswolds.

St. Albans Thirty minutes from King's Cross Station (25 miles), St. Albans is an old Roman stronghold, with ruins and rose gardens.

Salisbury is one-and-a-half hours from Waterloo Station (84 miles), with a wonderful old cathedral and many crooked little streets; Stonehenge is a short drive away.

Stratford-upon-Avon From Paddington Station to Stratford takes about 3 hours (91 miles). This is Shakespeare's town—he was born, married, and buried there—and the town is devoted to him, but has other attractions as well.

Windsor Thirty minutes from Waterloo Station (20 miles), and you can see the storybook castle by the Thames, plus a fine old town with good pubs. The playing fields of Eton are nearby.

NOT TO BE MISSED IN LONDON: A Highly Subjective List

- The British Airways London Eye (see page 176)
- The British Museum (see page 178)
- The Globe Theatre (see page 187)
- Hampton Court Palace (see page 190)
- Museum of London (see page 204)
- The National Portrait Gallery (see page 207)
- St. Paul's Cathedral (see page 216)
- The Science Museum (see page 217)
- The Tower of London (see page 225)
- Victoria and Albert Museum (see page 226)
- Westminster Abbey (see page 229)
- Hyde Park on Sunday (see page 237)
- St. James's Park (see page 240)
- A street market on the weekend (see page 341)

Romantic London

One really doesn't associate romance with London in the way one might with Paris or Venice, but that's not to say there aren't some romantic places to seek out with your beloved. Judging by the snogging (kissing) that goes on in Hyde Park, I'd have to say that taking a blanket, a jug of wine, and your special someone to the park for a lie around in the sun is one of London's favorite pastimes for couples, and it's free. If you need exercise, get in a paddle-boat built for two and tool around the Serpentine. Take a night cruise along the Thames, or sit on a bench at sunset on the Thames at the end of Oakley Street, watch the birds circling overhead, and wait for the lights to illuminate the spectacular Albert Bridge.

A romantic restaurant would be **Momo** (zone 8; 25 Heddon Street, off Regent Street, W1; (0207) 434-4040; tube: Oxford Circus); it's a middle-eastern restaurant done exquisitly in *Arabian Nights* fantasy style. The quite expensive **Pont de la Tour** (zone 5; Butler's Wharf, 36D Shad Thames,

SE1; (0207) 403-8403; tube: London Bridge or Tower Hill) has good food and wonderful views of Tower Bridge, which can be pretty romantic, unless you truly only have eyes for each other.

The most romantic hotels are **The Portobello** (ask for the room with the round bed) and **The Gore** (request The Venus, the Tudor, or the Miss Ada suite). And, of course, you can't go wrong at the **Ritz** for romance—check out the weekend break prices and tell them you want a honeymoon-type room or, better still, a suite (see Part Three, "Hotels," for more information).

Agent Provocateur (zone 10; 16 Pont Street, SW1; (0207) 235-0229; tube: Sloane Square) sells *very* sexy underwear that's erotic and sophisticated at the same time. And for chocolate massage-oil bars and bath salts for two, go to **Lush** (zone 7; Unit 11, Central Piazza, Covent Garden; (0207) 240-4570; tube: Covent Garden) or in **Chelsea** (zone 11; 123 King's Road, SW3; (0207) 376-8348; tube: Sloane Square).

Oh, Such a Perfect Day

What constitutes a perfect day in London will naturally depend on who's in your party and what your keenest interests are. One person's poison is another one's mead, as they say. But if I were to try to conjure up a day that would hit as many of my personal favorite high notes as possible, it would go something like this:

Breakfast at Patisserie Valerie—the croissants are unlike those anywhere else, and the cappuccino is strong and very French. Although there are other branches in London (in Soho and Marylebone), the one at which to start the perfect day is in zone 10 in Knightsbridge, 215 Brompton Road (phone (0207) 823-9971; tube: Knightsbridge). Buy your morning papers from the Press Bureau next door and check out the huge selection of magazines.

After breakfast, go look at the Brompton Oratory Church (zone 11). It's an amazing edifice, with small chapels lining the enormous hall, and a rotunda to rival St. Paul's. Go through the church yard and out to Ennismore Gardens, which you'll take up to Hyde Park, a couple of blocks away. Amble around the park, go to the riding ring and see if any of the queen's guards are exercising their horses or rehearsing any ceremonies. Go feed a duck or two at the Serpentine.

Exit the park at Exhibition Road and head for the Victoria and Albert Museum down the street (opens at 10 a.m.). Wander around the stained-glass windows upstairs, sit in the Fakes and Forgeries Statue Court, and go admire the William Morris tea room. If the weather's good, sit in the Pirelli Courtyard for a spell, then walk or take a taxi up Sydney Street to the Chelsea Town Hall. Across from the hall is an antiques center in which you can browse; next to it is Daisy and Tom's, a wonderful place to buy British books for your little friends. And then, if the weather's warm, have lunch outside at the Chelsea Marketplace.

Stroll down the King's Road toward Sloane Square, maybe do a little window shopping, and catch the 11 bus wherever possible. Take the 11 past all the great sights: Westminster Abbey, Big Ben, Whitehall, Trafalgar Square, up Fleet Street, to St. Paul's. If you have the energy, climb up to the top of St. Paul's and enjoy the view. If not, just have a seat in the church and admire the craftsmanship that went into this magnificent building, or perhaps rest in the courtyard of the church and watch the tourists. Catch a bus towards Trafalgar Square and go to Leicester Square to buy half-price theater tickets at the kiosk there for that evening. There's no saying what plays will be available, but it's always great to see an Oscar Wilde or Noel Coward play if possible: so very, very English. Check to see what stars are performing: you may get the pleasure of seeing Judi Dench, one of the Redgraves, or Maggie Smith tread the boards.

Then, depending on the time, your next move would be a toss up between having tea at the Ritz or Fortnam and Masons, or doing some brass-rubbing at St. Martin-in-the-Fields' in the crypt. It's a real treat: you pick out one of the many medieval brass plates with engraved images, get a piece of paper and some waxy chalk, and rub the chalk over the plate, making a print of the design. Take your time with the rubbing, enjoying the atmosphere and the pastime. Buy some gifts in the wonderful shop (there's two—one at the brass-rubbing area and one in the other part of the crypt). Then walk over to Covent Garden and watch the buskers (street entertainers) at work. Dinner at last. For the atmosphere and the Yorkshire pudding, try Rules, the oldest surviving restaurant in London (zone 7; 35 Maiden Lane, WC2; (0207) 836-5314; tube: Charing Cross). Yes, it's a tourist trap, but it is also redolent of a long-gone era, with the photos and cartoons on the wall charting its history since it opened in 1798. And where else can you get grouse, woodcock, and partridge?

You will love the play, especially because you will have paid half price for some perfectly decent seats. You will love how they sell delicious ice cream right in the theater at the intermission, and you will be proud of yourself for already ordering your refreshments before the play started and finding them waiting for you at the bar at intermission. When the play gets out at 10:30 or 11 p.m., walk over to Ronnie Scott's (zone 7; 47 Frith Street, W1; (0207) 439-0747; tube: Tottenham Court Road) and listen to jazz until it's time to call a minicab and go back to your fabulous hotel (The Gore, Hazlitt's, Covent Garden, or Blakes) to go to sleep. Hazlitt's is right across the street.

Walking in and around London

Walking is by far the best way to experience London. Grab a map and your camera, select a starting point, and just begin to explore. You never know what you may find once you move off of London's bustling main thoroughfares: a cobbled alleyway with a quaint cafe, a medieval church, or even a dreamy view across the river. Below are a number of suggested walks covering a diverse range of areas. Many cross the paths of some great London attractions and can create an entire day's worth of wandering if you decide to stop off and visit some of the sights along the way.

You might also want to try out **The Original London Walks** (phone (0207) 624-3978 or 794-1764; fax (0207) 625-1932; london.walks@ mail.bogo.co.uk; www.london.walks.com), which features scores of themed walks built around Jack the Ripper, ghosts of London, lost palaces, The Beatles, rock and roll, literary London, the swinging sixties, Princess Diana, Charles Dickens, and so many more. You can pick up a leaflet at most hotels or check for daily events in *Time Out*. Another company is **Stepping Out** (phone (0208) 881-2933; fax (0207) 405-6036; www.walklondondirect. co.uk). Both themed-walk companies have excellent guides and offer a huge selection of walks, both day and night.

Walking on Your Own

If you prefer to walk at your own pace, try the walks we've outlined here.

ZONE 3, CITY OF LONDON: THROUGH THE CENTURIES

Time to Allow 3–4 hours depending on indoor visits
Distance Approximately 1.5 miles
Sights Museum of London; St. Botolph, Aldersgate; Postman's Park; St. Bartholomew-the-Great Church; National Postal Museum; Christ Church, Greyfriars; St. Paul's Cathedral; Guildhall (including Guildhall Clock Museum and Guildhall Art Gallery); St. Lawrence Jewry
Tube St. Paul's or Barbican

This walk gives just a glimpse of the vast array of architecture that has evolved in London over the centuries, from the ancient Roman wall that once enclosed the fourth-century city of Londinium, to the skyscrapers of the modern financial district. Begin your wanderings at the Museum of London, looking out from the museum's terrace, where you are surrounded by concrete and glass. This is twentieth-century London, with heavy traffic and office buildings. This is a London that would make a Londoner from the last century (or even from just before the Blitz) weep with confusion and sorrow. However, if you know where to look, you will glimpse bits of Old—the London of medieval peasants, Renaissance grandeur, and Victorian sentimentality. A stop at the museum is great for getting your bearings on London's diverse historical eras.

After enjoying an engaging few hours of history, head across the traffic circle to Aldersgate. Locate Little Britain Street on the right, on whose corner sits St. Botolph Church. The church's classical Georgian interior is a glorious contrast to its bland and unassuming exterior. Turn right as you exit the church and enter Postman's Park. This hidden churchyard was dedicated by the Victorians in 1900 as a memorial to "heroes of everyday life" who died in acts of bravery. In the center of the intimate park, you will find the protected wall of memorials. One epitaph reads, "Saved a lunatic woman from suicide at Woolwich Arsenal, but was himself run over by the train." Exiting the park on the opposite side, turn right onto King Edward Street, then follow Little Britain around to the left to where it deposits you in Smithfield Square.

In medieval times, the marketplace of Smithfield Green was thriving with merchants, peddlers, peasants, and livestock. Jousts, tournaments, horse fairs, and hangings have all been held here. To your left is St. Bartholomew's Hospital. Begun in 1123 as a priory and hospice, it is London's oldest hospital. Out front is a memorial to Sir William Wallace, known to many as Braveheart. If you venture inside the hospital's main entrance, you will find the small hospital church of St. Bartholomew-the-Less and an eighteenth-century courtyard. Back out on the square and to your right you will see a half-timbered, tudor gatehouse. Through here is a gem of medieval London, the Priory Church of St. Bartholomew-the-Great, also dating back to 1123. Don't miss the opportunity to take a look at this breathtaking example of original twelfth-century Norman architecture.

Making your way back to Little Britain, turn right onto King Edward Street, using the dome of St. Paul's Cathedral before you as a guide. Past Postman's Park and the National Postal Museum, at the end of Little Britain, are the remains of Christopher Wren's Christ Church, Greyfriars. Originally built in 1691, it was destroyed during air raids in World War II. Today, the tower and walls enclose a lovely garden whose trellises mark the original location of the church columns and center aisle. Cross Newgate Street and turn left. Beyond the tube station entrance is the churchyard of St. Paul's Cathedral. Vastly different from medieval St. Bart's, Christopher Wren's Renaissance masterpiece is the second largest cathedral in the world. Stop here to see the glorious interior or perhaps climb the dome for unparalleled city views.

Wandering back through the churchyard, turn right and head east on Cheapside. Cross over and make a left on Wood Street and then follow Milk Street as it bears to the right. This area was another of London's medieval marketplaces, although the only remnants are the street names—Bread Street, Milk Street, Honey Lane—to remind you of its past. Just ahead is the entrance to Guildhall, the headquarters for the Corporation of

London. Behind the bleak twentieth-century facade lies the impressive Great Hall, open 10 a.m.–4:30 p.m. Monday through Friday. Next door, the Guildhall Library houses a clock museum (open 9:30 a.m.–4:30 p.m., Monday through Friday) and a remarkable art collection. Also, if you can catch it open, be sure to stop in and see the spectacular interior of the Church of St. Lawrence Jewry located on the main road, whose name is derived from its location on the site of London's early Jewish ghetto. Finally, follow King Street south to Victoria Street. Turn right and end your walk at Mansion House tube station.

ZONE 1, OLD HAMPSTEAD VILLAGE

Time to Allow 2 hours

Distance Approximately 1.5–2 miles

Sights Church Row, St. John's-at-Hampstead, Fenton House, Admiral's House, Burgh House, Flask Walk and Well Walk, Downshire Hill, Keats House, Hampstead Heath, Hampstead High Street

Also Nearby Freud Museum, Kenwood House

Tube Hampstead

The history of Hampstead has always been tied closely to its hill, its heath, and its healthy environment, and in the early 1700s, Hampstead became a booming spa town. The area's iron-rich water was said to cure all manner of ailments and you could purchase flasks of the vile-tasting stuff for 3p a bottle or bathe in it at one of the local bathhouses. Today, narrow streets lined with lovingly restored eighteenth-century homes help the village retain much of its charming Victorian atmosphere.

Arriving in Hampstead via the underground, you come up London's deepest (and creakiest) elevator shaft near the top of Hampstead Hill in the village center. Heath Street and Hampstead High Street stretch before you, lined with shops, cafes, and restaurants—definitely a great are in which to stop for tea at the end of your walk. Exiting the tube station, cross over and turn left on Heath Street, then right on Church Row, one of the best-preserved streets in London. Notice the grand wrought-iron work, the remains of early eighteenth-century oil lampstands, and the intricately detailed windows over many of the homes' main entrances. These fan lights, illuminated from behind by candles, helped identify one's home after dark in the days before street lighting. Famous residents here included George du Maurier, Gracie Fields, and H. G. Wells. At the end of the line of trees sits St. John–at-Hampstead, consecrated in 1747. Take some time to wander the graveyard and church then head up Holly Walk.

At the top of the hill on the right, St. Mary's Church is nestled among a row of homes. One of London's oldest Roman Catholic churches, its discreet location is due to its existence before religious tolerance was granted in 1829. Make a right and follow Mt. Vernon down to where it meets up with Hampstead Grove. Turn left. Another worthwhile stop is Fenton House on the right. This wonderfully preserved seventeenth-century home today houses an exquisite collection of Asian, European, and English china, needlework, and furniture, but its finest attraction is its unique collection of early musical instruments, including Handel's harpsichord. Beyond Fenton House, turn left onto Admiral's Walk. Look carefully at the house and you will see the nautical alterations made by Lieutenant Fountain North in 1775. North adapted the roof to resemble the deck of a ship, complete with flagstaff and cannon, which were fired to celebrate naval victories. P. L. Travers and Walt Disney fans should find this all vaguely familiar; the character and home of Admiral Boom in *Mary Poppins* was based on this eccentric individual.

At the end of Hampstead Grove, where it runs into the main thoroughfare of Heath Street, you will find a small reservoir on your left. Whitstone Pond, built in 1856, allowed Londoners who had successfully navigated the steep muddy roads to the hilltop to clean their carriages by walking their horses down the ramps and through the pond. Crossing Heath Street, begin your journey down the hill and alongside Hampstead Heath, turning right at Squire's Mount and passing some lovely cottages, which date to 1704. Continue on Cannon Lane, turning left on Well Road, so named for the spring that gave the town its reputation for health. Famous residents here included D. H. Lawrence, J. B. Priestly, and John Constable. Turning left on New End Square brings you past Burgh House, the 1703 home of Hampstead Spa's physician, William Gibbons. Today the building is a lovely local museum, meeting place, and exhibition space. There is a small tea room downstairs if you are needing a snack or rest. To your left is Well Walk and to your right, Flask Walk. Just up Flask Walk on your right is a bathhouse that was actually in use by some locals until the late 1960s. Cross Well Walk and enjoy a downhill stroll on Willow Road. At the bottom, turn right on Downshire Hill.

Another picturesque street lined with nineteenth-century homes and gardens, its centerpiece is St. John's-at-Hampstead Church, opened in 1823. If open, it is worth taking a quick peek inside. Turning left on Keats Grove brings you to our last stop. John Keats lived in Hampstead from 1818 to 1820, and it is here that he produced many of his most famous works. The home is carefully restored and decorated as Keats would have known it, and the intimate museum is a wonderful tribute to his short, tragic life. Upon leaving Keats House, turn left and head back up Keats Grove, then left again on Downshire Hill. Make a right on Rosslyn Hill and enjoy some window shopping or stop in one of the many cafes on your way back toward the Hampstead tube station, just a five-minute walk up the road.

<u>**ZONES 7 AND 9, ROYAL LONDON: From Palace to Parliament**</u>

Time to Allow 3–4 hours

Distance Approximately 2.5 miles

Sights Royal Mews, Queen's Gallery, Buckingham Palace, St. James's Park, Cabinet War Rooms, Admiralty Arch, Trafalgar Square, National Gallery, National Portrait Gallery, St. Martin–in-the-Fields Church, Royal Horse Guards, Banqueting House, 10 Downing Street, Cenotaph, Houses of Parliament, St. Margaret's Church, Westminster Abbey

Tube Victoria

This walk takes you past many of London's most popular sights. London's history, royalty, and fabulous architecture are thoroughly represented as we travel throughout Westminster, the home to London's monarchy and Parliament. The walk affords plenty of opportunities to stop along the way, so the length of the walk depends entirely on your stamina.

Begin your walk at Victoria tube station. Turn right on Buckingham Palace Road, following signs for the palace. Just beyond Lower Grosvenor Place you will find the entrance for the Royal Mews on the left. Housed here in the palace stables is an impressive display of royal carriages; the oldest, made in 1762 for George III, is still used for coronations. Just past the Royal Mews is the Queen's Picture Gallery, a changing exhibition space for the royal monarch's incredible collection of privately owned works of art. Continuing on, you will soon arrive in the palace forecourt, much of which is today a busy traffic circle.

Buckingham Palace has been the official London residence of the sovereign since George III bought the place from Lord Buckingham in 1762. The palace is home and office for Her Majesty, and its elaborately decorated rooms are in continuous use for state affairs, official receptions, ceremonial occasions, and Parliamentary meetings. See the attractions listing for opening times, and be sure to fit a visit into your schedule if possible. North of the palace is Green Park, but you need to locate St. James's Park, to the right of The Mall, as that is our next area to explore.

Enter the park by Birdcage Walk, and wander east along the pond's edge. St. James's is the oldest of London's parks. It started life as part of the private grounds of St. James's Palace, but was opened to the public during the reign of the Stuart monarchs. Cross over the bridge, stopping to take in the stunning views of the palace to the west and the Horse Guards Parade to the east. As you continue to walk along the path beside the lake, the London Eye ferris wheel, Westminster Abbey, and St. Stephen's Clock Tower can be seen through the trees, wildlife skitter past or glide by on the water, and if you're lucky, the sun will shine a few rays through the clouds above. Charles II, Samuel Pepys, and John Milton have all enjoyed such views (except for that of the London Eye, of course, whose elegance I am sure they would have loved). The most famous residents of the park are the pelicans, who have delighted visitors to the park since the seventeenth century. Every afternoon they parade across the lawn on Duck Island to receive their daily fish dinner, and they thoroughly enjoy the sanctuary provided here, along with the 20 or more other species of duck and goose that call St. James's home.

As you reach the other side of the park, continue on, crossing Horse Guards Road. Just in front of you, King Charles Street ends in a pedestrianized stairway, and to the right of this is the entrance to the Cabinet War Rooms. Winston Churchill and his cabinet carried out operations here during World War II. From the War Rooms, turn right on Horse Guards Road, passing the Horse Guards Parade, where the Changing of the Guard occurs daily at 11:30 a.m. (Sunday at 10 a.m.). Never take the daily changing of the guard as a given: it is frequently cancelled (call (0207) 799-2331 for recorded information). Turn right on The Mall and walk under Admiralty Arch and into Trafalgar Square. In the center stands Nelson's Column, the memorial to Britain's best-loved national hero, Admiral Lord Horatio Nelson, who defeated Napoleon at the Battle of Trafalgar in 1806. The square is the location for frequent political demonstrations, London's annual Christmas tree lighting, and New Year's countdowns. Behind is the National Gallery, where you could spend hours enjoying one of the world's greatest art collections. To the right is the eighteenth-century church of St. Martin-in-the-Fields, definitely worth a stop. Its simple but elegant interior offers free lunchtime concerts. Downstairs, the church's Cafe-in-the-Crypt provides soups and sandwiches.

Leaving Trafalgar Square, walk down Whitehall (the street directly opposite the National Gallery). You will pass the front of the Horse Guards Building, with its guards at attention, and almost directly opposite is the Banqueting House, all that remains of the great palace at Whitehall, which burned to the ground in 1698. Prior to this loss, the palace was the site of numerous historical events, such as the marriage of Henry VIII to Anne Boleyn and the execution of Charles I during the English Civil War. Others who have lived here included Cardinal Wolsey, Oliver Cromwell, Charles II, and William III and Mary II. Further along on the right is 10 Downing Street, home of Britain's prime minister, although you are not likely to see much, because the street is guarded and gated. The Cenotaph, in the middle of Whitehall, is Britain's memorial to those who died in World War I. It is the focal point of the country's Remembrance Day ceremonies, which include two minutes of silence throughout the entire country on the eleventh minute of the eleventh hour of the eleventh day of the eleventh month each year.

Not far ahead, you will begin to see the towers of the Palace of Westminster coming into view. Once you have arrived in Parliament Square, you have a number of choices before you. You can wander out onto Westminster

Bridge for the best views of Westminster Palace and St. Stephen's Tower. You can sit in on debates in the Houses of Parliament or explore the sixteenth-century St. Margaret's Church (within whose walls Sir Walter Raleigh is laid to rest). And take the opportunity at walk's end to enjoy inspiring hymns sung by the Westminster Boys Choir during the daily choral even-song at Westminster Abbey, possibly the most visited tourist sight and certainly one of the most beautiful churches in London.

For Museum Lovers

If you love going to museums, you already have a lot in common with typical Londoners. London is crammed with wonderful museums, many of which are free of charge, many more of which were free until the mid-1970s, but that's another story. There have been plans afoot to scrap museum admission fees within the next few years, but it's one step forward, two steps backwards, as the government argues with the musem officials. We continue to keep our fingers crossed.

There's a remarkable website that details current and upcoming exhibitions at 2,000 museums in London and across the country; it also offers virtual tours of the permanent collections of the museums featured. It's a great way to see some of the smaller, harder-to-visit museums without leaving your desk. The website's goal is to represent Britain's entire cultural history—no small undertaking. Visit it at www.24hourmuseum.org.uk.

Saving Money on Museum Admissions

There are ways to save on the admission fees of museums. One way is to go after 4:30 p.m., when visitors can enter free of charge for the remaining hour or so until closing time. Another way is the London Pass, a program launched by the London Tourist Board in 1999 that affords entry into more than 40 fee-charging attractions, free travel on tubes, trains, and busses, a color guide to London, and £5 worth of free telephone calls. A one-day pass costs £18 for adults and £11 for children; a three-day pass costs £42 for adults and £22 for children; and a six-day pass costs £72 for adults and £34 for children. You would have to do a lot of museum hopping to make it worth it. Passes can be purchased at www.Londonpass.com or at the British Visitor Centre (1 Regent Street, south of Picadilly Circus). The London Pass has taken the place of the old White Card and Go See passes, which are no longer available. It is important to note that many museums in London may be changing to a no-fee policy in 2002. Be sure to check the status of this plan on the website of the London Tourist Board (www.londontouristboard.com): if they have gone ahead with the free-museums scheme, the London Pass may not be worth it.

LONDON ATTRACTIONS CHART

Name	Type	Author's Rating	Zone
Albert Memorial	Outdoor memorial	★★	13
Apsley House (The Wellington Museum)	Historic home and museum	★★★	8
Bank of England Museum	Museum of money and banking	★★	3
Bethnal Museum of Childhood	Large museum of toys	★★★	4
Big Ben Clock Tower	Monument Not rated		9
The British Airways London Eye	Observation wheel	★★★★★	5
British Library at St. Pancras	Replacement for reading rooms at the British Museum	★★★★	15
British Museum	Among the most famous museums in the world	★★★★★	2
Buckingham Palace	Stately home of the queen	★★½	9
Burgh House	Museum with exhibitiion and concert space	★★	1
The Cabinet War Rooms	description needed	★★★	9
Carlyle's Museum	Historic home and museum	★★★	11
Changing of the Guard	Grand old tradition	★★	9
Chiswick House	Stately home and gardens	★★★	12
Clink Exhibition	Recreation of a medieval prison	★	5
Courtauld Institute	Gallery Museum	★★★	2
Cutty Sark	Restored sailing clipper ship	★★★	6
Design Museum	History of design of everyday items	★★	5
Dickens House	Historic home and museum	★	2
Freud Museum	Historic home and museum	★★★	1
Gilbert Collection	Museum of decorative arts	★★★	7
The Globe Theatre	Reconstructed Shakespearean theater	★★★★	5
Guards Museum	Military museum	★★	9
Guildhall	Corporate headquarters for the City of London	★★	7
HMS Belfast	Royal Navy battle ship from WWII	★★	5
Hampton Court Palace	Royal palace	★★★★★	12
Hermitage Rooms	Museum	★★★	7
Hogarth's House	Historic home	★★	12
Houses of Parliament	Britain's working chambers of government	★★	9
Imperial War Museum	British military experience	★★	5
Dr. Johnson's House	Historic home and museum	★	2

LONDON ATTRACTIONS CHART

Name	Type	Author's Rating	Zone
Kensington Palace State Rooms	Stately home of Kensington Gardens	★★★★	13
Kenwood House (The Iveagh Bequest)	Georgian villa and art gallery	★★★★	1
Lambeth Palace	Historic home	★★★	5
Leighton House Museum and Art Gallery	Historic home	★★★★★	13
Linley Sambourne House	Historic home	★★★	13
London Aquarium	Wonderland of fish	★★★★	5
London Dungeon	Horror attraction	★	5
London Transport Museum	Interactive museum of trams, buses, and trains	★★★★	7
London Zoo	Modernized old zoo	★★★	15
Madame Tussaud's Waxworks	World-famous wax museum	★★	14
Millennium Bridge	Footbridge across the Thames	★★★	3 and 5
The Monument	Commemorating the Great Fire of 1666	★★★★	3
Museum of London	Museum of London history	★★★★	3
National Gallery	Art gallery	★★★★★	7
National Maritime Museum and Queen's House	Largest maritime museum in the world	★★★★	6
National Portrait Gallery	Famous faces from British history	★★★★★	7
Natural History Museum	Old and modern exhibits	★★★	11
Old Bailey	London's central criminal courts	★★	3
Old Operating Theatre, Museum, and Herb Garret	Museum of old medical equipment	★★★★	5
Pollack's Toy Museum	Castle-like adventure into toys past	★★★★	14
Queen's Gallery, Buckingham Palace	Art gallery	★★★	9
Royal Academy of Arts	Museum and exhibition venue	★★★★	8
Royal Greenwich Observatory	Location of world's Prime Meridian	★★★	6
Royal Mews, Buckingham Palace	Where royal carriages and queen's horses are kept	★★★	9
Royal Naval College	Example of Renaissance architecture	★★★	6
St. Bartholomew-the-Great	London's oldest monastic church	★★★★	3
Science Museum	Museum	★★★★★	11

LONDON ATTRACTIONS CHART

Name	Type	Author's Rating	Zone
St. Paul's Cathedral	London's most prominent cathedral	★★★	3
Sherlock Holmes Museum	Museum	★★★★	14
Sir John Soane's Museum	Historic home and museum	★★★★★	2
Somerset House	Historic home and art galleries	★★★★★	2
Southwark Cathedral	Small medieval cathedral	★★★	5
Syon House	Historic home Brentford, Middlesex	★★★	
Tate Britain	Museum of English painters	★★★★★	9
Tate Modern	Museum of international modern art	★★	5
Tower Bridge	Offers terrific views	★★	3 and 5
Tower of London	Ancient fortress	★★★★★	3
Victoria and Albert Museum	Museum of decorative arts	★★★★★	11
Wallace Collection	Private collection of 19th-century Anglo-French art	★★★★	14
The Wellington Arch	Small, specialty museum of architecture	★★★	10
Westminster Abbey	Historically important church	★★★★	9
Windsor Castle	Queen's country house Windsor, Hertsfordshire	★★★★	

Museums and Attractions

Important note: Please be sure to call the following places before you go; opening times can be subject to change without notice.

For a look into London's parks and green spaces, see "Green and Pleasant Lands: Parks of London" on page 232. Also, at the end of this chapter is a profile of Greenwich.

Albert Memorial

Type of Attraction Outdoor memorial to a beloved prince consort
Location zone 13; Kensington Gardens, west of Exhibition Road, SW7; tube: High Street Kensington
Admission Free
Hours Daily, dawn to dusk

When to Go A sunny day, or at night when the floodlights are on

Special Comments Bring binoculars so you can see the amazing detail of the high parts of the memorial.

Overall Appeal by Age Group

Pre-school ★★	Grade School ★★	Teens ★★
Young Adults ★★	Over 30 ★★	Seniors ★★

Author's Rating ★★

How Much Time to Allow 30 minutes, plus time to hang around on the steps. It's a good people-watching place, where talented inline skaters congregate on weekends.

Description and Comments This memorial, built by a grieving Queen Victoria after her husband's death from typhoid at the age of 42, is no small thrill to see, as it had been covered in plastic and scaffolding for the last decade while being restored. It had been stripped of its gold in 1915, so we are in the privileged position of being the first generation in almost a century to see it in all its exuberant neogothic gilded glory (it cost three times as much to build as one of the finest churches built in Kensington at the same time and caused an uproar in Parliament). There are some Londoners who find the entire thing hideous and are appalled at the millions of pounds spent for its conservation. But whatever one might think of its artistry, it is a visual knockout. Check it out at night with the floodlights on it to appreciate a view the Victorians were denied.

The memorial can be seen from many angles in Hyde Park and Kensington Gardens, but don't imagine you have experienced its full flavor until you have looked the buffalo square in the eye.

Touring Tips Make this part of your Kensington Palace/Gardens and Hyde Park day.

Apsley House (The Wellington Museum)

Type of Attraction Former home of the duke of Wellington

Location zone 8; 149 Piccadilly, W1; tube: Hyde Park Corner

Admission £4.50 for adults; free for children under age 12; £3 for concessions

Hours Tuesday–Sunday, 11 a.m.–5 p.m.; last entry at 4:30 p.m.

Phone (0207) 499-5676

Website www.vam.ac.uk

When to Go Anytime

Special Comments There is no wheelchair access, but there are steps into house and between floors. If you walk along the pedestrian subway below Hyde Park Corner, you can see the story of Apsley House and the duke of Wellington rendered on the tiles on the wall, a good way to prepare for the visit to the house, which lacks descriptive commentary.

Overall Appeal by Age Group

Pre-school ★	Grade School ★★	Teens ★★
Young Adults ★★★	Over 30 ★★★	Seniors ★★★

Author's Rating ★★★

How Much Time to Allow 45 to an hour, more if you really love old masters

Description and Comments This grand house used to be known as 149 Piccadilly until it was given to the duke of Wellington as a splendid reward for his military successes in the Napoleonic Wars. While the Hyde Park Corner traffic circle whirls in front of the house, the windows in the back of Apsley House look out onto a serene vista of Hyde Park, the rose gardens, and the occasional horseback riders. Apsley is of interest to art lovers for the works it houses of such old masters as Velázquez, Goya, and Rubens, along with some lesser luminaries. The basement houses a collection of political cartoons that will teach you about the duke and his times.

Touring Tips   This is a very small, quick-hit kind of place, and it fits in well with a walk through Hyde Park and a visit to the Wellington Arch, before moving on through Green and St. James's Parks.

Bank of England Museum

Type of Attraction Historical displays tracing the rise of banking
Location zone 3; Threadneedle Street, EC2 (museum entrance on Bartholomew Lane); tube: Bank
Admission Free
Hours Monday–Friday, 10 a.m.–5 p.m.; closed weekends and bank holidays
Phone (0207) 601-5545
Website www.bankofengland.co.uk
When to Go Anytime
Special Comments Disabled friendly, with portable ramps available on request
Overall Appeal by Age Group

Pre-school —	Grade School ★★	Teens ★★
Young Adults ★★	Over 30 ★★	Seniors ★★

Author's Rating ★★
How Much Time to Allow 1 hour
Description and Comments   This is the only part of the massive fortress that is the Bank of England, known as "The Old Lady of Threadneedle Street," that mere mortals can enter. One display shows the evolution of the banknote from 1694—when the bank was formed to lend money to the government to pay for King James II's war against France— to the present; much of the currency used over time can be viewed here. Another display is modeled after the first bank and includes mannequins of wigged clerks and a huge fireplace behind mahogany counters. A video shows real footage from the building of the present bank in the 1930s, and there are interactive computer screens that provide a lot of information. Be warned: the displays require quite a bit of reading, as well as a particular interest in money and banking.

Bethnal Museum of Childhood

Type of Attraction Largest museum of toys in the world
Location zone 4; Cambridge Heath Road, E2; tube: Bethnal Green
Admission Free
Hours Daily except Friday, 10 a.m.–5:50 p.m; closed Friday
Phone (0208) 980-2415 (recording); (0208) 983-5200 (duty officer)
Website www.museumofchildhood.co.uk
When to Go Anytime

Special Comments Call ahead to arrange wheelchair access (phone (0208) 983-5205). Art workshops for children over age 3 and a soft play area for children ages 5 and under are available only on weekends.

Overall Appeal by Age Group

Pre-school ★★★	Grade School ★★★	Teens ★★★
Young Adults ★★★	Over 30 ★★★	Seniors ★★★

Author's Rating ★★★

How Much Time to Allow 90 minutes

Description and Comments Housed in a building directly across the street from the Bethnal Green tube station (a big plus when dragging children along), the Museum of Childhood is part of the Victoria and Albert Museum, and is, unlike the V&A, still free. It has an unparalleled collection of children's toys and accessories: doll houses from as far back as the seventeenth century, model trains, hobby horses, old mechanical games and toys (you must pay 20p to use them), dolls of every possible kind, teddy bears, and even old-fashioned prams and nursery furniture. Not surprisingly, the children seem to prefer pumping the mechanical toys full of coins to admiring the antiquities behind glass. There is a new interactive exhibition called "Our Planet," which is aimed at those ages 5–14.

Big Ben Clock Tower

Type of Attraction Look-only clock tower; enduring symbol of London

Location zone 9; Parliament Square, SW1; tube: Westminster

Admission One cannot enter the tower

Hours 24 hours a day you

Website www.londontouristboard.com

When to go When you're in the area

Description and comments In the first edition of this book, I failed to include an entry on Big Ben, earning me the well-deserved wrath of a few readers. I assumed that everyone knows that Big Ben is not an attraction, but just a beautiful piece of architecture that you can set your watch to. But of course it must be covered in a guide book to London, as it is the most recognizable symbol of the city, and replicas of Big Ben are at the top of most visitors' must-have souvenir list.

In 1834, the old Palace of Westminster burned to the ground and Parliament decided to build itself a Gothic style replacement. The clock tower was part of the grand plan, but due to its exacting specifications, construction took some time and was beset by difficulties. Big Ben refers in fact to the actual bell that chimes, and it was Big Trouble from the start. The first bell cast cracked almost immediately—possibly due to the weight of the clapper—and had to be recast in a smaller format. The clock's hands were too heavy to move, and also had to be replaced. The bell cracked again, and was silent for three years, until a solution was found in 1862. Big Ben has been ringing out ever since.

The British Airways London Eye

Type of Attraction The world's biggest observation wheel

Location zone 5; in Jubilee Gardens, next to County Hall by Westminster Bridge, on the south bank of the Thames; tube: Westminster or Waterloo

Admission £9.50 for adults; £7 for seniors and the disabled; £5 for children ages 5–16; free for kids under age 5

Hours February–March, daily, 10:30 a.m.–7 p.m.; March–May, daily, 10:30 a.m.–8 p.m.; May–September, daily, 10 a.m.–10 p.m.

Phone (0870) 500 0600

Website www.ba-londoneye.com

When to Go Anytime; it's best on a sunny day or clear night

Special Comments This is not for those suffering from vertigo; it is very high and can make one feel quite exposed. It is disabled friendly.

Overall Appeal by Age Group

Pre-school ★★★	Grade School ★★★★★	Teens ★★★★
Young Adults ★★★★★	Over 30 ★★★★★	Seniors ★★★★★

Author's Rating ★★★★★

How much time to allow If you haven't ordered tickets ahead of time, you may have to wait in line for as long as an hour, depending on the season and the weather. If you have reserved tickets (by phone or website), you can pick them up easily, and then you must wait about a half hour for boarding. The rotation takes 30 minutes.

Description and comments Definitely London's most successful attraction designed to celebrate the new millenium, the London Eye is a colossal (450 feet high) silver wheel sprouting clear pods that hang off the frame. There is a boarding area from which you enter the pods. Each of the 32 pods carries about 25 people, with benches for those who wish to sit. The design and the effect are surprisingly elegant and graceful; the wheel soars above the old buildings of Westminster and the South Bank. It moves slowly and majestically up, until its zenith of 450 feet, at which point passengers can see a good 25 miles away on a clear day. It's an amazing view of London.

Touring Tips You must order tickets a few days in advance, which is a problem with the unpredictable London weather. You choose the day and the time you wish to "board" (British Air uses aeronautical terms rather endearingly, calling the ride a "flight"); then you show up with your credit card and retrieve your tickets from one of the machines located to your left as you come into the office. A word of caution: the glass pods can be stiflingly hot on sunny summer days. Combine your visit with a trip to the aquarium or lunch at the Marriot Hotel's dining room with the river view.

British Library at St. Pancras

Type of Attraction New location of reading rooms (manuscript-archive collections) formerly housed in the British Museum (see profile below)

Location zone 5; 96 Euston Road, NW1; tube: King's Cross

Admission Free

Hours Public areas are open Monday and Wednesday–Friday, 9:30 a.m.–6 p.m.; Tuesday, 9:30 a.m.–8 p.m.; Saturday, 9:30 a.m.–5 p.m.; and Sunday, 11 a.m.–5 p.m.

Phone (0207) 412-7000

Website www.bl.uk

When to Go Anytime

Special Comments Full wheelchair/disabled access

Overall Appeal by Age Group

Pre-school —	Grade School ★★	Teens ★★
Young Adults ★★★	Over 30 ★★★	Seniors ★★★★

Author's Rating ★★★★
How Much Time to Allow I hour

Description and Comments   The embattled (and expensive: £500 million!) project to move the reading rooms from their beautiful, longtime niche at the British Museum was one of those necessary concessions to age that no one really wanted to make. However, since the opening, visitors and readers have been grudgingly admitting that it is a vast improvement over the cramped old quarters. Even Prince Charles, who scorned the exterior as "a collection of brick sheds groping for significance," was impressed with the interior. The fact is that, however lacking in aesthetics the place may be, it's still a veritable Aladdin's cave of treasures, and an improved one at that. Manuscripts such as the Lindisfarne Gospels from the tenth century, James Joyce's first draft of *Finnegan's Wake*, a copy of the Magna Carta from 1215, the Gutenberg Bible, and plenty of documents related to the greatest English writer of all, Shakespeare, are only some of the magnificent materials on view here.

The library offers to the public a fine bookstore, a cafe, and three exhibition galleries. There's the John Riblat Gallery, in which are displayed some of the library's most ancient and valuable manuscripts and maps. There's a wonderous room called "Turning the Page," in which a computer allows you to virtually flip through four texts: the Lindisfarne You can listen to James Joyce and other authors reading from their work, and to music of all types, too. In the Pearson Gallery of Living Words are educational exhibits, one of which explores the history of writing; another is a reading area, with a good display of children's literature. There are a few interactive, fun things to do, such as design a book or check out the evolution of recorded music. The third gallery houses the Philatelic Collections, with 8 million items. This is a bit too arcane for me, but pure heaven for stamp collectors.

Touring Tips   This is not a tourist attraction really: it is for people who love and respect books, so take care who you take along with you. Sign up for a guided tour to see the parts of the library not open to the public.

The British Museum

Type of Attraction Colossal museum housing treasures of the British empire
Location zone 2; Great Russell Street, WC1; tube: Tottenham Court Road
Admission Free
Hours Saturday–Wednesday, 10 a.m.–5:30 p.m.; Thursday and Friday, 10 a.m.–8:30 p.m.
Phone (0207) 636-1555
Website www.british-museum.ac.uk
When to Go Early mornings
Special Comments Obtain a leaflet from the information desk for details about wheelchair accesibility; wheelchairs are also available to borrow. The new Queen Elizabeth II Great Court opened in December 2000 and has improved the museum immensely.
Overall Appeal by Age Group

Pre-school ★★★★	Grade School ★★★★	Teens ★★★★★
Young Adults ★★★★★	Over 30 ★★★★★	Seniors ★★★★★

Author's Rating ★★★★★

How Much Time to Allow 2–4 hours

Description and Comments There is no doing the British Museum justice in a guide book. It is the number-one tourist attraction in London, with over 7 million visitors a year and really must be experienced in person, multiple times if possible. The museum today houses than 50,000 items in 100 galleries, and it all began when Sir Hans Sloane bequeathed his remarkable collection of art and artifacts to the state in 1753, and the earl of Oxford's rare manuscripts were added to the mix. The collection grew rapidly, as it became the scholarly and patriotic thing to do to leave one's finest possessions to the museum, and the museum repeatedly benefited from England's greatest empire-booty-looting years. Even the stolen goods of Napoleon's empire-building campaigns were placed here after the British defeated the French at Alexandria during the Napoleonic Wars.

At the British Museum, you can travel to the ends of the globe, throughout centuries of humankind's time on earth, and see just about every little thing that we've thought up along the way: mummies, pottery, clocks, painting, tools for war and peace, sculpture, personal decoration, household goods, treasures of gold and precious stones, and far more. Not only does are there artifacts from practically every civilization throughout time, but they are of the greatest import. The Rosetta Stone, the Lindow Man, the Egyptian mummies, and prehistoric pieces are just a few of the finds that have literally changed history and now reside here.

The building itself contributes to the museum's appeal. Recently remodeled, it features at its center the Queen Elizabeth II Great Court, as it is officially known, which is the largest covered square in Europe, with over 3,000 panes of glass sheltering an area the size of a soccer field. This courtyard has not always been accessible, for it was slowly filled in with the materials of the round, domed Reading Room of the British Library. When the Library was finally removed to St. Pancras in 1997 (see preceding profile), the courtyard space was reclaimed. This lovely Court stays open after the galleries close.

The museum also offers numerous gift shops, many benches and tables on which to rest your tired bones, and a restaurant at the top of the couryard that lends wonderful views. It's lovely on a sunny day, and quite atmospheric during more tpically English weather. To make the most of your visit, do study the website, which will have all the hours of all the shops, cafes, restaurants, exhibitions, and special lectures.

Touring Tips It's far too big to try to cover in one visit, so consult the map and the interests of your group before heading to the galleries, and use the compass multimedia system in the Reading Room to help plan your tour. There's a good guide book sold in the excellent bookstore. And as with most museums, getting there before the school buses arrive is key. It is hard to gaze with the proper wonder at the Rosetta Stone when you're being jostled by an army of uniformed schoolchildren.

Buckingham Palace (see profiles for Queen's Gallery and Royal Mews, both on premises)

Type of Attraction Stately home of the Queen
Location zone 9; Buckingham Palace Road, SW1; tube: Green Park
Admission £11 for adults; £5.50 for children ages 5–16; free for children under age 5; £27.50 for a family ticket
Hours August–September, daily, 9:30 a.m.–4:30 p.m.

Phone (0207) 799-2331 for recorded information; (0207) 321-2233 for credit-card ticket purchases; and (0207) 839-1377 for general inquiries/group booking
Website www.royal.gov.uk
When to Go If you purchase tickets from the ticket office in Green Park, go at 9 a.m. The lines are murder otherwise.
Special Comments Wheelchair users are required to arrange a visit in advance. I personally wouldn't inflict this tour on a preschooler, although they assure me that the young'uns seem to love it.
Overall Appeal by Age Group

Pre-school ★	Grade School ★★	Teens ★★
Young Adults ★★★	Over 30 ★★★	Seniors ★★★

Author's Rating ★★½

Description and Comments Buckingham House was purchased by King George III in 1761 from the duke of Buckingham. Like most real estate, the three most attractive points were location, location, location. Situated between St. James's and Hyde Parks, with a tree-lined avenue affording views of Westminster and even St. Paul's Dome, it was like a country estate in the city (or near the city, as west of the house was still country). It was a private residence, the official court remaining—as it does to this day, if only in name—that of St. James's. When George IV ascended the throne, he had his favorite architect, John Nash, remodel it in the grandiose style you see today.

There are only two months in which you can view the state rooms at Buckingham Palace, so plan accordingly. In 1996, Queen Elizabeth II decided to open some of the palace to the public to pay for the restoration of Windsor Castle, which was severely damaged by a fire in 1992. I suspect that they may have paid for the work several times over by now. There are 7,000 visitors a day, seven days a week, for eight weeks, paying over £10 a head—well, you do the math.

It's an amazing spectacle, even more so when you ponder that for all the years of the palace's existence, loyal subjects of the Crown never had a prayer of setting foot in these august precincts, and now they're letting the likes of you and me in to eyeball the queen's goods. And what goods they are: treasures of painting, sculpture, furniture, and decoration beyond description, so I won't even try. (Neither do they. You have to buy the official guidebook to know what you are looking at; there are no signs anywhere.) I will say that after a while, I felt rather unsettled, if not revolutionary, by the endless, priceless display. And there are hundreds of other rooms you're not allowed to see. The views through the numerous French doors are magnificent; you can look out along the back garden rolling regally along, a piece of ye olde English countryside within earshot of the roar of Hyde Park Corner.

Warning This is not an attraction for everyone, not least because of the ridiculous lines you have to wait in. It's a lot of money and a lot of effort for what is essentially an inert stately home. You could feel equally, if not more, satisfied with a good book on the palace.

Touring Tips Don't bring in any bags, so you can avoid the baggage security check. Before your tour time, do go buy the official guide from the gift shop next to the palace at the Queen's Gallery—you'll save yourself a wait on the way into the palace. I repeat: it's important to get this book if you want to know what is what, because just as in your own home, there are no labels on the goods. The guides are there to answer questions, and they're very knowledgeable. There's no guided tour per se; you just go in and follow the group. The time designated for your entry will be printed on your ticket; don't bother lining up until you're about 15 minutes beforehand. You might wander around the gift shop or St. James's Park in the meantime.

Burgh House

Type of Attraction Lovely period home/arts center providing exhibitions, concerts, and lectures
Location zone 1; New End Square, Hampstead, NW3; tube: Hampstead
Admission Free
Hours Wednesday–Sunday, noon–5 p.m., bank holidays, 2–5 p.m.
Phone (0207) 431-0144
When to Go Anytime
Overall Appeal by Age Group

Pre-school ★	Grade School ★	Teens ★
Young Adults ★★	Over 30 ★★★	Seniors ★★★

Author's Rating ★★
How Much Time to Allow One hour to see Hampstead Museum exhibit; other times depend on lecture or concert lengths

Description and Comments The meandering streets of Flask Walk and Well Walk are picturesque reminders of when Hampstead was a thriving spa village. To step out of the sometimes brisk Hampstead breeze, you might stop at this well-maintained Queen Anne home, where a modest museum of local history along with other, changing exhibitions are housed. The house is much more well known among the locals for its ongoing series of concerts, including opera, chamber music, and jazz. (Call for a current schedule.) There is also a charming tea room downstairs.

Touring Tips See our walking tour of Old Hampstead Village (pages 166–167) for other sights worth visiting in the area.

The Cabinet War Rooms

Type of Attraction World War II shelter for Churchhill and his cabinet
Location zone 9; Clive Steps, King Charles Street, SW1; tube: Westminster or St James's Park
Admission £5.40 for adults; free for children under age 16; £3.90 for seniors and students; admission includes audioguide
Hours April–September, 9:30 a.m.–5:15 p.m. daily; October–March, 10 a.m.–5:15 p.m. daily
Phone (0207) 930-6961
Website www.iwm.org.uk, click on Cabinet War Rooms
When to Go Anytime
Special Comments Good disabled access, including wheelchairs on loan and accessible toilets
Overall Appeal by Age Group

Pre-school ★	Grade School ★★	Teens ★★★
Young Adults ★★★	Over 30 ★★★	Seniors ★★★★

Author's Rating ★★★

How much time to allow I hour

Description and comments This is the shelter in which Winston Churchill met with his staff, heads of state, and military personnel during the six years of World War II, when Hitler's bombs rained with grim regularity on London. Churchill's historic broadcasts to buck up the public were made from this site, and desperate decisions that could have turned the war against the Allies were strategized in these rooms. From the sandbags that line the front of the shelter to the old telephones and notepaper on Churchill's desk, this is an unusually close encounter with the reality of the war in London. When the war ended, the lights were turned off and the door shut, and the rooms remained exactly as they were left until the 1980s, when they were opened to the public. The attraction offers a good audio tour, or you can get a booklet with which to go through the rooms. This is a must for the WWII veteran or buff.

Touring Tips Combine with a visit to St. James's Park.

Carlyle's Museum

Type of Attraction Victorian home of the sage of Chelsea
Location zone 11; 24 Cheyne Row, SW3; tube: Sloane Square
Admission £3.50 for adults; £1.75 for children under age 16
Hours March 29 through November 2: Wednesday–Sunday and bank holidays, 11 a.m.–5 p.m.
Phone (0149) 475-5559
When to Go Anytime it's open
Special Comments It's an old house with steep stairs; no wheelchair access
Overall Appeal by Age Group

Pre-school ★	Grade School ★★	Teens ★★
Young Adults ★★★	Over 30 ★★★	Seniors ★★★

Author's Rating ★★★
How Much Time to Allow 60–90 minutes

Description and Comments It's likely that the name Thomas Carlyle may not mean anything to most people these days; he was a great essayist and historian in his own time (1795–1881), known and admired by all the Victorian literati. His house was a salon of luminaries such as Charles Dickens, George Eliot, Alfred Lord Tennyson, and Frederic Chopin, drawn as much by the sage of Chelsea's wisdom as by the famous wit of his wife, Jane. What is marvelous about the house, in the absence of any great feeling for its former owner, is that it was made a museum only 15 years after Carlyle's death, and so has an abundance of authentic minutiae—a hat hung on a hook, clothing in a drawer—that is lacking in most literary shrines of this sort. All the furnishings are authentic, and the atmosphere is beyond the wildest dreams of a Victoriana-phile.

Touring Tips Be sure to look at all the blue plaques around here to see the kind of neighbors Carlyle enjoyed.

Changing of the Guard

Type of Attraction A grand old London tradition
Location zone 9; In the forecourt of Buckingham Palace, at the end of Pall Mall, SW1; tube: Green Park, then walk directly through the park to the palace

Admission Free

Hours April–July: daily at 11:30 a.m.; August–March: every other day at 11:30 a.m.; be sure to call for information

Phone (0207) 799 2331

Website www.royal.gov.uk

When to Go Arrive by 10:30 to get a good place by the railings or on the statue of Victoria, especially in the summer on a nice day

Special Comments The pageant is cancelled in very wet weather

Overall Appeal by Age Group

Pre-school ★	Grade School ★★	Teens ★★
Young Adults ★★	Over 30 ★★	Seniors ★★

Author's Rating ★★

How Much Time to Allow The actual ceremony lasts 40 minutes, but if you want to get a good vantage point, you may want to show up an hour earlier

Description and Comments: The Queen's Guard, often accompanied by a band, leaves Wellington Barracks at 11:27 and marches along Birdcage Walk to the Palace, where they ... well, change. I'm not crazy about this attraction even though I love horses and history. There's something so annoying about the hordes of people standing around, very few of whom can get a good look at the ceremony, and the ones pressed up against the railings looking relatively miserable for all the waiting they've had to do. That said, I can recommend the statue of Victoria for a vantage point that isn't quite as desperate and uncomfortable as the scene around the palace railings. (I'm talking about the summer months; in the winter, it's not quite so bad). If it's too crowded for you around the palace, go to the Horse Guards Parade on Horse Guards Parade Road, which is on the far eastern perimeter of St James's Park (tube: Embankment or Charing Cross). There is held a less-elaborate ceremony at 11 a.m. Monday–Saturday and at 10 a.m. on Sundays. The Queen's Life Guards leave the Hyde Park Barracks at 10:30 a.m Monday–Saturday and at 9:30 a.m. on Sundays, and march most impressively through Hyde Park Corner, Constitution Hill, and The Mall.

Touring Tips: If it's too crowded one day and you can't get a good view, save it for the next.

Chiswick House

Type of Attraction Stately home with major gardens in west London

Location zone 12; Burlington Lane, W4; tube: Turnham Green, or Chiswick by rail

Admission £3.50 for adults; £1.70 for children under age 16

Hours April–September: daily, 10 a.m.–6 p.m.; October–March: Wednesday–Sunday, 10 a.m.–4 p.m.

Phone (0208) 995-0508

When to Go In good weather; the garden is splendid

Special Comments Limited disabled access; call for details

Overall Appeal by Age Group

Pre-school ★	Grade School ★	Teens ★
Young Adults ★★	Over 30 ★★	Seniors ★★

Author's Rating ★★★

How Much Time to Allow 1 hour

Description and Comments It's a bit of a hike from either the train station in Chiswick or the tube at Turnham Green, but for anyone interested in Palladian design and eighteenth-century, over-the-top splendor, this is the place. Built in 1725 by Lord Burlington and William Kent, it has at its heart an octagonal room with a dome that is classically symmetrical. Its original purpose was more to show off Burlington's extensive art collection than to live in, but alas, most of those treasures have long since been retired to museums. However, the decoration, carvings, and statuary that remain are magnificent, and the William Kent ceilings are as sumptuous as those he did at Kensington Palace. In summer, the gardens are spectacular, filled with wonderful follies—mock ruins that were all the rage in the eighteenth and nineteenth centuries, ponds, statues, benches, and formal gardens.

Touring Tips This can be combined with a trip to Hogarth's House and a visit to Chiswick High Street.

Clink Exhibition

Type of Attraction Re-creation and exhibition of a medieval prison
Location zone 5; 1 Clink Street, SE1; tube: London Bridge
Admission £4 for adults; £3 for seniors, students, and children under age 16
Hours Daily, 10 a.m.–6 p.m.
Phone (0207) 403-6515
Webpage: www.clink.co.uk
When to Go Anytime
Special Comments This attraction is not accessible to those in wheelchairs or baby strollers, as the entrance to the basement site is down a rather dark flight of stairs, and the exhibit itself includes a number of narrow doorways that must be stepped over
Overall Appeal by Age Group

Pre-school †	Grade School ★	Teens ★
Young Adults ★	Over 30 ★	Seniors ★

† Too creepy for preschoolers
Author's Rating ★
How Much Time to Allow 30 minutes

Description and Comments Be warned: this place is a rip-off. The Clink began as a dungeon for disobedient clerics, debtors, and prostitutes. The exhibition presents itself as a re-created medieval dungeon and includes some dismal cell re-creations, diagrams of medieval torture devices, and fact boards on some of the prison's prior inhabitants. Though one might think that the ghoulish subject matter would be of high interest to grade-school kids and teens, most of the information must be read from the mounted displays, something kids seem to grow weary of too quickly.

Touring Tips If you do decide to explore this area, be sure to include a stop at Southwark Cathedral and Shakespeare's Globe Theatre, both within only a few minutes walk of the Clink Exhibition.

Cutty Sark

Type of Attraction Last of the great sailing clipper ships, restored
Location zone 6; Greenwich Pier; Docklands Light Railway: Greenwich
Admission £3.50 for adults; £2.50 for children, students, and seniors; £8.50 for family

Hours Daily, 10 a.m.–5 p.m.; last admission at 4:30 p.m.
Phone (0208) 858-3445
Website www.cuttysark.org.uk
When to Go Early
Special Comments Access for the disabled is limited to the entrance level of the ship, as the ship contains stairways that may prove difficult for some to maneuver.
Overall Appeal by Age Group

Pre-school ★★	Grade School ★★★★	Teens ★★★★
Young Adults ★★★	Over 30 ★★★	Seniors ★★★

Author's Rating ★★★
How Much Time to Allow 45–90 minutes

Description and Comments First launched in 1869, the *Cutty Sark* spent seven years in the China tea trade, but actually became famous as a wool- merchant ship in the years that followed, able to sail from England to Australia in only 72 days. The ship's main hold contains a history of this well-known tea clipper (there's a small gift shop there, too), but it is the lower hold that most impresses with the largest collection of merchant-ship figureheads in Britain. The colorful display was amassed by Captain John Cumbers of Gravesend, better known as Long John Silver. Tours of the ship can be arranged at no additional charge simply by asking. Children love to explore the restored ship's cabins, which give an alarming indication of the difference in class between captain and crew.

Touring Tips From the *Cutty Sark*'s bow you can also see the much smaller *Gipsy Moth IV*, in which Francis Chichester first sailed solo around the world.

Design Museum

Type of Attraction Four floors featuring the design of everyday items
Location zone 5; 28 Shad Thames, Butler's Wharf, SE1; tube: Tower Hill or London Bridge
Admission £5.50 for adults; £4 for children; £15 for a family ticket (2 adults and 2 children)
Hours Monday–Friday, 11:30 a.m.–6 p.m.; Saturday and Sunday, 10:30 a.m.–6 p.m.
Phone (0207) 378-6055
Website www.designmuseum.org
When to Go Anytime
Special Comments Wheelchair/disabled accessible
Overall Appeal by Age Group

Pre-school ★	Grade School ★	Teens ★
Young Adults ★★	Over 30 ★★	Seniors ★★

Author's Rating ★★
How Much Time to Allow 60–90 minutes

Description and Comments This is, in my opinion, a specialist's museum. Many might argue with me on that, saying that all people must have some interest in seeing a variety of interestingly designed chairs or a collection of well-made appliances, but I know many people who would snort at such an assertion.

Be that as it may, the museum is well attended and appreciated by Londoners and tourists, who flock here to look at the mass-produced designs of the twentieth century that we've lived with, perhaps without even noticing what they really looked like. One need only look at the collection of evolving TV sets to see that our household items have their own histories, which are inextricably linked to our domestic memories. Cars, office furniture, radios, and household utensils are all part of a permanent collection, which is added to regularly and shares the modern, bright space with a rota of exhibits, such as those covering the modern movement in Britain and 40 years of the mini-automobile. New ideas and design breakthroughs are highlighted here. The Design Museum was created by restaurant and furniture king Terence Conran, on the south bank of the Thames by Tower Bridge, and the cafe and restaurant have splendid views.

Touring Tips   Unless you are quite specifically interested in design, I wouldn't spend the money on this museum.

Dickens House

Type of Attraction   Literary shrine to the great Charles Dickens
Location   zone 3; 48 Doughty Street, WC1; tube: Russell Square
Admission   £4 for adults; £2 for children; £7 for a family ticket
Hours   Monday–Saturday, 10 a.m.–5 p.m.
Phone   (0207) 405-2127
Website   www.dickensmuseum.com
When to Go   Anytime
Special Comments   The house contains numerous steps and no wheelchair access
Overall Appeal by Age Group

Pre-school ★	Grade School ★	Teens ★
Young Adults ★	Over 30 ★★	Seniors ★★

Author's Rating   ★
How Much Time to Allow   40 minutes

Description and Comments   I am a big Dickens fan, and I was hoping for more from this museum; it is sad that London, the city that Dickens made real for so many readers, doesn't have a better temple to him. Dickens actually only lived in this house for two years, so his spirit certainly does not walk these floors the way you sense Carlyle's does in his house. There are manuscript pages that are exciting to see, lots of wonderful illustrations from his books and portraits of the writer, and these can make it worth the trip. The gift shop sells some fine old and new editions of Dickens and some of his contemporaries.

Touring Tips   Watch the video in the basement first; it's very good.

Freud Museum

Type of Attraction   English home of famous psychoanalyst Sigmund Freud
Location   zone 1; 20 Maresfield Gardens, South Hampstead, NW1; tube: Finchley Road
Admission   £4 for adults; free for children under age 12
Hours   Wednesday–Sunday, noon–5 p.m.
Phone   (0207) 435-2002
Website   www.freud.org.uk
When to Go   Anytime
Special Comments   Limited access for disabled; no lift to upper floor

Overall Appeal by Age Group

Pre-school ★	Grade School ★	Teens ★
Young Adults ★★	Over 30 ★★	Seniors ★★

Author's Rating ★★★

How Much Time to Allow 2 hours

Description and Comments Founder of the basic concepts behind what is known as psychoanalysis, Sigmund Freud brought terms like "free association," "id," and "ego" into general use. The house at 20 Maresfield Gardens, Hampstead, was Freud's home for the last year of his life, after he fled the Nazis in Vienna in 1938. It continued to be home to his daughter, Anna, until her death in 1982, and on her request, it now celebrates the life and work of her father. Inside, each room is carefully decorated as it had been in 1938, and the museum contains all of the possessions from Freud's former home in Vienna in which he had lived for over 47 years. The exhibition's centerpiece is Freud's library and study, including his famous analytic couch and numerous antiquities.

Touring Tips A wonderfully informative video is available for viewing upstairs. The 45-minute film, partially narrated by Anna Freud, contains silent black-and-white footage of Freud at home in Vienna as well as a description of the family's harrowing escape in 1938.

The Globe Theatre

Type of Attraction Magnificently reconstructed Shakespearean theater

Location zone 5; New Globe Walk, Bankside, SE1; tube: Mansion House or London Bridge

Admission The Globe Exhibition and guided tour cost £7.50 for adults, £6 for seniors and students, £5 for children ages 6–16, and are free for children under age 5; a family ticket is £23. Prices for performances run from £5 (standing room) to £27 (tiered seating)

Hours Daily, 10 a.m.–5 p.m.; check with the box office for performance times and dates

Phone (0207) 902-1500

Website www.shakespeares-globe.org

When to Go Anytime

Special Comments The exhibition is easily accessible for individuals in wheelchairs.

Overall Appeal by Age Group

Pre-school ★	Grade School ★★	Teens ★★
Young Adults ★★★	Over 30 ★★★★	Seniors ★★★★

Author's Rating ★★★★

How Much Time to Allow 1–2 hours for museum and tour

Description and Comments Brilliantly reconstructed as an almost exact replica of its former self (and founded by the late American actor and director Sam Wanamaker), The Globe officially opened in 1998 and is a delightful place to learn about the world's greatest playwright, William Shakespeare. In his day, Shakespeare's plays were also performed at The Rose and occasionally The Swan, but it was at The Globe that Shakespeare made his literary name. The tour of the theater, often led by actors and very well done, describes marvelous details about Elizabethan theater and the notorious Bankside area. Performances run in the summer months, and are held outdoors, under natural light, as they used to be. The Globe Exhibition was opened in 2000 and is located beneath the theater. The exhibit contains a fact-filled museum on the life and times of the bard, including some amazing tools used to make the building. It focuses as well on the actors and the audiences who have made Shakespeare's plays so enduring. The complex also contains a cafe, as well as a more upscale restaurant with a view of the river and the City.

Touring Tips   The box office says that the best seats for performances are not seats at all but the standing area in front of the stage, where the "groundlings" stand, the actors may mingle, and the rain may pour (don't worry; they sell rain ponchos).

Guards Museum

Type of Attraction Small museum appealing to military enthusiasts
Location zone 9; Wellington Barracks, Birdcage Walk, SW1; tube: St. James's Park
Admission £2 for adults; free for children; £4 for a family ticket
Hours Daily, 10 a.m.–4 p.m.
Phone (0207) 414-3271
When to Go Anytime
Special Comments Phone ahead to arrange to use lift to bypass steps
Overall Appeal by Age Group

Pre-school ★★	Grade School ★★	Teens ★
Young Adults ★	Over 30 ★	Seniors ★

Author's Rating ★★
How Much Time to Allow 30–40 minutes

Description and Comments   This museum dedicated to the Queen's Guards (some of whom perform the famous "changing of the guard" ceremony, see Changing of the Guard) is sure to warm the hearts of young people interested in the army or of military personnel interested in history. The guards have been around for about 300 years, since the days of King Charles II. The museum is small, but the shop is great for toy soldiers.

Guildhall
(including Clock Museum, Art Gallery, and Library Bookshop)

Type of Attraction Corporate headquarters for the City of London
Location zone 7; Gresham Street; tube: St. Paul's, Mansion House, or Bank
Admission Free
Hours Guildhall: Monday–Friday, 10 a.m.–5 p.m.; Guildhall Clock Museum and Library Bookshop: Monday–Saturday, 10 a.m.–5 p.m., Sunday, noon–4 p.m.
Phone (0207) 332-1456
Website www.cityoflondon.gov.uk
When to Go Anytime
Special Comments Partial access for disabled
Overall Appeal by Age Group

Pre-school ★	Grade School ★★	Teens ★★
Young Adults ★★	Over 30 ★★	Seniors ★★

Author's Rating ★★

How Much Time to Allow 1–1½ hours

Description and Comments Guildhall has witnessed traitors' trials and heroes' welcomes, freedom ceremonies and glittering state occasions. The seat of London's municipal government for over 800 years, it is still used for official ceremonies, state banquets, and the annual installation of the lord mayor of London. Although surrounded by twentieth-century government offices and largely reconstructed after a World War II bombing, the Great Hall still impresses. Its walls are original and date to the fifteenth century. An array of monuments line the hall in honor of national figures from the past 3 centuries, and banners of the 12 Great Livery Companies hang from above. The complex itself also houses over 700 examples of time-keeping in its rather small Clock Museum; its Art Gallery houses the Corporation of London's impressive collection of works depicting London life from the fifteenth century to the present. (The Corporation of London has a website for its extensive Art Gallery collection, entitled "Collage:" www.collage.nhil.com.)

Touring Tips The fifteenth-century crypt and nineteenth-century Old Library are generally off-limits to the public, but it is well worth asking if it might be possible to see them. Guided tours include these spots. Before you leave, be sure to stop and see the splendid interior of St. Lawrence Jewry and other sights in the area, which are described in our "City of London: Through the Centuries" theme walk, on pages 164–166.

HMS Belfast

Type of Attraction Perfectly preserved Royal Navy battle ship from World War II that is permanently moored in the Thames
Location zone 5; Morgans Lane, Tooley Street, SE1; tube: London Bridge
Admission £5 for adults; free for children under age 16
Hours March–October: daily, 10 a.m.–6 p.m.; November–February: daily, 10 a.m.–5 p.m.
Phone (0207) 940-6328
Website www.livesights.com
When to Go Weekdays; call to see if any class trips are scheduled
Special Comments They've made every effort to make most of the ship accessible to disabled, but there are many areas that are impassable for wheelchairs
Overall Appeal by Age Group

Pre-school ★★	Grade School ★★★	Teens ★★★
Young Adults ★★	Over 30 ★★	Seniors ★★

Author's Rating ★★
How Much Time to Allow 90 minutes
Description and Comments A bit of floating history, the HMS *Belfast* was built in 1938 and pressed into service at the D Day landings. Decommissioned in the 1960s, the HMS Belfast is run by the Imperial War Museum. It's a popular tourist attraction, although its appeal is not universal. You can explore all seven levels of this huge battleship and check out the boiler room, the cabins, and the gun turrets, as well as exhibitions and videos about life on board in 1943 and the history of the Royal Navy. Boys of all ages tend to love this ship, and those very interested in World War II may find it an enlightening experience.

Hampton Court Palace

Type of Attraction London's most impressive royal palace
Location zone 12; East Molesey, Surrey, approximately 12 miles outside of central London; tube: Richmond, then R68 bus; British Rail (accessible from Waterloo Station): Hampton Court)
Admission £10.50 for adults; £7 for children ages 5–15; £31.40 for familes; prices include admission to the gardens and maze
Hours March 25–October 27: Monday, 10:15 a.m.–6 p.m. and Tuesday–Sunday, 9:30 a.m.–6 p.m.; October 28–March 24: the palace closes on Monday at 4:15 p.m. and at 4:30 p.m. all other days
Phone (0208) 781-9500
Website www.hrp.org.uk
When to Go Anytime
Special Comments Disabled access, including ramps to the Tudor kitchens, access to some areas of the gardens, lifts to the first floor, and equipped toilets
Overall Appeal by Age Group

Pre-school ★★	Grade School ★★★	Teens ★★★★★
Young Adults ★★★★★	Over 30 ★★★★★	Seniors ★★★★★

Author's Rating ★★★★★
How Much Time to Allow Head out early to give yourself the full day to enjoy Hampton Court and time to arrive back in London for dinner or perhaps a trip to the theater.

Description and Comments One of the nicest things about Hampton Court Palace is its location. If you have been running all over the city of London, deciphering bus schedules and tube maps, a trip outside this fast-paced metropolis is a relaxing treat.

The powerful and influential lord chancellor to Henry VIII, Cardinal Wolsey, built Hampton Court Palace in 1516 and proceeded to live there quite lavishly. In 1528, after Henry inquired about such an extravagant home for a member of the clergy, Cardinal Wolsey offered it to the king. After Wolsey failed to secure from the pope Henry's much-desired annulment from Catherine of Aragon in 1529, Henry accepted his offer, no doubt with a malicious glee. Henry created the enormous Tudor kitchens, and redesigned the chapel. Alterations were also made by the famous architect Christopher Wren, under the direction of William and Mary, and further changes were instigated by Queen Anne. The result allows palace visitors to clearly distinguish some of the most important design styles in England's history.

The palace is organized into six walking tours, and then there are still the gardens and maze in which to wander. With all this to see, your best bet is to decide whether you want to start inside or out. I usually find that after an hour or two inside the vast halls I need get outside for a bit and can then return to more fully enjoy the rest of the palace. Costumed guides offer tours of Henry VIII's apartments, the King's and, in summer, Queen's apartments at no additional charge; this is always a good way to start your visit, as the fascinating story of Hampton Court is immediately brought to life by these experienced historians. If you prefer to head out on your own, audio guides of Henry's apartments and the Tudor kitchens are also available at no additional cost.

Of significant interest in Henry's Great Hall are the hammer-beam ceiling and stunning medieval tapestries. The rather plain hallway leading to the king's chapel is the Haunted Gallery and claims to be the wandering ground for the ghost of Henry's fifth wife, Catherine Howard.

Outside, you have a wide choice of garden styles to match the rooms they surround. The grandest of these is William III's Fountain Garden; on the south side is the Privy Garden. Beyond this are the sunken Pond Gardens and Tudor-style Knot and Herb Gardens, while on the opposite side of the palace can venture into the less manicured Wilderness, with its evergreens and the ever popular maze, originally laid out in 1714.

Touring Tips A sunny day makes Hampton Court's ornate gardens a fantastic picnic spot for families. Alternately, you might head to the Tiltyard Tearoom for an enjoyable light meal, or wander beyond the Lion Gates for a number of cozy pubs, all serving some wonderfully traditional lunchtime fare. Hampton Court is easily reached by train from Waterloo or Wimbledon Stations, but if you have time, the best way to approach the palace is by water. Boat tours up the Thames run in the summer months from Richmond (for a half-hour ride) or Westminster (for a full hour-long excursion). Approaching the palace in this manner affords an unequaled view of the majestic King's Apartments, the magnificently cultivated Privy gardens, and the vast park areas that once served as Henry's private hunting grounds. For river-tour schedules and pricing information call (0207) 930-4721.

Hogarth's House

Type of Attraction The satirist and painter's summer home and engravings
Location zone 12; Hogarth Lane, Great West Road, W4; tube: Turnham Green or British Rail to Chiswick
Admission Free
Hours April–October: Tuesday–Friday, 1–5 p.m., Saturday and Sunday, 1–6 p.m.; November–March: Tuesday–Friday, 1–5 p.m. Closed Monday and the month of January
Phone (0208) 994-6757
When to Go As part of a day in Chiswick (Chiswick House is a short walk away)
Special Comments Disabled accessible
Overall Appeal by Age Group

Pre-school ★	Grade School ★	Teens ★★
Young Adults ★★	Over 30 ★★	Seniors ★★

Author's Rating ★★

How Much Time to Allow 1 hour

Description and Comments If you go to Chiswick House in the morning, you might want to visit Hogarth in the afternoon. It used to be a quiet, country retreat for the brilliant painter and satirist William Hogarth, but is now located on a particularly busy section of the A4 motorway. More than 200 of Hogarth's most famous prints are here, including *Marriage a la Mode*, *A Rake's Progress*, and *A Harlot's Progress*, and it's quite delightful to take your time over them in this setting that the master called home for 15 years, until his death in 1764.

Touring Tips Make this visit part of your trip to Chiswick, and see Chiswick House as well.

Houses of Parliament: House of Lords and House of Commons

Type of Attraction Britain's working chambers of government

Location zone 9; Parliament Square, SW1; tube: Westminster

Admission Free, except for prebooked tours

Hours House of Lords: the public is admitted to the Strangers' Gallery Monday–Wednesday, beginning at 2:30 p.m., Thursday beginning at 3 p.m., and occassionaly on Fridays, beginning at 11 a.m. To the House of Commons, Monday–Wednesday, 2:30 –10:30 p.m., Thursday, 11:30 a.m.–7:30 p.m., and Friday, 9:30 a.m.–3 p.m. Check whether the House is sitting by calling (0207) 219 4272. Question Time (accessible by special prebooked tickets) takes place Monday–Wednesday, 2:30–3:30 p.m., and Thursday, 11:30–12:30 p.m. The Prime Minister answers questions 3–3:30 p.m.

Phone Commons info at (0207) 219-4272; Lords info at (0207) 219 3107

Website www.parliament.uk (go to Index and click on the letter "V" for visits)

When to Go When the Houses are not in recess (they recess at Christmas, at Easter, and from August to the middle of September)

Special Comments Security is very tight. Allow plenty of time to clear security checks. Do not bring food, drinks, mobile phones, or pagers. They will allow you in with a camera as long as it stays in your bag; absolutely no photography is permitted

Overall Appeal by Age Group

Pre-school †	Grade School †	Teens ★★
Young Adults ★★	Over 30 ★★★	Seniors ★★★

† Not appropriate for young children.

Author's Rating ★★

How Much Time to Allow 1–2 hours, depending on how long you'd like to observe the debates (allowing at least 30 minutes to clear security)

Description and Comments The first Parliament was convened in 1254 and consisted of lords, bishops, abbots, knights, and local citizens. Today's Parliament, closely based on its predecessors, includes the sovereign, the House of Lords (which used to be made up of hereditary peerage members, but now must be elected or appointed to their positions) and the House of Commons (members elected from their respective English, Welsh, Scottish, and Northern Irish communities). The current buildings in which they meet, built between 1840 and 1860, have become the most recognized trademarks of London.

Touring Tips Do use the website to plan your visit, because admission policies are currently being updated and the place may be temporarily closed to visitors. Call to get the latest information. If you want to do more than witness debates, consider arranging in advance to receive permits that allow you unchaperoned access as you follow a printed guide through splendidly decorated lobbies, corridors, the grand Westminster Hall, and the two Houses. If the Houses are in recess, tours will be granted Monday–Saturday, 9:15 a.m.–4:30 p.m. When the Houses are in session, tours will be scheduled only for Friday (you can also pay £25 for a personal guide). For tours while the Houses are in session, you must write a few months in advance to: Parliamentary Education Unit, Norman Shaw Boulevard (North), London SW1A 2TT. Be sure to include the exact dates of your visit, the total number in your party (not to exceed 16 people), your home address, and your London address and telephone. Permits will be mailed, so be sure to allow enough time.

If you can't get into the Houses of Parliament for any reason, visit Jewel Tower (zone 9; Abingdon Street, by Westminster Abbey; phone (0207) 222-2219), where you can see, for a small fee, an interactive virtual reality tour of both Houses. It's open 10 a.m.—4 p.m. in winter and 10 a.m.—6 p.m. in summer.

Imperial War Museum

Type of Attraction Highlights twentieth-century British military actions
Location zone 5; Lambeth Road, SE1; tube: Elephant and Castle or Lambeth North
Admission £5.50 for adults; free for children under age 16 and seniors; £13 for a family ticket
Hours Daily, 10 a.m.–6 p.m.
Phone (0207) 416-5320
Website www.iwm.org.uk
When to Go Anytime
Special Comments Limited access for disabled; wheelchairs can be booked by calling (0207) 416-5397
Overall Appeal by Age Group

| Pre-school ★ | Grade School ★ | Teens ★★ |
| Young Adults ★★ | Over 30 ★★ | Seniors ★★ |

Author's Rating ★★
How Much Time to Allow 1 hour

Description and Comments Housed in the famous former lunatic asylum known as Bedlam, the Imperial War Museum is an oddly appropriate present tenant, dedicated to the madness that is twentieth-century war. It is a sobering museum, especially the section on the liberation of Belsen, part of the permanent exhibit on the Holocaust completed in 2000. Overall, it was hard not to be offended by the blithe displays of the awful hardware of destruction: guns, tanks, zeppelins, V2 rockets, bombers. You are given insight into the horror of war by the re-creation of the sights and sounds and smells of the Blitz, a clock counting down the numbers of war deaths in this century, and the nightmare of life in a World War I trench, but then it seems you are invited to appreciate the machinery of it. Perhaps by way of making some definite statement on the side of pacifism, the Imperial War Museum has created a beautiful Peace Garden on its grounds, which was dedicated by the Dalai Lama in May 1999.

Dr. Johnson's House

Type of Attraction Literary attraction in historic house
Location zone 2; 17 Gough Square, EC4; tube: Blackfriars
Admission £4 for adults; £3 for children ages 10–16; free for children under age 10; £9 for families
Hours May—September: Monday–Saturday, 11 a.m.–5 p.m.; October—April: Monday–Saturday, 11 a.m.–5 p.m.
Phone (0207) 353-3745

Website www.drjh.dircon.co.uk
When to Go Anytime
Special Comments No wheelchair access; steep stairs
Overall Appeal by Age Group

Pre-school ★★   Grade School ★★   Teens ★★
Young Adults ★★   Over 30 ★★   Seniors ★★

Author's Rating ★★
How Much Time to Allow 27 minutes for video, 10–15 minutes for the house

Description and Comments I like Samuel Johnson more than the average bloke on the block, but even I wasn't overly impressed by this house, the only surviving domicile of the 17 he lived in. I might have felt differently had the admission been free; however, I do respect and support the fact that this house on prime property has managed to avoid the wrecking ball for 250 years. This alone makes it worth the visit and the price. Dr. Johnson spent 11 years in this house working on his famous dictionary, but the house falls short of providing the kind of atmosphere that makes a literary museum come alive. There aren't a whole lot of artifacts or furniture, although the collection of mezzotints and books on Johnson are impressive. You must watch the video, very well done and interesting, which does make the remarkable Johnson and his biographer, Boswell, come to life. All of the above, however, is subject to change, as the house is undergoing a major renovation.

Kensington Palace State Rooms

Type of Attraction Stately home in the middle of Kensington Gardens
Location zone 13; Kensington Gardens, Broad Walk; tube: Kensington High Street
Admission £8.80 for adults; £6.30 for children ages 5–16; free for children under age 5; £26.80 for families
Hours April through September: daily, 10 a.m.–5 p.m; October through March: daily, 10 a.m.–4 p.m.
Phone (0207) 937-9561
Website www.hrp.org.uk
When to Go Morninsg in summer; anytime in winter
Special Comments There are wheelchair-accessible toilets and a ramp to Orangery, but many steps inside the palace. Upstairs is inaccessible.
Overall Appeal by Age Group

Pre-school ★★   Grade School ★★★   Teens ★★★★
Young Adults ★★★★   Over 30 ★★★★   Seniors ★★★★

Author's Rating ★★★★
How Much Time to Allow 1½ hours

Description and Comments Kensington Palace is the former home of Princess Diana, and the place where Princess Victoria was told that she had become queen. It's not a grandiose palace like Buckingham or Windsor, which makes it in some ways more interesting. It was built in 1605 and sold to King William and Queen Mary in 1689 as a country escape from the noxious fumes of Whitehall, which were aggravating the king's asthma. The monarchs immediately hired Christopher Wren and Nicholas Hawksmoor to improve the house. Queen Anne later added more improvements, such as the Orangery, which was her "summer supper house," and acres of gardens. George I turned

what was essentially a country estate into a palace, and it's fascinating to note the difference between the homey oak-paneled dining room of William and Mary and the over-
the-top decor of William Kent's innovations. George II was the last monarch to make
Kensington Palace a primary residence, as Buckingham Palace became the townhouse of
choice to succeeding kings and queens. King George II and Queen Caroline made extensive additions to the gardens that can be enjoyed today, such as Broad Walk, the Round
Pond, and the Serpentine. In 1841, the gardens were opened to the public, when the
palace became a source of "grace and favour," apartments for offshoots of the royal family, as it remains.

You can see the bedroom in which Princess Victoria lived with her mother, the
duchess of Kent, until she was 18 and made queen. There are some fine examples of furniture and brilliant trompe l'oeil ceiling paintings and murals by William Kent. Two oddities
that must be seen are the wind dial by which King William III could tell how fast his ships
might be approaching, and the massive clock in the Cupola Room that used to play tunes
by Handel, Corelli, and Geminiani, and which, even minus this feature, represents a marvelous marriage of sixteenth-century technology and art.

There is a court-dress exhibition that takes the viewer through the sartorial styles and
often bizarre traditions of being presented at court. On a modern note, there are some
dresses of the present queen that highlight just how distant the glamorous royal past of
Kensington Palace is.

Touring Tips   Make this part of a day in the park. Early birds get the worm here, but it's
also nice to come later in the day and follow up your visit with tea at the Orangery next
door. Be sure to take advantage of the audio tour, as it's very thorough and interesting.

Kenwood House (The Iveagh Bequest)

Type of Attraction World-class art gallery in an elegant Georgian villa
Location zone 1; Hampstead Lane, Hampstead Heath, NW3; tube: Archway or Golders
Green
Admission Free
Hours April to September: daily, 10 a.m.–6 p.m.; October to March: daily, 10 a.m.–4 p.m.
Phone (0208) 348-1286
Website www.english-heritage.org.uk
When to Go Anytime, but preferably on weekdays and in good weather so you can
enjoy the Heath
Special Comments Call (0207) 973-3372 to arrange limited wheelchair access.
Overall Appeal by Age Group

Pre-school ★	Grade School ★★★	Teens ★★★
Young Adults ★★★	Over 30 ★★★	Seniors ★★★

Author's Rating ★★★★
How Much Time to Allow 2 hours in the house, plus time for tea or a walk around the
grounds and on the Heath. It's a good day out.

Description and Comments Kenwood is the most elegant exponent of architects
Robert and James Adams's early Georgian design. It is gorgeous, with Adams and Chip-
pendale furniture and decoration, the stunning masterpieces on the walls, and exceptional
views all year long.

Built in 1700, the house changed hands several times, until brewery magnate Edward Guinness, earl of Iveagh, purchased it to display his extensive collection of seventeenth-century Dutch and Flemish and late eighteenth-century British paintings, including works by Sir Joshua Reynolds, George Romney, J. M. W. Turner, Gainsborough, and Raeburn. There are a number of absolutely unmissable old masterpieces here, such as Rembrandt's *Self Portrait* and Vermeer's *The Guitar Player*. As an art gallery, it is right up there in the top ten of London. A number of somewhat quirky displays of miniature portraits, jewelry, ceramics, and 1,300 Georgian shoe buckles have also been donated by a variety of collectors.

Touring Tips   Combine this visit with a trip to Hampstead Village and the Heath. If you're visiting in the summer, combine it with the weekend concerts.

Lambeth Palace

Type of Attraction   Thirteenth-century home of archbishop of Canterbury
Location   zone 5; Lambeth Palace Road; bus number 3 or number 159, both via Whitehall and Westminster, would drop you just near the palace. Lambeth North tube station is a bit of a walk.
Admission   £6.50 per person
Hours   Usually midafternoons on Wednesday and Thursday only
Phone   (0207) 898-1200
When to Go   By prearranged tour only (see details below)
Special Comments   Requests for permission to see the palace must be made in writing to: Events Administrator, Lambeth Palace, Lambeth Palace Road, London SE1 7JU. Expect to book up to 18 months in advance!
Overall Appeal by Age Group

Pre-school †	Grade School ★	Teens ★
Young Adults ★★★	Over 30 ★★★	Seniors ★★★★

† Not appropriate for preschoolers
Author's Rating   ★★★
How Much Time to Allow   1½ hours

Description and Comments   A medieval gem on the south side of the Thames, Lambeth Palace has been the home to the archbishop of Canterbury for seven centuries. The palace is well off the beaten path of most tourist routes, due to the fact that it is not open to the public as a tourist site. However, if you are of a mind to see something that even most of the locals haven't, you should arrange to visit.

The buildings date back to the thirteenth century, and its halls have echoed the footsteps of many notable Britons. Among them are Thomas More and Oliver Cromwell. The palace's most impressive building is the early seventeenth-century library, with its exceptional hammer-beam roof, where you are surrounded by shelf after shelf of ancient books and illuminated manuscripts, some dating back to the ninth century. Also worth seeing are the ancient chapel and crypt.

Touring Tips   The palace allows visits at select times to prearranged groups only. You can request permission to join a group already booked for a tour, assuming that the group has not reached its limit of 30 people. Requests should be made in writing as much as 18 months in advance! Indicate the dates you will be in London and to ensure a speedy reply, and enclose a self-addressed envelope (airmail stamped, if necessary). Tours are given by residents of the palace and last about 70 minutes.

Leighton House Museum and Art Gallery

Type of Attraction House of pre-Raphaelite painter Lord Frederick Leighton
Location zone 13; 12 Holland Park Road; tube: High Street Kensington, then bus 9, 10, 27, 33, or 49 to Odeon Cinema, then walk through Holland Park
Admission Free; £3 for audio tour
Hours Monday–Saturday, 11 a.m.–5:30 p.m.; closed Tuesday
Phone (0207) 602-3316
Website www.rbkc.gov.uk/leightonhousemuseum
When to Go Anytime
Special Comments Not wheelchair accessible; many steps to top floor
Overall Appeal by Age Group

Pre-school ★	Grade School ★	Teens ★★
Young Adults ★★	Over 30 ★★	Seniors ★★

Author's Rating ★★★
How Much Time to Allow 30 minutes

Description and Comments If you are a true lover of the pre-Raphaelites (Edward Burne-Jones, John Millais, of course Frederick Leighton, and others) this is a must see. Lord Leighton, whose magnificent painted hallway can be seen in the Victoria & Albert Museum, dedicated his home as "a private palace devoted to art." The main attraction is the Arab Hall, which is a Victorian fantasy of the Middle East, with Isniuk tiles, elaborately carved and gilded woodwork, and the mosaic frieze. There is a wonderful sunken fountain in the middle of the room, which furthers the impression of a courtyard straight out of the pages of *The Arabian Nights*. The top floor is Leighton's old studio, and the huge windows, skylights, and dome are clearly the heart's desire of any nineteenth-century painter. There's a good collection of Victorian paintings on the lower floor, including Leighton's *Roman Mother;* upstairs you can see temporary exhibits of a widely varied nature. The house is sadly lacking in furniture and knick-knacks, and despite the stuffed peacock in the hall, one wishes for more of the decorative exuberance that must have obtained when Lord Leighton lived here.

Touring Tips Combine this with a trip to Holland Park and the Linley Sambourne House.

Linley Sambourne House

Type of Attraction Perfectly preserved home of Victorian punch cartoonist
Location zone 14; 18 Stafford Terrace, Kensington, W8; tube: High Street Kensington
Admission £3 for adults; £1.50 for children
Hours March 1–October 31: Wednesday, 10 a.m.–4 p.m. and Sunday, 2 p.m.–5 p.m. Closed November 1–February 28.
Phone (0207) 602-3316
Website www.rbkc.gov.uk/linleysambournehouse
When to Go Anytime it's open

Special Comments Lots of stairs and no wheelchair access. Closed until 2002 for renovations. Call ahead.

Overall Appeal by Age Group

Pre-school ★	Grade School ★★	Teens ★★
Young Adults ★★★	Over 30 ★★★	Seniors ★★★

Author's Rating ★★★

How Much Time to Allow 1 hour

Description and Comments This place is a veritable time machine, plunking one smack down in the middle of the late Victorian\early Edwardian era, with the sumptuous clutter that incited the backlash of modernism. William Morris designs adorn both walls and floors, and there are a few stained-glass windows to love. A predominant thought on seeing the vast collection of clocks, vases, gim-cracks, and knickknacks was of pity for the poor servant in charge of dusting. The immense aesthetic weight of all the pretty possessions can be a bit tiring, but it is an amazing piece of preservation.

Touring Tips Combine with a trip to Holland Park and/or to the Frederick Leighton House.

London Aquarium

Type of Attraction Wonderland of fish on the bank of the Thames

Location zone 5; County Hall, Riverside Building, Westminster Bridge Road, SE1; tube: Westminster or Waterloo

Admission £8.75 for adults; £5.25 for children; free for children under age 3; £25 for families

Hours Daily, 10 a.m.–6 p.m.(last entry at 5 p.m.); bank holidays, 10 a.m.–6:30 p.m.

Phone (0207) 967-8000

Website www.londonaquarium.co.uk

When to Go Avoid weekends and school holidays if possible; go early

Special Comments Fully accessible for disabled persons. To avoid steps, go around building to Belvedere Road to reach entrance. Picnic area available.

Overall Appeal by Age Group

Pre-school ★★★★	Grade School ★★★★	Teens ★★★
Young Adults ★★★	Over 30 ★★★	Seniors ★★★

Author's Rating ★★★★

How Much Time to Allow 2 hours

Description and Comments In a most unlikely conversion, a portion of London's County Hall (also the former home of the Greater London Council) became three dimly lit and atmospheric floors of enormous tanks filled with sea life and freshwater fish of every kind. The Atlantic tank holds 800,000 liters of water and tons of sharks, eels, and stingrays. It's most impressive, although I felt badly for the magnificent sharks whose snouts have been damaged by hitting the glass walls. There's a petting pool for kids to stroke manta rays, who actually seem to invite these caresses. In the Pacific tank, even bigger than the Atlantic, reside more sharks, rays, groupers, and smaller fish. The piranha tank is interesting, especially at dinner time, when you get to see what a real-life feeding frenzy looks like (call ahead to find out feeding times for various fish).

This is not the most amazing aquarium in the world by a long shot, and if you have access to a good one where you live, you might as well leave this off your list, but it has been proven to me time and again that, when it comes to taming small children, fish take the cake.

Touring Tips There's a McDonald's next door, with its own entrance to the aquarium. There's also a wonderful gift shop for every budget.

London Dungeon

Type of Attraction Dummy-driven yuck-fest with historical pretenses
Location zone 5; 28–34 Tooley Street, SE1; tube: London Bridge
Admission £10.95 for adults; £6.95 for children
Hours March–September: daily, 10 a.m.–8 p.m.; October–February: daily, 10:30 a.m.—5 p.m.
Phone (0207) 403-7221
Website www.thedungeons.com
When to Go Weekdays as soon as it opens; it gets pretty crowded midday
Special Comments Wheelchair access; don't bring small children
Overall Appeal by Age Group

Pre-school †	Grade School ★	Teens ★★★★
Young Adults ★★	Over 30 ★★	Seniors ★

† Too scary for pre-schoolers
Author's Rating ★
How Much Time to Allow 90 minutes

Description and Comments I am the first one to line up for the weird and horrible—the only thing I didn't yawn over at Madame Tussaud's was the Chamber of Horrors—but this place hit me the wrong way. The relentless gore without context was disturbing, and the "Jack the Ripper Experience" was just plain offensive. The hordes of French teenage boys who were there during my visit seemed to find it hilarious. They cheered wildly when we saw a dummy guillotined. There's a little boat ride that takes you on a trip to Traitor's Gate, which at least gets you off your feet for a bit. The best part was the gift shop, where I picked up a life-size skull candle and some fun Halloween stuff.

Touring Tips Drop off the teens here and go wait for them in the Bella Pasta across the street, or take a look at nearby Southwark Cathedral while the youngsters do their thing.

London Transport Museum

Type of Attraction A fun, interactive museum of trams, buses, and trains of old and new London
Location zone 7; 39 Wellington Street, off Covent Garden Piazza, WC2; tube: Covent Garden, Leicester Square
Admission £5.95 for adults; free for children
Hours Daily, 10 a.m.–6pm; opens at 11 a.m. on Friday
Phone (0207) 379-6344
Website www.ltmuseum.co.uk
When to Go Anytime

Special Comments Wheelchair and stroller access; cafe and gift shop

Overall Appeal by Age Group

Pre-school ★★★★	Grade School ★★★★	Teens ★★★
Young Adults ★★★	Over 30 ★★★	Seniors ★★★

Author's Rating ★★★★

How Much Time to Allow I hour

Description and Comments This is one of the best venues for kids in London, and adults love it, too. Although many might yawn at the idea of a museum dedicated to that most prosaic feature of urban life, public transportation, this museum is so cleverly and earnestly organized that it's impossible not to get swept up in the fun of it. From horse-drawn stagecoaches and omnibuses that you can climb on, to buses that you can pretend to drive and underground switches you can pretend to throw, this is an interactive museum that most kids will love. You're given a ticket to be stamped at numbered sites until you've filled up your card and seen all there is to see. There are videos of old-time trams and buses and a wonderful short film on the touching last trip of the last tram in London, with everyone singing "Auld Lang Syne." There's so much for adults to learn here, too, such as why the fares on buses and trains in London have to be so complicated and that 40,000 people took the first underground line on its first day. (Alas, we don't find out why you can wait forever for your bus and then three will come all at once).

The gift shop has a huge selection of great postcards and underground posters and a wealth of books about London's transport. You can get just about anything here with the London Underground map on it, even slippers.

Touring Tips Buy the museum guide if you have children under age 12—there's a fun pull-out section with games and educational pursuits in it. Combine this trip with a visit to Covent Garden, also fun for the kids, especially on weekends. Call or visit their website to check for lectures, tours, films, and family activities.

London Zoo

Type of Attraction Modernized old zoo set at the edge of Regent's Park

Location zone 15; Regent's Park; tube: Camden Town

Admission £10 for adults; £7 for children ages 3–15; £28 for a family ticket

Hours March–September: Monday–Saturday, 10 a.m.–5:30 p.m.; October–February: 10 a.m.–4 p.m.; open until 6 p.m. on Sunday

Phone (0207) 722-3333

Website www.zsl.org

When to Go When it's warm and not raining

Special Comments Wheelchair access

Overall Appeal by Age Group

Pre-school ★★★★	Grade School ★★★★	Teens ★★★
Young Adults ★★★	Over 30 ★★★	Seniors ★★★

Author's Rating ★★★

How Much Time to Allow 2 hours

Description and Comments The London Zoo is supposedly in some financial trouble, as there are no significant subsidies from the government to help it operate. It is trying its best, and the education that it provides on endangered species is invaluable, as is the experience of seeing Asian lions, lemurs, and rhinos in the flesh; it makes the possible loss of these animals to extinction all the more horrific. The zoo has tried hard to be the best it can be and has created a small but full environment of hooved, winged, and four-legged friends, but it may have already seen its day. Of course this might just be true for all zoos that have been unable to completely conform to the new ideas of keeping animals in captivity in a humane way—a concept that could be considered a contradiction in terms.

Opened in 1828, the zoo has clearly evolved from the old animals-in- cages standard, but it can't be all things to all animals, as is clear from the Bactrian camel, used to the torrid aridity of the Gobi Desert, standing listlessly in the chilly, damp air of London or from the gorilla rocking back and forth, giving his viewers reproachful looks. On a brighter note, the reptile house is magnificent, with cobras, pythons, and even alligators in nicely designed environments, plus a teaching center with snake skins and things made from the hides of unfortunate animals. The aquarium is also quite comprehensive and well housed. There are a lot of monkeys and a petting zoo for children. The shop is fantastic and will fulfill all your animal-paraphernalia needs, with books, stuffed animals, knick-knacks, gimcracks, and geegaws.

Madame Tussaud's Waxworks and the London Planetarium

Type of Attraction World-famous display of wax dummies, chosen most arbitrarily

Location zone 14; Marylebone Road, NW1; tube: Baker Street

Admission £12 for adults; £8.50 for children under age 16; £9.50 for seniors; free for children age 4 and under. Combination tickets to waxworks and London Planetarium: £14.45 for adults; £10 for children under age 16; £11.30 for seniors

Hours Daily, 10 a.m.–5:30 p.m. Opens at 9:30 a.m. on weekends, bank holidays, and summer weekdays

Phone (0870) 400-3000 to book tickets in advance and avoid the queue (for £1 extra on each ticket) or (0207) 935-6861

Website www.madame-tussauds.com

When to Go They advise that you go in the afternoon, but there always seems to be a line there, no matter what the time, even a half hour before it opens. Go a day before or book over the phone and get a ticket so you can get in the prepaid line. Forget the weekends.

Special Comments Limited wheelchair access: call in advance (0207) 935-6861

Overall Appeal by Age Group

Pre-school ★★	Grade School ★★★	Teens ★★★
Young Adults ★★★	Over 30 ★★★	Seniors ★★★

Author's Rating ★★

How Much Time to Allow 1 hour

Description and Comments I am not the one to talk to about Madame Tussaud's, because I found it ridiculous—I might have been more pleased with it if it were not for the lines, the price, and the milling hordes inside. I also think that it may have been more interesting in the days before film, when one really didn't know what the personages of the day looked like. However, I have many friends who loved it, so I decided to try to give it the benefit of the doubt. It's certainly one of London's most visited attractions. As you walk in you see a "garden party" presided over by mostly British celebs, and not the big ones. I defy any American to tell me who Chris Evans or Lenny Henry are (and they're the A-list celebs here). However, there was also Arnold Schwarzenegger, Dudley Moore, and some sports figures who may ring a bell. I liked the section on the history of the wax works, where you got to see the unfortunates who'd been decommissioned and decapitated and ended up with their heads on the shelf: Liza Minelli, Nikita Krushchev, Sammy Davis Jr., and W. C. Fields were but a few. The making of these wax works is fascinating. We got to see how Jerry Hall came to be formed, with video and all; interestingly, there's no sign of her ex anywhere—how gratifying that must be for her. It seemed to me that the 1970s were a particularly bad time for making dummies (see the movie stars and American presidents) but the 1990s proved to be something of a golden age. Some of the newer dummies are frighteningly real, down to the gleam in the eye. One can't say for sure about the verisimilitude of the old ones, like Voltaire, but I must say that Princess Diana's is a pretty good imitation. I loved the surreal display of the duke of Wellington staring down at the wax effigy of his old nemesis, Napoleon, an event that actually transpired.

There is a pretty silly ride in a miniature black taxi that rushes you through the history of London (from Elizabeth I till now) at a breakneck pace. All you can do is giggle as you fly along. Things improved (for me anyway) in the Chamber of Horrors, over which is the Dante inscription, "All Hope Abandon, Ye Who Enter Here!"—a sentiment perhaps more fitting for the end of the queue outside. It is a sobering and disturbing exhibit, which manages to even approximate the smell of unwashed bodies and despair (also reminiscent of the queue outside) in the prison section. But of all the horrors, murderers, and bloodiness, there is surely nothing more chilling than the display of Madame Tussaud herself, lantern held aloft, searching a mountain of decapitated bodies for the head of her former employer, Marie Antoinette. I think they should dump the celebrities and make the museum all about the madame: the young Marie Grosholtz Tussaud started out in the late 1700s assisting a doctor who specialized in making wax anatomy forms. Her talent for portraiture was so extraordinary that she was hired to teach art to the children of the doomed king and queen of France. When the French Revolution came, she was imprisoned (rooming with the future Josephine Bonaparte) and marked for the guillotine. Marie was saved by those who thought to have her make death masks of the aristocrats, many of whom she had known. She spent many a night poking through the bloody corpses for the heads she was commissioned to work on. What a way to make a living.

In an interesting juxtaposition, you are moved from the stomach-turning Chamber of Horrors straight into the cafe. The gift shop is big, but there's not much to buy, even for a gift-shop aficionado like myself.

Touring Tips   As I said, book a ticket in advance by phone or in person, so that you can avoid the lines, or at least minimize waiting time.

Millennium Bridge

Type of Attraction A footbridge across the Thames linking the Tate Modern with St. Paul's Cathedral

Location zones 3 & 5; Upper Thames Street on north bank of river; Bankside on south side of river; tube: Mansion on north, London Bridge on south

Admission Free

Hours 24/7
Phone London Tourist Board for info: (0207) 932 2000
Website www.londontouristboard.com
When to Go Anytime, but sunny days are best
Special Comments Wheelchair accessible
Overall Appeal by Age Group

Pre-school ★★★	Grade School ★★★★	Teens ★★★
Young Adults ★★★	Over 30 ★★★	Seniors ★★★

Author's Rating ★★★
How Much Time to Allow Fifteen minutes to cross it very slowly

Description and Comments   At press time, the Millennium Bridge had not yet been re-opened for foot traffic. It opened to great fanfare in 2000, but when the people spilled over its shimmering expanse, it started swaying dangerously, throwing some people to the ground, and it had to be closed for re-engineering. It's the first new bridge to be built over the Thames since 1894, and it's closed to motor vehicles. The original cost of £16 million keeps going up as the engineers and architects try to address its instability. It does seem that some of these grandiose millennium plans (the under-visited dome and the New Year's River of Fire fireworks, as well as the poor bridge) are just plain cursed. It was amusing to watch the architect blame the engineers and the engineers blame the architect when the bridge started swinging to and fro. Aesthetically, it certainly is pleasing, forming what architect Lord Norman Foster envisioned as a "blade of light," but until we can actually cross it without being tossed into the Thames, we must reserve judgement. It will be convenient for visitors and residents alike, who have always had to choke on traffic fumes when crossing the Thames.

Touring Tips   It will be a great way to cover the City and Southwark in one day.

Millennium Dome

The Millenim Dome exhibition has come and gone, and the fate of the bulbous growth has yet to be determined—maybe sports arena, maybe visitor's center or technology park; we shall see.

The Monument

Type of Attraction Tower commemorating the Great Fire of 1666
Location zone 3; Monument Street, EC3; tube: Monument
Admission £1.50 for adults; 50p for children under age 16
Hours Daily, 10 a.m.–6 p.m. (last admission at 5:40 p.m.)
Phone (0207) 626-2717
When to Go In summer, between 10 and 11:30 a.m. or between 4 and 5 p.m.; anytime during winter
Special Comments Pass on this if you are: a preschooler, out of shape, infirm in any way, already tired, or afraid of heights and close quarters.
Overall Appeal by Age Group

Pre-school —	Grade School ★★	Teens ★★★
Young Adults ★★★★	Over 30 ★★★	Seniors *Depends*

Author's Rating ★★★★

How Much Time to Allow 20 minutes

Description and Comments The Monument, at 202-feet high, was once as visible as St. Paul's Dome, which was certainly no coincidence, as Christopher Wren designed both. It was built to commemorate the Great Fire of 1666 that was actually responsible for making Wren, King Charles II's chief surveyor, one of London's most prolific architects. If laid down on its side, the Monument would reach directly to the spot on Pudding Lane where the fire started. It also has a precise linear relationship to St. Paul's, no doubt a touch that Wren relished.

The 311 steps to the top take about 5 minutes to walk, though it seems much longer. The stairs are pie shaped, which makes passing on them a little delicate. There is no stated etiquette for who takes which part of the steps as the climbers and descendants squeeze by each other, but the guard assured me that good manners and awareness are all that's necessary to negotiate the pass. I went on a rainy day when only a few hardy souls were to be seen, and I had no problem with passing the few that I did. There are three or four window seats on which to take a little breather while ascending. The view is quite fine—spectacular in fact—and the best possible place from which to see Tower Bridge. Sadly, the views of the Tower of London and the whole of St. Paul's have been severely compromised by newer buildings. I was assured by a taxi driver that the view used to be much more amazing. He also told me that his four-year-old son was completely freaked out by the height. Look down the stairwell when you get to the top—it's like an Escher drawing or something out of Alfred Hitchcock's *Vertigo*.

Touring Tips Bring a camera, and don't forget to pick up your certificate as you leave, commending you on your climb.

Museum of London

Type of Attraction Museum covering thousands of years of London history
Location zone 3; London Wall and Aldersgate; tube: St. Paul's or Barbican
Admission £5 for adults; free for children under age 16; tickets valid for re-admission for one year
Hours Monday–Saturday, 10 a.m.–5:50 p.m., Sunday, noon–5:50 p.m.
Phone (0207) 600-3699 or 600-0870
Website www.museumoflondon.org.uk
When to Go Anytime, although you may be navigating around large groups of school-children if you go to early on weekdays while school is in session; after 2:30 p.m., they're gone.
Special Comments Good handicap accessibility with a number of ramps and lifts for all floors.
Overall Appeal by Age Group

Pre-school ★★	Grade School ★★★★	Teens ★★★★
Young Adults ★★★★	Over 30 ★★★★	Seniors ★★★★

Author's Rating ★★★★
How Much Time to Allow 2–3 hours

Description and Comments The Museum of London tells the story of London from its first settlers back in 4,000 B.C. to the present, using a variety of eye-catching displays and fascinating reconstructions. Its chronologically themed tour route allows visitors to explore more closely the time periods each finds most intriguing. This museum is kid friendly, with some interactive or tactile displays. A few not-to-be-missed exhibits include a large section of London's fourth-century town wall, located outside but incorporated into the museum's Roman London exhibition through a window overlook, the 1757 gilded Lord Mayor's Coach, and re-created nineteenth-century street scenes and shops.

There are exhibits here that can be quite fascinating—a recent one had to do with Londoners' bodies over the centuries and displayed skeletons, corsets, and bones ravaged by such diseases as rickets and syphilis. It is a very well-presented museum, and it manages to make London's history feel quite intimate. There's a real cell from Newgate Prison that is perfectly chilling, and the Victorian shops give one the strangest sense of déjà-vu. The displays about the years of the Blitz are riveting. If you are even slightly interested in London's history, this museum is a must see; if you're not, you will be after a visit. The gift shop has a huge assortment of books on London and English history for all ages. There's a good cafe, too.

Touring Tips   For an introduction to many of the exhibitions and information on current exhibits check out the museum's website. Also, call ahead to find out how many schools are booked to visit the day of your visit—if it's a lot, come after 2:30 p.m.

National Gallery

Type of Attraction Splendid art gallery of 700 years of European painting
Location zone 7; Trafalgar Square, WC2; tube: Leicester Square or Charing Cross
Admission Free, though there is a charge for special exhibits
Hours Daily, 10 a.m.–6 p.m.; late view, Wednesday till 9 p.m.
Phone (0207) 839-3321
Website www.nationalgallery.org.uk
When to Go Anytime, but avoid major exhibits on weekends
Special Comments Wheelchair accessible
Overall Appeal by Age Group

Pre-school ★	Grade School ★★★	Teens ★★★
Young Adults ★★★★★	Over 30 ★★★★★	Seniors ★★★★★

Author's Rating ★★★★★
How Much Time to Allow As much as you can physically handle

Description and Comments   This is one of those amazing art museums in which you see the original of some utterly familiar image—Holbein's The *Ambassadors*, Van Gogh's *Sunflowers*, or Monet's *Water Lily Pond*—practically every time you turn around. It is the repository of about 2,300 works from 700 years of European art; you can spend hours gazing at paintings by Titian, Rembrandt, Carravagio, Vermeer, Velazquez, Michelangelo, Da Vinci, Van Eyck, and other old masters too numerous to mention. As if that weren't enough, the East Wing is filled with Impressionists, featuring some 50 paintings on a sort of permanent loan from the Tate Gallery. You'll see Seurat, Pissarro, Gauguin, Degas, Corot, and others. The collection is laid out quite methodically, and excellent inscriptions accompany each painting. The special exhibits are always worth the fee, and do get yourself a headset to listen to the tour.

The National Gallery was founded in 1824 under King George IV, when the government purchased 38 important paintings—from artists such as Raphael, Van Dyck, and Rembrandt—from the estate of John Julius Angerstein. The building was commissioned with a few strange requirements, such as the cupola crowning the front portico, initially ridiculed as a mustard pot, with the two bell towers on either side looking like pepper shakers. The architect, William Wilkens, was also asked to use a portion of a former royal palace in his design, so the slightly ungainly appearance may be due to these requests. Built on the site of the old King's Mews.

The new Sainsbury's Wing houses the oldest paintings, dating from 1260 to 1510. Don't miss Jan Van Eyck's *Arnolfini Marriage* in Room 56, and look for the artist reflected in the mirror. The West Wing has paintings dating from 1510 to 1600, including Tintoretto's *St. George and the Dragon*. The North Wing (paintings from 1600 to 1700) has dedicated Room 27 to Rembrandt and includes other seventeenth-century geniuses whose paintings have an almost supernatural power that no reproduction can capture. The East Wing takes us from 1700 up to 1920, with Canaletto and Turner's land- and seascapes giving way to the English portraits and social scenes of Gainsborough, Reynolds, and the prodigious Hogarth, whose series *Marriage à la Mode* can be seen here. Rooms 43–45 are always crowded with Impressionism fans looking at Rousseau's *Tropical Storm with Tiger,* Renoir's *Umbrellas,* Van Gogh's *Chair,* and so many more. Picasso is represented in Room 46, though there are no really major items here, except for *Minotauromachia.*

There's a Pret a Manger in the basement for excellent sandwiches and salads, and in the Sainsbury Wing is a more upscale restaurant serving decent food. The gift shops, one big and one little, are filled with the most wonderful collection of books, postcards, and calendars, and must be visted.

Touring Tips   Take advantage of the lectures and recorded tours available here; they are great aids. There is also a computer in the Micro Gallery, where you can look up and print out information about the art and artists.

National Maritime Museum and Queen's House (see also profile for Royal Observatory)

Type of Attraction   Largest maritime museum in the world
Location   zone 6; Romney Road, Greenwich (Docklands Light Railway: Greenwich)
Admission   Prices quoted include combined entrance to Maritime Museum, Queen's House, and Royal Greenwich Observatory (profiled separately): £10.50 for adults; £8.40 for seniors and students; free for children age 5–16; add £1.50 for combination ticket to include the *Cutty Sark*
Hours   Daily 10 a.m.–5 p.m.
Phone   (0208) 312-6565
Website   www.nmm.ac.uk
When to Go   Anytime on weekdays; early in the day on weekends
Special Comments   Fully accessible with lifts for disabled, touch talks for visually impaired, and sign-interpreted talks. Call for details.
Overall Appeal by Age Group

Pre-school ★★★	Grade School ★★★★	Teens ★★★
Young Adults ★★★★	Over 30 ★★★★	Seniors ★★★★

Author's Rating ★★★★
How Much Time to Allow   2–3 hours for the museum and 1–2 hours for Queen's House Millennium Exhibition

Description and Comments   The National Maritime Museum was restructured and revitalized just in time for the new millennium. Its new galleries include lots of interactive displays exploring the impact of the oceans on our daily lives, as well as our destructive impact on the seas. Exhibitions include the re-creations of steerage and first-class cabins and deck sections from an oceanliner, thousands of ship models, hundreds of navigational instruments, and galleries devoted to the history of British naval conquests and accomplishment. Of particular interest to adults is the elaborate Horatio Nelson exhibition, which pays homage to the famous admiral who defeated Napoleon at the Battle of Trafalgar. Kids, however, will have to be dragged out of the All-Hands Gallery, a fascinating interactive collection of exhibits, tools, and experiments of nautical principles. The fun includes raising and lowering signal flags, working a crane to load a ship's cargo, or attempting some deep-sea engineering.

The Queen's House, adjacent to the museum, has undergone major refurbishment and presents a beautiful architectural triumph of seventeenth-century architect Indigo Jones. The Queen's House is now a venue for the appreciatoin of maritime-related art work, with exhibits regularly mounted. The interior of the house has been restored to the days of Charles II, and the Royal Apartments on the upper floor are especially dazzling.

Touring Tips   The museum offers a wide range of children's educational workshops and activities, many free of charge. There are Pirate Workshops, the Crowsnest Club for those under age six, and Shipmates for those age seven and older. For details and a full schedule of planned events call (0208) 312-6608, or write the National Maritime Museum, Greenwich, London SE10 9NF.

The National Portrait Gallery

Type of Attraction   Collection of the most famous faces in British history
Location   zone 7; 2 St. Martin's Place, W2; adjacent to the National Gallery; tube: Leicester Square or Charing Cross
Admission   Free (except for special exhibitions)
Hours   Monday–Wednesday and Saturday–Sunday, 10 a.m.–6 p.m.; Thursday and Friday 10 a.m.–9 p.m.
Phone   (0207) 306-0055
Website   www.npg.org.uk
When to Go   Anytime
Special Comments   Very accessible to disabled individuals
Overall Appeal by Age Group

Pre-school ★	Grade School ★★	Teens ★★★★
Young Adults ★★★★	Over 30 ★★★★	Seniors ★★★★

Author's Rating   ★★★★★
How Much Time to Allow   2–3 hours

Description and Comments   Of all the museums that London has to offer, the National Portrait Gallery holds particular appeal. First of all, it's free and in the middle of a very interesting area. It's across the street from St. Martin-in-the-Fields Church, and sitting at the right-hand side of the National Gallery, just off Trafalgar Square. It's quite manageable in a couple of hours, unlike the eight miles of the Victoria and Albert or the grand halls of the National Gallery. Its size allows for relaxed browsing without the feeling that you must rush or you won't see everything. The NPG gives the casual student of England a direct line to its history through the faces of its most interesting and important people.

An escalator takes you to the top, where there is displayed a historical who's-who of England that includes the lean faces of the early medieval kings; the Tudors, with Holbein's imagery of Henry VIII (and his many wives); the Stuarts in the seventeenth century; the nineteenth-century Victorians; and, finally, portraits and photos of the current royal family. Andy Warhol's 4x4 image of Queen Elizabeth II is a bit of a lark, while the famous portraits and photos of Diana, Princess of Wales, with her death date below them, are really quite poignant.

As you take this visual voyage through the ages, notice the changing styles of portraiture and what kinds of people each age deemed worthy of portraiture. You will see people from various disciplines—science, literature, politics, art, and entertainment—whose contributions to English life reached far beyond this small island. With the help of the NPG sound guides, the amount of history you absorb will change how you perceive London's most famous sights. In 2000, a refurbishment added to the museum's appeal, with the escalator replacing the stairs and lifts, a new wing and extension giving the collection new lustre, and a good restaurant on the top floor offering glorious views over Trafalgar Square and beyond.

Touring Tips   In addition to the more pricey roof restaurant, there is also the Portrait Cafe in the basement. Combine your visit with a trip to the National Gallery next door.

Natural History Museum

Type of Attraction   Exhibits on the history of the natural world
Location   zone 11; Cromwell Road, South Kensington, SW7; tube: South Kensington
Admission   £9 for adults; free for children up to 17 years of age; free to all between 4:30 p.m. and 5:50 p.m. Monday–Friday, and after 5 p.m. on weekends
Hours   Monday–Saturday, 10 a.m.–5:50 p.m.; Sunday 11 a.m.–5:50 p.m.
Phone   (0207) 938-9123
Website   www.nhm.ac.uk
When to Go   Anytime during the weekdays, although watch out for lines of buses along Cromwell Road, which indicate hordes of schoolkids; weekends can be quite crowded, so go early
Special Comments   Complete disabled access
Overall Appeal by Age Group

| Pre-school ★★★ | Grade School ★★★★ | Teens ★★★ |
| Young Adults ★★★ | Over 30 ★★★ | Seniors ★★★ |

Author's Rating ★★★
How Much Time to Allow 2 hours or more

Description and Comments   As part of the South Kensington cultural revolution of the nineteenth century, the Natural History Museum was formed by the British Library's collections of Sir Hans Sloane, which were divvied up and sent to South Ken in the 1860s. It's a grand old institution, housed in a majestic building that, in itself, makes the visit worthwhile. Notice the animal statues on the outside, and the terra-cotta monkeys and other beasts climbing on stone vines in the lobby. It has all the hallmarks of a gothic cathedral, an impression that architect Alfred Waterhouse intended, to inspire the proper reverence for nature. It is a huge place, full of many surprises and some really fine examples of educational curating, such as the Ecology Gallery, in which you walk through a rain forest. It has plenty of interactive, permanent displays and temporary exhibits, some of which have been very good, such as the one on human biology. The newly remodeled Earth Galleries (entrance on Exhibition Road) are entered via a long escalator that goes through a model of the earth and features a re-creation of a convenience store in the Kobe earthquake. The Earth Galleries are full of see-and-touch educational exhibits, which is fine with kids, but perhaps not so wondrous for adults. I am much more impressed with some of the older artifacts: dioramas of exotic animals, including the extinct dodo bird, and cabinets full of butterflies, all the bounty brought back from the far-flung reaches of the empire, much of which is utterly irreplaceable and of great scientific importance. The dinosaur exhibit is quite good, and of interest to old and young alike. It is set out in such a way that one follows along paths and climbs up stairs, which keeps the kids active and happy, while the parents can take the time to read the information posted there. The gift shops are excellent for children's educational toys and books, as well as geological booty.

Touring Tips   Be sure to look at the entire front of the building on Cromwell Road: in a witty reflection of the statues of artists that adorn the front of the neighboring Victoria and Albert Museum, the Natural History Museum has statues of animals on its facade. If the line at the Cromwell Road entrance is long, enter at the Earth Galleries on Exhibition Road.

Old Bailey

Type of Attraction   London's central criminal courts
Location   zone 3; Old Bailey Street, EC4; tube: St. Paul's
Admission   Free; children under age 14 not admitted
Hours   Monday–Friday, 10:30 a.m.–4:30 p.m.; closed for lunch from 1–2 p.m.
Phone   (0207) 248-3277; ask for List Office
Website   www.courtservice.gov.uk
When to Go   Arrive for the times given. The public gallery in each courtroom has a limited number of seats, and bailiffs may not allow access once court is in session.
Special Comments   Security searches are routine. Do not bring backpacks, cameras, food, mobile phones, or pagers. These items are prohibited, and there is no cloak room for storing them.
Overall Appeal by Age Group

Pre-school †	Grade School †	Teens ★★
Young Adults ★★	Over 30 ★★★	Seniors ★★

† Not appropriate for children.
Author's Rating   ★★
How Much Time to Allow   As much time as your interest in the proceedings dictates

Description and Comments   Although most interesting to those with a background in law, the cases held in London's Old Bailey are criminal cases, and just about anyone will find both the content of the cases and the etiquette of the British courtroom intriguing for some length of time. Wigged and traditionally robed barristers address each other as "friend" and the judge as "milord," and politely assert their cases while the defendant sits at the rear of the courtroom, visibly separated from the "gentlemen's proceedings" going on in front of him.

The Old Bailey was built on the site of Newgate Prison, the noxious and notorious prison that held criminals (of the innocent and guilty variety) and public executions from the twelfth century until it was destroyed in 1902. Not the best feng shui for a court, one might say, with God only knows how many desperate ghosts hanging around. This court saw the spectacle of Oscar Wilde's trial—"the butterfly broken on a wheel"—as well as those of the Yorkshire Ripper and the wife killer, Dr. Crippen.

Touring Tips   The entrance to the public galleries is off of Newgate Street and down Old Bailey, past the original courts building and its contemporary addition, to Warwick Passage on the left. Call ahead to find out what cases are currently on the docket and at what point in the proceedings they are. Dial the number above and then ask for the List Office.

Old Operating Theatre, Museum, and Herb Garret

Type of Attraction   Haunting museum of old medical equipment and an early Victorian operating theater
Location   zone 5; 9A St. Thomas's Sreet, SE1; tube: London Bridge
Admission   £3.50 for adults; £1.75 for children; £8 for a family
Hours   Daily, 10:30 a.m.–5 p.m.
Phone   (0207) 955-4791
Website   www.thegarret.org.uk
When to Go   Anytime
Special Comments   The stairs in this old house are very, very steep. There is no wheelchair access.
Overall Appeal by Age Group

Pre-school †	Grade School ★	Teens ★★
Young Adults ★★★	Over 30 ★★★	Seniors ★★★

† Not appropriate for preschoolers.
Author's Rating   ★★★★
How Much Time to Allow   1 hour

Description and Comments   In a tiny old house in a street by London Bridge is one of the most fascinating medical museums in London. You must climb up some rather treacherous steps to reach the musty old attic, in which you'll find displayed many of the gruesome medical instruments used before the days of anesthesia; these were quite sickening to see. Around the room are sheaths of herbs—comfrey for healing bones, penny royal for nausea, willow bark from which aspirin was derived, and elderflowers for what ails you.

The centerpiece of the museum is the operating theater from the early nineteenth century, a case study for postoperative septicity from the days before Dr. Lister figured out the germ theory. The table is made of wood, and under it is a box of sawdust, which the surgeon would kick where necessary to catch the blood; there's a small washbasin in which hands were washed after the operation; the room is ringed by semicircular levels of observation areas into which medical students would be crammed like sardines to stand and watch. This is not a place for the faint of heart. The gift shop is packed with interesting books on herbal remedies.

Touring Tips   Include this museum with a trip to Southwark.

Pollock's Toy Museum

Type of Attraction Castle–like adventure into toys of the past
Location zone 14; 1 Scala Street, W1P; tube: Goodge Street
Admission £3 for adults; £1.50 for children
Hours Monday–Saturday, 10 a.m.–5 p.m.
Phone (0207) 636-3452
Website www.pollocks.cwc.net
When to Go Anytime, but call and check to see if a school group is planned
Special Comments This museum consists of six rooms on three floors connected by very steep stairs; it is not disabled or wheelchair accessible.
Overall Appeal by Age Group

Pre-school ★★	Grade School ★★★★	Teens ★★★
Young Adults ★★★	Over 30 ★★★★	Seniors ★★★★

Author's Rating ★★★★
How Much Time to Allow 1 hour

Description and Comments   I can't say it better than Robert Louis Stevenson: "If you love art, folly, or the bright eyes of children, speed to Pollock's." Okay, so he was actually referring to Benjamin Pollock's famous toy theaters of the nineteenth century, but he probably would have been even more hearty in his approval of the Toy Museum. It contains not only Mr. Pollock's cunning toy theaters but five further rooms of toys of every description, as well as displays along the steep staircases. There is probably not one square foot in the place that doesn't display some charming toy, poster, or board game. You'll see rocking horses, American automatic money boxes, Magic Lanterns, ancient jack-in-the-boxes, toy soldiers, folk dolls from around the world, doll-house rooms, puppets, teddy bears, even space toys. There are no interactive displays, but it's small and delightful enough to keep children well entertained for the time it takes to look through, though adults may want to linger longer. There's a shop on the ground floor with books, toy reproductions, and other fun stuff. Buy generously and support this priceless collection.

Touring Tips   Combine this with a trip to the nearby British Museum

Queen's Gallery, Buckingham Palace

Type of Attraction Rotating exhibition of the Queen's treatures
Location zone 9; Buckingham Palace, SW1; tube: Victoria, Green Park, or St. James's Park
Admission £5 for adults; £3 for children
Hours Daily, 9:30 a.m.–4:30 p.m.; closed between exhibitions, so call ahead
Phone (0207) 839-1377
Website www.royal.gov.uk
When to Go Anytime, but it can be crowded in summer
Special Comments At present it is not wheelchair accessible, but when the new wing opens in spring 2002 to celebrate the Queen's Golden Jubilee, it will be disabled friendly.
Overall Appeal by Age Group

Pre-school ★	Grade School ★	Teens ★★
Young Adults ★★★	Over 30 ★★★	Seniors ★★

Author's Rating ★★★

How Much Time to Allow Presently 40–60 minutes

Description and Comments It is difficult to discuss the Queen's Gallery, as the planned expansion will make it a horse of a different color entirely. Currently, it is a small gallery space with a constantly changing collection from the queen's treasure chest of world-class paintings, and your enjoyment of it depends on your appreciation of whatever is on view. In the past, they have shown watercolors by British artists, the art of Albion, and drawings of Michelangelo and Da Vinci. When the new wing is opened, it will show a larger selection from the queen's collection, which includes 20,000 drawings by old masters, such as Holbein, Canaletto, Da Vinci, Michelangelo, Carracci, and more; 10,000 old masters' paintings, including such artists as Rembrandt, Vermeer, Holbein, Brueghel, Van Dyck, and Rubens; royal portraits by Gainsborough, Reynolds, and Wilkie, as well as George Stubb's magnificent equine portraits; 30,000 English watercolors, a possible half a million prints, and countless sculptures, glass and porcelain works, books, and Fabergé trinkets. They also plan to exhibit some of the astonishing furniture, porcelain, and other decorative art the Royal Family has picked up over the centuries. A cafe is in the works too. So keep your fingers crossed that it opens as planned, and prepare to be dazzled.

Touring Tips The gallery is a great way to pass the time while waiting for the Buckingham Palace tour.

Royal Academy of Arts

Type of Attraction Venue for the world-famous Summer Exhibition of contemporary artists, record-breaking exhibitions of major artists and art themes, and a small but fine permanent collection of past academicians

Location zone 8; Burlington House, Piccadilly, W1; tube: Piccadilly Circus, Green Park

Admission £6–8 for adults, depending on exhibition; £2.50 for children ages 12–18; £1 for children ages 8–11

Hours Daily, 10 a.m.–6 p.m.; open until 10 p.m. on Friday

Phone (0207) 300-8000 (recorded information); (0207) 300-5760 or (0207) 300-5761

Website www.royalacademy.org.uk

When to Go The biggest crowds will be when there's a very popular exhibition; weekends are normally crowded. Go in the morning if possible.

Special Comments Wheelchair access

Overall Appeal by Age Group

Pre-school ★	Grade School ★	Teens ★★★
Young Adults ★★★★	Over 30 ★★★★	Seniors ★★★★

Author's Rating ★★★★

How Much Time to Allow It depends on the exhibit, but 2 hours is a good estimate

Description and Comments The academy is housed in the beautiful old Burlington House, off Piccadilly. The courtyard usually features some exhibit of sculptures, often marvelously at odds with the Palladian grandeur of this last few surviving eighteenth-century palazzos. This was England's first art school, founded by Gainsborough and Reynolds, among others, in 1768. To be counted among the academicians was the highest mark of success. Today, it continues its tradition as a venue for new artists by hosting the 200-year-old Summer Exhibition, in which painters and sculptors compete for the honor of displaying their work to an appreciative audience, many of whom come to buy. It's a bit of a hodge podge and scorned by many of the chattering classes (critics and journalists) and most of the artists who don't get in the exhibit. But everyone keeps trying to win a place on the wall.

The exhibits are usually excellent. One record-breaking exhibit was the Monet show in which people had to be let in on a timed basis, and for the last couple of days, they had to keep the academy open for 24 hours. A less popular but no less interesting show was of the whimsical Victorian paintings of faeries. A permanent collection includes work from past academicians, as well as its most significant treasure, Michelangelo's marble frieze of Madonna and child.

Touring Tips   For £30, you can become a Friend of the Royal Academy, which allows you use of the very pleasant Friends' Room, free admission plus a guest, and, most importantly, you can jump the queue for the blockbuster exhibitions. You also get to feel quite virtuous as a much-needed patron of the arts. Call the academy ahead of time, or just come to the Friends' Desk and sign up.

Royal Greenwich Observatory

Type of Attraction   Location of the world's Prime Meridian (0 degrees longitude)
Location   zone 6; Blackheath Avenue, hilltop of Greenwich Park; Docklands Light Railway: Greenwich
Admission   £6 for adults; £4.80 for seniors and students; free for children under age16; Add £1.50 for combination ticket to include the *Cutty Sark*
Hours   Daily, 10 a.m.–5 p.m.
Phone   (0208) 312-6565
Website   www.nmm.ac.uk
When to Go   Anytime
Special Comments   Not all observatory buildings are fully accessible. Special-access days are arranged with BSL signed tours and touch sessions. For details call (0208) 312-6522.
Overall Appeal by Age Group

Pre-school ★	Grade School ★	Teens ★★★
Young Adults ★★★	Over 30 ★★★	Seniors ★★★

Author's Rating   ★★★
How Much Time to Allow   1–2 hours

Description and Comments   In 1675, Charles II appointed John Flamsteed his Astronomer Royal, with the specific mandate to create better navigational maps for the British empire. Christopher Wren then designed and built an observatory for him on the highest point of the king's royal hunting grounds in Greenwich. Today, this small complex of buildings is a popular museum. You can place yourself in two hemispheres at the same time as you straddle the Prime Meridian, a favorite photo op for visitors. The museum's oldest part, Flamsteed House, is the restored home of the first Astronomer Royal. Its main galleries tell a variety of the bizarre methods once used to help ships' captains determine their location at sea and the increasingly important race to discover longitude. The remaining buildings contain a number of astronomical tools and telescopes, including Britain's largest, in the impressive Telescope Dome.

Touring Tips Planetarium shows are given at 2:30 p.m. on weekdays.

Royal Mews, Buckingham Palace

Type of Attraction Where the royal carriages and queen's horses are kept
Location zone 9; Buckingham Palace Road, SW1; tube: St. James's Park or Victoria
Admission £4.60 for adults; £2.50 for children; £11.80 for a family ticket
Hours Monday–Thursday; noon–4 p.m. During Palace State Rooms opening in August and September Monday–Thursday 10.30 a.m.–5 p.m. Closed Friday–Sunday. Subject to sudden closures, so be sure to call first.
Phone (0207) 930-4832
Website www.royal.gov.uk
When to Go See hours above
Special Comments Disabled are free, and there is good wheelchair access. Call disabled info at (0207) 839-1377
Overall Appeal by Age Group

Pre-school ★★	Grade School ★★	Teens ★★
Young Adults ★★	Over 30 ★★	Seniors ★★

Author's Rating ★★★
How Much Time to Allow 40 minutes

Description and Comments It's a small attraction and only open a few hours a week, but I urge any horse-and-carriage fancier to go take a look, if only to see the most elegant, cleanest stables in the entire world. Designed by John Nash, the stables retain a Georgian perfection, with freshly painted stalls of a pale yellow and lovely wrought-iron lamps. The horses are just as magnificent as you would expect: strong, perfect, and glossy. How they handle the oddly narrow riding ring is anyone's guess, but what the ring lacks in practicality, it makes up for in beauty. The royal coaches and automobiles are just mind boggling, especially the gold state coach built for George II in 1761, which is still in use. There's a room with some of the most admirable tack and saddles ever made, in which is also displayed sketches and photos of royal public occasions.

Touring Tips Try to make this part of your trip to Buckingham Palace, as you can get a combined ticket at a reduced rate.

Royal Naval College

Type of Attraction Extraordinary example of Renaissance architecture and interiors
Location zone 6; King William Walk, SE10; tube: Greenwich, on Docklands Light Railway
Admission Free
Hours Daily, 10 a.m.–5 p.m.
Phone (0208) 269-4741
Website www.greenwichfoundation.org.uk
When to Go Anytime
Special Comments Since the RNC is still owned by the Royal Navy, be prepared to have your bags searched on entry as part of security procedures

Overall Appeal by Age Group

Pre-school ★	Grade School ★	Teens ★★
Young Adults ★★★	Over 30 ★★★	Seniors ★★

Author's Rating ★★★

How Much Time to Allow Approximately 30 minutes

Description and Comments The Royal Naval College sits majestically on the banks of the Thames and is well worth exploring. Most of the property is off limits to the public, but the college's spectacular Painted Hall and Royal Chapel are hidden treasures that should definitely be sought out. The buildings of the RNC were begun by Christopher Wren as a new palace for Charles II, but endured numerous revisions before their eventual development as a naval hospital for disabled seamen. It was with these altered plans that the riverfront view of the Queen's House behind it was preserved. The magnificent Painted Hall in the west wing was decorated by Sir James Thornhill and contains a glorious ceiling painting and walls covered in artwork that has a remarkable three-dimensional quality. In the east wing is the Royal Naval Chapel with equally exquisite interiors.

Touring Tips Go on a weekend when you can also visit the Greenwich market.

St. Bartholomew-the-Great

Type of Attraction London's oldest monastic church

Location zone 3; Little Britain Street, off West Smithfield, EC1; tube: St. Paul's or Barbican

Admission Free; donations gratefully accepted

Hours Monday–Friday, 8:30 a.m.–4 p.m.; Saturday, 10:30 a.m.–1:30 p.m.; Sunday, 2–6 p.m. Regular Sunday services are at 9 a.m. and 11 a.m. (choral), with beautifully sung choral evensong at 6:30 p.m.

Phone (0207) 606-5171

Website www.greatbarts.com

When to Go Anytime

Special Comments It is best to approach the church from Little Britain Street. If coming from the direction of St. Paul's, you will pass St. Bart's Hospital on your left, and the church will be on your right just as you come into the square at Smithfield. Look for the rustic Tudor gatehouse on your right.

Overall Appeal by Age Group

Pre-school ★	Grade School ★	Teens ★★
Young Adults ★★★	Over 30 ★★★	Seniors ★★★

Author's Rating ★★★★

How Much Time to Allow 30–45 minutes; twice that if you are staying for a service

Description and Comments After spending the morning at St. Paul's Cathedral, a great way to continue exploring London is to wander around to a few other nearby churches. It was in this manner that I first found what still remains my favorite London church. The Priory Church of St. Bartholomew–the-Great is the oldest remaining church in London's square mile. This exquisite medieval church was founded in 1123 by Rahere, Henry I's court jester. Upon being cured of malaria while on a pilgrimage to Rome, Rahere had a vision of St. Bartholomew and vowed to build a monastery in his honor. Its ancient

Romanesque architecture transports you back to an earlier time. Standing in the doorway, as you look in toward the magnificent medieval stonework, you can almost hear the cattle being herded out on Smithfield Green, or excited peasants gathering for the public executions, jousts, and tournaments that were commonly held there. Moving forward into the church chancel, you are spellbound by images of early monastic life, from the thick Norman pillars to the medieval baptismal font. Looking up, you can glimpse "William Bolton's Window," just to the right of the altar. A former prior, Bolton created a private room here so that he could observe parishioners' weekly donations to the alms box.

Touring Tips   St. Bartholomew's is renowned for having an exceptional choir. Try to schedule your arrival to coincide with Sunday evensong.

St. Paul's Cathedral

Type of Attraction   London's most prominent cathedral
Location   zone 3; Ludgate Hill, EC4; tube: St. Paul's or Mansion House
Admission   Cathedral, galleries, and crypt entry: £5 for adults; £4 for seniors and students; £2.50 for children. Self-guided tours (with cassette) and guided tours are also available. Call to check prices.
Hours   Visitors to cathedral: Monday–Friday, 9 a.m.–5:15 p.m.; galleries open at 9:30 a.m.; choral evensong occurs weekdays at 5 p.m. and Sunday at 3:15 p.m. Call the cathedral for other mass times.
Phone   (0207) 236-4128
When to Go   Early in the day on weekdays to avoid the crowds and catch the best chances for clear-sky views from the dome
Special Comments   Good disabled access to cathedral's nave and crypt, but there is no lift access to the galleries
Overall Appeal by Age Group

Pre-school ★	Grade School ★★	Teens ★★
Young Adults ★★★	Over 30 ★★★	Seniors ★★★

Author's Rating   ★★★
How Much Time to Allow   30 minutes to 1 hour, depending on whether you plan to climb to the top of the dome

Description and Comments   There was once a Roman temple to the goddess Diana on the site of the present St. Paul's, but even such ancient sanctity did not put the succeeding buildings out of harm's way; the first church was destroyed by fire in around 660. The second was demolished by Vikings. The huge wooden cross was struck by lightning in 1382, and in 1561 a spire was also toppled by lightning. During Henry VIII's reformation, the church turned into a kind of public marketplace. A bishop described the nave in 1560: "The south side for Popery and Usury; the north for Simony [buying and selling pardons]; and the horse-fair in the middle for all kinds of bargains, meetings, brawlings, murders, conspiracies; and the font for ordinary payments of money." The Great Fire of 1666 destroyed the third incarnation of St. Paul's Cathedral, along with four-fifths of the city. King Charles II's surveyor-general, Christopher Wren, became responsible for designing its replacement, and this became his masterpiece. The cathedral was finished in a mere 35 years (the first cathedral to be completed by a single architect), and its stone English baroque style, despite being dwarfed by the encroachments of skyscrapers, still dominates the neighborhood. The dome is one of the highest in the world, at 360 feet, and second in size only to St. Peter's Basilica in Rome. Its lantern weighs a massive 850 tons.

Inside the cathedral, there are mosaics and frescoes, the *Light of the World* by Holman Hunt, Jean Tijou's grand sanctuary gates, and the intricate choir- stall carvings designed by the most skilled wood craftsman of the day, Grinling Gibbons. The crypt is the resting place of—among other notables—Lord Admiral Horatio Nelson, the duke of Wellington, and Wren himself, whose son composed the Latin inscription on his tomb: "Reader, if you seek his monument, look around." Also in the crypt are the cathedral shop and a small cafe.

The 530 steps that take you to the top of St. Paul's are worth the effort, especially if you are lucky enough to have a clear, or even sunny, day. It is an easy walk to the Whispering Gallery, the first of the three levels, where words whispered on one side of the gallery can be clearly heard on the other. On the second level, the external Stone Gallery provides telescopes and benches, but it is the uppermost Golden Gallery that offers the most spectacular views of London. To see them, however, you must submit to considerably more nerve-racking climbing.

Touring Tips If your interest in Christopher Wren is inspired by St. Paul's, there are a number of other charming examples of his seventeenth-century work, many of which are just around the corner. Some of those closest to the cathedral include: St. Mary-le-Bow (Cheapside), St. Bride's (Fleet Street), and Christ Church (Newgate Street), whose tower is all that remains. A lovely garden now fills what was once the nave.

The Science Museum

Type of Attraction Abundant collection of scientific/technological odds and ends that add up to a fascinating experience

Location zone 11; Exhibition Road, SW7; tube: South Kensington

Admission £7.90 for adults; free for children under age 16

Hours Daily, 10 a.m.–6 p.m.

Phone (0207) 942-4000

Website www.sciencemuseum.org.uk

When to Go Avoid school holidays and weekends, unless you're there at 10 a.m. It's one of London's most popular museums, so go early or on weekdays.

Special Comments Good wheelchair and disabled access; call the Disabled Persons Enquiry Line at (0207) 938-9788.

Overall Appeal by Age Group

Pre-school ★★★★	Grade School ★★★★	Teens ★★★★
Young Adults ★★★★	Over 30 ★★★★	Seniors ★★★★

Author's Rating ★★★★★

How Much Time to Allow As much as you can spare—you could easily spend all day here, there's so much to see. If you're there with children who want to play in the interactive areas, plan to spend at least 3 hours.

Description and Comments You don't need any particular interest in things scientific to love this most comprehensive collection displaying the progress of technology and science from the dawn of time to today. It is dauntingly large and there is a lot to read, but it allows you to travel, from an early hour glass in the time gallery, to the Apollo 10 Command Module in the exploration-of-space exhibit. Moving exhibits include a miniaturized field with examples of plowing carried out by a number of small tractors, and a stupendously huge mill engine in the middle of the East Hall. You can watch Foucault's pendulum swinging away in the staircase by the East Hall, or check out a replica of a turn-of-the-century pharmacy in the area that focuses on the art of medicine. The supermarket Sainsbury's has contributed a "Food for Thought" exhibit that examines every aspect of nutrition, the strangest being the mannequins of a young man and a young woman, showing what food they consumed in a month, how much sweat, feces, and urine they excreted, and how much their hair and nails grew.

Downstairs in the basement is a wonderful place to bring the young children: there's a hands-on gallery where children between ages three and six can build things with giant Legos and play with trucks and trolleys. You'll never get them out of there, which may be why the museum suggests starting at the top and moving downward.

Touring Tips   If you arrive and find a line, go across the street to the Victoria and Albert Museum or the Natural History Museum, and come back late in the afternoon (it's free after 4:30 p.m.), when the families have taken their tired kids home.

Sherlock Holmes Museum

Type of Attraction   Re-creation of fictional Victorian bachelor's house
Location   zone 14; 221B Baker Street, NW1; tube: Baker Street
Admission   £6 for adults; £4 for children under age 16; free for children under age 7
Hours   Daily, 9:30 a.m.–6:30 p.m.
Phone   (0207) 935-8866
Website   www.sherlock-holmes.co.uk
When to Go   Anytime, especially if you're waiting for Madame Tussaud's to open or are on your way to the London Zoo
Special Comments   No wheelchair access; numerous, steep stairs
Overall Appeal by Age Group

Pre-school ★	Grade School ★	Teens ★★★
Young Adults ★★★	Over 30 ★★★	Seniors ★★★

Author's Rating ★★★★
How Much Time to Allow 30–40 minutes

Description and Comments   I am a Sherlock Holmes fan, and I am also a sucker for anything from the nineteenth century. But even if you are none of the above, I think you'll find this a charming, if expensive, little stop. The self-guided (and short) tour through the little house is like stepping back in time: there are fires laid in all the rooms, which are bursting with curios and furniture, much in the way described in the stories by Sir Arthur Conan Doyle. It is a funny experience, seeing this fictional place brought to life; by the time you leave you may think there really was a Sherlock Holmes. The decor is wonderful. There's the violin he so famously played, close at hand in the study, leg irons on the bed by a valise half packed, a medical corner for Dr. Watson, a remarkable early typewriter, and a turn-of-the-century telephone. Even the attic is perfect, stuffed with leather goods, hat boxes, and other items we're all too young to remember. Items from the stories are displayed with appropriate quotes from the books, and there's an extraordinary chess set in gold and silver with characters from the books as the pieces. You can buy a similar set (though not in metal) in the gift shop, which is full of mugs, tea towels, games, pipes, and deerstalker caps. There are a few valuable books—early editions and the like—but if you don't see what you want, go across the street to the Sherlock Holmes Memorabilia Company shop across the street, where they have some impressive first editions.

Touring Tips Time your visit so you can have a traditional tea in the charming Hudson's Victorian Dining Room, which is attached to the museum.

Sir John Soane's Museum

Type of Attraction Fascinating, eccentric collection of sculpture, art, and antiquities belonging to neoclassical architect Sir John Soane
Location zone 2; 13 Lincoln's Inn Fields, WC2; tube: Holborn, Central line
Admission Free
Hours Tuesday–Saturday, 10 a.m.–5 p.m.; stay open the first Tuesday of each month from 6–9 p.m.
Phone (0207) 405-2107
Website www.soane.org
When to Go Anytime, although there is an excellent tour of the museum on Saturday at 2:30 p.m., which is limited to 20 people. It is advised that you arrive early to secure a spot.
Special Comments The museum is not handicapped accessible, as it was formerly the private home of Sir John Soane and was directed to be left as he had it. You will even be asked to leave backpacks at the front desk so there is less chance of knocking over any of the hundreds of items that can be seen in each room. This attraction is not recommended for very young children with the tendency to touch everything.
Overall Appeal by Age Group

Pre-school †	Grade School ★	Teens ★★★
Young Adults ★★★★★	Over 30 ★★★★	Seniors ★★★★★

† Not appropriate for young children
Author's Rating ★★★★★
How Much Time to Allow 1½–2½ hours

Description and Comments Many in London consider this their favorite museum. As small as it is, you can visit this nondescript residence numerous times, with treasures in every conceivable cranny, and discover new things to love about this collection each time. Situated just a stone's throw from one of the early Inns of Court, Sir John Soane bought and reconstructed the Georgian homes at 12, 13, and 14 Lincoln's Inn Fields and began filling them with a rather eccentric collection of art and antiquities. His architectural talent is seen in much of the unique floor plan of number 13, which includes a glass-domed roof and central atrium that allow light over three floors as well as in the Soanes' dining room and breakfast parlor, both of which incorporate an unusual display of mirrors that reflect light and add illusions of space.

Other remarkable aspects of the collection include the series of paintings by William Hogarth, entitled the *Rake's Progress* and *Election,* in an impressive picture gallery of false and hidden walls; a mock medieval monk's parlor containing gloomy casts and gargoyles; and the sarcophagus of Seti I surrounded by rows of antique statuary. Saturday's hour-long tour takes you through all of this and into number 12 as well, where you can see Soane's enormous research library, complete with architectural plans for the Bank of England, Whitehall, and parts of the treasury, along with numerous models of Pompeiian temples.

Touring Tips If you can't manage the Saturday tour, definitely strike up a conversation with any of the museum curators. They are very friendly and love to talk about the plethora of items acquired by Sir John Soane. It is the only way to really appreciate the amount and variety of items you see housed in this small townhouse.

Somerset House (including Courtauld Institute Gallery, Gilbert Collection, and Hermitage Rooms)

Type of Attraction Hugely magnificent edifice with river views, a classical courtyard, a river terrace, and three separate art galleries

Location zone 2; Strand, WC; tube: Covent Garden; Temple (except on Sunday)

Admission Free for Somerset house and grounds. Courtauld Institute Gallery: £4 for adults, £3 for seniors; admission is free on Monday between 10 a.m. and 2 p.m. Gilbert Collection: £4 for adults, free for children under age 18 (an audio guide and magnifying glass are included in the price). Combined-admission adult tickets for the Courtauld Gallery and Gilbert collection are £7. Hermitage Rooms: £6 for adults and £4 for concessions. Children under age 18 are admitted free of charge to all galleries.

Hours Somerset House and all galleries are open daily, 10 a.m.–6 p.m. and on Sunday from noon to 6 p.m. During the summer, the house itself and its terrace and courtyard stay open on Friday till 10 p.m.

Phone Somerset: (0207) 845 4600; Courtauld: (0207) 848-2526; Gilbert: 020 7420 9400; Hermitage: (0207) 845 4630

Websites www.somerset-house.org.uk; www.courtauld.ac.uk; www.gilbert-collection. org.uk; www.hermitagerooms.com

When to Go The courtyard and terrace of the house are splendid on a sunny day; inside galleries are great anytime, but see special comments about the Hermitage Rooms.

Special Comments The house and the galleries are all wheelchair accessible. Special sign-language talks are also offered occassionally; call (0207) 848-2549 for details. Because the Hermitage Rooms are small, the tickets are sold for timed slots, on the hour and on the half hour; about 60 at a time can go in. Also, check the Hermitage website to be sure they are not in the middle of staging a new exhibit; the exhibits are shown in ten-month cycles.

Overall Appeal by Age Group

Pre-school ★★★	Grade School ★★★	Teens ★★★
Young Adults ★★★★★	Over 30 ★★★★★	Seniors ★★★★★

Author's Rating ★★★★★

How much time to allow This depends on whether you go to any or all of the art galleries and upon how long you stroll around or linger in the cafes or on the terrace. You could spend the day here.

Description and comments Somerset House is one of the great jewels in London's architectural and historical crown. It was opened to the public in 2000, after a lengthy and expensive renovation that included adding the Gilbert Collection and the Hermitage Rooms to its long-standing Courtauld Gallery Institute. The site of Somerset House has a long history, going back to 1547; in addition to the galleries, it now houses a fair number of cafes, gift shops, and places to sit and watch the Thames flow by.

The Courtauld Gallery is an integral part of the Courtauld Institute of Art. The gallery originated out of textile magnate Samuel Courtauld's private collection from the 1930s, but has grown considerably since that time. It is most famous for its priceless Impressionist works, which include Van Gogh's *Self Portrait with Bandaged Ear,* Degas's *Two Dancers,* Renior's *La Loge,* and Manet's *Déjeuner sur l'herbe.* It is worth noting however, that the medieval and early Renaissance works in galleries 1 and 2 are also quite impressive, with paintings by Brueghel, Bellini, and Rubens.

The Gilbert Collection is a museum of decorative arts, housing Sir Arthur Gilbert's mammoth collection of gold, silver, and mosaics. There are silver items here to rival the Victoria & Albert's collection, and I don't know where in the world there could be more "micro-mosaic" tables, artwork, and snuff boxes. A staggering amount of work went into these pieces, and I would advise that you take the magnifying glass on offer to fully appreciate what's here.

In the Hermitage Rooms are exhibited selections from the great Hermitage Museum of St. Petersburg, Russia, and the exhibit changes every ten months. When I visited, the treasures of Catherine the Great, who founded the museum with her art collections in 1764, were featured, including her jewellery, antiquities, toiletry cases, decorative items, and paintings. Even at the hefty admission price of £6, if you are a museum lover, this is a must go; it's a long way to the St. Petersburg.

Touring Tips The Courtauld offers a fantastic educational booklet called "Courtauld Gallery Trail," available at the admissions desk, that instructs children (aged 5–12) in the study of the gallery's fine-art collection by asking practical questions about how to look at and learn from the paintings. Plan on having lunch or tea while at the Somerset House.

Southwark Cathedral

Type of Attraction Small medieval cathedral with famous literary ties
Location zone 5; Montague Close, Southwark, SE1; tube: London Bridge
Admission Combined exhibition and audio tour: £5 for adults; £1.50 for children under age 12
Hours Monday–Saturday, 10 a.m.–6 p.m.; Sunday, 11 a.m.–5 p.m.
Phone (0207) 367-6700
Website www.dswark.org
When to Go Anytime
Special Comments Disabled access; permits must be obtained from welcome desk for photography or videotaping
Overall Appeal by Age Group

Pre-school ★★	Grade School ★★	Teens ★★
Young Adults ★★★	Over 30 ★★★	Seniors ★★★

Author's Rating ★★★
How Much Time to Allow 1–2 hours

Description and Comments Although it has only been a cathedral since 1905, parts of this building date back to the twelfth century, when it was the Augustinian priory church of St. Mary Overie. In the time span between, the cathedral has been frequented by many notables of the day. William Shakespeare attended mass here regularly, and his brother, Edward, is interred in the choir aisle. A chapel is dedicated to the founder of Harvard Univeristy, John Harvard, who was born in Southwark and baptized in the church in 1607. In addition, there is the tomb of poet John Gower, a contemporary of Chaucer, and a memorial to Shakespeare that includes a glorious twentieth-century stained-glass window depicting almost two dozen of Shakespeare's most famous characters.

As part of the £10.9 million Southwark Cathedral Millennium Project, a new exhibition using technology such as computers to look at artifacts and films, interactive cameras contrasting today's view from the top of the cathedral tower with views since the 16th centiry, and an amazing 24-hour time lapse 360 degree view from London Bridge. The new meets the old rather handily at this exhibit. There's also a shop and a restaurant.

Touring Tips Southwark Cathedral makes a nice stop if you are wandering around the Southwark area, especially if you have already been to Shakespeare's Globe Theatre.

Syon House

Type of Attraction Home and landscaped grounds of former duke
Location outside zones; Syon Park, Brentford, Middlesex; tube: Gunnersbury
Admission House and garden: £6.25 for adults, £5.25 for children; free for park only
Hours Gardens: daily, 10 a.m.–5:30 p.m.; house: Wednesday, Thursday, and Sunday, 11 a.m.–5 p.m.
Phone (0208) 560-0881
Website www.syonpark.co.uk
When to Go In nice weather in spring, summer, or fall for gardens; anytime for the house
Special Comments No provisions made for disabled access in house; garden center and cafe in the grounds are fully accessible
Overall Appeal by Age Group

Pre-school ★	Grade School ★	Teens ★
Young Adults ★★★	Over 30 ★★★	Seniors ★★★

Author's Rating ★★★
How Much Time to Allow 2 hours, depending on weather

Description and Comments Set in 200 acres of landscaped park, Syon House was built on the site of a medieval monastery. In 1539, Henry VII disolved the abbey, and for a while it was used as a prison for Katherine Howard, his fifth wife, before her execution. In 1597, Henry Percy, the ninth earl of Northumberland took possession of Syon House, and it has remained in the family ever since. In 1761, Robert Adam, one of the most popular and respected architects of his day, remodeled the house to create a fashionable and neoclassical interior. Many paintings are on display, including works by Van Dyke, Gainsborough, Reynolds, and Lely. Recently, private apartments and state rooms have been opened to the public for the first time, by the present duke of Northumberland (the twelfth). In the eighteenth century, the riverside gardens were landscaped by the great Capability Brown to include an extensive collection of rare plants and trees. There is also a lake and a rose garden, and the Great Conservatory, which was consturcted in 1820.

Touring Tips   You can also go see the London Butterfly House, and for the kids, there's the Aquatic Experience and Snakes and Ladders (a play area). See separate listing in Part Seven, "Children's London," for further details.

Tate Britain

Type of Attraction Museum of English painters
Location zone 9; Millbank, on Thames, SW1; tube: Pimlico
Admission Free, though donations are eagerly accepted; there's a charge for special exhibits
Hours Daily, 10 a.m.–5:50 p.m.
Phone (0207) 887-8000 (recorded information); (0207) 887-8008
Website www.tate.org.uk
When to Go Anytime, but avoid midday if there's a big exhibition on
Special Comments Access-for-disabled leaflet is available at information desks. Parking spaces and wheelchairs are available, but must be booked in advance.
Overall Appeal by Age Group

Pre-school ★	Grade School ★★	Teens ★★★
Young Adults ★★★★	Over 30 ★★★★	Seniors ★★★★

Author's Rating ★★★★
How Much Time to Allow 2 hours or more

Description and Comments   The old Tate Gallery was changed in the spring of 2000, when the international modern art was moved across the river to the new Tate Modern (see separate profile) at the Bankside Power Station. This left a completely marvelous collection of English painters and sculptors from the sixteenth to the early twentieth century here at Tate Britain. The building itself is quite impressive, with Poseidon situated between a lion and unicorn on the roof, stately columns adorning the entrance, and halls of beautiful marble and design. In October 2001, a new extension opened five new galleries, another entrance and shop, and better visitor facilities. There are plenty of benches from which to enjoy the paintings and the ambience. All the great British artists are here: Hogarth, Stubbs, Reynolds, Blake, Burne-Jones, Constable, and even an honorary Englishman, the American expat James Whistler. The pride of the collection is J. M. W. Turner, whose paintings and memorabilia fill the Clore Gallery. The gift shop has an excellent selection of books, gifts, and postcards, and the cafe is top notch—remember that spending money in either helps support this excellent, free art gallery and its sister gallery across the river, the Tate Modern.

Tate Modern

Type of Attraction Museum of international modern art
Location zone 5; 25 Sumner Street, Bankside, SE1; tube: Southwark or Blackfriars
Admission Free, except for special exhibitions, lectures, and films
Hours Sunday–Thursday, 10 a.m.–6 p.m.; Friday and Saturday, 10 a.m.–10 p.m.
Phone (0207) 887 8008
Website www.tate.org.uk
When to Go Anytime

Special Comments Individuals with wheelchairs or strollers should use the north entrance from river walkway or the west entrance on Holland Street. To reserve a parking space or wheelchair, call (0207) 887 8888.

Overall Appeal by Age Group

Pre-school —	Grade School ★★	Teens ★★
Young Adults ★★★	Over 30 ★★★	Seniors ★★★

Author's Rating ★★★

How Much Time to Allow 1–2 hours

Description and Comments Housed in the old Bankside Power Station, the Tate Modern is the new (opened in 2000) national museum formed from the old Tate's (now called the Tate Britain) modern art collection, from 1900 to the present day. The work of Dali, Picasso, Matisse, Duchamp, Warhol, and Rothko are here, among many other names prominent in modern art. The views from the museums are wonderful, taking in the Millennium Footbridge and St. Paul's across the Thames. The museum itself is strangely echoing, possibly too big for its britches, and the starkness of the rooms make the starkness of some of the modern art that much more alienating (to me, anyway). There are good exhibits here, two cafes and an expresso bar, a large shop in Turbine Hall, and an overall interesting architectural conversion from power station to art gallery. I was put off by the space itself; I am a fan of a warm, dark, and cosy museum, so I should probably disqualify myself right now from being the final word on the Tate Modern. Coming soon is a river-bus service running between Tate Modern and Tate Britain.

Touring Tips If the footbridge is finally open when you come, take it across the river to St. Paul's for an entirely different use of huge echoing space.

Tower Bridge

Type of Attraction History of the bridge and a walk across the top of it

Location zone 3; Tower Bridge, SE1; tube: Tower Hill or London Bridge

Admission £6.25 for adults; £4.25 for children age 5–15; £18.25 for family tickets

Hours April–October: daily, 10 a.m.–6:30 p.m.; November–March: daily, 9:30 a.m.–6 p.m. (last admission is 75 minutes before closing)

Phone (0207) 378-1928; (0207) 407-9191 (recording)

Website www.towerbridge.org.uk

When to Go Early morning or around 4 p.m.

Special Comments Disabled access; call for details and to make plans

Overall Appeal by Age Group

Pre-school ★	Grade School ★	Teens ★
Young Adults ★★	Over 30 ★★	Seniors ★★

Author's Rating ★★

How Much Time to Allow 90 minutes

Description and Comments This is the bridge that everyone thinks is London Bridge, and what the American investors thought they were getting when they bought London Bridge in the 1970s to put up in the Arizona desert. Were they ever disappointed to get the real, boring London Bridge. Tower Bridge was built in 1894 and remains a beautiful piece of architecture, as well as a marvel of engineering. It is adequately appreciated from the ground, and I don't really think all that much is gained by waiting in the interminable lines to go in it, but if you can get in without waiting for more than half an hour, it's worth a look. They seem to be straining to provide a tour of some length, with a kind of corny multimedia trip through time to the bridge's inception, but the old films are fun to watch, and the history of how they ended up using this design is interesting, but probably not to small children. However, once you get let out on the walkway high above the Thames, with views everywhere, you can't help but be glad you visited.

Touring Tips   If there's a huge line—one that reaches out onto the bridge —go enjoy the south riverside cafes and stores or go to the Tower of London and return when the line has reached inside the ticket area, which is, according to the staff, usually around 4:15 p.m.

The Tower of London

Type of Attraction   Ancient, history-rich fortress on the banks of the Thames
Location   zone 3; Tower Hill, EC3; tube: Tower Hill
Admission   £11.50 for adults; £7.50 for children; free for children under age 5; £31 for a family ticket
Hours   March to October: Monday–Saturday, 9 a.m.–5 p.m., Sunday 10 a.m.–5 p.m.; November to February: Sunday and Monday, 10 a.m.–4 p.m. and Tuesday–Saturday, 9 a.m.–4 p.m.
Phone   (0207) 709-0765
Website   www.hrp.org.uk
When to Go   The lines get pretty ferocious in the summer; line up early or go later in the day
Special Comments   Lots of difficult stairs and passageways. A limited number of wheelchairs are available; ask at the group ticket office.
Overall Appeal by Age Group

Pre-school ★	Grade School ★★★★	Teens ★★★★
Young Adults ★★★★	Over 30 ★★★★★	Seniors ★★★★★

Author's Rating ★★★★★
How Much Time to Allow   3 hours or more

Description and Comments   The first time I entered the Tower of London through the Middle Tower, I literally went weak in the knees. To an American with more than a passing interest in English history, a trip to the tower is a transcendent experience. There has been much written about how tourist ridden it is, but I never found that to be a mitigating factor in my awe and appreciation of it. Yes, it is usually packed with howling school-children and tourists; yes, there are gift shops and snack bars all over the place; and yes, some of the attempts at historical verisimilitude are corny. But this is still one of the most important sites in all of England and was the scene of dramas beyond counting. Numerous guidebooks will tell you that it's hard to feel the essential grimness of the place with all the happy sightseers around, but I say that with a little imagination and focus, you can sense the ghosts that plague this place of imprisonment, torture, and death.

As anyone who lives there after dark can tell you, the place is lousy with ghosts, and not the happy kind. Macaulay, the nineteenth-century historian, wrote of the small burial ground by the Chapel of St. Peter Ad Vincula: "In truth, there is no sadder spot on earth as this little cemetery. Death is there associated, not, as in Westminster Abbey and St Paul's, with genius and virtue . . . but with whatever is darkest in human nature and in human destiny, with the savage triumph of implacable enemies, with the inconstancy, the ingratitude, the cowardice of friends, with all the miseries of fallen greatness and of blighted fame." It does make you shiver when you hear the roll call of the imprisoned and beheaded: Thomas More, Anne Boleyn, Lady Jane Grey and her husband, Queen Catherine Howard, a host of lords and ladies whose only crime was to end up on the wrong side of the monarch. There were also kings of Scotland and France, William Wallace (alias Braveheart), King Henry VI, the two little princes murdered in their sleep (presumably by their uncle, Richard III), Sir Walter Raleigh, and countless victims of religious persecutions. It is, for all its present serenity and beauty, a place soaked in centuries of blood.

The tower was started as a simple fortification on the Thames in 1066 by William the Conqueror, and grew over the years to include 13 different towers, numerous houses, walks, armories, barracks, and greens, all surrounded by a moat. The moat was drained in 1843 due to the mephitic stink of it, but there are plans afoot to fill it in again, which would be quite pleasing to the eye. The Yeoman Warders, also known as Beefeaters, have been at the tower since the 1300s and are now an invaluable source of information about the tower. They are happy to answer questions, and you may attach yourself to any group that is being entertained and enlightened by a Beefeater. There are Yeoman Warder talks and free tours every day; the Lanthorn Tower and the Middle Tower have information boards outlining the day's talks, tours and events. You will see ravens there. They are a very important part of the tower, and have been kept here with wings clipped for over 600 years. The legend goes that if the ravens should ever leave, the tower will fall and England will be in great danger. There is one there at present, named Thor, who has somehow been trained to imitate human speech, so any disembodied "Hellos" you hear will not always be the work of the ghosts.

One of the most famous sights at the tower is the Crown Jewels. I was not all that interested in them—the line can be awfully long, and while the crowns and scepters are interesting as historical emblems, they are strangely lifeless. Seeing them was not nearly as gratifying as reading the scratched graffiti—in English and Latin—of the unfortunate prisoners in Beauchamp Tower, or sitting under a tree in one of the greens absorbing the atmosphere. It's a good place to hang around, so take your time. The audio tours are great and can be done at your own pace, and the guide book is an excellent investment.

Touring Tips   There is a security check that slows down the entrance; if possible, leave your knapsack or bag at home when you visit.

Victoria and Albert Museum

Type of Attraction Breathtaking collection of decorative arts and design
Location zone 11; Cromwell Road (second entrance on Exhibition Road), South Kensington, SW7; tube: South Kensington
Admission £5 for adults; free for children under age 18; free to all between 4:30 p.m. and 5:50 p.m.
Hours Monday, 10 a.m.– 5:50 p.m.; Tuesday–Sunday 10 a.m.–5:45 p.m.; Wednesday and Friday open until 10 p.m.
Phone (0207) 942-2000
Website www.vam.ac.uk
When to Go Anytime

Special Comments Wheelchair access is from the Exhibition Road entrance; there are ramps over most of the many small sets of steps

Overall Appeal by Age Group

Pre-school ★★★   Grade School ★★★   Teens ★★★

Young Adults ★★★★★   Over 30 ★★★★★   Seniors ★★★★★

Author's Rating ★★★★★

How Much Time to Allow As much as possible

Description and Comments The Victoria and Albert Museum is the jewel in the South Kensington Museumland's crown. It houses the most engaging assortment of treasures, and although it has been criticized for not having a strict enough focus, that is precisely its charm. It could be the enormous attic of some mad uncle, wealthy beyond all measure, indiscriminately collecting anything and everything of interest that might make his home more beautiful. You have an endless choice of things to see: armor, religious artifacts, stained glass, sculptures, wood carvings, jewelry, musical instruments, iron work, furniture, glass work, clothing, paintings, photographs, and whatever special exhibit is being held at the time, always very well mounted.

The original V&A was part of Prince Albert's grand scheme to make South Kensington a center for arts, science, and learning. When it opened in 1852, funded by the Great Exhibition of 1851, Prince Albert envisioned the South Kensington Museum, as it was known then, to be a repository of applied arts—items that happily married beauty and utility. Such restrictions were hopeless from the start, as treasures started arriving from all over the empire and thousands of legacies. As you wander around the museum—and I believe that's the best way to go, although many would guide you toward the introductory tours that occur daily—you might bear in mind the fact that there are millions more objects d'art, paintings, photographs, clothing, textiles, and so on stored away in the basement.

By 1899, the old housing for the collection was clearly unfit, and work was begun on the present building, named by Queen Victoria, who never passed up an opportunity to honor her long-departed husband. She didn't live to see it completed ten years later, but she presides over its Cromwell Road entrance like a secular version of the Virgin Mary, who tops the Brompton Oratory Church next door. There has been talk about finding a more appropriately descriptive name for this wonderful museum, but I think that evoking the quintessential couple of that inquisitive, acquisitive nineteenth-century British empire is perfect. The building is a real beauty, inside and out, and any visit to the museum should always include a few moments to appreciate the grace of the main-entrance dome, the Fakes and Forgeries' immense halls and skylights, the Pirelli Courtyard, and especially the areas that, in a less populated age, served as the museum's eateries: the Poynter, Gamble, and Morris rooms. These rooms are simply magnificent.

The restaurant downstairs is excellent. The front lobby now has a small cafe in which you can admire the astonishing glass chandelier. The gift shop is wonderful; there's also a children's gift shop downstairs by the restaurant.

Touring Tips On Wednesday (depending on the season, call (0207) 942-2209 to make sure it's on), there's a Late View, with a limited number of galleries open, a lecture in the beautiful old lecture hall past the Silver Galleries, and a gallery talk. The restaurant is open and has candles on the table, and live music is played there as well as in the front hall. It's a wonderful way to pass a Wednesday evening.

The weekends feature a Family Cart, with activities for children. It's extremely entertaining and educational for kids of every age.

The Wallace Collection

Type of Attraction   Collection of nineteenth-century Anglo-French art
Location   zone 14; Hertford House, Manchester Square, W1; tube: Bond Street
Admission   Free
Hours   Monday–Saturday, 10 a.m.–5 p.m.; Sunday, noon–5 p.m.
Phone   (0207) 935-0687
Website   www.the-wallace-collection.org.uk
When to Go   Anytime
Special Comments   Good disabled access including an outdoor ramp, lifts to the upper floors, and mostly uncluttered rooms in which it is easy to maneuver
Overall Appeal by Age Group

Pre-school ★	Grade School ★	Teens ★★
Young Adults ★★★	Over 30 ★★★★	Seniors ★★★★

Author's Rating   ★★★★
How Much Time to Allow   1–3 hours

Description and Comments   The Wallace Collection is tucked away in a lovely Georgian square between Regent's and Hyde Parks. The second marquess of Hertford leased the home, now Hertford House, in 1797, for the good duck shooting available in the area. Today, Hertford House holds the combined acquisitions of five generations of marquesses of Hertford. Between 1750 and 1880, this family formed what has become one of the most impressive collections displaying quintessential aristocratic lifestyle and artistic taste in the nineteenth century.

The collection is displayed over this French chateau's two main floors, and some areas are worthy of special note. Galleries 2, 3, and 4 contain some fabulous pieces of Louis XIV furniture and art. A remarkable European Renaissance armory is housed in Galleries 8, 9, and 10, and Gallery 11 is devoted to Asian arms, armor, and art. Hertford House's largest room, Gallery 22, offers one of the finest displays of European paintings to be seen anywhere in the world. This impressive gallery, formerly called "The Long Picture Gallery," houses works by such masters as Titian, Poussin, Rembrandt, Rubens, Van Dyck, and Velázquez. Even if the house were empty of treasures, it would still be worth visiting to see the carved mantlepieces and elegant design of this architectural paragon of a bygone era.

Temporary exhibits, new educational facilities, new galleries, and a cafe, along with certain engineering reconstructions, were part of an intensive Centenary Project in 2000 that cost over ten million pounds. It was money well and wisely spent, making this good small museum a great small museum.

Touring Tips   Free public lectures and tours on various aspects of the collection are given on weekdays and weekends. Tours usually last about 45 minutes and give good insight into the styles and history of the artists and their times. If you are on a tight schedule, call for touring times, or just arrive and wander on your own until a tour begins.

The Wellington Arch

Type of Attraction Architectural and London-related items in the arch
Location zone 10; in the middle of Hyde Park Corner roundabout, SW1; tube: Hyde Park Corner
Admission £2.50 for adults; £1.30 for children; £1.90 for concessions
Hours April–September: daily, 10 a.m.–6 p.m.; October: daily, 10 a.m.–5 p.m.; November–March: Wednesday–Sunday, 10 a.m.–4 p.m.
Phone (0207) 973 3494
Website www.english-heritage.org.uk
When to Go Anytime
Special Comments The entrance is on the south side inside of the arch, a small doorway with no banners or big signs announcing its position. You reach the island either through the subways, or at the street crossing in front of the Lanesborough Hotel.
Overall Appeal by Age Group

Pre-school —	Grade School ★	Teens ★
Young Adults ★	Over 30 ★★	Seniors ★★

Author's Rating ★★
How Much Time to Allow Depending upon your interest, 30 minutes to an hour

Description and Comments   This is one of those specialty museums for either architectural historians or London-obsessed cranks (I count myself in the latter group). It's worth a go, as it's relatively inexpensive, and if you combine it with a visit to Apsley House across the way, it will leave you feeling as if you know all there is to know about that corner of London. There are a couple of films running in loops that have wonderful old shots of Hyde Park Corner from the horse-and-cart era to the present; and the moulds from the magnificent statue on top of the arch are most inspiring. But the best thing about it are the views to be had from the observation platforms. The look in at the tennis courts in the "backyard" of Buckingham Palace was a first for me; and the views of the London Eye and Westminster are nice too. A photo display of Londoners' snapshots of their city is riveting, and the reason I ended up spending thtere an hour. I wouldn't want to be there in a crowd, though; it's mighty small.

Touring Tips   If you go from Apsley House to the Arch via the tube (follow signs for Green Park), you get the story of the duke of Wellington recapitulated in tile on the walls, as well as a hour-to-hour description of the battle of Waterloo, for which the duke is famous.

Westminster Abbey

Type of Attraction England's historically most important church
Location zone 9; Broad Sanctuary, just off of Parliament Square; tube: St. James Park or Westminster
Admission Free admission for services or to visit the nave and cloisters; royal chapels and tombs: £6 for adults; £3 for students and seniors; £2 for children; £12 for family; Chapter House, Pyx Chamber, and museum: £1 with royal chapels admission or £2.50 for adults, £1.90 for students and seniors, and £1.30 for children
Hours Royal chapels are open Monday–Friday, 9 a.m.–3:45 p.m., Saturday, 9 a.m.–1:45

p.m. (Closing times given are for last admission.) Chapter House, Pyx Chamber, and museum hours are Monday–Saturday, 10 a.m.–3:30 p.m. The abbey is closed before special services, on Sundays (except for services), December 24–28, Good Friday, and on Commonwealth Observance Day.

Phone (0207) 222-5152

Website www.westminster-abbey.org

When to Go Early mornings on weekdays, especially during the busy summer months. If you really hate crowds in close spaces, make a quick call to be sure you aren't arriving at the same time as 3 tour groups.

Special Comments Audio guides are available in seven languages for £2.50, Monday–Friday, 9:30 a.m.–3 p.m. and Saturday, 9:30 a.m.–1 p.m.

Overall Appeal by Age Group

Pre-school ★	Grade School ★★★	Teens ★★★★
Young Adults ★★★★	Over 30 ★★★★	Seniors ★★★★

Author's Rating ★★★★

Additional Tips My favorite way to experience Westminster Abbey is to arrive around 3:30 p.m. and then wander the cloisters (especially the lovely Little Cloister) before returning to the nave to wait for the 5 p.m. evensong. It is worth waiting at the head of the line (which starts to form at about 4:15 p.m.), as the first evensong attendees are seated in the stately choir stalls where the atmosphere and view of the Westminster Boys Choir is the best.

How Much Time to Allow 1½–2 hours for audio guides; evensong is about 45 minutes

Description and Comments Since the Abbey is one of the most popular tourist sights in London, the key here is to avoid touring when it is mobbed. You lose sight of the beauty of the interiors (displaying at least four different eras of architecture), the sheer numbers of people buried here (over 3,000), and the incredible amount of history that this building has seen (for over 900 years) when you are moving in a sluggish single file line through the chapels. Instead, try to start off your day with a visit or, as I mentioned above, end your day with one.

Since 1998, the primary entrance to the Abbey has been through the North Transept, which gives a rather disjointed image of the Abbey on first glance. I suggest that you immediately head back toward the West Front entrance so that you can see the Abbey as it was meant to be viewed. From this perspective you can clearly see the majesty of the tallest nave in England (at 102 feet). In front of you is the Tomb of the Unknown Soldier and to your right is a fourteenth-century portrait of Richard II, the oldest known image of a monarch painted from life. As you head back toward the North Transept, also called Statesmen's Aisle, you pass through Musician's Aisle and end up back near the admissions and information desks. From here you move in a mostly single-file line through the smaller chapels of Elizabeth I and Innocents Corner and head toward the fantastic display of English perpendicular architecture that makes up the Henry VII Chapel. The elaborately carved choir stalls here are dedicated to the Knights of the Order of the Bath, whose banners and helmets decorate the stalls. Among the notable names buried in this chapel alone are Henry VII and his wife; King George II and Queen Caroline; Henry VIII's only son, Edward VI; and James I and his lover, George Villiers, the first nonroyal to be buried in this part of the Abbey.

As you head along the south aisle of Henry VII's chapel, you can see the tombs of Mary

Queen of Scots; Lady Margaret Beaufort, Henry VII's mother; as well as William and Mary, Queen Anne, and Charles II. Walking back toward the nave, you pass the oak throne dating back to 1300 called the Coronation Chair, which has been used in every royal coronation since then. Just beyond this point, tombs and gatework hide much of the Abbey's most famous tomb, the shrine of St. Edward the Confessor. Unfortunately, this tomb, although recently restored, remains closed to the public. The South Transept of Poet's Corner, however, continues to be a favorite of visitors and contains the grave slabs of, among many others, Geoffrey Chaucer, Robert Browning, Alfred Lord Tennyson, Charles Dickens, Rudyard Kipling, and Thomas Hardy, as well as impressive memorials to William Shakespeare and George Frideric Handel. The last person to have been buried here was Sir Laurence Olivier, who died in 1989.

After exploring the Abbey's interior, be sure you find your way out to the cloisters, where the monks worked, studied, and lived. Visiting on a cold day gives you insight into the hearty constitution these early scholars must have had. Today, the cloisters contain a small shop and cafe. English Heritage also runs a small area just off the east cloisters. This includes the Chapter House, which was the original meeting place of the House of Commons until the time of Henry VIII, and the Pyx Chamber, which served as the sacristy and royal treasury of the earliest church.

Touring Tips   Before you enter the Westminster Abbey, take the time to enjoy its lesser-known neighbor. Many people head straight for the entrance and fail to even notice St. Margaret's Church, which shares the churchyard. Built in 1523, this tiny church's simple and uncluttered interior will contrast sharply with the Abbey's appearance as an overflowing mausoleum.

Photography is not permitted in any part of the Abbey at any of the times mentioned above. If you are a camera buff and will not settle for putting postcards in your albums, plan your visit for Wednesday between 6 and 7 p.m. At this special time, admission is half price and amateur photography is permitted, although no tours or audio guides will be available.

Windsor Castle

Type of Attraction   The queen's country house, a mighty fine old castle
Location   Windsor, Hertsfordshire, outside London (British Rail: Waterloo Station to Windsor Riverside)
Admission   £11 for adults; £5 for children ages 5–16; free for childen under age 5
Hours   March–October: daily, 10 a.m.–5:30 p.m., last admission at 4 p.m.; November–February: daily, 10 a.m.–4 p.m., last admission at 3 p.m. St. George's Chapel closed Sunday
Phone   (0175) 318-3118
Website   www.royal.gov.uk
When to Go   Always call first! Windsor Castle is subject to regular, annual, and sudden closures due to various royal ceremonies and events. The month of June is particularly susceptible to this sort of thing. Otherwise, go anytime, but show up early before the tour groups.
Special Comments   Limited wheelchair access, lots of walking
Overall Appeal by Age Group

Pre-school ★	Grade School ★★	Teens ★★★
Young Adults ★★★★	Over 30 ★★★★	Seniors ★★★★

Author's Rating ★★★★

How Much Time to Allow Half a day, plus time to wander in Windsor

Description and Comments In November 1992, the world saw film footage of Windsor Castle with smoke and flames pouring out from behind its distinctive crenelated keep and foremen running to and fro with priceless paintings and furniture. The fire destroyed over 100 rooms, and it took 5 years to repair the terrible damage done to the ancient castle. Even if you don't normally like gaping at castles, you might make an exception of Windsor, for the restoration of the gutted and devastated castle—burnt to its medieval stone walls, with roofs collapsed—is a marvel in itself, and the exhibition that describes the process is remarkable.

William the Conqueror, who also built the Tower of London, chose the site in Windsor for a fortress to protect London from western invaders. The castle has been continually inhabited for the past 900 years, and many additions—and deletions, too, through other fires—have been made over those years.

It is presently a place of overwhelming splendor and tremendous riches, which might be best summed up by the awesome Queen Mary's Dolls' House. This is big luxury on a small scale: Sir Edward Luytens designed the multistory doll house in the 1920s, and it took three years and a thousand craftsmen and artists to complete it. It has running water, electric lights, a working elevator, actual miniature books, fine art, gorgeous furniture, and even two tiny thrones with crowns on them.

Another attraction at Windsor is St. George's Chapel, started in 1475; its a stunning example of great medieval architecture, with stained-glass windows of unparalleled beauty. Ten monarchs are buried within its precincts, and there are some stupendously crafted sarcophagi. The crests and banners of the Knights of the Order of the Garter are all there, and you get a feel for the ritual and pageantry that have propped up the ruling classes of England for centuries.

Touring Tips Be sure to make time to wander around the pleasnt town of Windsor.

Green and Pleasant Lands: Parks of London

On the weekends, when the museums and tourist attractions are packed, go to the parks and soak up the gratifying English appreciation for nature tame and wild. Part of London's appeal as a city is its careful conservation of greenery—whether in its many squares or its enormous parks. For more information, contact The Royal Parks Agency at (0207) 298-2000 or go to www.royalparks.gov.uk.

PARKS	DESCRIPTION	ZONE
Green Park	Between Hyde Park and St. James's Park	9
Hampstead Heath	Enormous expanse of country	1
Highgate Cemetery	Overgrown Victorian graveyard	1
Holland Park	54-acre landscaped park	13
Hyde Park	350-acre people's park	10
Kensington Gardens	Gardens, walkways, fountains, palace	13

Kew Gardens (The Royal Botanic Gardens)	Botanical extravaganza	12
Regent's Park	490-acre elegant park	3
Richmond Park	London's largest park	12
St. James's Park	Oldest royal park in London	9

Green Park

Type of Park Expanse of green lawn and old trees
Location zone 9; between Piccadilly and Constitution Hill (between Hyde Park and St. James's Park); enter at Hyde Park Corner; tube: Green Park
Admission Free
Hours Daily, 5 a.m. to midnight
When to Go Anytime; don't miss spring bulbs and blazing autumn foliage

Description and Comments As happened with St. James's Park, Green Park was reclaimed from the marshy meadows that surrounded the Tyburn River. Originally purchased by Henry VIII for enclosed grazing and hunting, the land was made into a formal park in 1667. It became a favorite place for duels and highwaymen, military parades, ballooning, and people watching. Green Park was opened to the public in 1826, and since then people have loved strolling along the east end of the park, admiring the fine mansions there, ending up at Buckingham Palace and St. James's Park. There are no flowerbeds in Green Park, but the crocuses in spring more than make up for that lack, and the 950 magnificent plane, oak, poplar, chestnut, and other varieties of trees to be seen there are completely pleasing. You may rent chairs there in the spring, summer, and fall, which makes a nice break from shopping or sight-seeing in the Piccadilly area. A refreshment stand is available at the Buckingham Palace end of the park, and toilets can be found by the Green Park tube station.

Hampstead Heath

Type of Park Enormous expanse of country in Greater London area
Location zone 1; Hampstead; tube: Highgate, then take 210 bus to West Gate
Admission Free
Hours Daily, 8 a.m. to dusk
When to Go Anytime; don't miss the spring blossoms and autumn colors

Description and Comments Though Hampstead Heath is not actually a park per se, it is a most remarkable place, covering a staggering 1,600 acres of undeveloped land and offering stunning views over London. There are hills, lakes, wild woods, and landscaped gardens. Hampstead Heath has so much to offer, not the least of which is Kenwood House, a stately home and art museum at the northernmost top of the heath. There are outdoor concerts in the summer on Saturday nights, which are followed by displays of fireworks. People bring blankets and picnic hampers and sit on a hill outside, while those who pay for tickets hunker down a little closer to the music. The Men's and Ladies' Ponds for swimming in the summer are part of a set of lakes along the Highgate border of the heath. There's also a pond for model boats and one for bird watching. Parliament Hill, across the bicycle track that cuts through the Heath, is the best place in London for viewing the Guy

London
Parks

N

① Green Park
② Hampstead Heath
③ Highgate Cemetery
④ Holland Park
⑤ Hyde Park

⑥ Kensington Gardens
⑦ Kew Gardens
⑧ Regent's Park
⑨ Richmond Park
⑩ St. James's Park

Fawkes' Day fireworks, and in all seasons has spectacular views of London. You can hardly believe you are even near an urban area in many parts of the heath, where mansions on hills look like castles and conspire to make you feel you are in a story book. You can get a good lunch at the Kenwood House outdoor cafe in the summer.

Highgate Cemetery

Type of Park Wildly overgrown Victorian graveyard
Location zone 1; located on either side of Swains Lane in Highgate, adjacent to Waterlow Park; tube: Archway, Northern line
Admission West Cemetery (access is as part of guided tours only) £3; East Cemetery £1
Hours West Cemetery, April to September: tours are given Monday–Friday at noon, 2 p.m., 3 p.m., and 4 p.m.; Saturday and Sunday, 10 a.m.–4 p.m. October to March: tours are given on weekends only, hourly, 11 a.m.–3 p.m. East Cemetery, April to September: daily, 10 a.m.–5 p.m. October to March: daily, 10 a.m.–4 p.m.
Phone (0208) 340-1834
When to Go Anytime, although they only allow 20 people on each weekend hourly tour, so if you arrive late you may find yourself wandering the East Cemetery for an hour. Also, the cemetery will close for funerals, so call to check before setting out.

Description and Comments Opened in 1839, Highgate Cemetery became "the" place to be buried for London's wealthy Victorian families, intellectuals, and artists. One of seven cemeteries designed and opened during this time of continued population explosion, it remains one of the most elaborate and stirring examples of Victorian statuary excess. Overgrown and badly vandalized, the West Cemetery was closed in 1975 and is now diligently cared for by the Friends of Highgate Cemetery. Lush vegetation fills what was once an open, rolling hillside, and volunteers continue to clear overgrown pathways and graves. This extensive foliage creates eerie shadows; this, combined with the cracked and toppled grave markers everywhere, give the cemetery its fabulously gothic atmosphere. Tour guides are well versed on the many famous residents of the cemetery as well as having a number of fascinating anecdotes that explain the elaborate and symbolic Victorian statuary. The cemetery's creepiest section includes the Egyptian Avenue and the Terrace Catacombs.

You can wander on your own in the East Cemetery, but it holds a less eerie charm. Still, it is nice to be able linger where you will and get up close to the graves, some of which contain the most interesting epitaphs. There is a £2 "camera permit fee" for those interested in capturing the morose views. It's best to go early in the day, hopefully on a day with some sun, as the shadowy effects can create fantastic photographic images.

Holland Park

Type of Park 54-acre landscaped marvel with a Japanese garden
Location zone 13; Holland Park, between Kensington and Shepherd's Bush; tube: Holland Park Avenue (then a 10-minute walk to park) or Kensington High Street and take westbound bus 9, 10, 27, 28, 31, or 49
Admission Free
Hours Daily, 7:30 a.m. to dusk

When to Go Anytime; there are camellias, roses, irises, and other blossoms in spring; dahlias in summer; and autumn leaves

Description and Comments Holland Park once housed the magnificent Holland House, more castle than mansion, where the literati of the early nineteenth century used to flock to mix with the politicians and aristocrats of the day. The house was bombed during World War II, but what remains are fascinating monuments to the past: the surviving wings of Holland House, one now a youth hostel, the wrought-iron gates that formed the entrance to the estate, the Orangery, the ice house from the 1770s, the summer ballroom that is now a restaurant called The Belvedere, the old stables, and the many walks and enclosures that make up Holland Park.

There is wonderful variety of flora and fauna here, thanks to Lord Holland—a venerable Victorian gentleman—and his great interest in planting and wildlife. He can be seen as styled by sculptor G. F. Watts, surveying his land, occasionally providing a roosting place for some of the 60 wild bird species that have been spotted in the park. One feature he never saw, which was created in 1991, is the Kyoto Garden, a perfect Japanese garden. The white peacocks gather in the Yucca Lawn, along with numerous rabbits. There is an adventure playground in the park that is a must-do for families with young children.

Hyde Park

Type of Park 350-acre park with expansive lawns
Location zone 10; bordered by Park Lane, Knightsbridge, and Bayswater Road; tube: Hyde Park Corner
Admission Free
Hours Daily, dawn to dusk
When to Go Anytime; there are roses in summer, crocuses and daffodils in spring, fall foliage in autumn, and atmospheric bare trees in winter

Description and Comments During the dissolution of the monasteries in 1536, Henry VIII grabbed a hunk of land from the manor of Hyde and enclosed it for his hunting pleasure. James I opened the park to aristocrats, who took the air daily, a habit that persisted into the early twentieth century, with Rotten Row—originally Route du Roi, king's road—resounding with the beating of hooves and the chatter of the idle classes. Once, Kensington Gardens was part of Hyde Park—and is still separated only by a roadway—but in the mid-1700s, Queen Caroline appropriated 200 acres to make suitable gardens for Kensington Palace.

Hyde Park today is a wonderful escape from the high-decibel traffic noise of Park Lane, Knightsbridge, and Bayswater. One enters the park from any one of those streets, and within minutes of walking toward the Serpentine, the watery heart of the park, a delightful quiet descends. There's so much to do in Hyde Park: There are biking and inline skating paths through and around the edge of the park (do not bicycle on any paths not marked with the outline of a bike); there are cricket and soccer pitches, there are tennis courts, paddle- and rowboats, and one can even ride through Rotten Row on horseback. During the warm months, there are numerous places to rent lawn chairs, and you can get a bite to eat at the Lido or the cafeteria at the east end of the Serpentine. The Rose Walk by Hyde Park Corner is magnificent in June, and the Italian Piazza, with fountains and statues by the

Bayswater side, is wonderful at all times. Speaker's Corner, at the northeast of the park, is hopping on Sunday, often featuring born-again Christians yelling at us to repent, no longer on soapboxes, but on little stepladders or overturned buckets. The queen's guards exercise their horses and rehearse their ceremonies in Hyde Park, on the south by Prince's Gate. It's an astonishing thing to be walking through the park and suddenly be set upon by a regiment of sword-waving, plume-hatted horsemen. Hyde Park in sunlight is the best place to be in London.

If you want to get from South Kensington to Piccadilly, or from Knightsbridge to Marble Arch, do yourself a favor and walk through Hyde Park.

Kensington Gardens

Type of Park Gardens, walkways, fountains, statues, and a palace
Location zone 13; Kensington Gore; tube: Kensington High Street
Admission Free
Hours Daily, dawn to dusk
When to Go Anytime, especially when Kensington Palace and the Orangery are open. In spring and summer there is the flower walk and great foliage in fall.

Description and Comments   Kensington Palace will probably be forever associated with the extraordinary event of public mourning for Princess Diana, when in the days after her death in Paris, people arrived and laid flowers in front of the palace that was her home. By week's end there was a sea of blooms and cellophane in front of the gates, and the trees nearby were festooned with pictures, poems, and flowers, and candles stood burning everywhere. A permanent tribute to the "People's Princess" is the Princess Diana Memorial Playground in the Northwest corner of the park, a state-of-the-art playground that is always filled to capacity.

By the side of the palace is a lovely sunken garden that can be looked at, but not entered. Before the Orangery, which is a good place for tea, are topiary trees that recall the Restoration; and the Round Pond on which children have sailed toy boats for generations brings Mary Poppins vividly to mind. By the bridge over the Sepentine is a statue of Peter Pan; author J. M. Barrie lived right by the park and the island in the middle of the lake is clearly the model for the Island of the Lost Boys.

The Broad Walk is good for inline skating, as is the area in front of the Albert Memorial. And if you're in the mood for art, the Serpentine Gallery has changing exhibits and a good bookshop.

Kew Gardens (The Royal Botanic Gardens)

Type of Park Botanical extravaganza with 30,000 species of plants and flowers planted over 300 acres; follies, water features, and conservatories
Location zone 12; southwest London on the Thames; tube: Kew Gardens
Admission £5 for adults; £2.50 for children ages 5–16; free for children under age 5; £13–21 for a family ticket
Hours Daily, 9:30 p.m.–5:30 in winter; open later in summer
When to Go Anytime of the year, although summer is the best time to get your money's worth

Description and Comments   The Royal Botanical Gardens at Kew were begun in the eighteenth century, when wealthy and royal folks began to move out of smelly, crowded London. The Botanical Gardens, originally developed for the pleasure of the royal family, intersected nicely with the global travels of adventurers such as Captain Cook, who brought home never-before-seen specimens of plant life, such as the geranium. The gardens have gone from strength to strength since then as one of the world's most remarkable and serious centers of botanical research.

The enormous glass Palm House is a treasure trove of exotic tropical plants, with two levels on which to wander through the huge fronds and steamy atmosphere. There's a tropical aquarium in the basement that furthers the impression of being in a foreign clime. The Water Lily House is also interesting, and a testament to the wide-ranging journeys of the English explorers. The Temperate House is an even more impressive structure than the Palm House, twice as large, and containing plants from each and every continent, some of which were planted at Kew in the middle of the nineteenth century.

There are identifying plaques on the trees and signs on the flower beds, so that a visit to Kew can be a real education in botany. Two art galleries, Kew Palace, a Japanese pagoda, and numerous follies and conservatories make Kew an outing at which you can easily spend the whole day. There are a few cafes to choose from, and believe me, you'll need refreshment after a long day at plant-viewing. It's a shame that Kew is right in the path of Heathrow—the impression of stepping back in time is continually spoiled by the noise of overhead jets.

Regent's Park

Type of Park   Playground of 490 acres with 6,000 trees
Location   zone 15; at end of Baker Street; for south entrance, take the tube to Regent's Park or Baker Street)
Admission   Free
Hours   Daily, 5 a.m. to dusk
When to Go   Anytime; there are flower gardens in spring and summer, autumn leaves

Description and Comments   Named for George IV, when he was mad King George's understudy monarch, Regent's Park was designed by John Nash as part of the grand plan for a garden city of terraced mansions with countrylike views. Started in 1811, the scheme ultimately failed, with only a portion of the terrace houses sold (and those were said to be of substandard quality). However, in 1835, the park was flourishing and was opened to the public. Although the neighborhood may not have turned out as Nash planned, it's still gorgeous, and few can resist the grace and beauty of the classically inspired white mansions of Cumberland Terrace that look out on the magnificent landscape.

Within the park you will find the home of the American ambassador, donated by the heiress Barbara Hutton and suitably fenced and secured; a boating lake with ornamental bridges and an island; a lake by Queen Mary's Rose Gardens, which are quite extraordinary and include a waterfall and an open-air theater; a number of lodges; a mosque; Regent's Canal; and of course, the London Zoo. In the summer there are concerts on the Bandstand and plays at the theater, bird-watching walks, puppet shows, and outdoor refreshments. The Royal Horse Artillery can be seen occasionally on Cumberland Green.

Primrose Hill, north of the zoo, is not officially part of Regent's Park, but can be accessed easily from there, and provides a lovely view of all London.

Richmond Park

Type of Park London's largest, featuring deer and ancient oak trees
Location zone 12; southwest London; tube: Richmond Station, then take bus 72, 265, 371, or 415
Admission Free
Hours Daily, 7 a.m. to dusk
When to Go Anytime

Description and Comments Richmond Park is a gargantuan 2,470-acre preserve in which 400 fallow deer and 250 red deer live and graze. It is an extraordinary place, a piece of rolling countryside a stone's thrown (seven miles from Charing Cross) from the center of a major metropolitan city, with wildlife still roaming freely. Richmond had its first royal connections when Henry VII rebuilt a fine old palace on the Thames; his granddaughter Elizabeth I died at the palace. In 1625, surrounding lands were seized and walled to give King Charles I a country asylum from the plague. His wall created much ill will among the neighbors, who had been used to grazing their animals on the land and using the common roads. The king tried to compensate by allowing foot traffic through the park and permitting the local poor to gather deadwood for their hearth fires. After the Civil War, the House of Commons voted to leave the park as undeveloped land, and so it has remained ever since. There were various skirmishes between the royals and the public over right of access, which were put to rest on the death of the last royal ranger, Edward VII in 1910. Today, Richmond Park is a testament to the admirable environmental protectionism of the British and provides for the visitor a wonderfully unchanged picture of a medieval hunting ground.

Be aware that the deer are not completely harmless and can be aggressive if they are bothered while tending young or during rutting season. There are refreshments found in the Pembroke Lodge Cafeteria from April through October, from 10 a.m. to 5:30 p.m. (7 p.m. on weekends). White Lodge houses the Royal Ballet School. There are a number of seasonal events that take place in Richmond Park—check a newspaper or Time Out to see when, what, and where. Pembroke Lodge often stages lunchtime concerts. The best time to see the wonders of Richmond Park may be during the height of the fall leaf change: The colors are incomparably fine.

St. James's Park

Type of Park Oldest royal park in London; a must-see for sightseers
Location zone 9; east of Buckingham Palace gates; tube: St. James's Park
Admission Free
Hours Daily, 5 a.m.–midnight
When to Go Anytime is excellent, but in summer it is the most floral, and there are concerts on the bandstand between May and August

Description and Comments St. James's is certainly London's most royal of all parks, lying as it does between Buckingham and St. James's Palaces. There is a view from Buckingham Palace and from the bridge in the middle of the lake that is just magical—it looks like our fondest fantasy of an enchanted fairy-tale kingdom, with the turrets and steeples of Whitehall in the distance. St. James is the place to go see birds; the famous pelicans are there, as well as a huge assortment of unusual feathered friends. The Ornithological Society of London donated some birds in 1837 and started this particular feature of this beautiful park.

A leper hospital, called St. James, was erected here in the 1400s. The Tyburn River flowed through this area, so the land was marshy and unsuitable for much more than hunting until King James I drained and planted the area as a pleasure garden, filling it with pelicans and other rara avis. He also had an exotic menagerie there, with crocodiles and elephants, for his court's entertainment. When Charles II returned from exile in France, he redid the park in a more formal, French manner, and opened St. James's Park to the public. It was embraced enthusiastically and began its long life as a favorite spot for Londoners to meet and stroll—although it did have its darker days when people hung laundry there, muggers prowled the bushes, and prostitutes conducted business. Its appeal was upgraded when George IV rebuilt Buckingham House to be a royal palace and had John Nash make the park a more beautiful and natural-looking place.

There is a children's playground on the southwest corner of the park, and The Cake House (open daily from 9:30 a.m. to 5:30 p.m.) is in the east end, north of the lake. There are concerts at the bandstand in summer, and the birds are there all year to be admired. Green-and-white striped deck chairs can be rented on an hourly basis between April and September.

Greenwich

In 1863, American author Nathaniel Hawthorne described the quiet town of Greenwich as "beautiful,—a spot where the art of man has conspired with Nature." No doubt he was thinking how the rolling hills of Greenwich Park create a glorious backdrop for Christopher Wren's splendid **Royal Naval College** and Inigo Jones's equally noble **Queen's House,** while Wren's other Greenwich project, the **Royal Observatory,** sits serenely on the park's highest hill. The streets of Greenwich are just perfect for strolling; whether you are wandering down historic Croom's Hill or over past St. Alfrege's near the town center, the area has retained much of its cozy village atmosphere. Weekends bring craft and antiques lovers of all kinds converging on the Greenwich Market or enjoying a boat ride on the Thames.

Greenwich is steeped in royal history. The park dates from 1433, and the Palace of Placentia once graced the riverside where the Royal Naval College now stands. Henry VIII and all three of his children, Mary I, Elizabeth I, and Edward IV were born here. In 1616, Jones began building the Queen's House as a Palladian country home at the bottom of the park for Charles II's wife, Henrietta Maria; Wren followed this up with the hilltop Observatory and the Naval College, which elegantly frames the Queen's House today. Just north of the town's center, the colossal Millennium Dome sits in anticipation of a new incarnation, now that the 2000 exhibition is done.

Getting There

Located only a few miles downriver from London, Greenwich is easy to reach and makes a delightful day trip for visitors. The town center provides a wide variety of book, art, and nautical shops as well as a diverse selection of restaurants from Vietnamese to Mexican to good old English pub food. On weekends, the Greenwich Market is teeming with craft stalls and, combined with the nearby flea market and secondhand book market, can allow for hours of browsing.

To get to Greenwich, catch Docklands Light Railway (DLR), a fully automated and electric overland tram car type of transport that leaves from Bank Street or Tower Hill. The trip is about 20 minutes from either station and in the summer includes a recording that guides you through the wharfs and docks of London's East End, leaving you at the Greenwich Pier or the Cutty Sark. By far, the most picturesque journey comes from a guided riverboat ride down the Thames, past views of St. Paul's Cathedral, Tower Bridge, and Docklands. Boats leave from Westminster, Charing Cross, and Tower Pier for Greenwich approximately every 45 minutes and take 40 minutes to an hour, depending on where you embark. Enquiries can be made by calling (0207) 930-4097 or (0207) 987-1185.

Finally, you can call the Greenwich Tourist Information Center at (0208) 858-6376, write them, or stop by their location at 46 Greenwich Church Street, London SE10 9BL, for information on guided tours in Greenwich, special events, or any additional information you may need.

Part Seven

Children's London

London with Children

London is a wonderful city for children, even jet-lagged ones who can't quite figure out when to go to sleep. Before you go to London, get out some English nursery rhymes or Dickens (depending on the age of your children) and introduce them to the wonders of London in letters. It will make it that much more exciting when you get here. Rent some good London's movies for kids: *101 Dalmatians* (not the animated one), *Oliver!*, *Mary Poppins, A Little Princess* (Shirley Temple version), *The Prince and the Pauper, A Christmas Carol* (the Muppets version is less scary than the old Alistair Syms one), and *The Princess Carabou* are just a few that can get them thinking about and looking at London. There's a brilliant website by the London Tourist Board at www.londontouristboard.com that provides a kid's-eye view of London and its attractions. I strongly recommend a visit to it by grade-school children.

London has an enormous selection of attractions for children of all ages. The museums are getting more interactive and attention-grabbing all the time. Even the staid old Victoria and Albert now features a fun cart on weekends to keep the kids busy, entertained, and actually learning something about the wonderful collection. Parents will enjoy the kids' attractions as much as the children will. Just maybe, if you give the kids a chance, they will find something great in the places that cater to a more mature palate, such as the National Portrait Gallery or the Globe Theatre. But don't count on it with the really little ones. With them it's just crowd control and riding on buses; they love the double deckers.

A "London Book"

A great idea to really get the kids paying attention and having fun is to start a "London book" before you even leave. Pick out a blank book, big enough to paste lots of things in, and write down the itinerary, paste in pictures of planes, get the stewardess to sign it, and so on. Then, everywhere you go, you can collect stubs and pamphlets and take plenty of photos. Get film developed at one-hour labs, and spend the evening helping with the scrapbook. Drawings, poems, thoughts, a leaf from Holland Park, a feather from the Serpentine—all these things can make a beautiful scrapbook that children will always love to look through. Get a disposable camera for your child to use to take his or her own photos; you'll be surprised at how much more they'll go in for sight-seeing when it has such a personal purpose.

Planning and Touring Tips

Here are a few ideas to bear in mind when planning a vacation with the little and not-so-little ones:

Age   Although the wonderful park playgrounds and certain tourist attractions of London have much to offer toddlers and preschoolers, the bulk of London's attractions are generally oriented to older kids and adults. Children should be a fairly mature six years old to get the most out of popular attractions such as the Imperial War Museum, the *HMS Belfast,* possibly even the Tower of London, and a year or two older to get much out of the art museums, cathedrals, and palaces that London has in such grand abundance.

Time of Year to Visit   If there is any way to swing it, avoid the crowded summer months. Try to go between late September and November or between early April and mid-June. If you have children of varying ages and your school-age kids are good students, consider taking the older ones out of school so you can visit during the less expensive, less congested off-season. Arrange special study assignments relating to the many educational aspects of London. If your school-age children are not great students and cannot afford to miss any school, take your vacation as soon as the school year ends in June.

Building Naps and Rest into Your Itinerary   London offers more attractions than you can possibly see in a whole week, so don't try to see everything in one day. Tour in the early morning and return to your hotel midday for lunch and a nap. Go back and visit more attractions in the late afternoon, or go to a park, or to The London Eye, which stays open till dusk in the summer; or take a bus tour that is easier on the legs. Don't pooh-pooh jet lag; children seem to suffer from it less than the adults, but they are thrown off-kilter by the time change. Try to get them on the right time by exposing them to plenty of sunlight and not letting them nap too long during the day.

Where to Stay   The best area to stay in when you're carting kids around is near a park—Hyde, Holland, or Kensington Gardens are good, and there are lots of inexpensive hotels around Paddington. Kids who will complain about tired feet and hunger will perk up amazingly when they see a swing set, have some room to kick a soccer ball around, or can watch horses ride by. It's important to get small children off the tourist trail for a few hours to rest and recuperate. Neglecting to relax and unwind is the best way to get the whole family in a snit and ruin the day.

With small children, you will be glad to have planned ahead. Make sure you get a hotel within a few minutes' walk to a tube station. Naps and relief from the frenetic pace of touring London are indispensable. Even if you do get some good downtime in a park, there is no true substitute for returning to the familiarity and security of your own hotel for the little ones. Children too large to sleep in a stroller will relax and revive better if you get them back to your room.

Another factor in choosing a hotel is whether or not it has a swimming pool. A lot of visitors to London assume that, like those in so many American destinations, London hotels automatically come with a pool. Nothing could be further from the truth. There are a few expensive ones that do; more to the point, there are many hotels that can steer you to a public pool or that have some arrangement with a health club. Call ahead to find out if there are any age restrictions on swimming. A swimming pool can be a lifesaver for both you and your kids, keeping you all happily busy and healthily exercising for hours. It's also great for dealing with jet lag.

Getting Around Getting around can be a bit of a hassle because of traffic congestion, hence decisions about how to get around and how much time to allow need to be made. Probably the most fun way is to take a bus. However, they are not all double deckers anymore, though these used to be the trademark London buses. But sitting on the top deck of a double decker is a great way to see London; plenty of sights and weird people for the kids to ogle at. The problem with buses could be that you might be stuck in traffic for hours, and the old-fashioned double-decker buses are not stroller-friendly, unlike the newer single-deck buses, which you can usually board without having to collapse your stroller. Fine if you have eight arms to struggle with the bags, baby, and other bits and pieces!

The quicker way to get around is via the tube. However, the system is neither disabled- or stroller-friendly. Strollers can be negotiated on the escalators, but there are a lot of stairs to deal with. This is fine if there are two or more adults in your group, but if you're alone, you could be left struggling, scooping up the whole stroller, with baby inside, to get up and down the stairs. It astounds me how many other passengers are quick to push or scurry by, rather than offer a helping hand.

If you are expecting a baby, don't expect people to surrender their seats for you. While heavily pregnant, often I had to stand while those already seated pretended not to notice my big belly, by burrowing deep into their copy of the *Evening Standard.* However, not all of us Brits are so rude. Despite all who pretend not to notice your plight, the odd person is willing to help.

It is worth noting that there are seats on the buses and tubes that are clearly indicated as priority seating for those with young children or the elderly. So, if no one has offered and you're feeling bold, you have every right to ask someone to move.

For short hops with the kids, a black cab might be the best idea (if walking is not an option, of course). Just remember that traffic is pretty appalling around all central areas during the day (Oxford Street, Marble Arch, Piccadilly, Bayswater, Knightsbridge, Chelsea, and Kensington), and these taxis are not cheap.

Stay Loose   As every parent has discovered by day three of their first baby's life, flexibility is everything in parenting, and that goes double for sight-seeing with children. Remember that having fun is not necessarily the same as seeing everything. When you and your children start getting tired and irritable, call a time out and regroup. Trust your instincts. What would really feel best right now? Another museum, a rest break with some ice cream, or going back to the room for a nap? The way to have a great vacation is to put the emphasis on being happy and having a good time, whatever that takes. You do not have to meet a quota for experiencing every museum or attraction, seeing every neighborhood and monument, or following every suggestion in the book. London has been here for a long time, and it's not going anywhere. Your kids' childhood, on the other hand, is a flash of lightning. Make sure their memories of London are happy ones, and they'll want to come back when they're grown up.

All for One and One for All   When you're traveling en famille, you are a moving unit made up of many differing tastes, abilities, and interests. Accept that energy levels vary among individuals and be prepared to respond to small children or other members of your group who poop out. Try not to let your own disappointment hurt the tired one's feelings. Maybe you can take turns with the other grown-up, if there is one with you, in taking the walking wounded back to the hotel, so that one of you can continue sight-seeing.

Setting Limits and Making Plans   The best way to avoid arguments and disappointments is to develop a game plan before you go. Establish some general guidelines for each day and try to get everybody excited about the plans. Be sure to include:

1. Wake-up time and breakfast plans.

2. What time you need to depart for the part of London you plan to explore.

3. What you need to take with you.

4. A policy for splitting the group up or for staying together.

5. A plan for what to do if the group gets separated or someone is lost.

6. How long you intend to tour in the morning and what you want to see, including fall-back plans in the event an attraction is too crowded.

7. A policy on what you can afford for snacks, lunch, and refreshments. This is very important in London, the most expensive of cities.

8. A target time for returning to your hotel for a rest.

9. If you rest, a target time for returning to the touring and for how late you will stay out.

10. Plans for dinner.

11. A policy for shopping and buying souvenirs, including who pays (parents or kids).

Be Flexible   Having a game plan does not mean forgoing spontaneity or sticking rigidly to the itinerary. Once again, listen to your intuition. Alter the plan if the situation warrants. Be prepared to roll with the punches.

Rain, Sunburn, and Dehydration   London's weather is changeable. Although it's not often terribly hot, it can get quite warm in the sun, and you can get a beauty of a sunburn. Carry a small bottle of sunscreen, or smear it on before you go out. Remember a bottle of water to rehydrate the happy campers. Rain is the biggest surprise in London; you never know when it's going to come, but chances are it will, if only for a sprinkle. The best and lightest protection is a plastic rain poncho; you can carry a few and not have as much weight or bulk as with a couple of umbrellas.

Blisters   Blisters and sore feet are common for visitors of all ages, so wear comfortable, well-broken-in shoes and two pairs of thin socks (preferable to one pair of thick socks). If you or your children are unusually susceptible to blisters, carry some precut Moleskin bandages; they offer the best possible protection and won't sweat off. When you feel a hot spot, stop, air out your foot, and place a Moleskin over the area before a blister forms. You'll probably find some in London in a pharmacy under a Dr. Scholl's display, but bring some with you just in case. Sometimes small children won't tell their parents about a developing blister until it's too late. Check out your preschooler's feet a couple of times a day—this penny's worth of prevention will be worth many pounds of cure to you and them.

Health and Medical Care   If you have a child who requires medication, pack plenty and bring it on the plane in a carry-on bag. A bottle of liquid Dramamine will come in handy to fight off motion sickness, which can affect kids who are normally fine in a car but may get sick in a plane, train, or boat.

A small first-aid kit, available at most pharmacies, will handle most minor cuts, scrapes, and splinters and is easy to pack. Grown-up and children's-strength aspirin or Tylenol, a thermometer, cough syrup, baby wipes,

a plastic spoon, a nightlight, and pacifiers will round out a small kit of health-
related items for people traveling with children or infants. Again, bring it from home. It's much more expensive to get these items in London.

If You Become Separated Before venturing out of your hotel room, sit down with your kids and discuss what they should do if they get separated from you while touring a museum or attraction. Tell them to find a uniformed guard and ask for help. Point out that the main entrance of most London attractions has an information desk where they should go if they temporarily get separated.

It's not a bad idea to dress the smaller kids in distinctive colors so you can find them with a quick scanning. It is also considered prudent to sew a label into each child's shirt indicating his or her name, your name, and the name of your hotel. The same thing can be accomplished less elegantly by writing the information on a strip of masking tape. Hotel security professionals suggest that the information be printed in small letters and that the tape be affixed to the outside of the child's shirt five inches or so below the armpit.

Rainy Days As you know, London is a pretty rainy place—certainly not as bad as its reputation (Rome actually has more inches per year), but it does come down. Museums and galleries are obvious solutions to the rainy-day blues; that old stand-by, the movies, is a good place to kick back. Whiteley's has an indoor ice-skating rink, and there are a few paint-your-own-pottery places that kids just love—see "Activities" below for names and numbers. You have to wait a day or two to pick up your finished pieces, so ask ahead how long it will take to fire your kids' work. There's also brass rubbing at St. Martin–in-the-Fields, a cheaper option, and the kids can take their rubbings with them when leaving the church. Look in *Time Out* under children's events, as there may be a puppet show or story-time reading where you can stay dry. You can also get *Kids Out,* published monthly, for some bright ideas. There's a phone number, Kidsline (0207) 222-8070, that will give you details of events, shows, museums, attractions, and workshops for kids. Also, the London Tourist Board has a 24-hour recorded service of what's on for children in London; phone (0839) 123-404 or (0839) 123-436.

The lists below are very general; obviously some kids will be of a more appropriate age to enjoy some attractions than others. I've left out some of the attractions that one can see in any city, such as zoos, arcades, and amusement parks.

Please note the museums that charge have some free-admission hours in the late afternoon—you'll only get an hour and a half, but that's about all many kids can take, and the savings are well worth it. These include the London, Victoria and Albert, Imperial War, Natural History, and Science Museums.

The Top 10 Most Popular Sights for Children

1. The British Airways London Eye

2. Science Museum

3. London Aquarium (toddlers and preschoolers are very entertained here; older ones might prefer something more Londonesque)

4. Museum of London

5. Museum of Childhood

6. *HMS Belfast*

7. Tower of London

8. London Transport Museum

9. Natural History Museum

10. British Museum

Also See

1. Imperial War Museum

2. Madame Tussaud's and the London Planetarium

3. The Rock Circus

4. The London Balloon

5. London Dungeon (for gore-loving adolescents)

6. All the military museums for children of that bent: Cabinet War Rooms, Imperial War Museum, Guards Museum, National Army Museum

The Top 10 Least Popular Sights for Children

1. Queen's Gallery

2. Kenwood House

3. Design Museum

4. Buckingham Palace

5. Dickens' House

6. Parliament

7. Portobello Road

8. Kensington Palace

9. Dr. Johnson's House

10. The Tate (both the Britain and the Modern)

Services for Families

Rental Equipment and Child Care

Chelsea Baby Hire (phone (0208) 540-8830) and **Nappy Express** (phone (0208) 361-4040) rent cribs, high chairs, double strollers (or buggies, as they're known here), along with toys, household products, and more. For child care, consider **Childminders** (phone (0207) 935-3000). You'll first pay a joining fee for the service, then an hourly rate. **Universal Aunts**

(phone (0207) 738-8937) can deal with any domestic need or crisis, like a good auntie should, including short-term baby-sitting needs. **Hopes and Dreams** (phone (0207) 833-9388) is an alternative to agency baby-sitters—it's a day nursery for kids, complete with organic food and big fun. Big prices, too. **Pippa Pop-Ins Excursions and Activities** (phone (0207) 385-2458) is another day nursey based in Fulham.

Activities

Paint Your Own Pottery

Kids can practice their creative skills at **Art 4 Fun** in the Creative Café. It serves food, and kids can paint many different things. There are several branches, including: 196 Kensington Park Road, W11 (zone 13; tube: Notting Hill); 444 Chiswick High Road, W4 (zone 12; tube: Turnham Green); and 172 West End Lane, NW6 (zone 1; tube: West Hampstead). All are open daily, 10 a.m.–7 p.m. Call (0208) 994-4800 or visit www.Art4Fun.com for details. Also try **Bridgewater Pottery Café** (zone 11; 735 Fulham Road, SW6; phone (0207) 736-2157; tube: Fulham Broadway).

Brass Rubbings

Brass Rubbing Centre (zone 7; Trafalgar Square, WC2; phone (0207) 930-9306; tube: Leicester Square) in the crypt of St. Martin-in-the-Fields offers a wonderful treat for kids age six and up. They can make their own souvenirs by rubbing a waxy chalk over paper that covers brasses with carved medieval motifs such as knights, dragons, crests, etc. **All-Hallows-By-The-Tower** (zone 3; Byward Street, EC3; phone (0207) 481-2928; tube: Tower Hill) is another option. The church, which was built in 675 A.D., has an interesting history. John Quincy Adams, the sixth president of the United States, was married here, and William Penn, founder of Pennsylvania, was baptized here. Check out the museum (with an audio tour available); it's good for kids, as it covers all sorts of exciting historical events, including the Great Fire of London (1666), complete with sound effects. Brass rubbing is done 11 a.m.–4 p.m. but call first.

Skating

Queen's Ice-Skating Rink (zone 14; 17 Queenway, W2; phone (0207) 229-0172; tube: Queensway or Bayswater) is a big rink. The minimum age of skaters allowed is three years.

Bookstores

Call the following to check on storytelling performances: **Books Etc.** (zone 14; Whiteleys Center, W2; phone (0207) 229-3865; tube: Queensway or

Bayswater) and **Children's Book Centre** (zone 13; 237 Kensington High Street, W8; phone (0207) 937-749; tube: High Street Kensington).

Playgrounds

Battersea Park is all over fun, plus a zoo (zone 11; Albert Bridge Road, SW11; take the tube to Sloane Square, then bus 19 or 137).

Coram Fields (zone 2; 93 Guildford Street, WC1; phone (0207) 837-6138; tube: Russell Square) is a famous playground adults may not enter without an accompanying child—and they mean it. Animals are on view, and it's open 9 a.m. to dusk.

Holland Park (zone 13; tube: Holland Park) is a multilevel adventure playground, with an area for kids under age eight and peacocks, too.

Hyde Park (zone 13; tube: High Street Kensington), east of Princes Gate, has good swings and play stuff, as well as paddle-boats in summer and Peter Pan all year.

Kensington Gardens (zone 13; tube: High Street Kensington) has the Princess Diana Memorial, a playground at the end of Broad Walk, and remote-control model boats to watch in the Round Pond.

Regents Park (zone 15; tube: Regents Park) has three playgrounds and two boating lakes, one of which is for children.

St. James's Park (zone 8; tube: Green Park) has a smallish playground by Birdcage Walk and plenty of pelicans and other birds to watch. The 3 p.m. feeding of pelicans is very popular.

Syon Park & London Butterfly House (tube: Gunnersbury or Kew Bridge rail, then bus 267 or 237) is an estate open daily, 10 a.m.–5:30 p.m. Older kids will appreciate the Butterfly House, but the younger ones will love Aquatic Experience (phone (0208) 847-4730), which features fish, reptiles, amphibians, and other small animals in their natural habitats. There's also **Snakes & Ladders** (phone (0208) 847-0946), an adventure playground. Check out the miniature steam train in the gardens. Call (0208) 560-0881 for Syon Park information and (0208) 560-0378 for Butterfly House information (tube: Gunnersbury or Kew Gardens, then bus 267 or 237).

Theaters

Little Angel Theater (14 Dagmar Passage, off Cross Street, N1; phone (0207) 226-1787; www.littleangeltheatre.com; tube: Angel or Highbury & Islington), the city's only permanent puppet theatre, which has been running for 40 years, is a delightful venue with a 100-seat auditorium. Weekend shows by the resident or visiting puppet companies are offered, as well as shows during Christmas and half-term holidays. Tickets are £6.50 adults and £5.50 children.

National Film Theatre (zone 5; South Bank, SE1; phone (0207) 928-3535; www.bfi.org.uk; tube: Waterloo or Embankment) runs matinee performances for children every weekend day from 3 to 4 p.m. Some weekends they have special workshops for children over age 6. Tickets are £5.50 adults and £1 children.

Polka Theatre for Children (zone 12; 240 The Broadway, SW19; phone (0208) 543-4888; www.polkatheatre.com; tube: Wimbledon or British Rail to South Wimbledon) seats 300 and also has an 80-seat adventure room for children under age 5, a small but unusual playground, a cafe, and a gift shop. With excellent disability access. Tickets, £5–12.

Puppet Theatre Barge (zone 14; Bloomfield Road, W9; phone (0207) 249-6876; www.puppetbarge.com; tube: Warwick Avenue) is a traveling puppet barge featuring old-fashioned string marionettes. It is moored in Little Venice, Maida Vale from November to May. Shows run on weekends and during school holidays, beginning at 3 p.m. Advanced reservations are recommended. Tickets are £6.50 adults and £6 children.

Transportation

The **Six 2 16 Car Club,** "London's First Children's Car Service," is really for kids who travel alone back and forth to school, but they can also ferry you and your brood around London (phone (0208) 830-2255; www.six-2-16.co.uk).

Where to Eat

Here are some kid-friendly places to eat:

Big East (zone 11; 332–334 Kings Road, SW3; phone (0207) 352-4071; tube: Sloane Square) is geared up for kids; there's a special menu, plus crayons to keep those hands busy. Kids prices are £5.95–8.95 and include unlimited soft drinks and some chocolate gooey thing.

Hard Rock Cafe (zone 8; 150 Old Park Lane, W1; phone (0207) 629-0382; www.hardrock.com; tube: Green Park or Hyde Park Center) has lots of loud music and rock memorabilia festooning every available surface. It may not be suitable for very young children. I took my five-year-old niece and she spent the whole time with her hands over her ears moaning about the noise, but her baby brother didn't mind at all! There is a special kids menu for £5.95 and crayons to distract them.

Luna Nuova (zone 7; 22 Shorts Garden, WC2; phone (0207) 836-4110; tube: Covent Garden) is a friendly pizzeria where kids can make their own pizza and help the chef during slower periods.

Maxwells (zone 7; 8–9 James Street, WC2; phone (0207) 836-0303; www.maxwells.co.uk; tube: Covent Garden) is in a great location, near the Covent Garden piazza, and has a special kids menu, crayons, balloons, and more. During some holidays, they decorate the restaurant and provide seasonally festive menus.

Rainforest Cafe (zone 7; 20 Shaftsbury Avenue, WC2; phone (0207) 434-3111; www.therainforestcafe.co.uk; tube: Picadilly Circus), an American import, is a great place for kids, with its children's menu (burgers, ribs, sandwiches) and special treats for parties (face painting, goodie bags, and more), all in a jungle-esqe setting.

Sticky Fingers (zone 11; 1A Phillimore Gardens, W8; phone (0207) 938-5338; www.stickyfingers.co.uk; tube: High Street Kensington) is owned by Bill Wyman (ex–Rolling Stones member) and offers a kids' menu for £4.95 that includes burgers, ribs, chicken, pasta, and more. Sundays are best, with face painting, balloons, and a generally fun atmosphere.

Smollensky's (zone 7; 105 The Strand, WC2; phone (0207) 497-2101; www.smollenskys.co.uk; tube: Charing Cross) on the Strand is the perfect place for kids, especially for Saturday and Sunday lunch. There's a play area, a creche for the really young ones, and endless entertainment, including magicians, clowns, face painting, computer games, and more.

TGI Friday's (zone 7; 6 Bedford Street, WC2; phone (0207) 379-0585; www.fridays.co.uk; tube: Covent Garden off Charing Cross), another American import that's family friendly, offers balloons, crayons, and children's menus, including a Sesame Street one that comes with a free toy. On weekends, there is face painting and a magician on Sunday. If you happen to be weaning, they offer free organic baby food.

Shopping for Children

Toys

Daisy & Tom (zone 11; 81 King's Road, Chelsea, SW3; phone (0207) 352-5000; tube: Sloane Square) is a great kids' store with toys, books, nursery furniture, a carousel, and a very cool hair-cutting salon. **Davenport's Magic Shop** (zone 7; 7 Charing Cross Underground Concourse, Strand, WC2; phone (0207) 836-0408; tube: Charing Cross) is still going strong after 100 years of selling magic. **Hamleys** (zone 8; 188–196 Regent Street, W1; phone (0207) 734-3161; www.hamleys.com; tube: Oxford Street or Picadilly Circus), with its seven floors, is said to be the largest toy store in the world. You've been warned. **Harrods** (zone 10; 87 Brompton Road, SW1; phone (0207) 730-1234; www.harrods.com; tube: Knightsbridge) has a remarkable selection of dolls, but watch that wallet. **Tridias** (zone 11; 25 Bute Street, SW7; phone (0207) 584-2330; tube: South Kensington) sell lots of interesting toys and small, inexpensive gimcracks.

Clothing

These stores tend to be like kids themselves—here one minute, gone the next. Most of the clothes stores listed in our first edition have gone belly up, so it's wise to call before you venture to the following stores. Most of the stores listed are included not because they have cheap deals, but because they have interesting and distinctive European selections: from Petit Bateau, Petite Ourse, Laura Ashley, and other British or French designers.

Brora (zone 11; 344 Kings Road, SW3; phone (0207) 352-3697; www.brora.co.uk; tube: Sloane Square) specializes in cashmere and woolen clothes for newborns and young children, along with their established adult line.

Caramel (zone 11; 291 Brompton Road, SW3; phone (0207) 589-7001; tube: South Kensington) offers lots of cute and trendy gear for children up to approximately eight years of age.

Clementine (zone 13; 73 Ledbury Road, W11; phone (0207) 243-6331; tube: Notting Hill Gate or Westbourne Park) specializes in French and Italian clothes for children of all ages.

Catimini (zone 8; 52 South Molton Street, W1; phone (0207) 629-8099; www.catimini.fr; tube: Bond Street) has cute clothes with unusual details, such as pockets that resemble dolls' faces and candy-shaped buttons. It carries clothing for children up to approximately 14 years of age.

Daisy & Tom (zone 11; 181–183 Kings Road, SW3; phone (0207) 352-5000; tube: Sloane Square) is a great kids shop with designer labels such as Petit Bateau, Miniman, and Damask. While you shop, kids can ride the carousel or get a haircut. Clothes are for children up to 10 years of age.

Jigsaw Junior (zone 13; 190 Westbourne Grove, W11; phone (0207) 229-8654; www.jigsaw-online.com; tube: Notting Hill) offers simple clothes for girls only from the successful Jigsaw chain of fashion stores. There are plenty of playthings in the store to keep young shoppers happy. Clothes are for children up to 13 years of age.

Mothercare World (zone 8; 461 Oxford Street, W1; phone (0207) 629-6621; www.mothercare.com; tube: Marble Arch or Bond Street), although a chain store, is a great place to snap up affordable home-brand basics and clothing featuring licensed characters such as Barbie, Action Man, and Winnie the Pooh. Additional branches abound. The shop also carries baby products (see next section).

Please Mum (zone 10; 85 Knightsbridge, SW1; phone (0207) 486-1380; tube: Knightsbridge) specializes in Italian designers, from Moschino to Versace, plus the Please Mum home-brand collection. Frilly, old-fashioned children's ball gowns are a uniqe offering. Clothes are for children up to 14 years of age.

Paul Smith for Children (zone 7; 40–44 Florral Street, WC2; phone (0207) 379-7133; www.paulsmith.co.uk; tube: Covent Garden) features this world-famous designer's funky collection, including bold duck, helicopter, and airplane prints, which really do look cool. Shoes are also available. Clothes are for children up to 16 years of age.

Tartine et Chocolat (zone 8; 66 South Molton Street, W1; phone (0207) 629-7233; tube: Bond Street) is the place to go if you're looking for more conservative outfits. You'll find double-breasted coats, velvet dresses, lots of blues for baby boys, and lots of pinks for baby girls at this Parisian boutique.

Shoes

Buckle My Shoe (zone 8; 19 St. Christophers Place, W1; phone (0207) 935-5589; www.bucklemyshoe.com; tube: Bond Street) has more cute delights for those tiny feet—funky animal print slippers, glittery sandals. Not cheap, but what the heck!

Baby Goods

Mothercare World is always heaving with expectant and established parents, stocking up on cribs, bedding, strollers, highchairs, bottles, diapers, toys, and more. Particularly handy are the bathroom stalls (big enough to push strollers into), a feeding area with bottle warmers, and a special room for nursing mothers complete with rocking chairs and a water dispenser. (See the entry in the "Clothing" section, above, for location information.)

Nursery Window (zone 11; 83 Walton Street, SW3; phone (0207) 581-3358; www.nurserywindow.co.uk; tube: South Kensington), which is not too pricey, specializes in nursery furnishings: cribs, bedding, curtains, and even wallpaper. All fabrics are designed and printed in the United Kingdom. There's also a mail-order service.

Part Eight

Dining in London

Ten years ago, if you had said you were going to London for the food, your friends would have advised a long period of rest and perhaps a visit to your doctor. The idea simply seemed crazy. Food in London, and in all of the United Kingdom, was famous for its brutally unyielding awfulness.

To say that things have changed is to make a gross understatement. London now boasts two restaurants with three Michelin stars (the highest accolade restaurateurs can receive) and has been described as one of the gastronomic capitals of the world. Well, you can argue that kind of point endlessly, and making comparisons with other cities is an academic exercise. But there's no denying that you can now eat better in London than at any time since the Romans arrived.

Asian and South Asian cuisines have always been a strong point in London, and they remain so—but they're even better now, especially Indian cooking. There's a bigger range than ever before, with more regional variety and a general emphasis on fresh ingredients cooked to order. The same can be said of Chinese food, another traditional area of strength. It's true also of French and Italian cooking. Even old-fashioned British food is taken with the greatest seriousness, again at every price level.

But if there's anything special about London's food at the moment, it's a phenomenon that's called modern British, or (the term used here) modern European cooking. Nearly everyone who pays attention to gastronomic trends will use some version of this term. Defining it precisely . . . well, that's another matter. But here's a rough working definition: classic European techniques (especially French and Italian) applied to top-quality ingredients that may—but don't necessarily—come from any corner of the globe.

London is well suited to the development of this kind of eclecticism in cooking. The ingredients are there because of the city's location within

Europe and its longtime connections with Asia. In addition, a widely traveled customer base provides a serious demand for good cooking. Some of the best chefs exploit these elements with amazing results. Some borrow widely from Asia and the Americas, with the results bordering on so-called fusion cooking. Some remain deliberately French and Italian in orientation, whereas others emphasize the British source of ingredients and inspirations. Modern European is the most interesting food being cooked in London now, and restaurants of this type feature prominently in these listings.

If eating out in London is better than ever, you should also be warned of the downside: it's expensive—even for Londoners, and especially expensive for traveling Americans, with the dollar weak against the pound sterling. It is nearly impossible to find a good three-course meal with a bottle of wine for under £25 a head, and even fairly basic restaurants have an annoying tendency to cost twice that amount if you drink more than the house wine. We wish it weren't so, but there's nothing to be done unless exchange rates and pricing policies change.

In the meantime, those who seek high quality at low prices should pay special attention to the list of gastropubs in the "More Recommendations" section. These are old-fashioned pubs, refurbished in a simple style, that place the greatest emphasis on good food rather than beer and crisps (potato chips). The top gastropubs are usually off the beaten track (one reason they can charge lower prices), but you should seek them out if you don't mind a bit of extra traveling. They are some of London's best bets for budget eating in totally relaxed surroundings.

At the other restaurants, there are ways to cut costs. Lunch is likely to be considerably cheaper than dinner, and some places have pre- or post-theater offers with limited choice and lower prices. With drinks making up a large part of many bills, look for house wines or order by the glass if that's all you want. And don't feel obliged to order a bottle of water (almost always marked up heavily) if tap water will please you just as well. If you're traveling with children but don't see a children's menu, ask if a child-size portion can be prepared, as many good restaurants will oblige.

The other big complaint about London restaurants is the quality of service, and there's a lot of merit in the complaint. Cooking skills have zoomed up, but there is a perennial shortage of well-trained, conscientious waiters. At expensive restaurants this should not (in theory) be a problem, but in others—well, you may be lucky and you may not. Complain if you feel it's warranted. You'll be doing the restaurant a favor. And if you get poor service at high prices, complain even more vociferously. It shouldn't happen but it does.

One final word is in order here. The restaurant profiles that follow were assembled during a period of tumultuous change in the London restaurant world. Restaurants accepted reservations one day and announced their closure the next. Chefs moved around at an unprecedented rate. Menus were changed fundamentally. New management moved in on well-established operations. The pace of change from week to week makes it inevitable that further change will have occurred by the time you hold this book in your hands—some months after the section was written. Needless to say, this is out of our control.

The Restaurants

Rating Our Favorite London Restaurants

We have developed detailed profiles for the best and most interesting (in our opinion) restaurants in town. Each profile features an easily scanned heading that allows you, in just a second, to check out the restaurant's name, cuisine, star rating, cost, quality rating, and value rating.

Cuisine This is actually less straightforward than it sounds. A couple of years ago, for example, "pan-Asian" restaurants in Washington, D.C. were serving what was then generally described as "fusion" food—Asian ingredients with European techniques, or vice versa. Since then, there has been a pan-Asian explosion, but nearly all specialize in what would be street food back home: noodles, skewers, dumplings, and soups. Once-general categories have become subdivided—French into bistro fare and even Provençal, "new continental" into regional American and "eclectic"—while others have broadened and fused: Middle Eastern and Provençal into Mediterranean, Spanish and South American into nuevo Latino, and so on. In some cases, we have used the broader terms (i.e., "French") but added descriptions to give a clearer idea of the fare. Again, though, experimentation and "fusion" is ever more common, so don't hold us, or the chefs, to too strict a style.

Overall Rating The overall rating is a rating that encompasses the entire dining experience, including style, service, and ambience, in addition to the taste, presentation, and quality of the food. Five stars is the highest rating possible and connotes the best of everything. Four-star restaurants are exceptional, and three-star restaurants are well above average. Two-star restaurants are good. One star is used to indicate an average restaurant that demonstrates an unusual capability in some area of specialization—for example, an otherwise unmemorable place that has great barbecued chicken.

Cost Our expense description provides a comparative sense of how much a complete meal will cost. A complete meal for our purposes consists of an appetizer, entree, and dessert. Drinks and tips are excluded.

Inexpensive	Less than £20 per person
Moderate	£20–50 per person
Expensive	More than £50 per person

Quality Rating   The food quality is rated on a scale of one to five stars, five being the best rating attainable. The quality rating is based expressly on the taste, freshness of ingredients, preparation, presentation, and creativity of food served. There is no consideration of price. If you are a person who wants the best food available and cost is not an issue, you need look no further than the quality ratings.

Value Rating   If, on the other hand, you are looking for both quality and value, then you should check the value rating. The value ratings are defined as follows:

★★★★★	Exceptional value; a real bargain
★★★★	Good value
★★★	Fair value; you get exactly what you pay for
★★	Somewhat overpriced
★	Significantly overpriced

Locating the Restaurant   At the end of the heading is a designation for geographic zone. This zone description will give you a general idea of where the restaurant described is located. We've divided London into the following 15 geographic zones (see pages xii–xxx for detailed zone maps).

Zone 1 North London: Hampstead, Highgate

Zone 2 Bloomsbury and Holborn

Zone 3 The City, Clerkenwell, and Barbican

Zone 4 East End: Spitalfields, White Chapel

Zone 5 South London: South Bank, Lambeth, Brixton

Zone 6 Greenwich and Docklands

Zone 7 Soho and the West End

Zone 8 Mayfair and Piccadilly

Zone 9 Victoria and Westminster

Zone 10 Knightsbridge and Belgravia

Zone 11 Chelsea and South Kensington

Zone 12 West London: Hammersmith, Chiswick, Richmond, Kew

Zone 13 Kensington, Holland Park, Notting Hill

Zone 14 Bayswater, Marylebone, Little Venice, St. John's Wood

Zone 15 Regent's Park and Camden Town

Payment   We've listed the type of payment accepted at each restaurant using the following codes: AMEX equals American Express (Optima), CB equals Carte Blanche, D equals Discover, DC equals Diners Club, JCB equals Japan Credit Bureau, MC equals MasterCard, and VISA is self-explanatory.

Who's Included   Restaurants in London open and close at an alarming rate. So, for the most part, we have tried to confine our list to establishments with a proven track record over a fairly long period of time. The exceptions here are the newer offspring of the demigods of the culinary world—these places are destined to last, at least until our next update. Also, the list is highly selective. Noninclusion of a particular place does not necessarily indicate that the restaurant is not good, only that we did not feel it ranked among the best in its genre. Detailed profiles of individual restaurants follow in alphabetical order at the end of this chapter.

LONDON RESTAURANTS CHART

Restaurant	Cuisine	Price	Overall Rating	Quality	Value	Zone
Alfred	British	Inexp/Moderate ★★		★★½	★★★	2
Arkansas Café	American	Inexpensive	★★	★★★	★★★★	4
Bank	Modern European	Moderate	★★★	★★★½	★★★	2
Belgo	Belgian	Inexp/Moderate ★		★	★★★	7
Bibendum	Modern	Expensive	★★★★	★★★★	★★	11
Blue Print Café	Modern European	Moderate	★★★	★★★★½	★★★	5
Boisdale Restaurant and Bar	British	Moderate	★★½	★★★	★★★	10
Cactus Blue	American/ Modern European	Moderate	★★★	★★★½	★★★★	11
Café Spice Namaste	Indian	Moderate	★★★★	★★★★	★★★★	4
Cambio Detercio	Spanish	Moderate	★★★	★★★½	★★★★	11
Cantina Vinopolis	Modern European	Moderate	★★½	★★★	★★★★	5
Le Caprice	Modern	Moderate	★★½	★★★½	★★★	9
Chez Gerard	French (Bistro)	Inexp/Moderate ★★		★★★	★★★	7
Chuen Cheng Ku	Chinese	Inexp/Moderate ★★		★★★	★★★★	7
Clarke's	Modern European	Moderate/ Expensive	★★★★	★★★★	★★★	13
Connaught Restaurant	French (Haute Cuisine)	Expensive	★★★★	★★★★½	★★★	8
Corney & Barrow	Modern European	Moderate	★★	★★★	★★★	2, 4
Fifth Floor	Modern European	Moderate	★★★½	★★★½	★★★	10
fish!	Fish/ Shellfish	Inexp/Moderate ★★½		★★★	★★★★	7
Le Gavroche	French (Haute Cuisine)	Expensive	★★★★½	★★★★½	★★★	8
Heartstone	Modern European	Inexp/Moderate ★★★½		★★★½	★★★★★	15
Ibla	Italian	Moderate	★★	★★★½	★★★★	14
The Ivy	Modern European	Moderate	★★★★	★★★★	★★★	7

LONDON RESTAURANTS CHART

Restaurant	Cuisine	Price	Overall Rating	Quality	Value	Zone
Joe Allen	American	Inexp/Moderate	★★½	★★★	★★★	7
Livebait	Seafood	Inexp/Moderate	★★★½	★★★½	★★★	5, 7
Mango Room	Caribbean	Inexpensive	★★½	★★★½	★★★★	15
Mash	Modern European	Inexp/Moderate	★★	★★★½	★★★	7
Matsuri	Japanese	Moderate/ Expensive	★★★½	★★★½	★★	9
Moro	Spanish/ Middle Eastern	Moderate	★★★★	★★★★	★★★★	3
Mr. Kong	Chinese	Inexp/Moderate	★★★½	★★★½	★★★★	7
Nobu	"New Style" Japanese	Expensive	★★★★	★★★★	★★	8
North Sea Fish Restaurant	Fish and Chips	Inexpensive	★½	★★½	★★★★★	2
L'Odeon	Modern European	Moderate/ Expensive	★★★½	★★★½	★★★	14
1 Lombard Street	Modern European	Expensive	★★★★	★★★½	★★★	3
Orrey	Modern European	Expensive	★★★★½	★★★★★½	★★★	14
Pied à Terre	Modern British/French	Expensive	★★★★½	★★★★★½	★★★	14
Pizza Express	Pizza	Inexpensive	★	★★	★★★★	1
Pollo	Italian	Inexpensive	★	★★	★★★★★	7
Pret à Manger	Sandwiches	Inexpensive	★	★★	★★★★	3
Prospect Grill	Modern European/American	Inexp/Moderate	★★★½	★★★½	★★★★★	7
Quaglino's	Modern European	Moderate	★★½	★★★	★★★	9
Rasa	Indian	Moderate	★★★½	★★★½	★★★★	8
Richard Corrigan at Lindsay House	British	Moderate/ Expensive	★★★½	★★★½	★★	7
Royal China	Chinese	Inexpensive	★★★	★★★	★★★★	14
Rules	British	Moderate/ Expensive	★★★	★★★½	★★★	7
Silks & Spice	Asian	Inexpensive/ Moderate	★★	★★★	★★★★	14
Spiga	Italian	Inexpensive	★★	★★★	★★★	7
Stanley's	British	Inexpensive	★★	★★★	★★★★	7
St. John	Modern British	Moderate	★★★★	★★★★½	★★★★	3
Tamarind	Indian	Moderate	★★★½	★★★½	★★★	8
Teatro	Modern European	Moderate	★★½	★★★	★★★	7
Veeraswamy	Indian	Moderate	★★★½	★★★½	★★★★	7
Wagamama	Asian	Inexpensive	★	★★	★★★★	2, 7
Wódka	Polish	Moderate	★★½	★★★	★★★	11
Zaika	Modern Indian	Expensive	★★★★½	★★★★★½	★★★	13

More Recommendations

Chinese

China City   (25A Lisle Street, WC2; (0207) 734-3388). Dim sum specialists by day, solid Cantonese menu in the evening. This is a good alternative if there's a long line at Chuen Cheng Ku (see page 273).

Fung Shing   (15 Lisle Street, WC2; (0207) 437-1539) features cooking similar in ambition to Mr. Kong (see page 284) and is capable of producing memorable dishes.

Harbour City   (46 Gerrard Street, WC2; (0207) 439-7120) serves superb dim sum and is good in the evenings as well. This place is very popular with the local Chinese community.

Hunan   (51 Pimlico Road, SW; (0207) 730-5712) is one of London's few Hunan specialists and is essential for devotees of that spicy cuisine.

Mandarin Kitchen   (14–16 Queensway, W2; (0207) 721-7946) is just across the street from Royal China (see page 292). It's dreary in decor but offers wonderful dim sum and special dishes.

Fish and Chips

Upper Street Fish Shop   (324 Upper Street, N1; (0207) 359-1401) is upmarket fish and chips in a trendy area that's popular with locals; they have great desserts in addition to sparkling-fresh fish.

Geales   (2 Farmer Street, W8; (0207) 727-7969) is long established but was recently given a makeover. This popular spot in fashionable Notting Hill is almost always crowded.

French

1 Lombard Street   (1 Lombard Street, EC3; (0207) 929-6611) is a big brasserie and a smaller, pricier dining room in a building that began life as a bank; the cooking can be sensational, and the location is good if you're exploring the City (London's financial district).

Gordon Ramsay   (68–69 Royal Hospital Road, SW3; (0207) 352-4441) boasts three Michelin stars, an extraordinarily talented chef, and a small space that means tables are hard to come by. It's one of the best in London, but with dizzying prices outside the set lunch. Anyway, it doesn't matter. You have to reserve tables a month in advance, and they're almost impossible to get!

The Square   (6–10 Bruton Street, W1; (0207) 495-7100). Some people consider the modern European cooking here among the best in London, and their views are legitimate. Only the pricey wine list and occasional wobbles of service excluded it from the main entries, but it should be a top choice for a special, expensive meal.

Gastropubs and Wine Bars

Cork & Bottle Wine Bar   (44–46 Cranbourn Street, WC2; (0207) 734-7807). The food is nothing special, but the wine list is amazing, and the Leicester Square location is as central as you can get. This is why the cramped basement rooms are always packed. It's good for a light bite and a drink before or after a movie or play.

The Cow   (89 Westbourne Park Road, W11; (0207) 221-0021). Prices are not especially low, but quality is especially high at this popular place near Notting Hill.

The Eagle   (159 Farringdon Road, EC1; (0207) 837-1353) is the first of the gastropubs and still one of the best, though its immense popularity means space is hard to come by; if you're nearby, pop in for classy Italian/French cooking.

The Havelock Tavern   (57 Masbro Road, W14; (0207) 603-5374) is a popular local pub in a nice residential area of Shepherd's Bush; it has great atmosphere and great food.

The Vine   (86 Highgate Road, NW5; (0207) 209-0038). The building doesn't look like much, but everything here is done fantastically well. It's not far from Parliament Hill Fields, the southeastern extension of Hampstead Heath.

Greek

Lemonia   (89 Regent's Park Road, NW1; (0207) 586-7454). London was once famous for its Greek restaurants, but most are a shadow of their former glory. This is one of the exceptions, constantly packed and worth visiting if you're going to be sight-seeing in Regent's Park, Camden Town, or Primrose Hill. Reservations essential.

Italian and Pizza

Condotti   (4 Mill Street, W1; (0207) 499-1308). In an expensive area (Mayfair), this is a cheap source of good pizza in an attractive space; the proprietor was one of the founders of Pizza Express (see page 288).

Purple Sage   (90–92 Wigmore Street, Wl; (0207) 486-1912) offers a central location and pizza that's sometimes inventive, sometimes classic, and always good; the changing roster of nonpizza dishes is also reliable and reasonably priced.

Riva   (169 Church Road, SW13; (0208) 748-0434) is way, way out in quasisuburban Barnes, but if you really love the finest Italian food and feel like a walk around one of London's loveliest neighborhoods, consider it a top destination.

Japanese

Kulu Kulu (76 Brewer Street, W1; (0207) 734-7316) is the first and best of London's kaiten sushi restaurants—where dishes are circulated on a conveyor belt and you pick what you want as it goes around. Some of the best sushi in town, and cheap, too.

Misato (11 Wardour Street, W1; (0207) 734-0808) is a small, simple place in Chinatown for a quick meal; don't expect anything astounding, but quality is good and prices are low.

Yoshino (3 Piccadilly Place, W1; (0207) 287-6622). The menu is all in Japanese, but the outstanding food (with good, cheap set menus) makes it worth the difficulty; a surprise in every sense.

Midde Eastern and Turkish

Al Hamra (31–33 Shepherd Market, W1; (0207) 493-1954) is popular with tourists and locals alike. This Middle Eastern restaurant specializes in meze (assorted small dishes); it sometimes disappoints, but when it's good, it's very good.

Patogh (8 Crawford Place, W1; (0207) 262-4015). Simple in decor but with exceptionally fine cooking, Patogh is one of the better Middle Eastern restaurants in an area that's crowded with them.

Ranoush Juice Bar (43 Edgeware Road, W2; (0207) 723-5929). This is London's first juice bar and still a source of excellent sandwiches, kebabs, and cakes, as well as a lovely range of delicious fruity drinks; great budget food.

Sofra (18 Shepherd Market, W1; (0207) 499-3320) is a large chain specializing in reasonably priced Turkish food. Service doesn't always achieve the high standards set by the food, but this branch is better than most—and the others are worth considering if you want something cheap and tasty.

Thai

Patara (9 Beauchamp Place, SW3; (0207) 581-8820) is one of the best Thai places in London and with prices that aren't too painful considering the ritzy area (Knightsbridge).

Sri Siam (16 Old Compton Street, W1; (0207) 434-3544). This old warhorse is very central, very popular, and still capable of doing good things when everything's working well.

Restaurant Profiles

ALFRED ★★

BRITISH | INEXPENSIVE/MODERATE | QUALITY ★★½ | VALUE ★★★ | ZONE 2

245 Shaftesbury Avenue, WC2; (0207) 240-2566; tube: Tottenham Court Road

Customers Mostly locals **Reservation** Recommended **When to go** Lunch or dinner **Entrée range** £11.25–14.50 **Payment** VISA, MC, D, DC, CB **Service rating** ★★½ **Friendliness rating** ★★★ **Bar** Yes **Wine selection** Adequate; beers are outstanding **Dress** Casual **Disabled access** Yes

Lunch Monday–Friday, noon–3:30 p.m.

Dinner Monday–Saturday, 6–11 p.m.

Setting & atmosphere Plain decor, Formica tables, livelier by day.

House specialties Whisky-cured Scottish salmon with Michaelmas salad; scallops in beer batter with black pudding and pea purée; Cumberland sausages, champ mash, and onion gravy; haggis (in season); apple Trinity burnt cream; sticky toffee pudding.

Summary & comments Alfred is owned by the same people who own Stanleys and has the same policy of serving down-to-earth British food at relatively low prices. The room itself is nothing special, but the food is solid and dependably well produced, with an emphasis on regional ingredients and preparations. There's no fusion cooking here, unless you count the mixing of different parts of Britain and a bit of Ireland thrown in as well. Fish and meat are the top priorities, underpinned by filling side dishes and garnished by particularly delicious relishes and chutneys. Desserts are equally solid and traditional; bread is baked on the premises. Haggis, served as an appetizer, is Scotland's famous dish of meat and oatmeal cooked in a lamb's stomach and served with neeps (turnips)—it is better than it sounds! The set menu, £13.90/£17 for two or three courses, is a tremendous bargain.

ARKANSAS CAFÉ ★★

AMERICAN | INEXPENSIVE | QUALITY ★★★ | VALUE ★★★★ | ZONE 4

Spitalfields Market, E1; (0207) 377-6999; tube: Liverpool Street

Customers Locals and American business community **Reservations** Not necessary **When to go** Lunch **Entrée range** £3.50–12.50 **Payment** VISA, MC, DC **Service rating** ★★★ **Friendliness rating** ★★★★ **Bar** Yes **Wine selection** Minimal but inexpensive **Dress** Shirt and shoes mandatory **Disabled access** Main dining room only

Lunch Monday–Friday, noon–2:30 p.m.; Sunday, noon–4 p.m.

Setting & atmosphere Roadhouse barbecue joint.

House specialties Barbecued ribs, brisket, sliced pork, chicken, burgers.

Entertainment & amenities Two-man rockabilly band, by arrangement only.

Summary & comments If you are suffering withdrawal symptoms for top-quality American barbecue, come to the Arkansas. The proprietor is a prize-winning barbecue chef from Maryland, and his specially imported pit barbecues turn out what is, by a margin of several hundred miles, the best ribs in town. As a matter of fact, there's no competition: if you don't believe us, ask the U.S. ambassador, who gets the Arkansas to cater parties at the embassy. Much of the meat comes from the United States, and the rest of it is from impeccably chosen sources (English, Irish, French). The totally laid-back atmosphere will make you feel at home. Vegetarians won't have much fun; everyone else will have loads of it.

BANK ★★★

MODERN EUROPEAN | MODERATE | QUALITY ★★★½ | VALUE ★★★ | ZONE 2

1 Kingsway, WC2; (0207) 379-9797; tube: Covent Garden or Holborn; www.bankrestaurants.com/westminster

Customers Mostly locals **Reservations** Recommended **When to go** Lunch or dinner **Entrée range** £8–26.50 **Payment** VISA, MC, AMEX, D, DC, CB **Service rating** ★★★½ **Friendliness rating** ★★★½ **Bar** Yes **Wine selection** Good **Dress** No code **Disabled access** Yes

Breakfast Every day, 7–10:30 a.m.

Brunch Saturday and Sunday, 11:30 a.m.–3 p.m.

Lunch Monday–Friday, noon–2:45 p.m.; Saturday and Sunday, 11:30 a.m.–3 p.m.

Dinner Monday–Saturday, 5:30–11 p.m.; Sunday, 5–9:30 p.m.

Setting & atmosphere The big, ultramodern room is almost always packed in the evening, both at the bar and in the restaurant.

House specialties Baltic herring, new potatoes, and Swedish mustard dressing; peppered foie gras, caramelized peach, toasted brioche; Thai spring roll, red curry sauce; lobster with mayonnaise; halibut fish and chips; spiced confit duck, duck liver, and rocket (arugula) salad; calves' liver, bubble and squeak, crisp prosciutto; chocolate fondant, mandarin sorbet.

Other recommendations Pretheater prix-fixe menu, breakfast, steak and chips, desserts.

Summary & comments Bank is one of London's big restaurants, occupying a huge site that was formerly a branch of one of the national banks. Despite its size, it manages to wear a human face, and its central location and extensive opening hours make it a very useful place to know about. Though the chef is French, the food takes on Italian, Asian, and ultratraditional British cooking—what's more, everything is done with consistent skill. Due to its size, Bank is not necessarily a place to linger in, though you can if you want to. The low-cost prix-fixe menu (available at lunch and in the evening until 7 p.m.) offers two courses for just £13.50 and three for £15.50. The wine list offers ample choices under £20, service is friendly, and the bar would not be out of place in any big American city. If you like buzz and bustle, chances are you'll like Bank.

BELGO ★

BELGIAN | INEXPENSIVE/MODERATE | QUALITY ★★ | VALUE ★★★★ | ZONE 7

50 Earlham Street, WC2; (0207) 813-2233; tube: Covent Garden

72 Chalk Farm Road, NW1; (0207) 267-0718; tube: Chalk Farm or Camden Town
www.belgo-restaurants.com

Customers Locals and tourists **Reservations** Recommended **When to go** Lunch or dinner **Entrée range** £5–16.95 **Payment** VISA, MC, AMEX, D, DC, CB **Service rating** ★★ **Friendliness rating** ★★½ **Bar** No **Wine selection** Adequate; beers are outstanding **Dress** Casual **Disabled access** Yes

Lunch Every day, noon–3 p.m.

Dinner Monday–Thursday, 5:30–11:30 p.m.; Saturday, 5:30 p.m.–midnight; Sunday, 5:30–10 p.m.

Setting & atmosphere Big, high-ceilinged subterranean room with view of the kitchen and a deliberately encouraged air of conviviality.

House specialties Croquettes de fromage; salade Liègoise; tomato crevettes; Belgian braised meats; mussels in all guises; Belgian crêpes and waffles.

Other recommendations The beer list.

Summary & comments Belgo is an incredible success story with a new location opening in New York. The formula is simple: Sell Belgian food and drink at low prices—with a helpful array of special offers to keep them even lower—and get the waiters to dress in monks' robes. Not everyone's a fan, and the food (especially more complicated dishes) can be of variable quality. But the simpler mussel dishes are usually just fine. What's more, you can wash them down with a truly stunning array of the great beers of Belgium, one of the world's great beer producers. Lunch is the best time for bargains, but pretheater diners (this is theater-land) should take advantage of the "Beat the Clock" offer Monday through Friday: from 6 until 7:30 p.m., three main courses are charged according to the time shown on your food order—that is, order at 6:43 and you pay £6.43. Not the greatest food in town, but likely to be decent—and certainly a notable bargain.

BIBENDUM ★★★★

MODERN | EXPENSIVE | QUALITY ★★★★ | VALUE ★★ | ZONE 11

Michelin House, 81 Fulham Road, SW3; (0207) 581 5817; tube: South Kensington;
www.bibendum.co.uk

Customers Locals, tourists, and gastronomes **Reservations** Recommended **When to go** Lunch for the cheapest option and lovely view; dinner for that special occasion **Entrée range** Lunch £15.50–25 **Payment** VISA, MC, AMEX, D, DC **Service rating** ★★★★½ **Friendliness rating** ★★★★½ **Bar** No **Wine selection** Excellent but expensive **Dress** Smart casual **Disabled access** Yes

Lunch Monday–Friday, noon–2:30 p.m.; Saturday and Sunday, 12:30–3 p.m.

Dinner Monday–Saturday, 7–11:30 p.m.; Sunday, 7–10:30 p.m.

Setting & atmosphere A large, wonderfully high-ceilinged art deco room in what was formerly the headquarters of the Michelin Tire Company. The decor is simple and contemporary, but the setting is dominated by the huge stained-glass windows, which let in a shower of light by day and offer a fine view.

House specialties Escargots de Bourgogne; sauté foie gras with turnip fondant; warm smoked eel with Jersey Royals and quails eggs; soupe de poisson; fish and chips; roast Bersse pigeon with lettuce, peas, and sauté foie gras; poulet de Bresse à l'estragon.

Other recommendations Set lunch (£28.50 for three courses), French and Italian desserts.

Summary & comments Bibendum was the first restaurant in Sir Terence Conran's soon-to-be empire, and it remains one of the best exponents of modern cooking in London despite the departure of founding chef Simon Hopkinson. You can come here for lunch or dinner knowing that you'll get superbly cooked food from ingredients of the highest quality, served with consummate professionalism that still manages to be friendly. As you can see from the dishes listed above, the orientation is French and classic, but Asian influences appear as well, as does solid Britishness (the fish and chips may be the best in London). This is what has brought food-fanatical Londoners back to Bibendum for years. There's only one complaint: cost. They're not ripping anyone off with the food prices (attention to detail is expensive, especially when success depends heavily on top-quality ingredients), but wine is marked up without mercy, making an evening meal here a very costly exercise. Is it worth it? Yes, for a rare and very special treat in exquisite surroundings—or for the much more affordable set lunch. There is also a small oyster bar and a separate café (both downstairs) where you can eat quickly and lightly.

BLUE PRINT CAFÉ ★★★

MODERN EUROPEAN | MODERATE | QUALITY ★★★★½ | VALUE ★★★ | ZONE 5

28 Shad Thames, SE1; (0207) 378-7031; tube: London Bridge or Tower Bridge; www.blueprintcafe.co.uk

Customers Mostly locals **Reservations** Recommended **When to go** Lunch or dinner **Entrée range** £11–19; set lunch: 2 courses £19.50, 3 courses £22.50 **Payment** VISA, MC, AMEX, D, DC, JCB **Service rating** ★★★ **Friendliness rating** ★★★★ **Bar** Yes **Wine selection** Very good **Dress** Informal **Disabled access** Yes

Lunch Every day, noon–3 p.m.

Dinner Monday–Saturday, 6–11 p.m.

Setting & atmosphere This attractive, modern room with big windows overlooking the Thames hosts a trendy clientele.

House specialties Pickled herrings; potato and cucumber salads; young garlic, goat cheese, and tapenade; hake, lentils, and salsa verde; rabbit, barley, turnip, peas, and bacon; crème brulée; orange and polenta cake; mascarpone.

Summary & comments The Blue Print is one of many restaurants in the Shad Thames area, and one of several in the empire of Sir Terence Conran (see Bibendum, page 267, and Quaglino's, page 290). It is also one of several with a sweeping view of the Thames, and for this reason alone it is worth a visit. But it's also cheaper than much of the local competition. And the food is consistently good, year after year: modern in style and with heavy emphasis on the Mediterranean, especially Italy. The seasons and the market are king here, so the menu changes twice daily to reflect what's available. Fish, pasta, and home-curing are strong points. The wine list is not huge but is carefully chosen and easily accommodates diners on a budget. In warm weather, beg for a table on the terrace.

BOISDALE RESTAURANT AND BAR ★★½

BRITISH | MODERATE | QUALITY ★★★ | VALUE ★★★ | ZONE 10

15 Eccleston Street, SW1; (0207) 730-6922; tube: Victoria; www.boisdale.co.uk

Customers Tourists and usually affluent locals **Reservations** Recommended **When to go** Lunch or dinner **Entrée Range** £9.50–25 **Payment** VISA, MC, AMEX, D, DC, CB **Service rating** ★★★½ **Friendliness rating** ★★★½ **Bar** Yes **Wine selection** Good **Dress** Smart casual **Disabled access** No

Lunch Monday–Friday, noon–2:30 p.m.

Dinner Monday–Saturday, 7–10:30 p.m.

Setting & atmosphere Dark wood and red paneling, clublike ambience, garden at rear open in warm weather.

House specialties Anything with a Scottish element, such as smoked salmon, smoked grouse, venison, Highland lamb, Aberdeen Angus beef.

Other recommendations Set menus.

Entertainment & amenities Late jazz bar, live music.

Summary & comments Boisdale has established itself as London's most serious champion of the food and drink of Scotland. The emphasis is on getting great ingredients, whether raw or cured, and presenting them to their best advantage. You can go for the simplicity of an Aberdeen Angus steak, grilled and served with béarnaise sauce, or venture into more modern territory if you're feeling adventurous. The kitchen does well with both approaches, and the cozy atmosphere makes a warmly attractive setting. If you're game enough to try haggis, one of Scotland's national dishes, this is probably the place to do it. Whisky lovers should note that Boisdale's Back Bar, open throughout the day, has London's largest selection of single-malt scotch; the selection of cigars is also notable. .

CACTUS BLUE ★★★

AMERICAN/MODERN EUROPEAN | MODERATE | QUALITY ★★★½ | VALUE ★★★★ | ZONE 11

86 Fulham Road, SW3; (0207) 823-7858; tube: South Kensington

Customers Mostly locals **Reservations** Recommended **When to go** Dinner is best **Entrée range** £9.95–15.95 **Payment** VISA, MC, AMEX, D, DC, CB **Service rating** ★★★

Friendliness rating ★★★★½ **Bar** Yes **Wine selection** Small but good **Dress** Smart casual **Disabled access** Yes

Open Monday–Friday, 5:30–11:45 p.m.; Saturday, noon–11:45 p.m.; Sunday, noon–11 p.m.

Setting & atmosphere Nicely decorated with wrought iron and Southwestern U.S. artifacts, this restaurant has an affluent, mostly young local crowd.

Entertainment & amenities Live funk/jazz Sunday brunch and Tuesday and Wednesday evenings.

Summary & comments Cactus Blue has lovely decor, good food, great drinks, and unusually low prices for this chi-chi part of town. The menu is modern Southwestern plus a smattering of Modern European, with appetizers and small plates followed by a short group of quesadillas and a longer list of main courses. And though the format may not be out of the ordinary, the cooking is: a tortilla is wrapped around confit of duck and served with apricot and ginger jam, for instance. A quesadilla might contain bronzed chicken with mango and jalapeño oil; grilled swordfish comes with tropical salsa and roast vegetable couscous. All very modern and executed with skill. Sunday brunch is a popular event among local residents, but evenings are better if you want a drink with your meal. They make some of London's best margaritas and have a good range of premium tequila by the shot. And the mostly American wine list tops out at £23 apart from champagne, so drinking here won't break the bank.

CAFÉ SPICE NAMASTE ★★★★

INDIAN | MODERATE | QUALITY ★★★★ | VALUE ★★★★ | ZONE 4

16 Prescot Street, E1; (0207) 488-9242; tube: Aldgate, Aldgate East, Tower Hill

247 Lavender Hill; (0207) 738-1717

Customers Mostly locals, especially businesspeople and aficionados **Reservations** Recommended **When to go** Lunch or dinner **Entrée range** Lunch £5.95–14.75 **Payment** VISA, MC, AMEX, D, DC, CB, JCB **Service rating** ★★★ **Friendliness rating** ★★★★ **Bar** Yes **Wine selection** Good **Dress** Casual **Disabled access** Yes

Lunch Monday–Friday, noon–3 p.m.

Dinner Monday–Saturday, 6:30–10:30 p.m.

Setting & atmosphere A nicely redecorated, high-ceilinged room in a nineteenth-century building.

House specialties Unusual curries from various Indian regions; tandoori dishes; breads; vegetarian dishes.

Other recommendations Weekly changing specialty menus.

Summary & comments Since 1995, chef Cyrus Todiwala has made Café Spice Namaste one of London's best places to find really serious Indian food. Indeed, he is one of the prime "modernizers" of this favorite British cuisine, raising standards in every aspect over the nondescript "curry houses" of the bad old days. The dishes on the regular menu cover nearly every area of the Indian subcontinent and are distinguished for their subtle, complex spicing and relative rarity on British menus. There is a weekly "specialty menu" as well, featuring a particular region, and the wine list is notable for its serious attention to matching every style of food on the menu. There are only two minor negative points to bear in mind. One is the location, which is out of the way. The other is an occasional problem with rowdy (affluent) clients, given the restaurant's proximity to London's financial center. Apart from that, there's no way to recommend Café Spice Namaste too highly.

CAMBIO DE TERCIO   ★★★

SPANISH | MODERATE | QUALITY ★★★½ | VALUE ★★★★ | ZONE 11

163 Old Brompton Road, SW5; (0207) 244-8970; tube: Gloucester Road

Customers Locals **Reservations** Recommended **When to go** Lunch or dinner **Entrée range** Lunch £12.50–15.50 **Payment** VISA, MC, AMEX **Service rating** ★★★★ **Friendliness rating** ★★★★ **Bar** No **Wine selection** Excellent, mostly Spanish **Dress** Casual **Disabled access** Restaurant only

Lunch Every day, noon–2:30 p.m.

Dinner Monday–Saturday, 7–11:30 p.m.; Sunday, 7–11 p.m.

Setting & atmosphere A cozy, comfortable basement room decorated with bullfighting motifs.

House specialties Oxtail, hake, suckling pig, tapas.

Summary & comments Cambio is one of London's best Spanish restaurants. The kitchen is equally adept at staple dishes, using the best and most authentic imported ingredients, and at reinterpreting classics with a modern slant. Lovers of tapas, the "little dishes" with which Spanish people love to begin an evening's festivities, should note that the selection and quality here are excellent—and the choice of sherries, the perfect partner for this kind of eating, is similarly broad. There have been a few personnel changes in the kitchen in recent years, but standards seem to have been kept high. And though there have been grumbles about service from some quarters, they are neither numerous nor serious enough to keep Cambio off your list of possibilities. Dessert lovers should note that while Spain does not always excel in that department, Cambio de Tercio almost always does.

CANTINA VINOPOLIS   ★★½

MODERN EUROPEAN | MODERATE | QUALITY ★★★ | VALUE ★★★★ | ZONE 5

1 Bank End, SE1; (0207) 940-8333; tube: London Bridge; www.vinopolis.co.uk

Customers Mostly locals **When to go** Lunch or dinner **Entrée range** £11.50–13.50 **Payment** VISA, MC, AMEX, DC, JCB **Service rating** ★★★ **Friendliness rating** ★★★★ **Bar** Yes **Wine selection** Enormous **Dress** Casual **Disabled access** Yes

Lunch Monday–Saturday, noon–2:45 p.m.; Sunday, noon–3:45 p.m.

Dinner Monday–Saturday, 6–10:15 p.m.

Setting & atmosphere Plain but comfortable decor in a converted industrial space with high, vaulted ceilings.

Summary & comments Vinopolis is London's "wine museum," and this is part of it (though run by an outside company). The museum has had a hard time commercially, but its catering side is a great success. Unsurprisingly, the wine list is huge—and all are sold by the glass. That would be reason enough to come here, since the location is good for the ever-increasing attractions of the Bankside area. The food supplies the rest of the reason for coming along: it can be really excellent with good ingredients treated with care, flair, and respect. French and Italian dominate, but there are a lot of New World features as well, and the prices are exceptionally reasonable. You can't easily spend more than £25–30 before drinks. And with all those wines by the glass, this can be one of the most reasonable high-quality meals in the area.

LE CAPRICE   ★★½

MODERN | MODERATE | QUALITY ★★★½ | VALUE ★★★ | ZONE 9

Arlington Street, SW1; (0207) 629-2239; tube: Green Park

Customers Celebrities, affluent locals **Reservations** Recommended **When to go** Dinner or Sunday brunch **Entrée range** £9.75–21.75 **Payment** VISA, MC, AMEX, D, DC **Service rating** ★★★ **Friendliness rating** ★★★ **Bar** Yes **Wine selection** Short but good **Dress** No code **Disabled access** Yes, but not to toilets

Lunch Monday–Saturday, noon–3 p.m.; Sunday, noon–3:15 p.m.

Dinner Monday–Saturday, 5:30 p.m.–midnight; Sunday, 6 p.m.–midnight

Setting & atmosphere Lively but low-key, modern room that is pleasant but of no great distinction.

House specialties Nearly everything on the menu, especially simple dishes such as fish and chips, salmon fishcakes, and eggs Benedict.

Summary & comments Le Caprice has a well-deserved reputation for serving food that reaches a high standard pretty consistently. But that is not the main reason that Londoners come here, even if it helps. Le Caprice is a supremely fashionable restaurant in a low-key, understated kind of way. It's the kind of place where, if the next table is occupied by a princess, two movie stars, and a Nobel Prize–winning novelist, no one raises an eyebrow. Well, not in a way that you would notice, anyway. This is surely one of the reasons why the rich and fashionable and celebrated love the place so much, just as they love its sister restaurant, The Ivy (see page 279). For us mortals, the possibility of star-gazing might be a bonus. But I have paid three visits with not a star in sight and have loved the place anyway. It is comfortable and well run, and the food can be outstanding. And when it isn't outstanding, it's still very good. Dinners are buzzy, while Sunday brunch is more laid-back.

CHEZ GÉRARD   ★★

FRENCH (BISTRO) | INEXPENSIVE/MODERATE | QUALITY ★★★ | VALUE ★★★ | ZONE 7

The Market, The Piazza, WC2; (0207) 379-0666; tube: Covent Garden;
www.chezgerard.com

Customers Locals and tourists **Reservations** Recommended **When to go** Lunch or dinner (restaurant), any time (bar) **Entrée range** Lunch £9.90–16.40 **Payment** VISA, MC, AMEX, D, DC, CB **Service rating** ★★½ **Friendliness rating** ★★★½ **Bar** Yes **Wine selection** Good **Dress** Casual **Disabled access** No

Lunch Monday–Saturday, noon–3 p.m.; Sunday, noon–3:30 p.m.

Dinner Monday–Saturday, 5:30–11:30 p.m.; Sunday, 5:30–10:30 p.m.

Setting & atmosphere Conservatory overlooking Covent Garden market with an open-air terrace in warm weather.

House specialties Steak, especially Châteaubriand and onglet (hanger steak), served with pommes frites.

Other recommendations Simple bistro-style dishes such as oysters, fish soup, snails, and Bayonne ham with pickles.

Summary & comments Groupe Chez Gérard, which has seven other branches in addition to this one, has a very simple formula: French-style steak, French-style pommes frites (better known as French fries), and French-style service. They usually do it very well, though there are variations from branch to branch, and prices are kept low enough to keep most people happy even if they run into occasional problems with cooking or service. Fish-eaters will always find at least one dish aimed at them, as will vegetarians, but these are the most variable options in terms of quality, and they are not—let's be frank— what Chez Gérard is about. Set menus can offer exceptionally good value: £15.95 for three courses at lunch or in the evening. Don't come here expecting the meal of a lifetime, but if you're a steak-lover this will be your home away from home.

CHUEN CHENG KU ★★

CHINESE | INEXPENSIVE/MODERATE | QUALITY ★★★ | VALUE ★★★★ | ZONE 7

17 Wardour Street, W1; (0207) 734-3281; tube: Leicester Square or Piccadilly Circus

Customers Locals and tourists **Reservations** Not necessary **When to go** Lunch is best **Entrée range** Lunch £6.30–16.80 **Payment** VISA, MC, AMEX, DC, CB **Service rating** ★★½ **Friendliness rating** ★★½ **Bar** No **Wine selection** Adequate **Dress** Casual **Disabled access** Restaurant only

Open Every day, 11 a.m.–midnight

Setting & atmosphere This huge establishment is very busy at lunch (especially weekends) and mostly quieter in the evening.

House specialties Dim sum, rice and noodles, fish, and shellfish.

Other recommendations Standard Cantonese dishes.

Summary & comments Chuen Cheng Ku has been packing happy eaters into its capacious rooms for a couple of decades now and shows no sign of flagging in popularity. The best thing here, without a doubt, is the dim sum: served daily until 5:45 p.m., it comes around on trolleys and offers a huge selection with quite consistent quality. Weekends are the busiest time. You can expect a line of 1–20 parties, but the crowd is well managed and waits rarely exceed 20 minutes. The large numbers of Chinese families show that the place is appreciated by those who know quality when they see it. Dinner is usually less busy and of solid rather than exciting quality—but certainly good enough to make CCK a top choice when you're in the area, as you're sure to be, at some point. If there are six or more of you eating, the nine-dish set menus offer excellent value and a simplified choice.

CLARKE'S ★★★★

MODERN EUROPEAN | MODERATE/EXPENSIVE | QUALITY ★★★★ | VALUE ★★★ | ZONE 13

124 Kensington Church Street, W8; (0207) 221-9225; tube: Notting Hill Gate

Customers Mostly locals **Reservations** Essential **When to go** Lunch or dinner **Entrée range** Lunch £14; dinner set menu £44 for 4 courses **Payment** VISA, MC, AMEX, D, DC **Service rating** ★★★★½ **Friendliness rating** ★★★★½ **Bar** No **Wine selection** Outstanding **Dress** Casual **Disabled access** Restaurant yes, toilets no

Lunch Monday–Friday, 12:30–2 p.m.

Dinner Monday–Friday, 7–10 p.m.

Setting & atmosphere Upstairs room is tiny and intimate; downstairs is big and bustling, with a view of the kitchen.

House specialties Menu changes daily.

Summary & comments No one in Britain understands Californian cooking better than Sally Clarke, who worked there years ago (at Chez Panisse and elsewhere) before moving back to London and opening her own place. She bases her cooking on the seasons and on what's available in the market on a given day. Thus, menus change every day, with a short carte at lunchtime and fixed menus (following the example of Chez Panisse) at dinner. The cooking is strong in baking (including some of the best bread in London), roasting, and char-grilling. Combinations are often simple, but they never fail to impress, partly because the execution is so skilled and especially because the ingredients are as good as money can buy. The lack of choice at dinner may be somewhat irritating. Phone in advance to find out what's on the menu; however, given enough warning they will happily provide alternatives if possible. The wine list is superb and not especially high priced. Clarke's is not cheap, but at its price level it is one of the best restaurants in London.

CONNAUGHT RESTAURANT ★★★★

FRENCH (HAUTE CUISINE) | EXPENSIVE | QUALITY ★★★★½ | VALUE ★★★ | ZONE 8

Carlos Place, W1; (0207) 499-7070; tube: Green Park;
www.savoy-group.co.uk/connaught/dining/restaurant.html

Customers Hotel guests, affluent tourists, and locals **Reservations** Essential **When to go** Lunch or dinner **Entrée range** Lunch £13.50–45 **Payment** VISA, MC, AMEX, D, DC, CB **Service rating** ★★★★★ **Friendliness rating** ★★★★½ **Bar** Yes **Wine selection** Excellent but expensive **Dress** Formal, jacket and tie for men **Disabled access** Limited

Lunch Every day, 12:30–2:30 p.m.

Dinner Every day, 6:30–10:45 p.m.

Setting & atmosphere Chandeliers and wood paneling help create a feeling of luxury and unsurpassable comfort; it's formal but not intimidating.

House specialties Classic French and British cooking, roasts from the trolley, game (in season).

Summary & comments Eating at the Connaught is not just a meal, it's an experience. The hotel dates back to Edwardian times and is accustomed to catering for royalty—the menu has a special symbol for dishes created by recently retired chef Michel Bourdin for the queen's silver jubilee (1977). This is about as indiscreet as they get at the Connaught, a place where the high and mighty come to eat, but everyone is treated like an honored guest. There are two places to eat, the Restaurant and the smaller, more intimate Grill with slightly different hours. It's a matter of personal preference, but one of the banquettes in the Restaurant is a perfect place to get a taste of Connaught-style luxury. The food is mostly old-fashioned, a combination of English and French presented side by side in a mixture of the two languages: filet de boeuf en croûte légère "Strasbourgeoise" and croustade d'oeufs de caille maintenon alongside Cornish crab bisque and bread and butter pudding. The cooking is never less than assured and can sometimes reach dazzling heights, and the service is as good as service ever gets. Let's be blunt: Outside the limited-choice set menus (£22.50–28.50 at lunch, £58 at dinner), the Connaught is very, very expensive unless you order the cheapest things on the menu. And the wine list doesn't help in the matter of budgetary restraint. But this is a unique restaurant, the likes of which you will not find anywhere in the United States. For this reason alone it's worth a visit.

CORNEY & BARROW ★★

MODERN EUROPEAN | MODERATE | QUALITY ★★★ | VALUE ★★★ | ZONES 2 & 4

116 St. Martin's Lane, WC2; (0207) 655-9800; tube: Leicester Square or Charing Cross

44 Cannon Street, EC4; (0207) 248-1700; tube: Mansion House; www.corney-barrow.co.uk

Customers Mostly locals **Reservations** Not necessary **When to go** Lunch or dinner **Entrée range** £9.50–13.50 **Payment** VISA, MC, AMEX, DC, CB **Service rating** ★★½ **Friendliness rating** ★★★ **Bar** Yes **Wine selection** Excellent **Dress** Casual **Disabled access** No

Open Monday–Wednesday, noon–midnight; Thursday–Saturday, noon–2 a.m.

Setting & atmosphere A bar with high stools is on the ground floor, with a more comfortable lively and casual brasserie upstairs.

Summary & comments If location is everything in retail, the St. Martin's Lane flagship branch of Corney & Barrow has got it made. It's across the street from the English National Opera, one minute from Trafalgar Square and its galleries, and five minutes from the theaters and cinemas around Leicester Square. Corney & Barrow is a group of wine bars, backed up by a retail and wholesale wine merchant of great distinction, so the wine list is predictably strong: plenty of choices under £20, a rarity for London, and interesting bottles from all over. But the food is serious, too. Menus change monthly, and the quality of the cooking is high. The set menus (lunchtime and 5–7 p.m. or 10–11 p.m.) are a major bargain at £11.95 for two courses or £13.95 for three. There are eight other branches in addition to the one listed above, mostly in zone 3. Worth bearing in mind when you're doing the sights.

FIFTH FLOOR ★★★½

MODERN EUROPEAN | MODERATE | QUALITY ★★★½ | VALUE ★★★ | ZONE 10

Harvey Nichols, 109 Knightsbridge, SW1; (0207) 235-5250; tube: Knightsbridge; www.harveynichols.com

Customers Locals, tourists, and shoppers **Reservations** Recommended **When to go** Lunch or dinner **Entrée range** £16–24 **Payment** VISA, MC, AMEX, D, DC, CB **Service rating** ★★★½ **Friendliness rating** ★★★½ **Bar** Yes **Wine selection** Excellent **Dress** No dress code **Disabled access** Yes

Lunch Monday–Friday, noon–3 p.m.; Saturday and Sunday, noon–3:30 p.m.

Dinner Monday–Saturday, 6–11 p.m.

Setting & atmosphere Smart, contemporary decor in the ultrachic Harvey Nichols department store, attracting fashion-conscious clientele at both lunch and dinner.

Summary & comments In-store eating does not get any better than the Fifth Floor. It's not just a pit stop after doing the rounds of Harvey Nichols but a destination in its own right, and very popular. Good design means you don't even notice you're in a store when you're eating here—not that there are many complaints about that. Prices are as serious as the cooking, though the entree range is distorted by the expense of roast lobster: most main dishes are in the £13–16 range. At lunchtime, two appetizers (a popular option) will cost little more than £15. Or take advantage of the prix-fixe lunch at £23.50 for three courses—a real bargain. Wine lovers are particularly well served by a list that includes all the bottles from the nearby HN wine shop. It's absolutely endless, as you can guess from the fact that the helpful "Little List" and "House Selection" contain over 40 bottles. Final note: the bar serves high-quality cocktails.

fish! ★★½

FISH AND SHELLFISH | INEXPENSIVE/MODERATE | QUALITY ★★★ | VALUE ★★★★ | ZONE 7

3B Belvedere Road, SE1; (0207) 234-3333

Cathedral Street, London Bridge, SE1; (0207) 234-3333; tube: Westminster; www.fishdiner.co.uk

Customers Locals and tourists, many families **Reservations** Call (0207) 234-3333 for all branches **When to go** Lunch or dinner **Entrée range** £8.50–16.95 **Payment** VISA, MC, AMEX, D, DC, JCB **Service rating** ★★★ **Friendliness rating** ★★★½ **Bar** In some branches, but designed for customers waiting for tables **Wine selection** Small, adequate, inexpensive **Dress** Smart casual **Disabled access** Yes

Open Monday–Saturday, 11:30 a.m–11 p.m.; Sunday, noon–10:30 p.m.

Setting & atmosphere Informal, modern dining rooms with a view of the kitchen.

House specialties Fresh fish, plainly cooked.

Entertainment & amenities Watching the chefs at work!

Summary & comments At the time of this writing there were six fish! restaurants in London and four more in other towns and cities. And there were plans afoot for several new openings both in and out of the capital. The expansion pays tribute to a formula that's proved immensely successful: buy top-quality fish, offer it steamed or grilled, and allow customers to choose the sauce (e.g. salsa, hollandaise, herb and garlic butter, and so on). There are a few appetizers, too, along the lines of rock oysters (£1 apiece), prawn (shrimp) cocktail (£6.95), and smoked salmon (£5.95); and there are a few concessions to meat-lovers among the main courses, as well as a few slightly more complicated fishy main courses. But the real emphasis is on the core concept, which is by far the best way to be sure of success. The restaurants are specifically designed with children in mind, and they make it possible to eat quickly if that's what you're after—the spartan decor won't make you want to linger endlessly, though of course no one will kick you out. These are just good, reliable restaurants that won't break the bank. Though it should be noted that bills can rise quickly if you eat a full meal with extra options such as side orders. All in all, this is one of London's more successful chains. You can get information and even make confirmed reservations at their website.

LE GAVROCHE ★★★★½

FRENCH (HAUTE CUISINE) | EXPENSIVE | QUALITY ★★★★½ | VALUE ★★★ | ZONE 8

43 Upper Brook Street, W1; (0207) 408-0881; tube: Marble Arch

Customers Locals and tourists **Reservations** Essential **When to go** Lunch or dinner **Entrée range** £27.80–34.60 **Payment** VISA, MC, AMEX, DC, CB **Service rating** ★★★★★ **Friendliness rating** ★★★★½ **Bar** Yes, for diners only **Wine selection** Excellent **Dress** Formal **Disabled access** No

Lunch Monday–Friday, noon–2 p.m.

Dinner Monday–Friday, 7–11 p.m.

Setting & atmosphere This downstairs room offers intimate comfort at both lunch and dinner; it's indisputably grand, but with the kind of ultraprofessional service that pampers without being intimidating.

House specialties Foie gras chaud et pastilla de canard à la canelle; Rable de lapin et galette au Parmesan; Le Palet de chocolat amer et praline croustillant.

Other recommendations Soufflé Suissesse, ragoût de langoustines parfumé au gingembre, agneau de lait rôti, le caneton Gavroche en pot-au-feu, set lunch.

Summary & comments Le Gavroche is one of London's most famous and most expensive restaurants. It is classic in every sense, even though the menu has been "modernized" in recent years. The service is among the best in London, priding itself on knowing what customers want before they themselves know they want it, and the care taken with every detail is astonishing. All this comes at a truly frightening price outside the set lunch, which at £40 per person includes three courses, half a bottle of wine, water and coffee, and service. Sure, that's pretty expensive, too. But with main courses alone costing £30 on average, lunch is the only way most people can afford Le Gavroche. It's worth that one splash-out, because this is a great restaurant of the old-fashioned, perfectionist kind. Bread, ice creams and sorbets, premeal tidbits—they're all outstanding. And the all-French cheese board is probably the best in London. Come here if you want to treat yourself.

HEARTSTONE ★★★½

MODERN EUROPEAN | INEXPENSIVE/MODERATE | QUALITY ★★★½ | VALUE ★★★★★ |
ZONE 15

106 Parkway, NW1; (0207) 485-7744; tube: Camden Town

Customers Mostly locals **Reservations** Advisable for dinner **When to go** Anytime
Entrée range £8.50–13 **Payment** VISA, MC **Service rating** ★★★★½ **Friendliness rating** ★★★★★ **Bar** No **Wine selection** BYO **Dress** Casual **Disabled access** Yes

Open Tuesday–Saturday, 8 a.m.–9 p.m.; Sunday, 10 a.m.–4 p.m.

Setting & atmosphere Simple but very attractive lilac-painted room with a skylight.

Entertainment & amenities Massage/aromatherapy/nutritional consulting in the basement.

Summary & comments No place in London remotely resembles Heartstone. Its operation is based on the desire to promote healthy living and eating, but it serves a far more diverse menu—and far better food—than you'll find in most places that share the same aim. They don't serve alcohol, though they're happy to see you bring your own, and there's a no-smoking policy— a rarity in London. Instead, on the drinks front, there's unlimited filtered water and juice combos fresh from the juicer. The whole place is serene; it makes you feel peaceful just to be there. But none of this would count for anything without the excellent food, good ingredients (often organic) expertly cooked (often on the grill) in the open-plan kitchen. Some of the offerings would be classified as wholefoods, but you can also get an awesome steak or rack of lamb. In short, Heartstone does not sermonize. It simply aims to present the best of everything in a way that satisfies both principles and the need for profit. And it succeeds. Note: There is a good place to buy wine a few doors down, and an even better one just five minutes away.

IBLA ★★

ITALIAN | MODERATE | QUALITY ★★★½ | VALUE ★★★★ | ZONE 14

89 Marylebone High Street, W1; (0207) 224-3799; tube: Bond Street

Customers Mostly locals, including many Italians **Reservations** Recommended **When to go** Lunch or dinner **Set Menus** Lunch £15 for 2 courses, £18 for 3 courses; dinner £30 or £35 **Payment** VISA, MC, AMEX, DC, CB **Service rating** ★★★ **Friendliness rating** ★★★★★ **Bar** Yes **Wine selection** Very good **Dress** Casual **Disabled access** Restaurant only

Lunch Monday–Friday, noon–2:30 p.m.

Dinner Monday–Saturday, 7–10:30 p.m.

Setting & atmosphere Delicatessen items are on sale in the front room, while an attractive, simply decorated, and exceptionally pleasant dining room is in the back.

House specialties Smoked foie gras terrine with pears in Sauternes jelly and braised endive; crab ravioli with poached eggs and black truffle; risotto with gremolada and paprika frogs legs in port-wine sauce; pan-fried fillet of red mullet in clam broth; pan-fried fillet of John Dory with courgette (zucchini) blossoms and crab; pigeon in consommé with spring vegetables; roast lamb noisettes in an oyster and Champagne sauce with soft goat cheese.

Summary & comments Ibla is a quiet, unassuming treasure. One of its many good points is that it attracts, in our experience anyway, more Italians than "foreigners"—which is always a good sign. Another good point is the charming service. And the main good point: modern Italian food with many French touches and ingredients. Cooking is imaginative but never contrived, and all the more enticing because prices are exceptionally low (especially at lunch) for this level of excellence. The dishes mentioned above should convey most of the idea. Scallops and rhubarb in a green tea jelly and steamed eel with veal marrow and apple-ginger chutney should complete it. The wine list is strong not only in Italy but in the rest of Europe and most of the New World, and it's extremely well priced. Set lunch offers fewer choices than dinner and somewhat simpler cooking. Diners on a budget who want one really special meal should consider Ibla. Cooking of this ambition isn't usually so inexpensive.

THE IVY ★★★★

MODERN EUROPEAN | MODERATE | QUALITY ★★★★ | VALUE ★★★ | ZONE 7

1 West Street, WC2; (0207) 836-4751; tube: Leicester Square

Customers Mostly locals **Reservations** Essential **When to go** Lunch or dinner **Entrée range** Lunch £9–23.50 **Payment** VISA, MC, AMEX, D, DC **Service rating** ★★★★ **Friendliness rating** ★★★ **Bar** For diners only **Wine selection** Good **Dress** No dress code **Disabled access** Restaurant only

Lunch Monday–Saturday, noon–3 p.m.; Sunday, noon–3:30 p.m.

Dinner Every day, 5:30 p.m.–midnight

Setting & atmosphere Exceptionally comfortable wood-paneled room with stained-glass windows, discreet and refined.

House specialties Simple classics such as steak tartare, calf's liver, smoked salmon with scrambled eggs, shepherd's pie, eggs Benedict, grilled or fried fish.

Other recommendations Salads, desserts, Asian dishes.

Summary & comments Let's get the bad news out of the way first. Getting a table at The Ivy is famously difficult. If you're planning a trip and are dying to eat here, it's advisable to reserve at least a month in advance. Why should this be? Here's the good news: The Ivy is a supremely wonderful place. The food is mostly simple but always executed with skill. Service is professional and efficient, though there are sometimes complaints about off-handedness. But The Ivy isn't just a place to eat and drink. It is also, for most people, a spot to do a bit of star-gazing. The rich and famous love it, and chances are reasonable that you'll spot a familiar face while enjoying your eggs Benedict or fish and chips. But don't stare, please. That wouldn't be in keeping with Ivy etiquette.

JOE ALLEN   ★★½

AMERICAN | INEXPENSIVE/MODERATE | QUALITY ★★★ | VALUE ★★★ | ZONE 7

13 Exeter Street, WC2; (0207) 836-0651; tube: Covent Garden

Customers Varied, locals and tourists **Reservations** Recommended **When to go** Anytime **Entrée range** Lunch £7–13.50 **Payment** VISA, MC, AMEX **Service rating** ★★★½ **Friendliness rating** ★★★★ **Bar** Yes **Wine selection** Small but good **Dress** Casual **Disabled access** No

Open Monday–Friday, noon–1 a.m.; Saturday, 11:30 a.m.–1 a.m.; Sunday, 11:30 a.m.–midnight

Setting & atmosphere Think of your favorite local bar/restaurant—the kind of place you go for a cheerful, noisy night out with friends—and you have it.

House specialties Black-bean soup; chopped chicken liver; Caesar salad; eggs Benedict or eggs Joe Allen; grilled sirloin steak with steak fries; brownies; cheesecake.

Other recommendations Anything cooked simply (which means just about everything on the menu), especially hamburgers, sandwiches, and salads.

Entertainment & amenities Piano player Monday–Saturday, 9 p.m.–1 a.m.; jazz Sunday, 8 p.m.–1 a.m.

Summary & comments Like its two other branches in Paris and New York, the London Joe Allen is a place to go for unpretentious, American-style food in a lively atmosphere. It's set in the heart of theaterland, and its theatrical connections are firmly cemented in the cheap precurtain menus (£12 for two courses, £14 for three courses) and the late opening hour. Actors come in from the nearby theaters after their performance, and if you're lucky you may find yourself eating Caesar salad next to someone you watched on stage an hour earlier. It's the spirited buzz that brings Londoners in rather than any fancy fireworks in the food. But the food itself is solid, rarely disappointing those who like simple classics done well, and the drinks list, though short, is enticing at every level.

LIVEBAIT   ★★★½

SEAFOOD | INEXPENSIVE/MODERATE | QUALITY ★★★½ | VALUE ★★★ | ZONES 5 & 7

43 The Cut, SE1; (0207) 928-7211; tube: Waterloo

21 Wellington Street, WC2; (0207) 836-7161; tube: Covent Garden; www.livebaitrestaurants.co.uk

Customers Locals and tourists **Reservations** Recommended **When to go** Lunch or dinner **Entrée range** £14.50–16.95 **Payment** VISA, MC, AMEX, D, DC, CB **Service rating** ★★½ **Friendliness rating** ★★★½ **Bar** Yes **Wine selection** Good **Dress** Casual **Disabled access** No

Lunch Every day, noon–3 p.m.

Dinner Monday–Saturday, 5:30–11:30 p.m.

Setting & atmosphere Black and white tiles, minimal decor, brash and fun and noisy.

House specialties Ever-changing selection of fish dishes and shellfish platters.

Summary & comments The original Livebait, in SE1, took London by storm when it opened in 1997. It has since been taken over by Groupe Chez Gérard, but standards have remained high. The Covent Garden branch is centrally located and duplicates the formula—a simple setting with fairly elaborate cooking—very successfully. The secret lies in wonderfully fresh fish, some from exotic sources and some local to the United Kingdom, which you will find cooked in exceptionally innovative ways (such as grilled bluefin tuna with celeriac and foie gras purée, pousse spinach, port and thyme sauce) and in classic presentations such as sumptuous shellfish platters of oysters, clams, crevettes, cockles, winkles, whelks, prawns, and crab. Service can slow down as the kitchen gets busy (especially in the evening), but it never fails in the friendliness department. Prices à la carte are not exactly cheap, but it's worth noting the set menu (from £16.50) available at lunch and both pre- and post-theater.

MANGO ROOM ★★½

CARIBBEAN | INEXPENSIVE | QUALITY ★★★½ | VALUE ★★★★ | ZONE 15

10 Kentish Town Road, NW1; (0207) 482-5065; tube: Camden Town

Customers Fairly young locals **Reservations** Recommended **When to go** Dinner is livelier **Entrée range** £8.50–11 **Payment** VISA, MC, CB **Service rating** ★★★ **Friendliness rating** ★★★★★ **Bar** Yes **Wine selection** Minimal **Dress** As you wish **Disabled access** Yes

Lunch Tuesday–Sunday, noon–3 p.m.

Dinner Every day, 6 p.m.–midnight

Setting & atmosphere Colorful decor with a handmade look; mostly young, trendy crowd.

House specialties Ebony chicken wings, marinated in chile, pepper, garlic, and soya; curry goat with hot pepper, scallions, garlic, pimiento, and spices; mango and banana brûlée.

Other recommendations Steamed green-lip mussels with ginger, scallions, garlic, and coconut; ackee and avocado with spinach, plantains, tomatoes, and olives; grilled barracuda with courgettes and coconut sauce.

Entertainment & amenities Great ska, reggae, and "jazz Jamaica" background music.

Summary & comments Camden Town is one of London's hip, casual areas. With the popular Camden Lock market nearby and Regent's Park not much farther away, it gets incredibly crowded, especially on weekends. A host of establishments cater for the crowds, but few match Mango Room for quality. Being here is just a pleasure: the music is wonderful, the staff is really friendly, and the food is good, filling, and cheap. Based in Caribbean cooking, Mango Room offers both traditional classics and modern variations in the spirit of gastronomic globalism. There's a bar next door with comfortable chairs and sofas. If you're in the area, Mango Room is a great place to eat or drink after sight-seeing and shopping. Consider beer or a fruit punch rather than wine from the short list and get set to enjoy yourself in laid-back surroundings.

MASH ★★

MODERN EUROPEAN | INEXPENSIVE/MODERATE | QUALITY ★★★½ | VALUE ★★★ | ZONE 7

19–21 Great Portland Street, W1; (0207) 637-5555

26B Albemarle Street, W1; (0207) 495-5999; tube: Oxford Circus

Customers Mostly young locals **When to go** Lunch or dinner, weekend brunch, late night **Entrée range** £7–14.50 **Payment** VISA, MC, AMEX, D, DC **Service rating** ★★½ **Friendliness rating** ★★★½ **Bar** Yes **Wine selection** Very good **Dress** Smart casual but relaxed **Disabled access** Ground floor only

Lunch Monday–Friday, noon–3 p.m.; Saturday and Sunday, noon–4 p.m.

Dinner Monday–Saturday, 6–11:30 p.m.

Bar Monday–Saturday, 11 a.m.–1 a.m.

Setting & atmosphere Futuristic, modern decor with high ceilings and a microbrewery in the ground-floor bar; fairly noisy when crowded.

House specialties Smoked swordfish with coconut pickled vegetables and red mustard leaves; roasted asparagus with quail's eggs and Pecorino shavings; pizzas; breads; salads; chargrilled meat and fish.

Other recommendations Fresh fruit drinks, microbrewed beer.

Entertainment & amenities DJ Thursday through Saturday nights.

Summary & comments Mash is lively, boisterous, and ultracool. And very popular with a mostly young clientele, who crowd into the ground-floor bar and upstairs restaurant by day and night. Some come for the excellent beers brewed on premises, and you can join a lunchtime tour on Saturday (12:30 p.m.) for a tour, tasting, and two-course lunch. Or you can just come in to eat and drink without the educational angle. Grilling over wood and pizzas baked in a wood oven are strong points of the hip, usually well judged cooking, from a short menu that does pretty well by vegetarians. The bar is a good place for a quick lunch, and there's also a deli counter where you can get meals to take out. Noise-phobics should avoid the restaurant in the evening, but everyone else will enjoy the good buzz and decent food.

MATSURI ★★★½

JAPANESE | MODERATE/EXPENSIVE | QUALITY ★★★½ | VALUE ★★ | ZONE 9

15 Bury Street, SW1; (0207) 839-1101; tube: Green Park; www.matsuri-restaurant.com

Customers Locals and tourists **Reservations** Recommended **When to go** Lunch or dinner **Entrée range** Lunch £13–30 **Payment** VISA, MC, AMEX, DC, CB **Service rating**

★★★½ **Friendliness rating** ★★★½ **Bar** Yes **Wine selection** Adequate; beer and sake better **Dress** Casual **Disabled access** Yes, for diners only

Lunch Monday–Saturday, noon–2:30 p.m.

Dinner Monday–Saturday, 6–10:30 p.m.

Setting & atmosphere Big, spacious main dining room and smaller sushi bar; elegant but relaxed.

House specialties Sushi and teppanyaki.

Summary & comments London has its full share of big Japanese restaurants catering to businesspeople with expense accounts as big as the Grand Canyon. You'll find a few of them in the "More Recommendations" section, along with some smaller places at significantly lower prices. This is a big place, but the prices are relatively reasonable and the quality is high. Sushi and sashimi are expertly prepared and can be ordered either à la carte at the bar or in various permutations of a set meal (from £14 and up). Most of the space is given over to teppanyaki tables, where your choice of fish, meat, and vegetables is prepared and cooked for you on a sizzling hot plate. Very theatrical, but also good food. There's even a nod toward fusion cooking, in the form of tuna tartar, foie gras "Japanese," and little dishes such as deep-fried chicken. The list of specialty brand sakes is intriguing, though not cheap. But then, top-quality Japanese never comes cheap.

MORO   ★★★★

SPANISH/MIDDLE EASTERN | MODERATE | QUALITY ★★★★ | VALUE ★★★★ | ZONE 3

34–36 Exmouth Market, EC1; (0207) 833-8336; tube: Farringdon or Angel

Customers Locals, both young and old **Reservations** Recommended **When to go** Anytime **Entrée range** £10.50–15.50 **Payment** VISA, MC, AMEX, D **Service rating** ★★★ **Friendliness rating** ★★★★½ **Bar** Yes, with tapas menu **Wine selection** Very good **Dress** Casual **Disabled access** Yes

Lunch Monday–Friday, 12:30–2:30 p.m.

Dinner Monday–Saturday, 7–10:30 p.m.

Drinks and tapas Monday–Friday, 12:30–10:30 p.m.; Saturday, 6:30–10:30 p.m.

Setting & atmosphere Casual and lively; high-ceilinged room with simple decor.

House specialties Everything cooked in the wood-fired oven, such as cod with Saffron rice, caramelized onions, and tahini; charcoal-grilled dishes like lamb kebab with egg and mint salad and bulgur; homemade breads and yogurt; tarts and other desserts.

Other recommendations Vegetarian dishes, well-chosen Spanish cheeses, braised dishes.

Summary & comments Since opening in 1998, Moro has become one of the hottest, coolest, and most popular restaurants in London. The area is off the beaten track as far as sight-seeing is concerned, apart from Sadler's Wells Theatre, but it is also increasingly trendy in a nicely bohemian way. Moro has played a part in this. It is popular because the food is really outstanding: if anyone has ever had a bad time there, we haven't heard about it. The prices are very reasonable for cooking of this quality. Based on the cuisine and culture of

Moorish Spain, when the country was under Islamic rule, the food has big, bold flavors and generous spicing. You can never tell what you'll find at Moro, because the menu changes weekly. But it doesn't matter: everything's delicious. Not a place for a quiet evening. Definitely a place for a memorable meal, in a bustling restaurant that shows why people enthuse about London's gastronomic renaissance.

MR. KONG   ★★★½

CHINESE | INEXPENSIVE/MODERATE | QUALITY ★★★½ | VALUE ★★★★ | ZONE 7

21 Lisle Street, WC2; (0207) 437-7341; tube: Leicester Square

Customers Mostly locals **Reservations** Recommended **When to go** Lunch or dinner **Entrée range** Lunch £6–26 **Payment** VISA, MC, AMEX, D, DC, CB **Service rating** ★★★ **Friendliness rating** ★★½ **Bar** No **Wine selection** Adequate **Dress** Casual **Disabled access** Restaurant

Open Every day, noon–2:45 a.m.

Setting & atmosphere Unexceptional if well-appointed Chinese decor; usually very busy.

House specialties Chef's specials, especially shellfish and hot-pot dishes.

Other recommendations Standard Cantonese dishes.

Summary & comments In an area crowded with Chinese restaurants, Mr. Kong stands out by virtue of its interesting and innovative cooking. The menu is long, but you don't need to look any further than the "Chef's Special" page—over 50 dishes, some of them found nowhere else. They seldom climb beyond the £12 mark, and there's enough to keep you happy and interested for a good half-dozen mealtimes. Adventurous eaters can sample baked frogs' legs, fish maw, or pig's intestines; seafood fans should have soft-shell crabs (an occasional special), clams in various guises, or steamed crab with rice wine. Even if you stick with more conventional dishes, you will be well fed. Though Mr. Kong is somewhat more expensive than most restaurants in the area, it's worth the money.

NOBU   ★★★★

"NEW-STYLE" JAPANESE | EXPENSIVE | QUALITY ★★★★ | VALUE ★★ | ZONE 8

19 Old Park Lane, W1; (0207) 447-4747; tube: Hyde Park Corner

Customers Businesspeople, tourists, the occasional celebrity **Reservations** Essential **When to go** Lunch or dinner **Entrée range** £11.75–27.50 **Payment** VISA, MC, AMEX, DC, CB **Service rating** ★★★½ **Friendliness rating** ★★★★ **Bar** Yes **Wine selection** Very good **Dress** Fashionable **Disabled access** Yes

Lunch Monday–Friday, noon–2:15 p.m.

Dinner Monday–Friday, 6–10:15 p.m.; Saturday, 6–11:15 p.m.; Sunday, 6–9:45 p.m.

Setting & atmosphere Ultraminimalist decor for an ultrachic clientele.

House specialties "Special appetizers" such as yellowtail sashimi with jalapeño and tomato rock shrimp ceviche; all traditional sushi and sashimi.

Other recommendations "Special dishes" such as black cod with miso and Inaniwa pasta salad with lobster.

Summary & comments Nobu is one-of-a-kind restaurant, even though there are two other branches (in New York City and Beverly Hills). If you know about those outlets for Matsuhisu Nobuyuki's extraordinary reworking of Japanese cuisine, then you know what to expect here. There are three things that come to mind, and the most important is startling innovation that almost invariably sends diners into raptures. This is like no other Japanese food, taking in influences from every corner of the globe, especially South America. But it's innovation that works, which is what counts. The second thing is chic: Nobu attracts entertainment people, and you may get to see one or two when you eat here. The third thing is the daunting expense. If you order a full meal, it's hard to come away without spending £50 or more on food alone, and that won't even fill you up. This means Nobu doesn't rate well for value. And there have been complaints about service. But it is an amazing place, and everyone should visit once: consider going for a sushi lunch, which shouldn't set you back more than £20 a head as long as you avoid alcohol. And one encouraging point: prices have not risen in two years!

NORTH SEA FISH RESTAURANT   ★½

FISH AND CHIPS | INEXPENSIVE | QUALITY ★★½ | VALUE ★★★★★ | ZONE 2

7–8 Leigh Street, WC1; (0207) 387-5892; tube: Holborn or King's Cross

Customers Mostly locals **Reservations** Not necessary **When to go** Lunch or dinner **Entrée range** £7.90–16.95 **Payment** VISA, MC, AMEX, DC **Service rating** ★★★ **Friendliness rating** ★★★★ **Bar** Yes **Wine selection** Adequate **Dress** Casual **Disabled access** Limited

Lunch Monday–Saturday, noon–2:30 p.m.

Dinner Monday–Saturday, 5:30–10:30 p.m.

Setting & atmosphere Charmingly old-fashioned room with wooden beams and a lively buzz.

House specialties Fish and chips, avocado prawn, seafood platter, scampi, salmon, Dover sole.

Other recommendations Traditional desserts.

Summary & comments Everyone visiting London should eat fish and chips at least once. And if you eat it here, you'll see why it's one of the national dishes. To succeed, a cook needs top-quality fish and potatoes, good batter and oil, and an intimate knowledge of the art of deep-frying. At North Sea, they have all the requirements. You can have your choice of fish either fried in batter or matzo meal, or plainly grilled. Don't be put off by the fear of frying (even if it's supposedly "bad for you"). Batter-fried cod at the North Sea is absolutely delicious, not leaden or greasy like some fried foods. If you want to be authentic, have a side order of pickled onion to go with it. Service is decorous and efficient, the wine list is short but good, and the homemade desserts are wonderful. If you have room for them, that is.

L'ODÉON ★★★½

MODERN EUROPEAN | MODERATE/EXPENSIVE | QUALITY ★★★½ | VALUE ★★★ |ZONE 14

65 Regent Street, W1, (0207) 287-1400; tube: Piccadilly Circus

Customers Locals and tourists, many families **When to go** Lunch, drinks, or dinner **Entrée range** £12.50–20 **Payment** VISA, MC, AMEX, D, DC **Service rating** ★★★½ **Friendliness rating** ★★★½ **Bar** Yes **Wine selection** Good **Dress** Informal **Disabled access** Yes

Lunch Monday–Saturday, noon–2:30 p.m.

Dinner Monday–Saturday, 5:30–11:30 p.m.

Setting & atmosphere Large, attractive second-floor room with good views (at some tables) of Regent Street.

Summary & comments This place has had many ups and downs. At the moment it's in an up phase—but the variability of the past must add a note of caution to the recommendation. With that out of the way, we can say that we've had some fine meals here—and fine drinks in the bar, which is the first thing you see after ascending stairs or escalators. The food has been French-oriented and ambitiously complex at certain points in the restaurant's history. At press time it was simpler and more Italian-based: spinach and mozzarella tart with rocket (arugula) salad; roast monkfish with rosemary and sun-dried tomato risotto; and wild mushroom ravioli with spinach, Parmesan, and truffle cream sauce should convey the general picture. Prices are not cheap on the carte, though they're not extortionate. But if you're on a budget, lunch and pretheater menus at £15.50 (2 courses) and £19.50 (3 courses) are there to help. If you stop in for a cocktail, you will probably want to stay for dinner. L'Odéon is a very appealing place.

1 LOMBARD STREET ★★★★

MODERN EUROPEAN | EXPENSIVE | QUALITY ★★★½ | VALUE ★★★ | ZONE 3

1 Lombard Street, EC3; (0207) 929-6611; tube: Bank; www.1lombardstreet.com

Customers Mostly well-heeled businesspeople from nearby offices, some tourists **Reservations** Essential for dinner, advisable for lunch **When to go** Lunch or dinner **Entrée range** £9.95–26.50 brasserie, £27.50–29.50 restaurant **Payment** VISA, MC, AMEX, D, DC, JCB **Service rating** ★★★★ **Friendliness rating** ★★★★ **Bar** Yes **Wine selection** Good **Dress** Smart casual

Open Monday–Friday, 7:30 a.m.–10 p.m.

Setting & atmosphere The brasserie is a large, attractive, high-ceilinged room filled with light by day; restaurant in back is small, quiet, and discreet.

Summary & comments I Lombard Street, a "listed" building of architectural importance, was a banking hall before it was a restaurant. By day its main room, the Brasserie, is one of London's lovelier places to eat, with high ceilings dominated by a glass cupola over the circular bar. And it is very popular with the local banking/business community: you may get lucky at lunch if you walk in without making a reservation, but usually the only place to sit is at the bar. The food and setting have earned a Michelin star, and when you taste chef Herbert Berger's cooking you will understand why. Tastes are big, and presentation is carefully thought out; the framework is French, but there are intelligent additions from global cuisines. The prices are also big: three courses will be £25–35 in the Brasserie and £50–55 in the Restaurant. But you can eat relatively cheaply if you don't want a full meal, and you'll appreciate the friendly, smiling service. If you're planning a single blow-out dinner during your stay, the Restaurant should be a serious candidate despite the expense. Otherwise, this is a good stopping-off point while you're touring the area.

ORREY ★★★★½

MODERN EUROPEAN | EXPENSIVE | QUALITY ★★★★½ | VALUE ★★★ | ZONE 14

55 Marylebone High Street, W1; (0207) 616-8000; tube: Baker Street; www.conran.com/eat

Customers Affluent locals from all over London **When to go** Lunch or dinner **Entrée range** £14.50–24 **Payment** VISA, MC, AMEX, D, DC, JCB **Service rating** ★★★★★ **Friendliness rating** ★★★★★ **Bar** Yes **Wine selection** Outstanding but expensive **Dress** Smart **Disabled access** Yes

Lunch Monday–Saturday, noon–3 p.m.; Sunday, noon–2:30 p.m.

Dinner Monday–Saturday, 7–11 p.m.; Sunday, 7–10:30 p.m.

Setting & atmosphere Long, narrow second-floor room with skylight; small adjacent bar; open-air terrace in good weather.

House specialties Terrine of foie gras, Sauternes gelée, pain Poi lane; brochette of langoustines, terrine of tomato and basil, sauce rouille; crispy duck salad, honey-mustard dressing; pavé of wild salmon en papillotte, peas, sorrel, and asparagus; Anjou pigeon en cocotte, ventrèche bacon, étuvée of peas and girolles; veal cutlet, Jerusalem artichoke, morels, and truffle jus; trio of crème brûlée; confit of apricot and liquorice.

Other recommendations Light dinner menu on the terrace, weather permitting (summer only); set lunch and Sunday set dinner menus.

Summary & comments Orrey is part of the large Conran group (see Quaglino's, page 290) and is universally regarded as the best of its restaurants for those seeking high-quality cooking in more intimate surroundings. The restaurant is small by Conran standards; the emphasis here is on the food rather than the buzz. And the kitchen consistently meets the high standards it sets itself: the cooking here is among the best in London, and sometimes reaches dazzling heights in inventiveness, seasoning, and presentation. It has a Michelin star, but probably deserves two. On the other hand, the prices are as dazzling as the food. It is alarmingly easy to spend £75 a head for a full meal with wine, and if you take on the five-star reaches of the fine but costly wine list, you can go a lot higher than that. But they also have many wines by the glass, and the set lunch (£23.50 for three courses) and set Sunday dinner (£28.50) are a bargain by anyone's standards. With service that combines military precision with a genuinely warm welcome, this is one of London's top stars.

PIED À TERRE ★★★★½

MODERN BRITISH/FRENCH | EXPENSIVE | QUALITY ★★★★½ | VALUE ★★★ | ZONE 14

34 Charlotte Street, W1; (0207) 636-1178; tube: Goodge Street; www.pied.a.terre.co.uk

Customers Locals, tourists, business community **When to go** Lunch or dinner **Entrée range** Lunch, £12–28; dinner, £39 for 2 courses **Payment** VISA, MC, AMEX, D, DC, JCB **Service rating** ★★★★★ **Friendliness rating** ★★★½ **Bar** No **Wine selection** Exceptional **Dress** Smart casual

Lunch Monday–Friday, 12:15–2:30 p.m.

Dinner Monday–Saturday, 7–11 p.m.

Setting & atmosphere Small, quiet room with simple decor.

House specialties Tasting menus at £60 (seven courses) and £70 (nine courses), with optional wines by the glass to match each course .

Other recommendations Set lunch at £19.50 (two courses) and £23 (three courses).

Summary & comments Pied à Terre is one of the most distinguished restaurants in London, and a survivor of numerous chef changes over recent years. While the chefs have changed, the food has remained remarkably consistent both in quality and style: the aim is for big, bold flavors with complex assemblies of many different elements. But the effect is always harmonious and carefully thought out. Menus change, so it's impossible to say what will be offered when you come, but here are a few dishes to give the idea: braised pig's trotter with warm pork rillette, apple and cinnamon purée with braised pork belly and caramelized apple salad; sea bream fillets with watercress purée, oyster beignet, and oyster velouté; mandarin parfait with lemon curd, citrus fruit sorbet, and salad. This is modern cooking at its most sophisticated and expert. And matching wine with food is taken very seriously. The only cautionary note is that some people find the white-walled room rather lacking in personality, but since you come here for amazing cooking, that shouldn't put you off.

PIZZA EXPRESS ★

PIZZA | INEXPENSIVE | QUALITY ★★ | VALUE ★★★★ | ZONE 1

70 Heath Street, NW3; (0207) 433-1600; tube: Hampstead; www.pizzaexpress.co.uk

Customers Locals and tourists **Reservations** Not necessary **When to go** Anytime **Entrée range** £4.95–7.75 **Payment** VISA, MC, AMEX, DC **Service rating** ★★ **Friendliness rating** ★★★½ **Bar** No **Wine selection** Minimal **Dress** Casual **Disabled access** Yes

Open Every day, 11 a.m.–midnight

Setting & atmosphere Relaxed, unpretentious, and notably child-friendly.

Summary & comments This branch is just one of dozens: There are over 200 branches nationwide. Its formula is very simple. There are 16 types of pizza, a couple of baked pasta dishes and salads, and a few side dishes. The thin-crust pizzas are smallish by American standards but good; the pasta dishes are acceptable if not exciting; main-course salads are so-so. In short, not a place to come for a special meal but when you want something cheap and fast. It is especially good for children, who are always made welcome. Art-lovers should note that they contribute 25p to the Veneziana Fund, formerly Venice in Peril, whenever they order a Veneziana pizza (onions, capers, olives, pine nuts, sultanas, mozzarella, tomato, £5.30).

POLLO ★

ITALIAN | INEXPENSIVE | QUALITY ★★ | VALUE ★★★★★ | ZONE 7

20 Old Compton Street, W1; (0207) 734-5917; tube: Leicester Square or Tottenham Court Road

Customers Locals **Reservations** Not necessary **When to go** Lunch or dinner **Entrée range** £3.70–6 **Payment** Cash or sterling travelers checks **Service rating** ★★ **Friendliness rating** ★★★★ **Bar** No **Wine selection** Minimal **Dress** Casual **Disabled access** No

Open Every day, noon–midnight

Setting & atmosphere Old-fashioned 1950s decor, charmingly run-down, very lively at all hours.

House specialties Pasta.

Summary & comments The reasons for including Pollo in this book can be summed up in three words: pasta, price, and character. The prices are so low they're almost surreal, especially in a city where nothing comes cheap. The pasta is consistently good, whether sauced or baked. And the character is just great, made equally by the cheerful staff and the customers who pile in for cheap eats anytime of day. It's a glimpse of a London that has nearly disappeared from most areas frequented by tourists, and it's worth a visit for that reason alone. If you think of it as an Anglo-Italian diner, you'll have the right idea. One of a kind, and useful for budget-watchers.

PRET À MANGER ★

SANDWICHES, ETC. | INEXPENSIVE | QUALITY ★★ | VALUE ★★★★ | ZONE 3

The Tower of London, EC3; tube: Tower Hill; www.pret.com/flash

Customers Locals and tourists **Reservations** Not necessary **When to go** Breakfast, lunch, or snack **Entrée range** 99p–£4.75 **Payment** VISA, MC, AMEX, D, DC, CB **Service rating** ★★★ **Friendliness rating** ★★★½ **Bar** No **Wine selection** None **Dress** Casual **Disabled access** Yes

Open Every day, 8:30 a.m.–6 p.m.

Setting & atmosphere Sandwich shop.

Summary & comments Pret à Manger isn't a restaurant but an outlet for fast food, mostly sandwiches, and part of a chain of over 75 in the capital. Sandwiches range from ultrasimple egg salad (called "egg mayonnaise" in Britain, 99p) to wraps filled with hummus and red pepper salad (£2.10) and even vegetarian sushi (£2.70) or deluxe sushi (£4.95). Cakes and desserts are decent; coffee could be a lot better. In short, nothing to set the heart racing, but it's good, it's cheap, it's quick, and it's everywhere. If you just want a light, quick refueling session, this is one place to get it.

PROSPECT GRILL ★★★½

MODERN EUROPEAN/AMERICAN | INEXPENSIVE/MODERATE | QUALITY ★★★½ | VALUE ★★★★★ | ZONE 7

4–6 Garrick Street, WC1; (0207) 379-0412; tube: Leicester Square

Customers Varied **Reservations** Advisable **When to go** Lunch or dinner **Entrée range** £9.95–15.95 **Payment** VISA, MC, AMEX, DC **Service rating** ★★★★ **Friendliness rating** ★★★★★ **Bar** No **Wine selection** Small but good **Dress** Casual **Disabled access** Restaurant only, not rest rooms

Open Monday–Friday, 11:45 a.m.–3:30 p.m. and 5:45–11:45 p.m.; Saturday, 11:45 a.m.–11:45 p.m.

Setting & atmosphere Small, intimate front room with booths and plush decor; simpler side room with tables only.

Summary & comments The Prospect has been a great success ever since it opened in 1999, and it's easy to understand why. Few neighborhoods have such an appealing, welcoming cheapish restaurant where the cooking is this good, and in the West End it's as rare as a snowman in August. The food is simple, specializing (as you'll guess from the name) in grilled meat, fish, and vegetables. Steaks and burgers are made with organic beef and cooked just as you order with great fries on the side. But roast dishes are also good, and desserts are of the stick-to-your-hips variety. It's worth phoning well ahead to get a table in the front room, with its red walls and superbly comfortable seating. The other room is fine, but this is the one that most makes you think you're in an American steak house of ancient pedigree. Diners on a budget should note that the set lunch and pretheater menus (£13.95 for two courses, £15.95 for three) are terrific bargains.

QUAGLINO'S ★★½

MODERN EUROPEAN | MODERATE | QUALITY ★★★ | VALUE ★★★ | ZONE 9

16 Bury Street, SW1; (0207) 930-6767; tube: Green Park; www.quaglinos.co.uk

Customers Locals and tourists **Reservations** Recommended **When to go** Lunch or dinner **Entrée range** £12.50–30 **Payment** VISA, MC, AMEX, D, DC, CB **Service rating** ★★½

Friendliness rating ★★ **Bar** Yes **Wine selection** Good **Dress** Smart casual **Disabled access** Yes

Lunch Every day, noon–3 p.m.

Dinner Monday–Thursday, 5:30 p.m.–midnight; Friday and Saturday, 5:30 p.m.–1 a.m.; Sunday, 5:30–11 p.m.

Setting & atmosphere Massive interior, with a street-level mezzanine bar (very popular) overlooking the sunken dining room; very noisy.

House specialties Plateau de fruits de mer (and all shellfish), grilled meats such as Châteaubriand.

Other recommendations Prix-fixe menus.

Entertainment & amenities Live music every night from 8 p.m.

Summary & comments Quaglino's was a famous bar/restaurant in the 1930s. On its reopening by Sir Terence Conran in the late 1980s, it started a fad for really huge London restaurants—several of them owned by Conran himself. Many people, however, think this is still the best of them. The kitchen is on view behind glass, and so are banks of the fresh seafood which is one of the restaurant's strengths. Because it's so huge, this is not a place for quiet conversation. It's buzzy, boisterous, and brash. Some people love this kind of place; others do not. But even if this is not your usual style of restaurant, Quaglino's is worth considering to see a style of eating that London has taken to its heart. The prix-fixe menus (lunchtime and pre- and post-theater) are the best choice if you're on a limited budget. Service can also slow down at busy times.

RASA   ★★★½

INDIAN | MODERATE | QUALITY ★★★½ | VALUE ★★★★ | ZONE 8

6 Dering Street, W1; (0207) 629-1346; tube: Oxford Circus

55 Stoke Newington Church Street, N16; (0207) 249-0344; tube: Manor House

Customers Locals and aficionados **Reservations** Recommended **When to go** Lunch or dinner **Entrée range** £6–10.95 **Payment** VISA, MC, AMEX, D, DC, CB **Service rating** ★★★½ **Friendliness rating** ★★★ **Bar** Yes **Wine selection** Small but good **Dress** Casual **Disabled access** Restaurant only

Lunch Monday–Saturday, noon–3 p.m.

Dinner Monday–Saturday, 6–11 p.m.

Setting & atmosphere Pleasant modern interior, simply decorated, friendly and informal.

House specialties Southern Indian vegetarian dishes.

Other recommendations Breads, pickles, and chutneys.

Summary & comments The original Rasa, in out-of-the-way Stoke Newington, has educated thousands of Londoners about the beauties of Keralan (southern Indian) vegetarian cuisine. The second branch, in W1, more centrally located, deserves a visit if you have the slightest interest in Indian food. You can ask them to put together a Kerala feast, which will give a good balance and range of dishes featuring different flavors and textures. Or choose for yourself among the dosas (filled pancakes), curries, and side dishes of rice, vegetables, and exquisite bread. The food is filling but not stodgy, and no one who eats it comes away unimpressed. If you like the idea but don't like vegetarian meals, there's a branch called Rasa Samudra (5 Charlotte Street, W1; (0207) 637 0222) specializing in Southern Indian fish and shellfish. The Stoke Newington restaurant has humbler decor, far lower prices, and a huge local fan club that can cause a long wait for tables.

RICHARD CORRIGAN AT LINDSAY HOUSE ★★★½

BRITISH | MODERATE/EXPENSIVE | QUALITY ★★★½ | VALUE ★★ | ZONE 7

21 Romilly Street, W1; (0207) 439-0450; tube: Leicester Square or Piccadilly Circus; www.lindsayhouse.co.uk

Customers Mostly locals **Reservations** Recommended **When to go** Lunch or dinner **Entrée range** Lunch only, £18–25; set menus £23 (lunch), £44 (dinner) **Payment** VISA, MC, AMEX, D, CB, JCB **Service rating** ★★★★ **Friendliness rating** ★★★★ **Bar** No **Wine selection** Excellent but expensive **Dress** Smart casual **Disabled access** No

Lunch Monday–Friday, noon–2 p.m.

Dinner Monday–Saturday, 6–11 p.m.

Setting & atmosphere Two stories of a townhouse decorated with quiet elegance; cozy and subdued but not stuffy.

House specialties Menu changes daily; meat is the strong point.

Summary & comments Richard Corrigan, the chef at Lindsay House, has long had devoted followers for his robust, sophisticated approach to modern cooking. After moving around a slew of London restaurants, he seems to have settled in here, giving his fans the kind of hearty food that they've come to expect from him. Corrigan is Irish, and his native tradition shows in a love of pork, offal, and Irish ingredients such as black pudding. But his cooking is also based in French classicism, and it is both refined and adventurous. There's a lot of fish, too, but it's perhaps not always as reliable as the meat. Desserts are a strong point. Prices are not low, on the menu or (especially) the wine list; this is a restaurant for a special occasion. And a few grumbles have been heard about lax service. But if you like hearty cooking, chances are you'll like the Lindsay House. They'll cook specially for vegetarians if asked.

ROYAL CHINA ★★★

CHINESE | INEXPENSIVE | QUALITY ★★★ | VALUE ★★★★ | ZONE 14

13 Queensway, W2; (0207) 221-2535; tube: Bayswater or Queensway

Customers Locals and tourists, many Chinese **Reservations** Not necessary **When to go** Weekend lunch or dinner **Entrée range** £5.50–40 **Payment** VISA, MC, AMEX, D **Service rating** ★★ **Friendliness rating** ★★½ **Bar** Yes **Wine selection** Excellent for a Chinese restaurant **Dress** Casual **Disabled access** Restaurant only

Open Monday–Thursday, noon–11 p.m.; Friday and Saturday, noon–11:30 p.m.; Sunday, 11 a.m.–10 p.m.

Setting & atmosphere Plush Chinese decor with lots of black lacquer and gold, comfortable seating; can be quite hectic when there's a crowd.

House specialties All shellfish, especially lobster (cooked in six different ways), scallops, and prawns; dim sum.

Other recommendations Chicken with cashews; sautéed chicken with black beans and chili; fillet steak with black pepper; hot and spicy veal; Royal China Dover sole; Royal China lotus leaf rice; chilled mango pudding.

Summary & comments Probably the best restaurant in this Chinese restaurant–crowded street, Royal China is also a cut above in comfort, and care has been taken with the decor, even if it is not to everyone's taste. But the food is to everyone's taste, as you'll see if you go along for dim sum. There are the usual dumplings and rolls, as well as special dishes rarely found elsewhere, and the quality is exceptional. The only problem is the crowds, which on weekends (especially Sunday) can lead to enormous lines outside. Go during the week for a more leisurely affair, and for dinner as well as lunch. Seafood is exquisite, and even the set meals (normally a no-go area) are good. Service can be a little abrupt but is better than at many comparable places. And the wine list is a surprise, as good as some upper-echelon European restaurants—and much cheaper!

RULES ★★★

BRITISH | MODERATE/EXPENSIVE | QUALITY ★★★½ | VALUE ★★★ | ZONE 7

35 Maiden Lane, WC2; (0207) 836-5314; tube: Covent Garden or Charing Cross; www.rules.co.uk

Customers More tourists than locals **Reservations** Recommended **When to go** Dinner is best **Entrée range** £16.95–22.50 **Payment** VISA, MC, AMEX, D, DC, JCB **Service rating** ★★★ **Friendliness rating** ★★★ **Bar** No **Wine selection** Small but good **Dress** Casual **Disabled access** Yes

Open Monday–Saturday, noon–11:30p.m.; Sunday, noon–10:30 p.m.

Setting & atmosphere Ornate old-fashioned decor with prints and statues, but modern lively bustle at busy times.

House specialties Game dishes, Aberdeen Angus beef.

Other recommendations Terrine of venison and wild rabbit; terrine of foie gras and pigeon; roast and confit Gressingham duck in a Bramley apple and five-spice chutney; roast fillet of Wild Highland red deer; poached finnan haddock with a mussel and saffron broth; raspberry trifle syllabub.

Summary & comments Rules has been serving food from this location since 1798. That by itself is not a reason to recommend it, and for years the restaurant served indifferent food to tourists seeking a taste of tradition. But it has had, for several years now, a French-trained chef of high quality who combines classic game and meat cookery with up-to-the-minute modern touches. The menu doesn't stand still, which is a good sign. There is less unusual experimentation than before, and fish lovers will find more choice. But many will choose the appetizing selection of meat and game. The selection of "feathered and furred game" (some from their estate in Scotland, which also occasionally supplies beef and pork) is as good as you'll find anywhere in London. Vegetarians should probably go elsewhere. If you want to try a classic, old-fashioned rib of beef, or steak and kidney pie (with or without oysters), Rules is one of your best bets.

SILKS & SPICE   ★★

ASIAN | INEXPENSIVE/MODERATE | QUALITY ★★★ | VALUE ★★★★ | ZONE 14

23 Foley Street, W1; (0207) 636-2718; tube: Oxford Circus or Great Portland Street

95 Chiswick High Road, W4; (0208) 995-7991; tube: Turnham Green; www.silksandspice.co.uk

Customers Locals **Reservations** Recommended **When to go** Anytime **Entrée range** £5.50–12.50 **Payment** VISA, MC, AMEX, D, DC **Service rating** ★★½ **Friendliness rating** ★★★★ **Bar** No **Wine selection** Cheap and adequate **Dress** Casual **Disabled access** Ground floor only

Open Monday–Friday, noon–11 p.m.; Saturday, 5:30–11 p.m.; Sunday, 5:30–10:30 p.m.

Setting & atmosphere Pleasantly scruffy decor with Southeast Asian ornaments; noisy and lively.

House specialties Lobster noodles, salmon salad, grilled prawns.

Other recommendations All noodles, all char-grilled dishes, dim sum, curries.

Summary & comments Silks & Spice began here and now has two other branches in addition to the ones listed above. It deserves its success. The feel is slightly student-y, with jazz/funk playing on the stereo, but customers are of all ages. They come for well-priced and delicious Asian food, mostly Thai and Malaysian with bits of China and Japan. Comfort is not a selling point: tables are close, and chairs won't make you feel sleepy. But as long as you don't expect luxury you will probably enjoy their long, varied menu. Most dishes are classified according to chile-heat, which is useful, and although portions aren't huge, you can easily eat a filling meal for under £15 before drinks. On the minus side, the large basement is the smoking area and gets very smoky when busy. On the plus side, the Oriental Express Menu (noon–7 p.m.) offers smaller servings at lower prices for people in a rush. If Silks & Spice is full, there's an excellent, moderately priced fish restaurant next door called Back to Basics.

SPIGA   ★★

ITALIAN | INEXPENSIVE | QUALITY ★★★ | VALUE ★★★ | ZONE 7

84–86 Wardour Street, W1; (0207) 734-3444; tube: Tottenham Court Road

Spighetta, 43 Blandford Street, W1; (0207) 486-7340

Customers Mostly locals, mostly young **Reservations** Recommended **When to go** Lunch or dinner **Entrée range** £8–13.50 **Payment** VISA, MC, AMEX, D, DC, CB **Service rating** ★★½ **Friendliness rating** ★★★ **Bar** No **Wine selection** Small but adequate- **Dress** Casual **Disabled access** Yes

Lunch Every day, noon–3 p.m.

Dinner Sunday–Tuesday, 6:30–11 p.m.; Wednesday–Saturday, 6:30–midnight

Setting & atmosphere Sleek, modern decor with view of the kitchen, informal and friendly.

House specialties Pizzas; angel hair pasta with prawns, rocket (arugula) salad, garlic, and chiles; char-grilled chicken breast with spinach and roasted potatoes.

Summary & comments Spiga, like its cousin Spighetta, is a friendly, low-priced outlet for top-quality pizzas baked in wood-burning ovens. And these are some of the best pizzas in town, whether a simple Margherita or topped with prosciutto and wild mushrooms. They make Spiga a top choice in this part of town when you want good, simple food in informal surroundings. But there's more to the place than pizza: Pasta dishes in particular also excel, and appetizers, fish, and meat are simple, but well executed. Friendly service, good coffee, and ample choice in cheap wines completes the picture. The only complaint is a tendency for service to flag when the place is busy. But plusses outweigh minuses by a very wide margin.

STANLEY'S ★★

BRITISH | INEXPENSIVE | QUALITY ★★★ | VALUE ★★★★ | ZONE 7

6 Little Portland Street, W1; (0207) 462-0099; tube: Oxford Circus

Customers Mostly locals **Reservations** Not necessary **When to go** Lunch or dinner **Entrée range** £8.50–10.95 **Payment** VISA, MC, AMEX, D, CB **Service rating** ★★½ **Friendliness rating** ★★★★ **Bar** Yes **Wine selection** Adequate; beers are outstanding **Dress** Casual **Disabled access** Yes

Open Monday–Saturday, noon–midnight

Setting & atmosphere Jolly and very informal.

House specialties "The Magnificent Seven" sausages, spit roast Welsh beef, saddle of lamb.

Other recommendations House "savouries," desserts.

Summary & comments Stanley's is known to Londoners as the place to eat sausages— seven varieties, ranging from plain pork through Caribbean-style, Thai-style, game, chicken, bratwurst, and even a vegetarian Glamorgan sausage. They're served up by friendly and skilled staff in a simple room that's also pleasing to the eye, with its red banquettes and booths. And the sausages are reason enough to go here. But the rest of the food is also worth a look—simple, using top ingredients, and consistently well prepared. The wine list is dominated by English wines (which will surprise you with their quality). You'd be much better off, however, drinking one or more of the outstanding beers from the United Kingdom or Europe. Stanley's is a low-priced star, one of the best in the West End. And early eaters should note that all sausage dishes cost £7 (a good discount) from 5:30 to 7 p.m.

ST. JOHN ★★★★

MODERN BRITISH | MODERATE | QUALITY ★★★★½ | VALUE ★★★★ | ZONE 3

26 St. John Street, EC1; (0207) 251-0848; tube: Farringdon;
www.stjohnrestaurant.co.uk

Customers Mostly locals **When to go** Lunch or dinner **Entrée range** £10–23.50 **Payment** VISA, MC, AMEX, DC **Service rating** ★★★★ **Friendliness rating** ★★★★★ **Bar** Yes, with full menu available **Wine selection** Very good **Dress** Casual

Lunch Monday–Friday, noon–3 p.m.

Dinner Monday–Saturday, 6–11 p.m.

Setting & atmosphere Big, minimally decorated rooms in a converted industrial building; almost always crowded.

House specialties Radishes and butter; brwan (head cheese); smoked eel and horseradish; roast bone marrow and parsley salad; smoked Gloucester old spot chop; pigeon and radishes; grilled veal chop, chicory, and anchovy; tripe and onions; Welsh rarebit; Eccles cake and Lancashire cheese; chocolate pot.

Summary & comments You can learn a great deal about St. John from reading the list of specialties; then again, the list might tell you very little if you're not already familiar with it. Perhaps a better way of understanding it is through the restaurant's motto, now famous in London: "Nose to tail eating." This is a place for people who love meat and fish, but especially meat. And not just meat but the bits of meat (pork especially) that fancy restaurants sometimes throw away—but which "peasant" cooks have always known and loved. Everything is described in few words, because the emphasis is on top-notch ingredients (many of them organic) prepared and cooked very simply. This is a style of cooking that St. John pioneered in London, and which has been much imitated. Prices are not high for cooking at this level— please note that most main courses are £10–16. The commitment to quality is unyielding and passionate. If your idea of great cooking means taking the best products available and treating them with simple respect, St. John may be your idea of heaven. Note: it's not a place for vegetarians, and the adventurous eater is better served than the squeamish.

TAMARIND ★★★½

INDIAN | MODERATE | QUALITY ★★★½ | VALUE ★★★ | ZONE 8

20 Queen Street, W1; (0207) 629-3561; tube: Green Park;
www.tamarindrestaurant.com

Customers Locals and tourists **Reservations** Recommended **When to go** Lunch or dinner **Entrée range** £13.50–28 **Payment** VISA, MC, AMEX, D, DC, CB **Service rating** ★★★
Friendliness rating ★★★ **Bar** Yes **Wine selection** Very good **Dress** Smart **Disabled access** No

Lunch　Sunday–Friday, noon–3 p.m.

Dinner　Monday–Saturday, 6–11:30 p.m.; Sunday, 6–10:30 p.m.

Setting & atmosphere　Chic, stylish decor sets the tone.

Summary & comments　There are no specialties or recommendations listed here because this is one of those rare restaurants where you'll be hard-pressed to order a bad dish. Tamarind produces fireworks in every department, from chutneys and pickles (available for sale in jars) through breads and rice, and on to the meat, fish, and vegetable dishes that make this one of the best Indian eateries in London (vegetarians could do very well just ordering rice, bread, and a selection of side dishes). Mind you, it's also one of the most expensive. A three-course meal with all the right side dishes can easily cost £40 before drinks. Part of that is paying for the setting, for a large and polished team of waiters, for rent in one of London's most exclusive areas; it also helps support the Michelin star that Tamarind received in 2001. But it's also paying for the best ingredients, cooked with exceptional skill and attention. If you want to find out how good Indian restaurant cooking can be and don't mind paying "European" prices for the pleasure, this is one of the three or four best places to do it. The "Group Menus," a large selection of dishes to be ordered by the whole table, are a good value at £34, £38, or £45 a head.

TEATRO ★★½

MODERN EUROPEAN | MODERATE | QUALITY ★★★ | VALUE ★★★ | ZONE 7

93–107 Shaftesbury Avenue, W1; (0207) 494-3040; tube: Leicester Square or Tottenham Court Road

Customers Mostly locals **Reservations** Recommended **When to go** Dinner is best **Entrée range** £12.50–16.50 **Payment** VISA, MC, AMEX, D, DC **Service rating** ★★★★ **Friendliness rating** ★★★★ **Bar** Yes **Wine selection** Very good **Dress** No dress code **Disabled access** Yes

Lunch　Monday–Friday, noon–3 p.m.

Dinner　Monday–Saturday, 6–11:45 p.m.

Setting & atmosphere　Modern interior of understated but exceptional elegance hosts a fairly chic clientele.

House specialties　Salmon and sorrel fishcakes with herb mayonnaise; pan-fried foie gras with mango salsa; roasted breast of Gressingham duck with orange and roasted endive; carpaccio of tuna with wild globe artichoke, noodles, and parsley salad; banana tarte tatin.

Other recommendations　Set lunch and pretheater dinner menus.

Summary & comments　Teatro opened in 1998, turning a 1960s building of no great distinction into one of the West End's smartest and most distinguished showcases for modern cooking. Service is eager and almost invariably efficient. The cooking has changed considerably since its opening, with a shorter and less complicated menu, and there have been reports of inconsistent quality. But the location can't be beat—right in the heart of Soho's theater-land—and prices are reasonable. Vegetarians are catered to with at least two options for both appetizers and entrees, but meat- and fish-eaters are spoiled for choice. And if you're an early diner, you're in luck here: lunch and pretheater dinner (till 7 p.m.) are just £11.50 for two courses or £14 for three.

VEERASWAMY ★★★½

INDIAN | MODERATE | QUALITY ★★★½ | VALUE ★★★★ | ZONE 7

Mezzanine Floor, Victory House, 99 Regent Street, W1; (0207) 734-1401; tube: Piccadilly Circus

Chutney Mary, 535 Kings Road, SW10; (0207) 351-3113; tube: Fulham Broadway; www.veeraswamy.com

Customers Mostly locals **Reservations** Recommended **When to go** Lunch or dinner **Entrée range** £9–13.50 **Payment** VISA, MC, AMEX, DC, CB **Service rating** ★★★★ **Friendliness rating** ★★★★ **Bar** No **Wine selection** Very good **Dress** No dress code **Disabled access** Restaurant only, not rest rooms

Lunch Monday–Friday, noon–2:30 p.m.; Saturday and Sunday, 12:30–3 p.m.

Dinner Monday–Saturday, 5:30–11:30 p.m.; Sunday, 5:30–10:30 p.m.

Setting & atmosphere Stylish, colorful room overlooking Regent Street; mostly young, fashionable crowd.

House specialties Mussels in coconut and ginger sauce; supreme of chicken with sesame; Malabar lobster curry with fresh turmeric and raw mango; white lamb curry from Kerala; tandoori chicken tikka sautéed in a sauce of tomato and onion; green chili and cheese naan.

Other recommendations Breads, condiments, set meals, special diabetic menu according to Ayurvedic principles.

Summary & comments Veeraswamy has been on this site for decades, but the quality-conscious Chutney Mary group took over and revamped it in 1998. They modernized everything from decor to menu to wine list, and the result is one of London's better Indian restaurants. The room is unusually attractive in the way it contrasts pale wood with deep, well-chosen color. Service is from a young, multiethnic crew, and the kitchen is staffed by specialists cooking the dishes of their own region. This means that any dish, whatever part of India it's from, is likely to be authentic. Vegetable and fish/meat/chicken dishes are given equal prominence and cooked with equal care, making Veeraswamy a particularly good place to come with a mixed group of vegetarians and meat eaters. Prices are reasonable, compared with other Indian restaurants at this level, and set-price offerings make them even better. If your time is limited and you can eat only at one Indian place, this is a good candidate.

WAGAMAMA ★

ASIAN | INEXPENSIVE | QUALITY ★★ | VALUE ★★★★ | ZONES 2 & 7

4A Streatham Street, WC1; (0207) 323-9223; tube: Tottenham Court Road

10A Lexington Street, W1; (0207) 292-0990; tube: Oxford Circus or
Piccadilly Circus; www.wagamama.com

Customers Mostly locals **Reservations** Not accepted **When to go** Anytime **Entrée range** £4.90–7.50 **Payment** VISA, MC, AMEX , D, DC, JCB **Service rating** ★ **Friendliness rating** ★★ **Bar** No **Wine selection** Minimal **Dress** Casual **Disabled access** No, but see below

Open Monday–Saturday, noon–11 p.m.; Sunday, 12:30–10:30 p.m.

Setting & atmosphere Spartan room with seating at long tables.

House specialties Soup noodles, fried noodles, dumplings.

Summary & comments This is the original branch of Wagamama; there are six others, and several outside London as well. The expansion tells the story of a phenomenal success based on a simple idea. Produce a menu that focuses on just a few things, make them consistently well, and cut out all the frills so you can sell them cheap. The focus is on noodles, mostly Japanese varieties such as ramen and udon. The frills that disappear are personal space (you sit at long tables with other diners) and flexibility. You're in a machine at Wagamama, and it's not a place to dawdle. But the meals are cheap and filling, and you can be in and out very quickly when you're on the go. Complaints usually deal with service, which has little to do with personalized attention and much more with keeping the machine working smoothly. The places can't be ignored for their quality and speed; just don't expect to feel pampered. Note: The other branches have disabled access.

WÓDKA   ★★½

POLISH | MODERATE | QUALITY ★★★ | VALUE ★★★ | ZONE 11

12 St. Albans Grove, W8; (0207) 937-6513; tube: High Street Kensington

Customers Mostly locals and fans **Reservations** Recommended **When to go** Lunch or dinner **Entrée range** £10.90–13.90 **Payment** VISA, MC, AMEX, DC **Service rating** ★★★ **Friendliness rating** ★★★★½ **Bar** Yes **Wine selection** Small but good and very reasonable **Dress** Casual **Disabled access** Yes

Lunch Monday–Friday, 12:30–2:30 p.m.

Dinner Every day, 7–11:15 p.m.

Setting & atmosphere Small rooms and plain decor; popular at both lunch and dinner, and very welcoming.

House specialties Traditional Polish dishes such as blinis, dumplings, and herring; extensive vodka list.

Other recommendations Cheap lunch menu (£10.90 for two courses, £13.50 for three courses); roast and grilled meats; daily specials.

Summary & comments London has a long tradition of hosting emigrés from Eastern and Central Europe, who have brought with them the richness of their national cuisines. Wódka is part of that tradition, but it is not a traditional restaurant: the setting is modern and so is the food, despite paying due respect to classic Polish fare. Thus, you'll find blinis alongside risotto, and pierogis alongside grilled swordfish; unusual ingredients such as foie gras and oysters are there with kasha and dill. This gives a meal at Wódka a welcome element of surprise, and it also means you can eat more lightly here than at many restaurants serving this type of cuisine. The area is affluent, but Wódka is unpretentious and very well priced, both at lunch and at dinner. Wine is priced to match the food, but aficionados will not be able to resist the vodkas that give the restaurant its name. There are around 30 on the list, including vodkas flavored on the premises (such as vanilla or pear).

ZAIKA ★★★★½

MODERN INDIAN | EXPENSIVE | QUALITY ★★★★½ | VALUE ★★★ | ZONE 13

1 Kensington High Street, W8; (0207) 795-6533; tube: South Kensington; www.zaika-restaurant.co.uk

Customers More tourists than locals **When to go** Dinner is best **Entrée range** £9.95–21.50 **Payment** VISA, MC, AMEX, D, DC, JCB **Bar** No **Wine selection** Good **Dress** Smart casual **Disabled access** Yes, but not to rest rooms

Lunch Monday–Friday, noon–2:30 p.m.; Sunday, noon–2:45 p.m.

Dinner Monday–Saturday, 6:30–10:45 p.m.

Setting & atmosphere Swanky, elegant Indian.

House specialties Dhungar machli tikka (tandoori smoked salmon); kala murg (grilled spiced chicken); zaika platter; tikhe machli (spice marinated sea bass); samundri khazana (Hawaiian soft-shell crab and seared spiced scallops with Indian risotto); lal mirch murg (spicy chicken masala); gilafi dum biryani (crusted lamb biryani).

Other recommendations "Jugalbandi" menu, tasting menu at £33.50 or £40 with selected wines.

Summary & comments This genuinely innovative Indian restaurant won rave reviews on opening in 1999, and in 2001 became one of London's first Indian possessors of a Michelin star. It's easy to see why Michelin liked them: chef Vineet Bhatia's food is less authentic Indian than a sophisticated, contemporary interpretation bringing in elements and ideas from outside the subcontinent. It pays careful attention to presentation and presents some interesting desserts (not an Indian strong point) to finish off the meal. And everything about the place reflects the ambition: decor, wine list, and some of the highest prices of any Indian restaurant in London. Lovers of traditional Indian food sometimes object to the liberties taken here, but if you're not a stickler for authenticity, you're likely to be very impressed.

Part Nine

Entertainment
and Nightlife

The London Scene

No other metropolis can rival London for the overall quality and quantity of its theaters, opera, ballet, concert halls, jazz venues, art galleries, antiques fairs, auctions, exhibitions, cinemas, cabarets, comedy clubs, television, historic buildings, historic walks, private clubs, nightclubs, pubs, shops, restaurants, and publishing houses. Many more books and magazine titles are published in the United Kingdom than in the United States, and Londoners enjoy four quality national newspapers—each on a par with the *New York Times*—and numerous tabloids, many of which are at least as trashy as America's worst.

Although London remains English in character, it has, since World War II, become a microcosm of the defunct British empire with one person in five now hailing from an ethnic minority. The Indian, Asian, and Afro-Caribbean influences on the London scene have helped make it as vibrantly international as New York.

As anyone who knows his or her James Bond is aware, gambling is legal in Britain. Along with the high-class and the seedy casinos, most high streets (the main shopping street of an area) have an easily recognizable Ladbrokes betting shop, where one might place a wager on the horses, cricket results, snow at Christmas, or even on such vital issues as who shot Phil on "Eastenders," the Cockney soap opera.

Soho, in zone 7, is the epicenter of London's nightlife, a dazzling conglomeration of practically everything London has to offer. Here's where you'll find the theaters, cinemas, pubs, clubs, and restaurants that have made London famous. But London's culture and night fun is not limited to this neighborhood by any means. Pick up copies of *Time Out, What's On,* or the Thursday supplement of *The Evening Standard, Hot Tickets,* to see what's going on where and when. (Check www.timeout.com before you arrive.)

Theater

London theater comes in three categories: The West End, London's equivalent to Broadway; off–West End, ditto; and fringe, which equals off-Broadway.

The West End

Although "the West End" refers to an area of central London, it also indicates cultural status and encompasses the **Royal National Theatre,** which is located south of the Thames (zone 5; South Bank, SE1; box-office (0207) 452-3000; information (0207) 452-3400; www.nationaltheatre.org.uk; tube: Waterloo). West End theaters are famous for their musicals and mainstream productions, but drama in the West End is of variable quality, ranging from the sublime to the overtly commercial.

However, the theaters of London's West End enjoy such renown that Hollywood actors able to command millions of dollars per film clamor to appear in them for a relative pittance and, more often than not, to mixed reviews. Nicole Kidman, Daryl Hannah, Jerry Hall, Kevin Spacey, and Ellen Burstyn are just a few of the movie stars who have lit up the West End recently.

Try www.officiallondontheatre.co.uk for a listing of current plays, plus reviews, phone numbers, and tips. You can even have a seating plan of the theater in which your choice is playing faxed to you.

When purchasing tickets for the theater, it is helpful to remember to never buy a ticket from a tout (essentially, a scalper type), because he or she will charge an astronomical sum for it. Instead, you should queue up in front of the discount ticket booth, a little house located on the south side of the grassy part of Leicester Square (tube: Leicester Square). It is a tan building with a clock on top of it. You can also identify it by the lines forming on either side of it. The west side is for night performances; the east side sells matinee tickets. They charge £2.50 per ticket for a service fee and accept cash or credit cards (no traveler's checks). The booth is open Monday through Saturday from 10 a.m. to 7 p.m., Sunday from noon to 3:30 p.m. (for matinees only). Be sure you go to this booth only and not one of the many shop fronts around Leicester Square that call themselves discount, but actually offer no deals at all.

Many theaters offer half-price tickets on Mondays and for dress rehearsals. Some also grant concessions to students and seniors. Queuing for return tickets before a performance can also sometimes yield a discount.

Tickets for West End musicals are elusive and expensive at £35, although you can obtain advance tickets with your credit card by phoning **Ticketmaster** (phone (0207) 344-4444 or visit www.ticketmaster.co.uk) and **Firstcall** (phone (0207) 420-0000 or visit www.firstcalltickets.com). However, booking fees add around 10% to the price of a ticket, and many theaters charge a telephone booking fee, which is often not mentioned in the listed price. Therefore, the least expensive way to acquire a ticket is to turn up at the box office in person. West End theaters are, obviously, at the top end of the market. The Royal National Theatre on the South Bank (see above for contact information) presents plays in repertoire so that, in any given week, at least five can be seen in one of the three theaters contained within its sprawling, neo-brutalist dimensions.

Under the direction of the former Royal Shakespeare Company and West End impresario Trevor Nunn, the National offers the widest possible range of work, encompassing classical as well as new and neglected plays from the whole of world drama. On the lighter side, the National also offers musicals and even works for children, six days a week throughout the year. The theater runs a repertoire of classic and contemporary productions that change seasonally. The box office is open Monday–Saturday, 10 a.m.– 8 p.m.

Royal Court (zone 11; Sloane Square, SW1; (0207) 565-5000; www.royalcourttheatre.com; tube: Sloane Square) has re-opened after an extensive and expensive refurbishment program. Though not based in the West End, the Royal Court is considered the most important venue for new writers in Britain and therefore deserves a big mention. There are two theaters: the "Downstairs" main theater and the "Upstairs" studio. There is also a funky new restaurant/bar. Performances are held Monday–Saturday at 7:30 p.m., and the Saturday matinee is held at 3:30 p.m. Tickets are £5–20.50. This is a great place to check out as an alternative to the West End theaters, and it's cheaper, too.

The Royal Shakespeare Company is the main conduit through which the immortal genius of the bard is imparted. The RSC also performs works from new and other classical writers in its repertoire, as long as they are relevant to Shakespeare. Recent triumphs include *Richard III,* with Robert Lindsay; *A Winters' Tale,* starring Anthony Sher; and a production of C. S. Lewis's *The Lion, The Witch, and the Wardrobe.* The RSC, whose home is in Stratford-upon-Avon, is based in the **Barbican Centre** (zone 3; Silk Street, EC2; (0207) 638-8891; information (0207) 638-4141; www.barbican. org.uk; tube: Barbican or Moorgate), which includes the enormous Barbican Theatre itself and a smaller space called the Pit. The Barbican box office is open 9 a.m.– 8 p.m., Monday–Saturday. Tickets are £5–34.

The authentic re-creation of **Shakespeare's Globe Theatre** (zone 5; New Globe Walk, SE1; (0207) 401-9919; www.shakespeares-globe.org; tube: Blackfriars), close to its original site, is the achievement of American expat actor Sam Wannamaker. Sadly, Wannamaker died shortly before the completion of the Globe's restoration. Although its basement remains open throughout the year to provide the world's largest exhibition devoted to the life and work of Shakespeare and the theater of his time, the roofless Globe's theatrical season is limited to May through September. The box office is open Tuesday–Saturday, 10 a.m.–6 p.m. Matinees are Saturday at 2 p.m. and Sunday at 1 p.m. or 6:30 p.m. (times alternate each week). Tickets are £5–27.

Restaurants in the vicinity of the larger theaters often offer preshow menus at reduced prices, as do some of the theaters themselves; the cuisine served up at the Royal National Theatre is particularly palatable.

Off–West End

Off–West End theaters often provide the most outstanding productions in terms of creativity because they offer writers, directors, and actors an artistic freedom that can sometimes be lacking in the more commercially motivated organizations. With emphasis firmly on the modern and avant garde, the **Almeida** (near zone 3; Almeida Street, N1; (0207) 359-4404; www.almeida.co.uk; tube: Angel) features cerebral drama from top writers and actors. The intimate, 105-seat **Bush Theatre** (west of zone 13; Shepherd's Bush Green, W12; (0207) 610-4224; www.bushtheatre.co.uk; tube: Shepherd's Bush or Goldhawk Road) is considered the next most important spot (after the Royal Court Theatre) for productions by new writers, many of whom have gone on to greater successes. Although tickets can be a bit pricey, the **Donmar Warehouse** (zone 7; 41 Earlham Street, WC2; (0207) 369-1732; www.donmar-warehouse.com; tube: Covent Garden) under the artistic direction of Sam Mendes has garnered raves from critics in recent years. Home to gay and lesbian productions, the **Drill Hall** (zone 7; 16 Chenies Street, WC1; (0207) 307-5060; www.drillhall.co.uk; tube: Goodge Street) welcomes everyone. The atmosphere of this intimate theater is brilliant. Monday evenings are for women only, and Thursday is a nonsmoking day. Ticket are £8–16. A small theater located above a pub, **The Gate** (zone 13; at The Prince Albert, 11 Pembridge Road, W11; (0207) 229-0706; tube: Notting Hill Gate) has a fine reputation for its low-budget yet high-quality drama from all over the world. Budding actors and directors relish the opportunity to work here and will happily do so for free, so great are the kudos. Performances run Monday through Saturday. Tickets are £6–12. **The King's Head** (zone 15; 115 Upper Street, N1; (0207) 226-1916; tube: Angel) is London's most venerable pub theater, frequently putting on top-quality, small-scale revues and musicals. Then, too, the King's Head also features hour-long luncheon plays that can be consumed along with your fish and chips; the place is open until midnight with live music in the bar.

Regent's Park Open Air Theatre (zone 14; Regent's Park, NW1; (0207) 486-2431 or (0207) 486-1933; www.open-air-theatre.org.uk; tube: Baker

Street) provides for those who like their theater al fresco. Set in the middle of the eponymous park and furnished with a bar and snacking facilities, this charming summer theater is an ideal venue in which to see the company' s vastly entertaining version of *A Midsummer Night's Dream.* The season kicks off on June 4, and tickets are £8.50–23. Be prepared, however, for the vagaries of British weather. Performances will be cancelled in torrential rain, but the show must always go on for Sunday performances.

Riverside Studios (zone 12; Crisp Road, W6; (0208) 237-1111 or (0208) 237-1000; www.riversidestudios.co.uk; tube: Hammersmith) overlooks the river Thames near Hammersmith bridge. There are three studio spaces: one seats 400, another seats 150, and the third is in permanent use for a TV show. In addition to the theatrical and dance productions, there is also a repertory cinema, a gallery, and a cafe overlooking the river. Standing in the shadows of the Old Vic theater, **YoungVic** (zone 5; 66 The Cut, SE1; (0207) 928-6363; www.youngvic.org; tube: Southwark) has become a successful venue, attracting big-name actors and touring companies such as the Royal Shakespeare Company. Shows run Monday through Saturday. Tickets are £9–25.

Fringe

Fringe theater can be found throughout London, but like British weather, is variable and generally of patchy quality. Still, the following theaters do provide the occasional ray of histrionic sunshine:

The small **Chelsea Theatre** (zone 11; Kings Road, SW10; (0207) 352-1967; www.theatrezone.org; tube: Sloane Square, then bus 211, 319, 19, 22; or South Kensington, then bus 49, 45) focuses on exciting new plays, which run 7–8 weeks at a time. A recent triumph included Tony Kushner's *Home-Body.* Performances are held Monday–Saturday, at 8 p.m. Tickets are £7–11. **The Finborough** (at Finborough Arms, Finborough Road, SW10; (0207) 373-3842; finboroughtheatre.itgo.com) is a small pub venue that hosts new writers, some of whom have ended up in the West End or on Broadway. They run two different plays every night, back to back. Performances are Tuesday–Saturday, at 7 and 8:30 p.m.; Sunday matinees occur at 2:30 and 4 p.m. Tickets are £4–10. Discounts are available for Tuesday performances. Credit cards are *not* accepted. Being so close to Picadilly, **Jermyn Street Theatre** (zone 7; 16b Jermyn Street, SW1; (0207) 287-2875; www.jermyn-streettheatre.co.uk; tube: Picadilly Circus) is a great alternative to a big West End production. This intimate, 70-seater venue hosts a mixure of shows, but musicals are the main feature. Performances are daily at 8 p.m.; Saturday and Sunday matinees are at 4 p.m. Tickets are £12–15.

The **New End Theatre** (zone 1; 27 New End, NW3; (0207) 794-0022; tube: Hampstead) is situated in upmarket Hampstead. Those with an ear for a good tune might investigate the musicals staged at **The Bridewell** (zone 3; Bride Lane, off Fleet Street, EC4; (0207) 936-3456; tube: Black-friars). New writing and a thriving bar can be found in plentiful supply at the legendary **Old Red Lion** (zone 15; 416 St. John Street, EC1; (0207) 837-7816; tube: Angel).

Although a tuxedo is no longer requisite attire when attending the theater, the British middle class still appears to dress more elegantly than Americans do, and black tie remains mandatory for any gala charity night where royals may be present. Certainly suits and smart dresses are the norm in West End and off–West End theaters, but you will not feel out of place in the egalitarian sneakers, baseball cap, and jeans.

Laughs in London

The British frequently congratulate themselves on their ironic sense of humor, and justly so; surely no other country has produced so many comic novelists of the caliber of Henry Fielding, William Makepeace Thackeray, Jane Austen, E. F. Benson, George Meredith, Anthony Trollope, Jerome K. Jerome, Evelyn Waugh, Tom Sharpe, Kingsley Amis, and, of course, the divine P. G. Wodehouse, to name only a few.

British humor extends even to some politicians, notably Alan Clarke on the right and Tony Banks on the left, both of whom are given to entertaining quips that would soon see them hounded out of office in overly earnest America. Winston Churchill was undoubtedly the wittiest of leaders and is emminently quotable, although many of his jokes were of a decidedly salty nature.

Britain's quality newspapers are also a good source of dry humor; outstanding writers include Matthew Paris of *The Times* and Auberon Waugh, Boris Johnson, and Craig Brown of the *Telegraph*. *The Londoner's Diary* in the *Evening Standard* is also amusing, as are the gossip columns in *The Telegraph* and *The Times*.

Although British sitcoms are currently in the doldrums, the BBC has an unrivaled roster of past triumphs. If you are staying in one evening, try renting videos of *Fawlty Towers, Black Adder, Yes Prime Minister, Jeeves and Wooster, Drop the Dead Donkey, Alan Partridge, Rising Damp, Only Fools and Horses, French and Saunders, The Comic Strip, The Fast Show,* and *Absolutely Fabulous*—they are all masterpieces of television comedy.

It is therefore not surprising that London has more comedy outlets than most cosmopolitan cities. The humor on display varies in quality and includes traditional improvisation and physical, surreal, and observational comedy. Most venues are replete with bars and restaurants, so should the acts occasionally fall short of the mark, you are at least spared the sufferings endured by those trapped in their seats of publicly funded avant-garde theaters.

Chuckle Club (zone 2; Houghton Street, WC2; (0207) 476-1672; tube: Holborn) is an itinerant comedy club that currently resides at the London School of Economics. Performances are held on Saturday only, starting 8:30 p.m. Tickets cost £6–8. The bar (which offers discount drink prices because this is a student venue) is open until 3 a.m., and after the comedy show there is a disco.

Comedy Store, at Haymarket House (zone 7; Oxedon Street, SW1; (0207) 344-0234; www.thecomedystore.co.uk; tube: Piccadilly Circus), is the venue from which alternative comedy exploded onto British television screens. Such stars as Jennifer Saunders (of *French and Saunders* and *Absolutely Fabulous*), Keith Alan, Ben Elton, and Ric Mayall began their careers here. The Comedy Store is open Tuesday through Sunday.

Comedy Cafe (in zone 3 at 66 Rivington Street, EC2; (0207) 739-5706; tube: Old Street) is one of the handful of clubs in London devoted entirely to comedy and takes the generous precaution of granting free admission on Wednesday, when new acts make their debuts. Comedy Cafe is open Wednesday through Sunday.

Jongleurs (zone 11; The Cornet, 49 Lavender Gardens, SW11; (0207) 564-2500; www.jongleurs.com; tube: Clapham Junction) is as popular as the Comedy Store, with an impressive line-up of performances that aren't all stand-up comedy. Shows are on Friday at 8:45 p.m., followed by a disco and late bar until 1 a.m. Saturday performances start at 7:15 p.m., with a late show at 11:15 p.m. Ticket prices are £11–14 on Friday and £9–12 on Saturday. As this venue is a bit far out, you might prefer its sister club in Camden Lock (see below).

A popular branch of the famous Jongleurs Battersea (see above), **Jongleurs Camden Lock** (Dingwalls, Middle Yard, Camden Lock in zone 15; Camden High Street, NW1; (0207) 564-2500; www.jongleurs.com; tube: Camden Town or Chalk Farm) is comfortable and busy, so book in advance. Shows on Friday start at 8:45 p.m., followed by a disco; on Saturday, performances start at 7:15 p.m. and 11:15 p.m. Ticket are £11–14 on Friday and £9–12 on Saturday.

Classical Music

London, arguably the music capital of the world, is endowed with four highly regarded orchestras, two internationally renowned arts establishments, numerous ensembles, and a correspondingly wide range of concerts.

Although the Barbican's London Symphony Orchestra remains the capital's leading ensemble, with the London Philharmonic only just behind, the South Bank Centre's London Philharmonic Orchestra has been gaining in strength. Then, too, the Royal Philharmonic Orchestra enjoys a distinguished history, despite having to get by without public funding. Many of the world's leading musicians flock to London stages, often for the city's frequent music festivals, especially the Henry Wood Promenade Concerts (more affectionately known as "The Proms"), held each year from July to September at the **Royal Albert Hall** (zone 13; Kensington Gore, SW; (0207) 589-3203 or 589-8212; www.royalalberthall.com; tube: Gloucester Road or South Kensington). The Albert is a prodigious Victorian building that sometimes plays host to pop gigs, the *Cirque du Soleil,* and even wrestling bouts. Yet it recalls the glories of its heyday during the Proms, when a splendid array of music is presented. Tickets for the promenade section (the area in the front of the stage without seating) are on offer for anywhere from a trifling £3 right up to £70.

The freshly refurbished **Royal Opera House** (zone 7; Covent Garden, WC2; recorded information (0207) 304-4000 or box office (0207) 240-1200; www.royalopera.org; tube: Covent Garden) is worth a visit just to see the beautiful building, and in fact they do offer tours of the House. They have classical productions of operas and ballets, and the price of the tickets is as breathtaking as the venue: up to £150! Recent operas have included "Parsival" and "Tosca;" balletic offerings have included "Onegin" and "The Nutcracker."

Wigmore Hall (zone 8 at 36 Wigmore Street, W1; (0207) 935-2141; www.wigmore-hall.org.uk; tube: Bond Street) is the best place in town to hear piano recitals and chamber groups. Although the hall was revamped not long ago, Wigmore continues to serve up a largely traditional fare. Tickets are £7–£30.

You might care to attend a lunchtime concert held every second Thursday in the converted church of **St. John's Smith Square** (zone 9; Smith Square, SW1; (0207) 222-1061; tube: Westminster). St. John's, near the Houses of Parliament, is nestled in an area of antique civility, and the church is possessed of a magical ambience.

It is easy to lose one's way down the labyrinthine corridors of that monster of modernism, the **Barbican Centre** (zone 3; Silk Street; (0207) 638-8891 or (0207) 638-4141; www.barbican.org.uk). Still, the fact that the Barbican has superb acoustics, is home to the London Symphony Orchestra, and hosts the "Great Orchestras of the World" series may grant courage to the intrepid. Other great orchestras that perform a wide range of classical music at the Barbican are the BBC Symphony Orchestra, the City of London Simfonia, and the English Chamber Orchestra.

Perched just above the Thames next to Waterloo Bridge, the **South Bank Centre** can be found in zone 5 at Belvedere Road, South Bank, SE1 (box office (0207) 960-4242; recorded information (0207) 633-0932; www.sbc.org.uk; tube: Waterloo). Its Royal Festival Hall (RFH1) is the main auditorium for symphony concerts; the smaller Queen Elizabeth Hall (RFH2) puts on semi-stage operas and chamber groups; and recitals as well as ensembles are performed in the intimate setting of the adjacent Purcell Room (RFH3). The South Bank Centre comes complete with restaurants, cafes, bars, and book and record shops. Ticket prices vary enormously. Please check with the box office.

Finally, we draw your attention to several open-air festivals held over the summer. First, the **Hampton Court Palace Festival** (outside zones; Hampton Court, East Molsey, Surrey; (0207) 344-4444; www.hamptoncourtfestival.com) is held in June. British Rails Hampton Court riverboat from Westminster or Richmond to Hampton Court Pier (April–October). The impressive historic palace grounds will prove most romantic to those imaginative souls who appreciate classical music. Tickets are £25–85.

The Holland Park Theatre (zone 13; Holland Park, Kensington High Street, W8; box office (0207) 602-7856; information (0207) 603-1123; www.operalondon.com; tube: High Street Kensington or Holland Park) stages an array of music, theater, and dance performances in one of London's loveliest parks. Guests are sheltered from the harmful effects of storm and sun by an enveloping canopy. The Holland Park Theatre is open June–August. Tickets are £10–30.

Dance & Ballet

When one thinks of dance in London, a flood of terpsichorean images come pirouetting to mind: *The Red Shoes,* Fontaine and Nureyev, Fred and Adele Astaire, Sadler's Wells, The Royal Ballet, Covent Garden, and the wonderful movie *Billy Elliot.*

Dance grew steadily in popularity throughout the 1990s, abetted by several festivals. **Dance Umbrella** (phone (0208) 741-5881; www.danceumbrella.co.uk) features contemporary dance from all over the world and normally runs during September and October for seven weeks. The events are hosted at various venues across London. **The Place Theatre** (zone 15; 17 Duke's Road WC1; (0207) 387-0031; www.theplace.org.uk; tube: Euston, Euston Square, or British Rail: Euston) hosts over 32 dance events annually, featuring British and international contemporary dance companies, with a platform for new and emerging choreographers. The theatre also features a special children's season.

Two of the largest and most active dance venues are the **Barbican Centre** and the **South Bank Centre** (see "Classical Music," above, for contact information).

The **Royal Ballet** hosts productions in the main theater of the **Royal Opera House** (see entries for the venue in the "Classical Music" and

"Opera" sections). Some of the performances on the agenda for 2001 and 2002 include *Don Quixote, Serenade Remanso, The Nutcracker, La Bayadere, Giselle,* and *Romeo and Juliet.* Expect to pay £10–60 for tickets.

The refurbishment of **Sadler's Wells** (Rosebury Avenue, EC1; (0207) 863-8000; tube: Chancery Lane) has been completed at last, and the more intimate and central **Peacock Theatre** (zone 2; Portugal Street, off Kingsway, WC2; (0207) 314-8800; www.sadlers-wells.com; tube: Holborn), which served as the interim house during the refurbishment, is now a permanent branch of Sadler's Wells. The revamped Sadler's Wells has extensive bars, state-of-the-art flying and lighting equipment, an ultraflexible stage—twice its original size—and an 80-seat orchestra pit, among other attractions. Tickerts are £8.50–35. Please note that the Peacock and Saddler's Wells tend to feature more contemporary ballet performances. Vast in scale, yet graceful in outline, the **London Coliseum** (zone 7; St. Martin's Lane, WC2; (0207) 632-8300; www.eno.org; tube: Charing Cross) is actually the **English National Opera** (ENO), but does present such leading dance companies as the English National Ballet and The Royal Ballet during its Christmas and summer seasons. Christmastime will feature *The Nutcracker.* See separate listing in "Opera," below.

Opera

The **Royal Opera House** (see "Classical Music," above, for contact information) was recently refurbished and expanded. The main theater is home to the **Royal Ballet,** but within the Royal Opera House there are two more intimate venues for opera and dance: the **Linbury Studio Theater** with 420 seats, and the **Clore Studios,** a 200-seater space, which is ideal for workshops and performances. At these smaller theaters one can see opera stripped to its essentials and for a more affordable price than the great productions in the main theater. Disability access has also improved. There is also the enticing Amphitheatre Bar and Restaurant, whose terrace overlooks Covent Garden. Ticket prices range from £4 for lunchtime performances and some severely restricted views of evening performances to £150 for the best seats. Go to www.royalopera.org for the latest information.

Home to the English National Opera, the **London Coliseum** (zone 7; St. Martin's Lane, WC2; (0207) 632-8300, www.eno.org; tube: Charing Cross) is a grand venue that tries to promote a populist image—with affordable ticket prices and challenging productions. While restoration work has already started and will continue until 2004, the building will not be closed, and every effor is being made to keep disruption to a minimum. The program for 2001–2002 included Prokofiev's *War and Peace,* Stravinsky's *The Rakes Progress,* and, of course, some old favorites, such as Mozart's *The Marriage of Figaro* and Gilbert and Sullivan's *The Mikado.* Here, the operas are sung in

English. Please note that the English Ballet takes over the Coliseum mid-December through mid-January. Tickets are anywhere from £3 to 52.50.

Live Jazz, Pop, and Rock

London is a matrix of performing talent, and on any given Saturday night there will be well over 100 gigs being played throughout the city. Tickets vary in price from a fiver or less for pop gigs, to more than £30 for a top pop attraction.

Again, as with the theater, you must never buy tickets from scalpers, because the practice is illegal and their merchandise is probably forged. It is always best to purchase tickets from the concert venue itself. You will usually not be charged a booking fee if you pay with cash.

The thriving London jazz scene has, over the years, given the world such international luminaries as John McLauglin, George Shearing, and Dave Holland, which is indicative of the talent found here. Numerous restaurants, bars, pubs, and cafes continue to pleasantly enhance their atmosphere with live jazz music; see *Time Out* and the *Evening Standard's Hot Tickets* magazine for details. Among the leading jazz venues for largely local talent (all of which are profiled in the following club section) are **Ronnie Scott's, The 606 Club, Vortex, Jazz Café, China Jazz, Pizza Express, Pizza on the Park,** and **Bull's Head.**

The Barbican and South Bank Centre often present top international (inevitably American) stars, and two big jazz festivals are held in the autumn: the **Soho Jazz Festival** and the **Oris London Jazz Festival.**

The **Notting Hill Carnival,** held in late August, is Europe's largest street festival and features huge sound systems pumping out reggae, rap, and drum bass. Be warned, though: this event is not for the agoraphobic or timid—there are entirely too many muggers, pick-pockets, and deranged people pumped full of alcohol for it to suit every sensibility.

Gargantuan rock structures include the 11,000-seat **Wembley Arena** (outside zones; Empire Way, Wembley, Middlesex; (0208) 902-8833 or (0870) 739-0739; www.wembley.co.uk/venues; tube: Wembley Park); the 20,000-seat **Earl's Court Exhibition Centre** (zone 11; Warwick Road, SW5; (0207) 385-1200, www.eco.co.uk; tube: Earl's Court); and the 12,000-capacity **London Arena** (zone 6; Limeharbour, Isle of Dogs, E14; (0207) 538-1212; www.londonarena.co.uk; rail: Docklands Light Rail, Crossharbour & London Arena). Of course, the sheer vastness of these coliseums tends to undermine the sonic and visual aspects of performance, and refreshments are overpriced. Still, if you must see the Rolling Stones or Robbie Williams, you'll go to these places.

Smaller-scale and hence more civilized venues are preferable in every way. The **Shepherd's Bush Empire** (near zone 12; Shepherd's Bush Green;

W12; (0207) 771-2000; www.ticketweb.co.uk; tube: Shepherd's Bush) had previously been the BBC Television Theatre before developing into a top popular music spot with an excellent sound system. The Empire has a three-tiered seating arrangement, but we suggest you acquire an upstairs ticket, as the ground floor slants downwards and you'd have to be a giant to see anything. Expect to pay £10–30 for tickets.

The **Brixton Academy** (zone 5; 211 Stockwell Road, SW9; (0207) 924-9999; www.brixton-academy.co.uk; tube: Brixton) has a 4,300-person capacity with a seated balcony and standing room at ground level. Many popular bands have selected to perform here, and the place has a good atmosphere. Madonna put this venue on the map last year. However, it does lie within one of London's more dodgy areas, so use common sense and don't go wandering around after the gig. Instead, head straight over to the nearby tube station or, better still, hail a black cab.

Dance Clubs

London has a huge range of nightclubs, offering everything from hard-core techno to smooth jazz to table-top dancers. London's clubs generally provide excellent quality. However, select clubs may sometimes refuse to admit you on the basis of a doorman's arbitrary decision.

Therefore, it may be a good idea not to set your heart on one club when there are so many to choose from. Only do make an early start—before 11 p.m.—then, should the doormen prove intractable, you have the option—indeed, satisfaction—of repairing to a rival club.

Many clubs offer reduced admission rates before 10:30 p.m., and it is easier to gain admittance at that hour. A club that is quiet at 11 p.m. can often be packed to the rafters by midnight.

Some clubs in London start late and carry on until 6 a.m., with their busiest period being between 11:30 p.m. and 2 a.m. If you intend to dine at the club, we recommend you book a table for 10 p.m., after which you will be permitted to stay on for the dancing. Not all clubs serve dinner; call the club and ask for information.

For disco dancing, the following clubs (all profiled in the following section) are recommended: **Embargo, Hanover Grand, Leopard Lounge, Ministry of Sound,** and **Cafe de Paris.**

Swing dancing comes in several categories in London. Ballroom dancing is held on Saturday afternoons and evenings and Sunday afternoons in such elegant venues as the legendary **Savoy Hotel** (zone 7; 1 Savoy Hill, WC2; (0207) 836-4343; www.savoygroup.com; tube: Embankment). This hotel holds a tea dance on Sunday (in the lobby) and a dinner/dance (in The River Restaurant) on Saturday and Sunday evenings. On some Saturday evenings (please note, not every week) they also host "Stomping at the

Savoy" (held in the lobby), where you can get on down to the sounds of the 1920s, 1930s, and 1940s. Due to popular demand, you will need to make reservations for all of the above. Tea dances are held at the **Palm Court** at the Meridien Waldorf Hotel on Aldwych, by Waterloo Bridge (zone 7; WC2; (0207) 836-2400; tube: Aldwych) on Saturday and Sunday, 4–6:30 p.m. Though formal gowns and black ties are no longer required, they do expect smart/casual attire. You also need to make reservations here.

Jump-Jive Nights are altogether more frenetic affairs, which is reflected in the zoot suits, army uniforms, and bobby socks donned by punters for bopping to music of the 1940s. Jitterbugs are held on Wednesday nights at **Notre Dame Hall** (zone 7; 5 Leicester Place, WC2; (0207) 734-6004; tube: Leicester Square), a top spot for swing dancing. In addition to swing bands, **Dover Street Restaurant and Bar** (zone 8; 8/10 Dover Street, W1; (0207) 629-9813 or 491-2958; www.doverst.co.uk; tube: Green Park) also books R&B outfits and dinner-jazz combos and samba, so you might want to phone ahead to find out which night would be most suitable for your visit. You will probably need to book in adavance. **The 100 Club** (zone 7; 100 Oxford Street, W1; (0207) 636-0933; www.the100club.co.uk; tube: Oxford Circus) features jump-jive dancing and early evening dance lessons on Monday. Admission is £8.

For Latin dancing you might wish to try La Salsa held on Friday nights at the **Loughborough Hotel** (Loughborough Road, Brixton; (0207) 771-3134 or 642-5806). The three packed floors of this chic South American venue feature a Brazilian bar, live bands, and classes beginning at 9:30 p.m. La Salsa entertains an integrated crowd consisting largely of regulars, and the atmosphere is harmonious. Take a black cab on your way there; at the close of festivities, the doormen will direct you to a reputable minicab firmonly 30 seconds away from the club.

Dancing the tango is a romantic way to spend an evening, and the best place in town to do so is at **Zero Hour** (zone 5; at the Dome, above Boston Arms pub, Dartmouth Park Hill, N19; pub (0207) 272-8153; dance teacher (0796) 645-7863; www.tangolab.com; tube: Tufnell Park). Argentinian tango is taught here on Wednesday from 7:15 p.m. to 9 p.m. (for all levels), and dancing to tango and other international sounds continues until midnight. The cost is £7.50 for classes and £5 for entry into the salon only. Another Latin hot spot is **Bar Rumba** (zone 7; 36 Shaftsbury Avenue, W1; (0207) 287-2751; www.barrumba.co.uk; tube: Leicester Square). Every night is dedicated to a different type of music and dance. Tuesday is "Rumba Pa'ti" night and includes salsa, merengue, and other Latin grooves. Kick off the evening with a dance class, starting at 6:30 p.m. Bar Rumba is open until 3 a.m., and admission is £3 for entry and £6 to attend a class.

Cuba (in zone 13 at 11 Kensington High Street, W8; (0207) 938-4137; tube: Kensington High Street) is a trendy, busy, noisy venue where you can stuff your face with tapas and Latin American food, then wear it off on the dance floor. Eating is not obligatory; there is a bar, too. Dancing takes place Monday–Saturday until 2 a.m. Cuba is open on Sunday, but the dance floor is closed. Admission is £3–£10. **Havana** (zone 11; 490 Fulham Road, SW6; (0207) 381-5005; tube: Fulham Broadway) plays Latin music every night, with salsa and merengue leading the way. The dress is smart/casual and is not particularly trendy—thus less intimidating, perhaps! Expect to book in advance on weekends. Admission is free on weekdays before 9 p.m. or all night if you are eating; weekend admission is £8. **Salsa** (zone 7; Charing Cross Road, WC1; (0207) 379-3277; tube: Leicester Square) hosts Latin evenings and classes all week long. Call for details. Admission is free on weekdays from afternoon until 9 p.m. and £4 thereafter; Friday and Saturday admission is £4 until 9 p.m. and £8 thereafter. If you are with a group of women, there's no lack of male partners. The dance floor is full of Algerian salsa fiends who will happily gyrate against you for hours at a time. Sounds a bit sleezy, but it's good, clean fun.

Bars and Pubs

The British are, generally speaking, formidable drinkers, with the pub having stood since time immemorial as the central institution in the British experience. And it is the golden rule of pub etiquette—respectful reserve—that has enabled people from all walks of life to mingle successfully.

Keeping pace with the British as they effortlessly knock back pint after pint is not an easy task for the uninitiated. Still, accomplished American boozers, after putting in an appropriate amount of time and practice, should be able to hold up their end of the proceedings. If, however, you have inadvertently permeated the wall of British reserve to strike up an acquaintance with some friendly natives in a pub, and it is your turn to spring for a round but you haven't finished your pint, it is better to swallow one's pride, rather than keep everyone waiting, and head over to the bar, cash in hand.

Incidentally, though it is not customary to tip bartenders in pubs, those serving expensive drinks in upmarket clubs and bars sprinkled across West London often do expect gratuity. And, although they have a vague understanding of what a Bloody Mary is, you will draw a blank from most British bartenders of you ask them for, say, a Cape Cod or even a Screwdriver. You will have to instead explain that it is vodka and orange juice and so on that you require. When your drink arrives, you will find to your dismay that spirits in Britain are, by law, served up in paltry amounts called gills or measures that are about the size of a thimble, so you might want to ask for a double.

It's no surprise that the British lead the world at the sport of drinking pints of beer. Their superb beer comes in a variety of appealing guises, including lager (light continental beer), bitter (rightly named Anglo-Saxon ale), mild (concocted with chocolate malt), cider (fermented apple juice), and shandy (half lager, half lemonade). Best of all are real ales, the boozy equivalent of organic whole-meal bread.

Pub food also can be surprisingly good, depending on the overall quality of the pub itself. Most pubs are strongly historical in ambience, with walls festooned with attractive eighteenth- and nineteenth-century bric-a-brac. In winter, many pubs have a roaring fire, and in summer, a beer garden.

Although bars with a special-hours certificate may remain open until 3 a.m., pubs tend to close at 11 p.m. on weekdays and at midnight on weekends. Britain, however, is forging ever closer ties with Europe, and British licensing laws are expected to soon be extended to match those of other EU member states.

If you wish to include a visit to an archetypal olde-worlde inn on your agenda, you could not do better than the **Prospect of Whitby** (zone 4; 57 Wapping Wall, E1; (0207) 481-1095; tube: Wapping). Whitby dates back to 1520 and is mentioned in Pepys's diary. The pub is renowned for its Elizabethan pewter bar, flagstone floors, cast-iron hearths, and small round windows. It is open daily, 11:30 a.m.–3 p.m. and 5:30–11 p.m.

A haven for journalists and scribblers of all types since before 1666, when it was singed by the Great Fire, **Ye Old Cheshire Cheese** (zone 2; 145 Fleet Street, EC4; (0207) 353-6170; tube: Blackfriars) is a storybook tavern replete with blazing fires, nooks and crannies, wooden floors, and sundry bars and dining sections. During your visit to Old Cheesy, you may as well raise a glass to previous regulars Thackeray, Johnson, Voltaire, Pope, and Tennyson. It's open noon–11 p.m. daily.

By contrast, **The Saint** (zone 7; 8 Great Newport Street, WC2; (0207) 240-1551; www.thebreakfastgroup.co.uk; tube: Leicester Square) is ultra-modern, with its patronizing door staff; chic, spotlit décor; and attractive cocktails and cuisine. It is open 5 p.m.–2 a.m. on weekdays and 5 p.m.–3 a.m. on weekends.

One venue worth visiting, with three great individual bars under one roof, is the **Hilton Hotel** (zone 8; Park Lane, W1; (0207) 493-8000; www.hilton.com; tube: Hyde Park Corner or Green Park). If Britain's inclement weather causes you to yearn for sunnier climes, you might like to go to the hotel's **Trader Vic's** (phone (0207) 208-4113) for an ersatz night on a South Pacific island. Home of the Mai Tai cocktail and delicious food, Vic's is something of a mood lagoon. It's open Monday–Saturday, 5 p.m.–12:45 a.m. and Sunday, 5–10:30 p.m. Alternately, you could venture up to the twenty-eighth floor to the chi-chi and romantic **Windows Bar and Restaurant** (phone (0207) 208-4021), which offers a great view of London. Please note smart/casual dress code (no jeans or sneakers) and you will need to make reservations if you wish to dine. Windows hours are Monday–Friday, 12:30–2:30 p.m. and 5:30 p.m.–2 a.m.; Saturday, 5:30 p.m.–3 a.m. Finally, the latest addition ot the Hilton bar scene is the Zen-trendy **Zeta Bar** (it has a separate entrance on Hertford Street; (0207) 208-4067). Cocktails are the specialty here—either non-alcoholic, delicious, health-inducing "liquid lunches," or the more lethal, alcoholic variety. Good bar food is also available. As the night wears on, a stricter door code is operated—but as long as you look affluent or super trendy, you'll have no problem getting in. Zeta Bar is open Monday–Tuesday, noon–1 a.m.; Wednesday–Friday, noon–3 a.m.; Saturday, 5 p.m.–3 a.m.; and Sunday, 5–10:30 p.m.

We now make mention of three exclusive venues to which you might not be admitted but ought to know about. First is the still fashionable **Atlantic Bar & Grill** (zone 7; 20 Glasshouse Street, W1; (0207) 734-4888; tube: Piccadilly Circus), open Monday–Friday, noon–3 a.m.; Saturday, 5 p.m.–3 a.m.; and Sunday, 6–10:30 p.m. You need to look smart and cool here. **The Metropolitan Bar** (zone 8; Old Park Lane, W1; (0207) 447-1000; tube: Hyde Park Corner) is awash with pop and soap stars and is open Monday–Saturday, 11 a.m.–3 a.m., and Sunday, 11 a.m.–10:30 p.m., though non-members aren't allowed in after 6 p.m. Finally, there's **Pharmacy** (zone 13; 150 Notting Hall Gate; (0207) 221-2442; www.pharmacy-london.com; tube: Notting Hill), a bar and restaurant decorated and part owned by Damien Hirst, Britain's most notorious conceptual artist. Pharmacy is open Monday–Thursday, 5:30 p.m.–12:45 a.m.; Friday, 5:30 p.m.–1:45 a.m.; Saturday, noon–1:45 a.m.; and Sunday, noon–midnight.

A Sexy City

The oldest profession has long flourished in London, with some of its more accomplished practitioners establishing links with the greatest names in England. Indeed, many noble lines were started by the illegitimate progeny of a royal sire and his concubine—an argument the Labour Party used in its abolishment of the right of hereditary peers to sit in the House of Lords.

Although prostitution is not as endemic as it was during its Victorian heyday (when even Tory Prime Minister Gladstone used to prowl the streets, supposedly in quest of fallen women in need of reforming), one cannot enter a telephone box in the central London of today without noticing the numerous salacious cards deposited within.

Soho is the sex center of London, and the area around Old Compton Street hosts quite a few sex shops and strip clubs. Beware of unlicensed venues, though, for they are, quite literally, tourist traps. A common practice of these establishments is to plant a siren-like hostess at the door who lures her victim inside for a drink and a show. The punter subsequently discovers that the bill for her orange juice and his beer comes to some astronomically unreasonable figure—and there are always a number of belligerent security staff on hand to ensure that customers pay up.

If you don't fancy the Soho scene, which is frankly still a bit sleazy, irrespective of local clean-up campaigns, the next safest bet would be the sex shows held at the following venues. These are mainly "saucy" cabaret shows or lap-dance clubs, which seem to be springing up all over the place.

Seemingly off the beaten track (though nothing a cab ride couldn't sort out), **For Your Eyes Only** (near zone 12; 28 Abbey Road, Park Royal, NW10; (0208) 965-7699; www.fyeo.co.uk; tube: Park Royal) is the place to go if you want your dancers to go the "full monty." On stage they perform topless, but if you book the girls for a private dance, they will happily strip right down to their birthday suits. It's open Monday–Wednesday, 7:30 p.m.–2:30 a.m.; Thursday–Saturday, 7:30 p.m.–3 a.m.

LA Confidential (near zone 12; 1 High Street, W5; phone (0208) 840-0616, www.laconfidential.co.uk) is a bit out of the way, but actually close to Heathrow if you're staying there, and not too far from town if you take a cab. Here the girls will do a couple of dances on stage, then private dances at the tables. Every other Thursday they stage an erotic cabaret. There's a reasonably priced bar and full restaurant. Open Monday–Thursday, 6 p.m.–2 a.m.; Friday, 6 p.m.–3 a.m.; closed weekends.

It's the usual drill at **Secrets,** aka **Secrets 1** (zone 12; 62 Glenthorne Road, W6; (0208) 563-7974; tube: Hammersmith): girls come on stage and prance around to a couple of numbers, then mingle among the customers for private dancing. **Secrets 3** (zone 2; 3 Grays Inn Road, WC1; tube: Kings Cross) is more centrally located and offers a secluded VIP area (the Hammersmith location is tables only). Secrets 1 is open from Monday to Saturday, 8 p.m.–2 a.m.; Secrets 3, from Monday to Saturday, 6 p.m.–2:30 a.m.

Spawned from an American-owned chain, **Spearmint Rhino** (zone 2; 161 Tottenham Court Road, W1; (0207) 209-4488; www.spearmint. rhino.com; tube: Goodge Street or Warren Street) is the latest addition to London's lap-dance scene. The club's interior is plush, spacious, and comfortable and attracts some five-star celebrities. The club boasts a bevy of 150 dancing beauties who each perform two numbers before private dancing. The club also includes a cocktail bar, five-star restaurant, and a gift shop. It's a classy joint, if this is your kind of thing, open Monday–Saturday, 11 a.m.–2 a.m., and Sunday, noon–midnight.

Stringfellow's (zone 7; 16 Upper St. Martin's Lane, Covent Garden, WC2; (0207) 240-5534; www.stringfellows.com; tube: Leicester Square), Peter Stringfellow's club, pays host to the mass-market sort of celebrity: soap stars, footballers, and Awms (actress/model/whatevers). The place is rife with 1980s glamour and pleasant enough in its way, particularly since Stringfellow's came into possession of a table-dancing license. It's open Monday–Saturday, 7:30 p.m.–3 a.m.

Sophisticats at Voltane (zone 8; 1 Marylebone Lane, W1; (0208) 201-8804 or 201-8968; tube: Bond Street) is presided over by the amiable Cat-man, David Simones, and was recently the subject of a seven-part television documentary; it features ballerinas and showgirls from all over the world. Indeed, Sophisticats has a distinctly Parisian decadence about it; in addition to the twice-nightly Catgirl cabaret, the club also provides table dancing, caviar girls, and cocktail waitresses. It is recommended, although since it is a private club, you must call first to see if you can get a reservation. It's open Monday–Friday, 8:30 p.m.–3 a.m.

Gaming in the United Kingdom

The gaming industry in Great Britain is one of the most carefully regulated in the world. All casinos across England, Scotland, and Wales are licensed under the Gaming Act of 1968, which stipulates that unless already a member or the guest of a member, a player must register at the casino 24 hours before entering to play. The Gaming Act is designed to protect the public purse from the perils of compulsive gambling. Or, in the strictest legalese: it is a legal requirement that the membership-application form is signed on the premises of the casino. A passport, driver's license, or other suitable identification is required. Authorization of all new memberships takes 24 hours. The casinos of London Clubs International begin with the magnificent **50 St. James** (zone 7; 50 St. James Street, SW1; (0207) 491-4678; tube: Piccadilly), which opened as London's first club built for the purpose of gaming, in 1828, and is, along with the legendary **Les Ambassadeurs Club** (zone 8; 5 Hamilton Place, W1; (0207) 495-5555; www.lci.com; tube: Hyde Park), at the top end of the market. These exclusive and lavishly appointed clubs are frequented by royalty, the aristocracy, and celebrated figures from the world of entertainment. Both clubs are open daily, 2 p.m.–4 a.m. The dress code prohibits jeans, and men are expected to wear coats and ties in the evenings.

Midmarket venues include the **Rendezvous Casino** (zone 8; 14 Old Park Lane, W1; (0207) 491-8586; www.ici.com; tube: Hyde Park), with its spacious gaming floor, French-influenced bistro, and relaxed sports bar; and **The Sportsman Casino** (zone 8; 40 Bryanston Street, W1; (0207) 414-

0061; www.clublci.com; tube: Hyde Park), designed in the style of a Mississippi riverboat. As well as offering roulette, blackjack, and baccarat, the Sportsman boasts a dice game that has proven to be particularly popular with American visitors. Both clubs are open from about noon until 4 a.m.; gaming begins at 2 p.m. The dress code is smart/casual; no jeans are allowed. Coats and ties are required for men in the evening.

The mass-market **Golden Nugget Casino** (zone 7; 22 Shaftesbury Avenue, W1; (0207) 439-0099; www.clublci.com; tube: Piccadilly) is the largest and busiest casino in the London Clubs group. It offers a fast-moving environment and fast food to go with it. The atmosphere of this casino is both friendly and informal. Games include roulette, baccarat, blackjack, and stud poker; it is open daily, 2 p.m.– 4 a.m.

Freeloader's Forum

Visitors to London rapidly discover the disparity in prices between goods and services purchased in America and their English equivalents. British merchandise is far more expensive due to a legalized swindle, the so-called Recommended Retail Price Index, whereby prices are fixed at scandalously high leves by agreement between manufacturers and retail outlets.

But please do not complain about Britain's rip-off prices to those working on the shop floor, because although company bosses are raking it in, the poor worker at the checkout counter makes considerably less than he or she would in America. Yet the British can also be generous, as evidenced by the bonanza of free activities taking place throughout London.

Free Music

Many churches in central London, such as **St. John's** (zone 7; Waterloo Road; tube: Waterloo), **St. Martin-in-the-Fields** (zone 7; St. Martin's Place; tube: Leicester Square or Charing Cross), and **St. Pancras Church** (zone 15; Euston Road; tube: Euston) offer free lunchtime classical concerts and recitals, as do music schools such as the **Royal College of Music** (zone 13; Prince Consort Road, SW7; (0207) 591-4314; www.rcm.ac.uk; tube: Gloucester Road or High Street Kensington) and the **Royal Academy of Music** (zone 14; Marylebone Road; (0207) 873-7300; www.ram.ac.uk; tube: Marylebone or Baker Street). Performances at the Royal College of Music are held Monday–Thursday at 1:05 p.m., and during term time they are held evenings at 7 p.m. Performances at the Royal Academy of Music are held daily at 1:05 and 5:05 p.m.

You can also hear a mixture of musical delights at the aptly named **Freestage at the Barbican** (zone 3; Silk Street, EC2; (0207) 638-8891; www.barbican.org.uk; tube: Barbican) and at the **South Bank's National**

Theatre (zone 5; South Bank, SE1; (0207) 452-3000; www.nationalthe-atre.org.uk; tube: Waterloo or Westminster) and **Royal Festival Hall** (zone 5; South Bank, SE1; (0207) 960-4242; www.sbc.org.uk). Performances at the Barbican are held daily at 1 p.m.; the National Theatre features music in the foyer area daily at 6 p.m. Performances in the foyer of the Royal Festival Hall run from 12:30 to 2:30 p.m. every day; they also feature jazz on Friday evenings at 7 p.m.

The **100 Club** (zone 8; 100 Oxford Street, W1; (0207) 636-0933; tube: Oxford Street) presents a well-liked series of swing and traditional gigs during Friday lunchtimes. Some bookshops also present free music. Try **Border's Books & Music** (zone 8; 197 Oxford Street, W1; (0207) 292-1600; tube: Oxford Circus) every Friday night, upstairs, at 6:30 p.m.; **Helter Skelter Music Bookshop** (zone 7; 4 Denmark Street, WC2; (0207) 836-1151; tube: Tottenham Court Road); and **Filthy MacNasty's Whiskey Cafe** (zone 2; 68 Amwell Street, EC1; (0207) 837-6067; www.philkav@globalnet.co.uk; tube: Angel) for a DJ on Friday nights and live music on Saturday evenings and Sunday afternoons.

Free Friday can be found at the **Cock Tavern** (zone 15; Phoenix Road, NW1; (0207) 387-1884; tube: Euston), where you can enjoy a variety of music and pints and alco-pops (frozen liquor on a stick) costing only £2, which is as cheap as can be found in London. Numerous bars, restaurants, and pubs also supply the customer with free music. Check *Time Out* and *Hot Tickets* for listings.

Free Comedy

Since the practice of adding canned laughter to television soundtracks was universally condemned, the BBC now requires a constant supply of jolly spectators willing to be audience members for their comedy productions. For free tickets—just imagine the fun you'll have telling everyone back home that you appeared on British TV—contact the BBC Ticket Unit at Room 30, Design Building, BBC TV Centre, Wood Lane, W12 7RJ; (0208) 576-1227.

Free Films

Free documentaries are sometimes shown at the **Whitechapel Gallery** (zone 4; Whitechapel High Street, E1; (0207) 522-7878; www.whitechapel.org; tube: Whitechapel). Art-house films are shown periodically on Saturday afternoon at the **Clore Gallery** inside the Tate Britain (for information, see profile in Part Six, "Sight-Seeing and Tours").

LONDON NIGHTCLUBS

Name	Description	Zone
Bagley's	Gigantic disco and bar	15
Brown's	Glamorous disco	7
Bull's Head	Jazz club	12
Cafe de Paris	London's most renowned club	7
Crazy Larry's	20-somethings dance hangout	11
Dover Street Restaurant & Bar	Large jazz restaurant and bar	8
Embargo	Designer dance club	11
Emporium	High-tech, ultramodern dance club	7
The Fridge	Brixton's most celebrated disco	5
Heaven	Gay dance club	7
Hippodrome	Tourist trap; dance club	7
Hanover Grand	Popular discotheque	8
Jazz Café	Modern jazz club	15
Ministry of Sound	U.K.'s most famous disco	5
Noise Bar	Industrial bar with DJ	7
Pizza Express	Intimate jazz club and restaurant	7
Pizza on the Park	Upmarket jazz cabaret and restaurant	10
Rock Garden	Techno and Top 40 dance club	7
Ronnie Scott's	London's premier jazz club	7
606	Jazz club and restaurant	11
Turnmill's	Late-night disco	3
Venom Zoo Bar	Bar and dance club	7
Vortex Jazz Bar	Jazz club and restaurant	3

Nightclub Profiles

BAGLEY'S

A GIGANTIC DISCO AND BAR

Who Goes There Youthful dancers and soaks

Zone 15   King's Cross Depot, York Way, N1; (0207) 278-2777

Cover Friday, £14–20; Saturday, £14 **Prices** Cheap by club standards **Dress** Smart/casual **Food available** Snacks

Hours Friday, 10:30 p.m.–6:30 a.m.; Saturday, 10:30 p.m.–7:30 a.m.

What goes on Sweat rises like smoke off the dance floor.

Setting & atmosphere Bagley's is colossal, with five dance floors, six bars, and something different going on in every room.

If you go You will be part of a heaving, throbbing mob of young movers in one of the many rooms.

BROWN'S

GLAMOROUS DISCO

Who Goes There Brown's has been an oasis to the stars for the last 12 years and continues to be so. Although ostensibly a private members' club, the public is permitted entrance on Friday and Saturday nights.

Zone 7   4 Great Queen Street, WC2; (0207) 831-0802

Cover £15 **Prices** Expensive, but then so is being a star **Dress** Fashionable **Food available** Catering available for large parties

Hours Friday and Saturday, 10:30 p.m.–4 a.m.

What goes on The club has a three-tiered social system: the downstairs dance floor is Midgard; the second floor is the Rainbow Bridge; and the VIP members' bar on the third floor is Asgard, home of the gods.

Setting & atmosphere   Loud, glamorous, and urgent.

If you go   Don't pester the celebs for autographs.

BULL'S HEAD

A JAZZ CLUB

Who Goes There The 25–55 age group; actors, musos, film and telly people

Zone 12   373 Lonsdale Road, SW13; (0208) 876-5241

Cover Anywhere from £4 to £10, depending on the celebrity of the band **Prices** Modest **Dress** In the words of the immortal Cole Porter, anything goes **Food available** Excellent Thai cuisine

Hours Monday–Saturday, 8:30–11 p.m.; Sunday, 2–4:30 p.m.

What goes on   Most of the modern greats have played here.

Setting & atmosphere   The Bull's Head is a beautiful pub facing the Thames that was built in 1684 with the stables—now the bistro—added on in 1700. The mood is convivial.

If you go   Offer to buy the musicians a pint.

CAFE DE PARIS

LONDON'S MOST RENOWNED CLUB

Who Goes There Everyone who is anyone in London

Zone 7   3–4 Coventry Street, W1; (0207) 734-7700

Cover £15 **Prices** Somewhat pricey **Dress** Elegant **Food available** French cuisine presided over by an ex–Anton Mosimann chef

Hours Closes at 3 a.m.

What goes on Live jazz music accompanies dinner, after which a DJ spins records for the more athletically inclined. The cafe is furnished with numerous bars.

Setting & atmosphere Since its launch in the 1920s, Cafe de Paris has been synonymous with high society—even the queen has given a party there. Such luminous performers as Marlene Dietrich, Maurice Chevalier, Fred Astaire, Noël Coward, Frank Sinatra, Edith Piaf, and your humble correspondent have graced its stage. Plush, opulent, and elegant, the Cafe's art deco design was influenced by the operas *Don Giovanni* and *La Bohème*. A 50-foot bar encompasses the oval ballroom, and the restaurant is highly regarded.

If you go You will be dining, drinking, and dancing in style. You may, however, need to know the right people to get in. Therefore we suggest that you circumvent all of the nonsense at the door by booking a table for dinner. Please do not turn up in your baseball cap and sneakers.

CRAZY LARRY'S

HATERS TO A HOORAY HENRY SET OUT TO GET DRUNK AND FIND GIRLS

Who Goes There Young twentysomethings

Zone 11   533 King's Road, Chelsea, SW6; (0207) 376-5555

Cover £10 **Prices** Not too bad, for London **Dress** Smart/casual **Food available** Snacks

Hours Wednesday, 8:30 p.m.–2:30 a.m.; Thursday–Saturday, 10 p.m.–2:30 a.m.

What goes on Fledgling clubbers just out of university to having a sweaty bop. It's a bit sporty, with its satellite video screen hookup. And Crazy Larry's is well known for its 1970s, 1980s, and 1990s nights.

Setting & atmosphere The decor is functional, as is the music. The object is to get the sporty young grads away from the bar and out onto the dance floor.

If you go Remember to say "yah" rather than "yo."

DOVER STREET RESTAURANT & BAR

A LARGE AND JUSTLY POPULAR JAZZ RESTAURANT AND BAR

Who Goes There Numerous personalities from the worlds of stage, film, television, and sport mingle with white-collar workers

Zone 8   8–10 Dover Street, W1; (0207) 491-7509

Cover Monday–Thursday, £7 after 10 p.m.; Friday and Saturday, £12 after 10 p.m. **Prices** Reasonable **Dress** Smart/casual; jeans and sneakers are not permitted **Specials** The Dover Street Restaurant gourmet menu, available for £45 per person (including music cover, service, and VAT), offers a glass of champagne on arrival followed by a tempting selection of French and English cuisine **Food available** French and Mediterranean cuisine served until 2 a.m.

Hours Monday–Friday, 5:30 p.m.–3 a.m.; Saturday, 7 p.m.–3 a.m.

What goes on Fine dining, live music, dancing, and DJs.

Setting & atmosphere Dover Street has been established as one of London's most atmospheric restaurants and jazz venues for over 20 years and has recently been refurbished to become the largest venue of its kind in the capital. This place swings.

If you go Remember to adhere to the dress code.

EMBARGO

CHELSEA'S ALWAYS-IN-VOGUE DESIGNER DANCE CLUB

Who Goes There The young Chelsea set

Zone 11   533b King's Road, SW10; (0207) 351-5038

Cover £10 **Prices** Slightly pricey **Dress** Stylish **Food available** A modern European restaurant serves dinner

Hours 9:30 p.m.–2 a.m.

What goes on Along with Circa in Mayfair, Embargo was opened by Rusty Egan and was therefore the vogue place to be during Rusty's tenure. Embargo still draws a classy celebrity crowd who dance the night away to thunderous house DJs.

Setting & atmosphere A modern designer club with clean, hard surfaces and mirrors, Embargo is often attended by beautiful young women.

If you go Don't disturb the beautiful young people.

EMPORIUM

MOST DISCOS WOULD LOVE TO HAVE THE DESIGN AND SOUND OF THIS PLACE

Who Goes There Sports stars and soap stars

Zone 7   62 Kingly Street, W1; (0207) 734-3190

Cover £10–15 **Prices** Expensive **Dress** Smart—no sneakers or jeans **Specials** You must be kidding **Food available** An expensive restaurant

Hours Closes on Saturday at 4 a.m.

What goes on The pop celebrities discuss show biz and football over deafening DJs while waiters dance attendance on them.

Setting & atmosphere A high-tech and ultramodern club glistening with the sheen of success.

If you go Browse through a few tabloids beforehand so that you'll be able to recognize the subjects of the latest scandals.

THE FRIDGE

BRIXTON'S MOST CELEBRATED DISCO

Who Goes There The clientele varies according to what is on during any given night, but the Fridge has been playing host to the gay and lesbian market for some time now

Zone 5   Town Hall Parade, Brixton Hill, SW2; (0207) 326-5100

Cover Friday, £8 before 8 p.m., £14 after; Saturday, £10–12 **Prices** Average **Dress** Casual **Food available** Fast

Hours Daily, 10 p.m.–6 a.m.

What goes on Dancing and trancing out to techno.

Setting & atmosphere A vast dance floor, a huge bar, capacious balconies, and the liberality of head honchos Andy and Sue have combined to make the Fridge a place to really let it all hang out. Highly recommended for the open minded. Renowned DJs spinning every night. Call for special-event information.

If you go Call a respectable minicab company to get home.

HANOVER GRAND

A POPULAR DISCOTHEQUE

Who Goes There Fashionistas on Thursday, while the house set attends on Friday and Saturday

Zone 8   6 Hanover Street, W1; (0207) 499-7977

Cover £8–12 **Prices** Uppish **Dress** Smart/casual **Food available** No

Hours Daily, 10:30 p.m.–5 a.m.

What goes on Roger Michael, one of London's top club promoters, welcomes the models and fashionable on Thursday nights for his Next Big Thing evenings, while Fresh 'n' Funky on Wednesday draws the dance crowd.

Setting & atmosphere The club has a capacity for 800 people, and the venue has three floors with the dancing taking place on ground level.

If you go Go on a Thursday.

HEAVEN

GAY PARADISE

Who Goes There Straights and gays

Zone 7   The Arches, Villiers Street, WC2; (0207) 930-2020

Cover £12 **Prices** Average **Dress** Flamboyant **Food available** Coffee bar–type sandwiches and munchies

Hours Daily, 10:30 p.m.–3 a.m.; Saturday, 10 p.m.–5 a.m.

What goes on A gay old time is had by all, even by the heteros, who are also dying to get into Heaven. Saturday night is gay night, but all are welcomed.

Setting & atmosphere The crowded rooms pulsate to techno music.

If you go Arrive before 10:30 p.m. Heaven is notorious for the length of its queues.

HIPPODROME

TOURIST TRAP

Who Goes There Unwary tourists

Zone 7   Leicester Square, W1; (0207) 437-4311

Cover £12 **Prices** Slightly pricey **Dress** Smart **Food available** Chinese restaurant

Hours Tuesday–Saturday, 9 p.m.–3 a.m.

What goes on Drinking, dancing, and flirting to top 40.

Setting & atmosphere A gigantic lighting rig, black mirrors, a large neon sign over the entrance, and a superb sound system playing chart toppers. Take advantage of the Saturday-night drink specials—buy one get one free.

If you go Don't admit it.

JAZZ CAFE

MODERN CLUB GEARED TOWARD RAP, SOUL, FUNK, AND JAZZ

Who Goes There 20–55-year-olds, depending on whether jazz or rap is featured

Zone 15   5 Parkway, N1; (0207) 916-6060

Cover £5–30 according to the popularity of the act **Prices** Average **Dress** Anything goes **Food available** Dinner is offered via a modern European menu

Hours The Jazz Cafe remains open until 2 a.m. on Friday and Saturday

What goes on This club's name is something of a misnomer, as is the radio station Jazz FM's. Both entities attempt to confer the superior artistic status of jazz on lesser forms of music. Thus the Jazz Cafe, on any given night, may have rap, soul, or funk bands performing rather than jazz groups. I therefore suggest that you consult the listings pages of *Time Out* or *Hot Tickets* magazine before going.

Setting & atmosphere The bar leads onto the dance floor, where there are some seats available. The restaurant is situated on the balcony overlooking the stage and projectors transmit arty neon images onto the awnings.

If you go Tell the soul band that is performing that you thought you were coming to a jazz club and then ask them to attempt a rendition of John Coltrane's "Giant Steps."

MINISTRY OF SOUND

THE UNITED KINGDOM'S MOST FAMOUS DISCO

Who Goes There Regulars who've been coming for over five years, as well as newcomers

Zone 5   103 Gaunt Street, SE; (0207) 378-6562

Cover Friday, £12; Saturday, £15 **Prices** Slightly expensive **Dress** Glamorous **Food available** None

Hours Friday, 10:30 p.m.–6 a.m.; Saturday, midnight–9 a.m.

What goes on Young to youngish clubbers bopping to monotonously loud and repetitious drum 'n' bass grooves.

Setting & atmosphere Ministry of Sound is a vast converted warehouse located in the not exactly salubrious boondocks of Elephant and Castle, so you must be sure to take a cab both there and back. You will need plenty of energy because this place will blow your head off. Check the listings pages of the press for the nights on which American DJs are imported to show the locals how it is done. You will find yourself dancing to everything from UK garage to R&B hits. Get ready for a fun time!

If you go Wear your dancing shoes.

NOISE BAR

ITS NAME IS APPROPRIATE

Who Goes There Gorgeous party people

Zone 7   10 Wardour Street, W1; (0207) 287-1010

Cover None **Prices** Average **Dress** Gorgeous **Food available** None

Hours Daily, 6 p.m.–3 a.m.

What goes on Punters attempt to converse while well-known DJs and their accomplices blast out drum 'n' bass records over the mixing desk.

Setting & atmosphere Situated at street level, Noise boasts a modern industrial interior. The bar's facade consists of curved Privalite glass windows, which, after an electrical current has been passed through them, can be either clear or opaque. The purple and copper bar dispenses a comprehensive list of premium-brand spirits, bottled beers, wines and champagnes, and an extensive cocktail list.

If you go Try either the Hurricane—a mixture of Bacardi, Myer's Dark, and tropical juices; or the Typhoon, made up of Amaretto Di Saronno, Archers Peach Schnapps, Blue Curaçao, grenadine, peach puree, and orange juice.

PIZZA EXPRESS

AN INTIMATE JAZZ CLUB AND RESTAURANT RECENTLY DUBBED "LONDON'S BEST LIVE MUSIC VENUE" BY *TIME OUT* MAGAZINE

Who Goes There Pizza and jazz lovers of both the tourist and local variety.

Zone 7   10 Dean Street, W1; (0207) 439-8722

Cover £10–20, depending on the status of the band **Prices** Average **Dress** Smart/casual **Food available** Pizza, pasta, lasagna, salad Niçoise, and so on

Hours Opens at 7:45 p.m., with shows beginning at 9 p.m., and closes at midnight.

What goes on Eighty percent of the bands booked are celebrated Americans of the status of Tal Farlow, Art Farmer, Kenny Garret, and Roy Haynes. Pizza Express also books top British talent such as Martin Taylor and Guy Barker.

Setting & atmosphere Pizza Express is an intimate basement club equipped with modern stage lighting and sound. The environment is friendly, sophisticated, and relaxed. The food and wine are excellent, and the music is superb. A memorable night out.

If you go You will enjoy yourself.

PIZZA ON THE PARK

AN UPMARKET JAZZ/CABARET CLUB/RESTAURANT

Who Goes There Generally an older crowd of the 45+ category

Zone 10   11–13 Knightsbridge, SW1; (0207) 235-5273

Cover £16–18 if you book in advance, £20 if you turn up at the door

Prices Fairly average, which is somewhat surprising considering the venue's posh location **Dress** Smart/casual **Food available** Yes

Hours Closes at midnight

What goes on Jazz and cabaret shows begin at 9:15 p.m. and end at 11:15 p.m.

Setting & atmosphere The club is located on the site of a Victorian tea shop, which was saved from demolition in 1986 by Peter Boizot. Boizot then commissioned Enzu Apicella to transform the place into a modern jazz/cabaret club. POTP is clubby, intimate, dimly lit, and freshly flowered.

If you go Try the wild Scottish smoked salmon, reputed to be the best in town.

ROCK GARDEN

TECHNO AND TOP 40 DANCE CLUB

Who Goes There Young trendies, European hipsters, and junior-year-abroad students, ages 18–35

Zone 7   The Piazza, Covent Garden WC2; (0207) 836-4052

Cover £5–12 **Prices** Relatively inexpensive for the area; check for drink specials **Dress** Trendy, but not over dressy **Food available** Full restaurant with excellent Mediterranean and American cuisine and service until 2 a.m. Outdoor seating overlooking the Piazza.

Hours Friday and Saturday, 5 p.m.–5 a.m.

What goes on Downstairs there are two rooms an air-conditioned techno room and a Top 40 room warmed by the body heat of the young dancers. Special club nights offer funk 'n disko and various other themes. The 2-for-1 deal on drinks and bar snacks (Monday––Saturday, 5 p.m.–7 p.m.) ensures that the impecunious students show up early.

Setting & atmosphere It has the feeling of a large European club in a small venue. The Covent Garden setting is atmospheric and convenient.

If you go Great music, drink specials, good crowd, all under one roof. Diners at the restaurant get in free.

RONNIE SCOTT'S

LONDON'S PREMIER JAZZ CLUB

Who Goes There Yuppies, buppies, musicians, and arty types come to hear the world's best jazz musicians in the downstairs club, while the younger set tends to congregate around the upstairs dance floor

Zone 7   Soho and the West End; 47 Frith Street, W1; (0121) 643-4525

Cover Varies. Free if you belong to the musician's union; £20 is normal for a Saturday **Prices** A little lower than average **Dress** Smart **Food available** A full menu of modern European cuisine and a la carte as well

Hours Daily, 8 p.m.–3 a.m.

What goes on Affluent diners and drinkers are serenaded by famous musicians downstairs while others choose to attend the upstairs disco. Doors open at 8 p.m. and the live shows start at 9:30 p.m.

Setting & atmosphere Ronnie's is pushing 40 now and is as close as London will ever get to the classic sort of jazz club you have seen in countless films.

If you go Prepare for an enjoyable evening.

606

A HIGHLY REGARDED JAZZ CLUB AND RESTAURANT OPEN FOR OVER 25 YEARS

Who Goes There Yuppies, buppies, and bohemians, young and old

Zone 11   90 Lots Road, SW10; (0207) 352-5953; www.606.co.uk

Cover There is no cover per se, but there is a music charge of £4.75 per person Sunday–Thursday, and £6 on Friday and Saturday, which is added onto the bill at the end of the night **Prices** Modest to reasonable **Dress** Casual **Food available** An extensive European-based menu, featuring a wide selection of meat, fresh fish, and vegetarian meals. The cuisine at the 606 has been praised by the Sunday Times and TV's The Restaurant Show, among others.

Hours Friday and Saturday, 8 p.m.–2 a.m.; Sunday, 8 p.m.– midnight; Monday–Wednesday, 7:30 p.m.–midnight; Thursday, 8 p.m.–1:30 a.m.

What goes on There are two jazz groups on each night from Monday through Wednesday playing from 7:30 p.m. until midnight. One band is featured, playing from around 8 p.m. until 11 p.m. The groups are selected from a variety of up-and-coming players and more established musicians. The music ranges from traditional to contemporary, with an emphasis on the modern.

Setting & atmosphere A basement club with a relaxed atmosphere, the 606 is a great place to take a date for a late supper and a bottle of wine.

If you go Don't ask any of the bands to play "Tie a Yellow Ribbon."

TURNMILLS

THE DISCO WHERE ALL-NIGHT CLUBBERS END UP

Who Goes There Hard-core club hoppers; Turnmills also hosts Trade, Britain's top gay night

Zone 3   63b Clerkenwell Road, EC1; (0207) 250-3409

Cover £10 on Saturday only **Prices** Lowish **Dress** Casual **Food available** Yes, bar food

Hours Friday, 10:30 p.m.–7:30 a.m.; Saturday, 10 p.m.–5 a.m.

What goes on In addition to the mandatory drinking and dancing, this club provides a few pinball machines.

Setting & atmosphere Candlelit tables and an Electronica bar area provide a refreshing contrast to the throbbing chaos of the dance floor.

If you go Take a taxi both there and back—if you last until 7 a.m. you will be in no condition to find your way home.

VENOM ZOO BAR

BAR AND DANCE CLUB

Who Goes There Eclectic range of regulars, from laborers to lawyers, and plenty of young tourists. Over 21 only.

Zone 7   13–17 Bear Street, Leicester Square, WC2; (0207) 839-4188

Cover Monday–Wednesday after 9 p.m., £3; Thursday, £4; Friday and Saturday after 9 p.m., £5, after 11 p.m., £8 **Prices** Average; about £3 a drink and less at happy hour **Dress** Trendy **Food available** Snacks

Hours Daily, 4 p.m.–3 a.m.

What goes on A mixed bag, very laid back. Everyone is there to have a great time. There are happy hours every night, and good dance music too.

Setting & atmosphere Two floors of fun. On the first floor, there is a bar area in which to mingle and meet friends. The basement floor has a huge dance floor surrounded by a few smaller bars to ease traffic flow.

If you go Beware of the throngs of Leiscester Square on the weekends—it's a zoo, so hold on to our valuables.

THE VORTEX JAZZ BAR

A HIGHLY REGARDED JAZZ CLUB-CUM-CAFE, BAR, AND RESTAURANT

Who Goes There Arty types

Zone 3   139–141 Stoke Newington Church Street, N16; (0207) 254-6516

Cover £4–10 **Prices** Reasonable **Dress** Informal **Food available** The cafe serves coffee, cappuccino, teas, cakes, and mainly vegetarian hot meals, soups, and salads

Hours Every day, 10 a.m. to midnight

What goes on The Vortex is so civilized that even its audience has been lauded by *The Times* for its educated and enthusiastic response to the mainstream to avant-garde jazz music presented there. The Vortex also plays host to special-guest club nights devoted to international music, cabaret, women musicians, and young contemporary artists. The club welcomes visiting musicians from America and mainland Europe.

Setting & atmosphere The Vortex is a first-floor venue in the heart of Stoke Newington. It's intimate, shadowy, and seedy with no nonsmoking areas.

If you go Carry a prominently displayed copy of Camus's *No Exit* with you.

Part Ten

Shopping in London

It's safe to say that everything is cheaper in the United States than in London. It's common that any Londoner going to America, from taxi drivers to investment bankers, takes an empty suitcase to fill with the comparatively low-priced clothing and household goods found in Anytown, USA. According to a survey done by the *London Times* in late 1998, Britons spend as much as 52% more for their cars than the least expensive EU equivalent; a shopping basket of groceries costs 36% more than the same goods in France, 54% more than in Germany, and 45% more than in America. A more recent (March 2001) and more informal survey done by the *Evening Standard* discovered that Londoners pay more than New Yorkers and Parisians for everything but deodorant, newspapers, and milk. And the foot-and-mouth disease of 2001 has caused the price of milk to rise.

So as not to completely dash your shopping dreams, let me hasten to emphasize that London has a vibrant shopping scene, with stores, stalls, and shops as far as the eye can see and some goods that are difficult to find elsewhere. Some of these things, like the hundreds of items with the Harrods name and logo plastered on them, you wouldn't necessarily want to find anywhere else, but others, like Liberty scarves, bespoke shirts from Harvie & Hudson, and bath products from Lush, are a must for the worldly shopper. If you come during the big sales, the best being during the month of January (there's also one in August), you just might be able to pay North American prices for stuff you can't readily get at home. These January and August sales are a retail tradition to make way for the next season of goods, but you can also expect some closing-down sales or minor spur-of-the-moment sales in any given month.

Wise Buys in London

The following items are worth buying in London because of their high quality or their unavailability in the United States. See our "Where to

Find" section later in this chapter for information on where to find these items.

Antiques

If you're smart and go to the early-morning Bermonsey Market, or check out the Camden Passage on Wednesdays, you'll find a huge selection in London at decent prices. See "Markets" starting on page 342. You once did not have to pay VAT on antiques, but alas, those days are over. You can get a deal, though, if you bargain and pay by cash.

Aromatic Body Stuff

Bath oils, salts, soaps, and scents in some cases cost less than in the United States. Culpepper the Herbalist, Neal's Yard Remedies, Floris, Lush, Crabtree & Evelyn, and Penhaligon are slightly cheaper here than in the few places they are sold in the States, and Boots the Chemist has its own line of goods of reasonable quality.

Bone China

Look in the stalls on Portobello Road in Notting Hill on Saturday market day, or at the Reject China Shops (phone (0207) 434-2502) for patterns you can't find in America. Even Harrods can provide some deals at sales times, and their stock is enormous. Crystal goods, too, can be cheaper than in the States.

Books

London is a city of readers, and there are thousands of bookstores that cater to readers with all possible interests. You can get books here that are only published in England, antiquarian volumes in gorgeous sets, and crates full of secondhand books. The old books are really worth your while. (I once saw a book from the 1600s with real bookworm-bore holes in it for £500. Problem was that it was in Latin.)

Children's Clothing

Some children's clothing may be, if not cheaper, of better quality and value than in the States. English smock dresses and French baby clothes are beautiful, and you don't have to pay VAT.

Designer Clothing

Secondhand, that is. There are tons of resale shops in which you can get "preowned" Chanel, Voyage, Gucci, Westwood, or whatever for reasonable prices. A lot of ladies seem to have worn these clothes twice and then moved on to the next big thing. There are outlets in which you might find semi-good deals on brand new English and French designer clothes, but it's an iffy business, dependent on exchange rates and the size of the VAT refund.

Fabrics

England has long been known for its gorgeous fabrics; try John Lewis or Peter Jones for the best deals on locally made material and things like trim and curtain swags.

Souvenirs of London

Yes, cheaper here than anywhere, naturally, but avoid the airport and museum shops. The best buys are on the street in stalls; Oxford Street, Leicester Square, Soho (Tottenham Court Road), and Piccadilly Circus are the places to look.

Stationery

Filofax, the personal organizer so well loved by well-heeled professionals in the States, is an indigenous English product and much cheaper here than anywhere else, especially at sale time.

Time to Shop

Stores in central London open late and close early. The usual times are 10 a.m. to 6 p.m., with a few opening at 9 a.m. (but closing at 5 p.m.), and a very few, like Waterstone's Bookstores, staying open until 9:30 p.m. (the Picadilly branch stays open until 11:30 p.m.). Some places, such as those in Covent Garden and some fashionable stores, don't open until 10:30 or 11 a.m.

There is a "late" night for shopping. Stores stay open until 7 or 8 p.m. on Thursdays on Oxford Street, Regent Street, and the West End. Just to keep you on your toes, Knightsbridge's and Chelsea's late night is Wednesday. Sunday is still relatively sacrosanct as a day of rest for shopkeepers, although more stores on the major shopping streets are starting to open for a half day, from noon to 5 or 6 p.m. Shockingly, Harrods has started breaking with tradition to open on Sundays during the weeks leading up to Christmas (can't imagine why). Street markets follow their own muse as far as opening hours and days go, as you'll see on pages 342–345.

Paying Up

All the major credit cards are taken at most shops. Some stores will take traveler's checks in British sterling, but they don't even want to hear about U.S. dollar traveler's checks. If they are kind enough to cash them, it may not be at a rate favorable to you. (Bring a passport to cash traveler's checks.) A good exchange rate is available at Harrods and at Marks and Spencer.

The credit card is a good way to go, as you'll have a record of your purchases and the exchange rate will be fair. The rate used will be that on the day the credit purchase clears the credit card company or bank. So don't think that just because the pound is down one day, you should run out and charge up a storm—it could go up again and cost you a pretty penny. But please, don't make yourself crazy over these things you can't control.

As for VAT

Value Added Tax is the mind-boggling 17.5% the British government adds on to the cost of all goods and services except for books, food, and children's clothing. Most goods will have the VAT already figured into the price on the tags, but other items, especially those sold at fancy knickknack stores and other high-priced shops, try to prevent total sticker shock by placing a discreet "+VAT" after all those zeros. If you have your goods shipped directly from the store, the VAT will be deducted from the price, but you'd have to be paying a lot of money to have the cost of shipping balance out. There's also the important subject of paying duty on your imported goods when you arrive in the United States. You are allowed $400 per person of goods duty free, and families may combine this allowance, so that a family of five is allowed $2000 worth of goods. The next $1,000 worth of goods gets charged a flat 10%—after that it will vary according to what type of import you're bringing.

Yes, you may be able to get a refund of some of the VAT you've paid, but it requires a little footwork. I'll let Her Majesty's Customs and Excise Department explain it all, but first, let me get this off my chest: It's true that VAT is expensive, and if you're buying a £1,000 watch or £600 silver salt-and-pepper shakers, go ahead, fill out the form, stand in the line, and get the refund. However, I see so many visitors spending a meager £50 or £100 in a museum shop or a clothing store and then spending valuable vacation time trying to get a refund that won't really amount to much. Consider that visitors use the public transport, walk on the sidewalks, enjoy the magnificent parks, take pictures of the changing of the guard—basically, they are taking advantage of all the fruits of the National Trust's hard work to make England worth visiting—and they think they are such savvy travelers for getting back less than £10 on every £100 they spend. I don't get it. Okay, I feel better. Here's how the VAT-refund process works.

Value Added Tax Refunds—The Official Story

Here are the highlights from a pamphlet entitled "Guide to Tax Free Shopping—the VAT Refund Scheme" (VAT/704/3/93), produced by Her Majesty's Ministry of Customs and Excise and published here by her kind permission.

What is the retail-export scheme?   When you visit the United Kingdom, you pay Value Added Tax (VAT) on most things you buy. The retail-export scheme allows you to obtain a refund of the tax on certain goods you intend to export from the European Community (EC).

Can I buy goods under this scheme? Yes, if you are an overseas visitor who:

- has not been in the EC for more than 365 days in the 2 years before the date you buy the goods; and
- you intend to leave the EC with all the goods in your personal luggage, within 3 months of the date you bought them.

How do I know which shops operate the scheme? The shops that operate the scheme usually have a sign in the window advertising the scheme as "tax-free shopping." If in doubt, ask for the "tax-free" sales assistant.

What must I do to obtain a VAT refund?

- ask the shop to complete a VAT or tax-free shopping form (this is very important, as without the form from the shop, you cannot get a refund);
- obtain an EC certification stamp when you leave the EC;
- mail or hand in your stamped forms to obtain your VAT refund.

Do I get all the tax back? Most shops charge a small administrative fee which will be deducted from the tax refunded to you.

What export documents will I be given? The shop will give you one of the following VAT-refund documents:

- the customs form VAT 407(1993); or
- a shop's or refund company's tax-free shopping form; or
- a retail-export scheme sales invoice.

These documents are available only from shops operating the scheme, and the shop from which you purchase the goods on which you intend to claim a refund must fill out a portion of the form it provides.

When must I export the goods? You must permanently export the goods from the EC within 3 months of purchase.

Do I have to carry all the goods bought under the scheme in my hand baggage? You should always carry items of high value, including jewelry, furs, cameras, watches, silverware, and small antiques, in your hand baggage. However, if the goods are too large to carry on board an aircraft you may pack them in your hold baggage. If you do this, you must contact the British customs export officer before you check in. The airline will tell you how to do this.

Do I get the VAT-refund document back? You must give the document and show the goods to Customs at the port or airport when you finally leave the EC. The Customs export officer will certify the document and return it to you so that you can get a refund. These procedures may take some time, so please arrive at least two hours before you are due to depart. (Author's note: I would make that three and a half hours in summer.)

What if I leave the EC on a through (transit) flight via another member state? There are special rules for goods being carried on through flights that leave the EC via another member state.

- Hand baggage: goods carried on as hand baggage and VAT-refund documents must be produced to customs in the member state of final transfer before leaving the EC. You would process your VAT goods in the United Kingdom, but keep the goods and documents handy for inspection when leaving the EC. The same applies for check-in luggage.
- Hold baggage: if you will be leaving the United Kingdom on such a flight and intend carrying large or heavy goods in hold baggage, you should ask the shopkeeper for a separate VAT-refund document for those goods. The goods and VAT-refund document must be produced to U.K. Customs before departure from the United Kingdom.

How do I get a refund? There are several methods to try for getting a refund. You may:

- mail the certified document back to the shopkeeper; or
- mail the certified document to a VAT-refunding company; or
- hand the certified document to a cash-refund booth at the point of departure, if the shopkeeper has authorized you to do so (a charge may be made for this service).

Important Reminder If you do not produce the goods and VAT-refund document to the customs export officer when you finally leave the EC, you will not get a refund of VAT.

The Unofficial Version

Only those who are not British subjects or citizens of other EU countries qualify for VAT refund, and they have to leave the country with their goods within six months.

You will not get the entire 17.5% back—it's more like 10–15% (plus an additional fee that you pay for the processing of the papers) and can actually be as little as 4% with some refund companies.

Ask what is the minimum you must spend in a given shop to qualify for the papers being filled out—it can vary, although the law puts the minimum at £50. Some shops will refuse outright, some will charge at least £5 for issuing the papers.

You must have the refund form filled out at the place of purchase! You cannot get it done anywhere else by anyone else. Bring your passport to the store.

There are refund companies that handle the VAT refund, and they have set the refund at different rates. The clerk can tell you which company the shop uses and help you decide whether it's worth your while or not.

You must show your VAT-refund purchases at the airport Customs, usually (and most easily) in carry-on luggage. Factor the size of the item against the amount of the refund times the degree of hassle you're willing to go through.

Go to the customs official to get the VAT papers before you check in your luggage.

Allow time for all the forms to be filled out—about five minutes for each one.

After you go through passport control, line up at the VAT desk to show them what you've bought and the papers that go with them.

You then get the papers back, mail them to the shop, or take them to the Tax-Free Europe desk. Tax-Free Europe is a tax-refund company that many stores are starting to use to expedite the VAT returns. They give you a cash refund at the airport, but a lot of your money stays in their hands. There's also VatBack, which will do a credit-card refund by mail; this takes about three months, but you'll get a bigger percentage back. They also give immediate cash back, at £8.60 for over £100 of goods or £18.50 for over £500 of goods.

If your VAT-refund items are too big to carry on, budget an extra hour at the airport, as you will need to have a security guard watch you go through passport control and then return the items to your airline for checking.

In the summer and after sales, there are often long lines at the VAT-refund desk at Heathrow, and this is getting worse all the time as people have started working the VAT-refund scheme in earnest.

There is also the possibility of getting the VAT refund from a hotel or holiday apartment, or from a car-rental agency; ask the concierge or the person with whom you book your travel arrangements for the forms and the information.

Salespeople's Attitudes and Behavior

Salespeople in London are (although one hates to make a generalization about such things) among the most laid-back in the world. It's not that they don't want to make a sale; it's just that they don't want to be perceived as pushing anyone to buy something. Except in a few upscale stores, where the staff is rigorously trained to look like they give a damn, the salespeople in London will surprise and perhaps bewilder you with their laissez-faire attitudes. Personally, I find it a relief from the kind of sales style in which you are forced to engage in banter (read: pressured to buy) with salespeople when all you want to do is have a look, but if you are in need of assistance, you will have to get used to approaching them. There's nothing malicious or lackadaisical about them, it's just that this is not a culture in which over-eager selling is admired. Even the famous funny East End sales patter at the markets is more a tradition of being quick and clever than it is of making a sale. The correct response is to be equally laid-back and not get demanding and rude—London salespeople are masters of the cold dismissal, and you won't win.

The Big Shopping Neighborhoods

Beauchamp Place and Walton Street   Located in zone 10 (take the tube to Knightsbridge), Beauchamp (pronounced "Beecham") Place is a swiftly changing street these days, due to skyrocketing rents and an everchanging economy. The **Reject China Shop** dominates the entrance to Beauchamp Place at Brompton Road, with two floors of china plates and accessories. As you make your way up the street, you'll find jewelry (**Dower & Hall, Follie Follie, The Watch Department, Hamilton & Inches**), shoes and purses (**Sergio Rossi, Franchetti Bond, Anello & Davide**), hats (**John Boyd**), secondhand and clearance designer clothes (**Bertie Golightly, Pamela's**), deluxe underwear (**Janet Reger**), and, of course, designers (**Bruce Oldfield, Isabel Kristiansen, Caroline Charles, Paddy Campbell,** and others). This is also the street on which to see fashionable women push food around on their plates at the restaurants **Floriana's** and **San Lorenzo.**

At the end of Beauchamp, make a right into Walton Street and get ready to really spend some money. **Baker and Spice** is a fantastic bakery that supplies many of London's finest restaurants; get something to take back to the hotel, like the garlic bread. There are trendy jewelers, a slew of interior decorators' shops full of wonderful curiosities, and a couple of decent restaurants. Try **Patrizia Wigan Designs** for children's clothing: There are always sale items that are so beautiful you'll buy something even if you don't have kids. There's **Stephanie Hopper,** who features old portraits whose faces have been erased and replaced with dog faces—very strange, and very popular with Americans apparently. **Chelsea Textiles Ltd.** has fiercely expensive and awesomely beautiful hand-embroidered reproductions of seventeenth- and eighteenth-century linens; **Tappisserie,** for wealthy craftspeople, has hand-painted needlepoint designs that are stunning. Reasonably priced monogrammed linen and unreasonably expensive Porthault sheets are at the **Monogrammed Linen Shop.** See also the extraordinary display of glass and crystal work by contemporary British artists at **The Room. Louise Bradley** and **The Wedding List Company** have everything a bride could want, and you can find jewelry for yourself at **Cox & Power.** Don't miss the slice of Italy at the **Farmacia Santa Maria Novella** (expertly hidden at 117) for creams, candles, and soaps. Everyone on the street is happy to ship their products to America, so if you want to buy new or antique children's furniture at **Dragons of Walton Street,** or fine Aubusson reproduction carpets at **Orientalist Carpets,** it's no problem to send them directly home.

Fulham Road   This area is found in zone 11; take the tube to South Kensignton. Before you get to the trendy **Joseph Boutique** at Brompton Cross, where Fulham Road actually starts, you'll pass some very haut monde stores of fashion: **Tokio, The Library,** and **NK Space** (two designer boutiques and a designer and cosmetics place). From the Bromptom Cross to Edith Grove, Fulham Road features a stretch of shops whose goods cover the gamut, from the height of fashion, antiques, and housewares, to the best used treasures, at the **Notting Hill Charity Shop.** It encompasses the so-called "beach," a block or so of pubs and restaurants that are popular with the twentysomethings. The Michelin Building houses the upscale housewares of **The Conran Shop,** as well as the restaurant **Bibendum,** named after the Michelin tire man, whom you can see immortalized in tile there. From there you can stroll along and look in windows containing housewares, tiles, and watches. **Voyage,** famous for its £1,200 trimmed cardigans and its locked-door policy that once turned away Madonna and Julia Roberts, has two stores here, one for women and one for men. Their members-only policy is supposedly a thing of the past, but it's still absurdly exclusive, and I wouldn't go there even if I won the lottery and wore a size 4. **Butler & Wilson** is an antique clothes and jewelry store that has a ton of tiaras, including a huge one on the top of the building. The jeweler **Theo Fanell,** a delightful wedding shop with secondhand dresses, and the upscale stationery store **Papyus** all precede the block devoted to expensive antiques. There's a good bookstore, **Pan Books,** past the **Virgin Cinema,** that stays open to 9:30 p.m., as does the best Italian deli in the world, **Luigi's.** Don't miss **Wok Wok,** with excellent Asian food served fast and easy. After the store **A Touch of Brass,** which sells guess what, you're on your way toward the antiques stores in the area.

New and Old Bond Streets (Zone 8, tube: Bond Street) Wow, what a stretch of real estate these streets (which are in zone 8 and can be accessed via the Bond Street tube stop) are! Starting from Oxford Street, New Bond Street starts off with a battery of designer shops and clothing boutiques, such as **Warehouse, Cecil Gee, Next, Guess, Emma Somerset, Armani, Cerruti 1881, Versace, Herbie Frogg** (this one's the so-called Sale Shop—the really expensive one is down the way on Old Bond), **Calvin Klein, Tommy Hilfiger, Miu Miu (Prada), Lanvin, Guy LaRouch, Thierry Mugler, Donna Karan, Yves Saint Laurent, Ermenegildo Zegna, Chanel, Ralph Lauren, Valentino, Nicole Farhi**—the list goes on and on. Suffice it to say they're all here. Not to mention designer shoes, fine art, jewelry (**Tiffany and Cartier,** natch), Hermès scarves, and so on. **Smythson of Bond Street** is a stationery store that begs your jaw to drop with its £23 pigskin mini-post-it-note holder, or the blank writing book for £59. There's a bench on the great divide (a pedestrian walkway) between New and Old Bond Streets, on which you will see two very realistic statues of Winston Churchill and Franklin Roosevelt. Old Bond is more of the same: exactly the same, in fact, in the cases of Donna Karan, Ralph Lauren,

Armani, Versace, and others. In case you forgot to spend £260 on a T-shirt on New Bond, you'll get a second chance on Old Bond.

Kensington Church Street (Zone 11, tube: High Street Kensington) This is the street of antiques, with shops stretching from Kensington High Street all the way to Notting Hill Gate. It's a great place to window shop and cruise in and out of the stores whose displays strike your fancy. As with all antiques stores, the inventory is always changing, but there are a few places that specialize in certain periods and styles. **The Pruskin Gallery** is known for its art nouveau, art deco, and 1940s objets d'art and furniture; **Patrick Sandberg** has eighteenth- and early nineteenth-century furniture and decorations; Meissen porcelain can be found at **Davies Antiques;** there's **Berwald Oriental Art;** and antique clocks and scientific instruments are sold at both **Raffety & Walwyn** and **Roderick Antique Clocks.** There are also wonderful mirror stores and a great crystal chandelier place. The prices can be quite high on this street, but it's fun to look, and you never know when you'll find something you really love. **Kensington Place Restaurant** is a popular eating spot on this street.

King's Road Located in zone 11 and accessible via the Sloane Square tube stop, this was the place to be in the 1960s and 1970s, when Mary Quant set up shop to sell her revolutionary miniskirts, and Vivienne Westwood kept changing the name of her and Malcolm McLaren's punk chic boutique. The Mary Quant place is now a coffee and snack shop, but the Vivienne Westwood store still has the fast-moving backward clock outside, and the floor inside still slants dangerously. King's Road is long and full of quickly changing boutiques and trendy stores, but there are some places that will, one can only hope, always be there. Starting at the Vivienne Westwood end (the western part near World's End) and heading to Sloane Square, you'll find thrift shops; **Oxfam, Trinity Hospice,** and **Imperial Cancer Fund** will have the occasional great buys. Some fabric stores along the way include **Anna French, Thomas Dave, Osbourn & Little,** and the **Designer's Guild. Wilde Ones** will take care of all your New Age needs, but at a steep cost. **Lello Bracio, Johnny Moke,** and the **Natural Shoe Store** offer the latest in shoes, both comfortable and stylish. **Old Church Galleries** has wonderful old and rare prints, and there are some good antiques and reproduction places along the way, including **Antiquarius,** a market housing many stalls with lots of goods. Check out **Steinberg and Tolkien** and be sure to go downstairs—they have the most amazing selection of vintage clothes in London, though it's more like a museum than a store, with prices to match. Other stores include **Marks and Spencer, Lush, Daisy and Tom's Childrens Store,** lots of boutiques for clothes, and at the end, **Peter Jones,** the stolid department store. Good restaurants are plentiful, and there's a **Starbucks,** too.

Sloane Street   There are two blocks of stores on this street (zone 10; tube: Knightsbridge) between Brompton Road in Knightsbridge and Sloane Square that are shockingly chock full of every hot designer you can think of. It's like a mini Bond Street: **Chanel, Dior, Dolce & Gabbana, Valentino, Prada, Lacroix, Tomasz Starzewski, Max Mara, Katharine Hamnett, Gianfranco Ferre, Armani, Ally Capellini, Alberta Ferretti, Tommy Hilfiger, Hermès,** and **Gucci.** If you don't find the designer store you need, there's always **Harvey Nichols** right at the end of the street. The street smells of money and lots of perfume.

Oxford and Regent Streets   The word that jumps to mind when I think of this area (zone 7; tube: Oxford Circus) is "boring." It has lots of chain stores, too many people, and a couple of flower and fruit stalls that are the only good reason to go here—although I must say that the department store **John Lewis** is usually my reason for being in the neighborhood. **Selfridges, Marks and Spencer, Dixons Electronics, Debenhams, The Body Shop, The Gap, Virgin Megastores**—these are not places that a tourist needs to go. However, turn the corner at Oxford Circus down Regent Street, and you will probably enjoy stopping in at **Liberty,** the Tudor-style department store that has a fascinating architecture and some interesting goods. **Hamley's,** the big toy store, is down the street; there's also a **Pastimes,** in which you can find really good gifts that exploit to the max our affection for a vanished Olde England. Avoid the **Disney Store,** but drop by the **British Air Travel Store** for its wonderful selection of travel goods and London books. **Burberry's, Jaeger,** and **Aquascutum** offer some high-class and high-priced clothing. Another good place to turn off Oxford Street is at St. Christopher's Place, a pedestrian alley full of fun shops and restaurants.

Markets

Markets cover a fair amount of space, so rather than addresses, we've given the tube stop, from where signs will direct you most efficiently.

Bermondsey Market   (zone 5; Bermonsey Square; tube: London Bridge and Borough) Open only Friday from 5 a.m. to 2 p.m., this market, also known as the New Caledonian, gives preference to the early bird, and that means arriving in pitch darkness to vie with the dealers buying antiques of every description, including clothing and jewelry. It's a serious place, and supposedly the "really good" stuff is gone before 9 a.m., but if you're not a dealer that shouldn't bother you. No credit cards are taken here; bring plenty of cash.

Brick Lane Market   (zone 3; Brick Lane; tube: Aldgate East, Shoreditch, or Liverpool Street) This East End market is open only on Sundays from 8 a.m. to 1 p.m. It is still kind of basic, without much of the sexy stuff, but it does have its fans. As the East End becomes more fashionable, the market shares in the gentrification, with hip, young designer gear vying with chipped crockery for your attention. Check it out on your way to the more predictable Spitalfields Sunday market.

Camden Market (Camden Town; tube: Camden Town) A word of warning about this market: it is now one of London's biggest tourist attractions, which means huge crowds of people. An absolute must for teens and twentysomethings, this market has very hip clothing, jewelry, records, and lots of curious-looking young people to watch. The whole of Camden has the most appealing vibration; it's almost like a latter-day Haight-Ashbury, complete with head shops, local crafts, incense, and Indian fabrics. There are plenty of good food stalls and cafes in the area and lots of outdoor seating in warm weather. Be sure to stop in at the **Victorian Market Hall,** which is open daily and has three floors of shops and stalls of everything from London souvenirs to antiques to books—something for everyone. Camden Market is open Thursday and Friday from 9 a.m. to 5 p.m. and weekends from 10 a.m. to 6 p.m.

Follow Chalk Farm Road to **The Stables,** a weekend market of antiques and secondhand goods.

Camden Passage Market (zone 3; Camden Passage; tube: Angel) Not to be confused with the above Camden Market, this market offers an interesting array of antiques and collectibles in outdoor stalls. It's open Wednesday from 10 a.m. to 2 p.m. and Saturday from 10 a.m. to 5 p.m., but the Passage itself has permanent antiques stores open all week. You can visit www.antiquescamdenpassage.co.uk.

Columbia Flower Market (zone 3; Columbia Road east of Ravenswood Street; tube: Old Street) Here you'll find lots of beautiful flowers, as well as gift, jewelry, and various other stalls. It's open from 8 a.m. to 1 p.m. on Sundays only.

The Apple Market (zone 7; tube: Convent Garden) Open daily from 10 a.m. to 7 p.m., this one is a must-see, especially on the weekends when the buskers (street entertainers) are around and throngs are milling. The market is set up in stalls and includes everything from crafts to woolens, with a juice bar and other food stalls thrown in. The brick structure that once housed the fruit, vegetable, and flower sellers is now given over to more upscale clothing, decoration, and body-care purveyors. On Monday, there is an antiques market that features lots of jewelry, silver, and knicknacks at relatively reasonable prices. A variety of craftspeople set up in the stalls depending on the day, and at Christmas even more stalls are set up around the piazza.

Greenwich Markets (zone 5; take Greenwich Docklands Light Rail (DCR) or Cutty Sark DCR from Tower Tube) There are a number of markets in Greenwich that are open on Saturday and Sunday from 9 a.m. to 6 p.m. You should have no trouble finding them, because the town is small and you just can't miss them. There's the crafts market in the center of town; the Bosun's Yard market, which also sells crafts and such; the Canopy Antiques Market, which is really a flea market with plenty of interesting junk; and the Greenwich Antiques Market, which has many stalls of vintage clothes, as well as a variety of collectibles and antiques.

Leather Lane Market (zone 2; tube: Chancery Lane) There has been a market on this site at Leather Lane for more than 300 years. As you may guess, it does have leather goods, and they're not too expensive either. Besides the clothing, the other stuff probably won't get your attention; it's mostly electrical and household items, CDs, and so on, but the market itself has a good atmosphere. It's open Monday through Friday from 10:30 a.m. to 2 p.m.

Petticoat Lane Market (zone 3; Middlesex Street and environs; tube: Liverpool Street) Open only on Sunday from 9 a.m. to 2 p.m., Petticoat Lane Market used to be located on a street of that name until the Victorian sensibilities became too delicate to handle the reference to ladies' unmentionables. Now there are tons of stalls—selling clothing, shoes, household goods, crafts, you name it—that line a number of streets in the area.

Portobello Market (zone 3; tube: Notting Hill Gate) Located on Portobello Road, from the Notting Hill end to the Ladbroke Grove end, this market is really several markets in one. The antiques market is held on Saturday from 7 a.m. to 6 p.m.; the general market is open Monday through Wednesday from 9 a.m. to 5 p.m.; the organic market takes place Thursday from 11 a.m. to 6 p.m.; and clothing and knickknacks are for sale on Friday from 7 a.m. to 4 p.m., Saturday from 8 a.m. to 5 p.m., and Sunday from 9 a.m. to 4 p.m. On Saturday, at the Notting Hill end, in addition to the stalls galore of antiques, the stores that are often closed on weekdays are open for business. There are a few multiple-dealer buildings that are worth a look, and do stop in at Neil Phillips for a gander at some great stained-glass windows. It's a major scene, so come early. As you head toward Ladbroke Grove, clothing takes over, and at the end of the street, you turn left on Westbourne Grove Road and walk through densely packed stalls of secondhand clothes, head shop–type paraphernalia, vintage shoes, food, and loud music.

St. Martin-in-the-Fields Market (zone 7; St. Martin's Lane; tube: Charing Cross) Have a look around when you're in the Trafalgar Square area, as this market is in the same zone. It's mostly clothing and teenage items, although one might find some nice and inexpensive secondhand velvet jackets from the 1970s. Lots of neo-hippie gear. While you're at it, go see the gift shops in the crypt of St. Martin-in-the-Fields Church and make a brass rubbing of one of the many Celtic and other designs.

Spitalfields Market (zone 3; Commercial Street between Lam and Brushfield; tube: Liverpool Street) Sunday is the best time for Spitalfields—both the general and organic markets are open, starting at 9 a.m. (The general market is also open Monday through Friday from 11 a.m. to 3 p.m., and the organic on Friday from 11 a.m. to 3 p.m.) Combine your trip to Spitalfields with one to the Petticoat Lane and/or Brick Lane Markets. Spitalfields has the most extensive offering of delicious organic foods, as well as lots of fast Indian and other international meals.

Walthamstow (Walthamstow High Street; tube: Walthamstow Central) Open Monday through Saturday from 8 a.m. to 6 p.m., Walthamstow is billed as Europe's longest daily street market, with 450 stalls and 300 shops. It's mostly ordinary consumer goods for a bargain, including food, clothes, electrical equipment, and the like, but it is fun to see. It also offers lots of delicious food stalls and, in the summer, live entertainment.

Department Stores

These are most like the American stores we know so well, although they're more expensive. John Lewis and Peter Jones (same store, different names) have everything you might need in life, and they claim to beat all other department store prices. Harrods pretends to have everything under the sun but really doesn't and charges at least a few quid more than John Lewis. Marks and Spencer has clothes and food and a limited selection of grocery items. Selfridges, Debenhams, and Harvey Nichols are somewhat similar to each other, all with lots of fashions, cosmetics, and a cafe or two.

Debenhams (zone 14; 334–338 Oxford Street, W1; (0207) 580-3000; www.debenhams.com; tube: Bond Street) Not much to come for, except a few designers. The store has numerous locations.

Fortnum & Mason (zone 9; 181 Piccadilly, W1; (0207) 734-8040; www.fortnumandmason.co.uk; tube: Green Park) You might not think of this as anything other than a food emporium, but in fact F&M has floors that carry clothing, clocks, and gifts above its ground floor stocked with jellies and jams. The interior is beautiful, and the cream tea is classic.

Harrods (zone 10; 87 Brompton Road, SW1; (0207) 730-1234; www.harrods.com; tube: Knightsbridge) Harrods made its reputatoin in the mid-nineteenth century as a goods emporium unparalleled in the Empire, capable of satisfying every possible whim: it once famously delivered a camel to a customer. It still has an impressive array of stock, but in my opinion, it takes itself too seriously with its dress code and charge for use of the rest room. The food halls are quite wonderful, with restaurants on the perimeters of the produce and prepared-foods stalls. Prices are high, except at its much ballyhooed sales.

Harvey Nichols   (109–125 Knightsbridge, SW1; (0207) 235-5000; www.harveynichols.com; tube: Knightsbridge) Beloved by rich fashionistas, Harvey Nichols offers floors of designer clothes, plus a good restaurant on the fifth-floor flood hall .

John Lewis/Peter Jones   (John Lewis is in zone 14; 278–306 Oxford Street, W1; (0207) 629-7711; www.johnlewis.co.uk; tube: Oxford Circus. Peter Jones is in zone 11; Sloane Square, SW1; (0207) 730-3434; tube: Sloane Square.) There's nothing fancy or trendy here, but they actually do carry everything, from picture hooks to computers, at good prices.

Liberty   (zone 7; 210–220 Regent Street, W1; (0207) 734-1234; www.liberty-of-london.co.uk; tube: Oxford Circus) A wonderful store, in the Tudor style that perks up the Georgian cool of Regent Street, Liberty is full of interesting items and home to the famous Liberty fabrics and to antiques.

Marks and Spencer   (main branch in zone 14; 458 Oxford Street, W1; (0207) 935-7954; www.marks-and-spencer.co.uk; tube: Bond Street) M&S, or Marks and Sparks as it's known, carries a lot of good stuff. With its own St. Michel name brand, it provides food and fashion. Apparently, their underwear is worn by 70% of all Londoners, and I can vouch for its comfort and design. I know of a few Americans who stock up whenever they're in town. Solid if unimaginative clothing is offered in every possible size. Branches are everywhere.

Selfridges   (zone 14; 400 Oxford Street, W1; (0207) 629-1234; www.self-ridges.co.uk; tube: Marble Arch) Thanks to a £100 million facelift in 1999 and the reorganizing efforts of a new director, Selfridges has regained a grip on its identity and now thoroughly lives up to the grand promise of its extravagant facade. Designer wear, silver, beauty products, furniture, as well as restaurants and a very comprehensive food hall, make this a satisfying shopping experience.

Where to Find . . .

Antiques

There are so many antiques stores in London, from White Chapel to Hammersmith, that an entire book could be devoted to listing them. What I will point you toward are the antiques arcades that are plentiful here, and let you wander through the great variety of antiques to be had among the stalls, including jewelry, books, clothing, furniture, clocks, silver, decorative arts, knickknacks, and more. See pages 342–345 for information about the larger markets that include antiques—Bermonsey, Camden Passage, and Portobello. Other antiques markets include:

Alfie's Antique Market (zone 14; 13-5 Church Street, NW8; (0207) 723-6066; tube: Edgeware Road) is open Tuesday–Saturday, 10 a.m.–6 p.m.

Antiquarius (zone 11; 131–141 King's Road, SW3; (0207) 351-5353; tube: Sloane Square) is open Monday–Saturday, 10 a.m.–6 p.m.

Bourbon-Hanby Antiques Centre (zone 11; 151 Sydney Street, SW3, on the corner of King's Road; (0207) 352-2106; www.antiques.co.uk/bourbon-hanby; tube: Sloane Square) is open Monday–Saturday, 10 a.m.–6 p.m. and Sunday, 11 a.m.–5 p.m.

Gray's Antiques Market and Gray's Mews Market (zone 8; off Oxford Street at 58 Davies Street, W1; (0207) 629-7034; www.graysantiques.com; tube: Bond Street) is open Monday–Friday, 10 a.m.–6 p.m.

Auction Houses

These can be a lot of fun, and you can also get some amazing items, as the treasures of the empire continue to pass through acquisitive hands. Bargains are not to be had by the likes of common folk, as the dealers know what they're doing and how to do it, but you can give it a go. Call to find out what is being sold and when, and go take a look at the catalogs to familiarize yourself with the prices. These are the four most prestigious auction houses in London, not to mention in the world: **Bonhams** (zone 10; Montpelier Street, SW7; (0207) 393-3900; www.bonhams.com; tube: Knightsbridge); **Christie's** (zone 11; 85 Old Brompton Road, SW7 (0207) 581-7611; www.christies.com; tube: South Kensington); **Phillips** (zone 8; 101 New Bond Street, W1; (0207) 629-6602; www.phillips-auctions.com; tube: Bond Street); and **Sotheby's** (zone 8; 34–35 New Bond Street, W1; (0207) 293-5000; www.sothebys.com; tube: Bond Street).

Beauty and Bath Stores

Culpepper the Herbalist (zone 7; 8 The Market, Covent Garden Piazza, WC2; (0207) 379-6698; tube: Covent Garden) sells bath salts, oils, teas, spices, essential oils—they've got it all here. A branch is located at 21 Bruton Street, W1; (0207) 629-4559. The entire line of eco-friendly Dr. Hauschka products can be found at **Renate** (zone 7; 4 Cheval Place, SW7; (0207) 589-1133; tube: Knightsbridge). You can also get a marvelous facial and massage there. **Lush** (zone 7; 7 & 11 The Market, Covent Garden Piazza, WC; (0207) 379-5423; tube: Covent Garden) is a wonderful place for chocolate massage bars, soaps by the hunk, fizzy bath bombs, and homemade oatmeal masks. It is made to look like a delicatessen and has very good gifts. A branch is at 123 King's Road, SW3; (0207) 376-8348. **MAC Cosmetics** (zone 11; 109 King's Road, SW3; (0207) 534-9222; www.maccosmetics. com; tube: Sloane Square) is a Canadian company that offers new, trendy makeup that doesn't cost the world. **Neal's Yard Remedies** (zone 7; 15 Neal's Yard, WC2; (0207) 379-7222; tube: Covent Garden) is a great place for homeopathic remedies, fresh herbs, essential oils, soaps, and hair-care products, all in beautiful blue glass bottles. Other branches are too numerous to mention, so call for information. **Space NK Apothecary** (zone 7; 37 Earlham Street, WC2; (0207) 379-7030; tube: Covent Garden) offers the latest and greatest in cosmetics and beauty products at its popular store. The apothecary also has many branches, so call for locations.

Bookstores

There are many chain bookstores in London, which have branches everywhere. Call to find the one nearest to you: **Books Etc.** (phone (0207) 404-0261); **Borders Books & Music** (phone (0207) 379-6838; www. borders.com); **Dillions** (phone (0207) 434-9617); **WH Smith** (phone (0207) 261-1708); and **Waterstones** (phone (0207) 434-4291).

Then there are the more unusual stores: **Atlantis Bookshop** (zone 2; 49a Museum Street, WC1; (0207) 405-2120; www.atlantisbookshop.demon. co.uk; tube: Tottenham Court Road) caters to a clientele interested in psychic research, witchcraft, and supernatural phenomena. Incredible deals are found in **Book Thrift** (zone 11; 22 Thurloe Street, SW7; (0207) 589-2916; tube: South Kensington), which specializes in fine-arts books for a fraction of the original cost. Buy immediately: when the stock is gone, it's gone for good. **European Bookshop** (zone 7; 5 Warwick Street, W1; (0207) 734-5259; www.esb.co.uk; tube: Piccadilly Circus) sells books and mags in most European languages. **Grant & Cutler** (zone 8; 55–57 Great Marlborough Street, W1; (0207) 734-2012; www.grant-c.demon.co.uk; tube: Oxford Street) has books, videos, cassettes, and more. About 200 languages are represented, so you're certain to find something you can understand.

Henry Southeran (zone 8; on the ground floor at 2 Sackville Street, W1; (0207) 629-6517; tube: Green Park) is the place to look for real antiquarian books. Within Henry Southeran is **The Folio Society Gallery,** where reproductions of fine, antiquarian books are available. The books are magnificent, well bound, and illustrated as in the old days, and the titles available are classics of every kind. The only catch is you have to join the society with the obligation to buy four books as the price of membership (the difficulty is limiting yourself to only four). The society, at the same address as Henry Southeran, can be reached by phone at (0207) 439-6151 or on the Internet at www.sotherans.co.uk.

Forbidden Planet (zone 2; 71–75 New Oxford Street, WC1; (0207) 836-4179; tube: Tottenham Court Road), billed as "The Science Fiction Entertainment Store," has got it all, from toys to videos to every kind of printed matter you can imagine. **French's Theatre Bookshop** (52 Fitzroy Street, W1; (0207) 387-9373; www.samuelfrench-london.co.uk; tube: Warren Street) has play scripts beyond compare and is a must for the theater student or aficionado.

Hatchard's (zone 8; 187 Piccadilly, W1; (0207) 439-9921; www.hatchards.co.uk; tube: Piccadilly Circus) is London's oldest bookstore, with a very fine selection and a great atmosphere. **Helter Skelter** (zone 2; 4 Denmark Street, WC2; (0207) 836-1151; www.skelter. demon.co.uk; tube: Tottenham Court Road) is a music bookshop with sheet music, mags, music-related art, and all possible fiction and nonfiction about the subject. **Librairie La Page French Booksellers** has everything for the French student, young and old (zone 11; 7 Harrington Road, SW7; (0207) 589-5991; tube: South Kensington). **Pan Bookstore** (zone 11; 158 Fulham Road, SW10; (0207) 373-4997; tube: South Kensington, then 14 bus toward Fulham) has lots of signed editions of recently published books.

Politico's (zone 9; 8 Artillery Row, SW1; (0207) 828-0010; www.politi-cos,co.uk; tube: St. James's Park) has great political paraphernalia, plus a fine selection of books on biography, reference, and history. **Stanford's** (zone 7; 12–14 Long Acre, WC2; (0207) 836-1321; www.stanfords.co.uk; tube: Leicester Square) has the biggest collection of maps, globes, and travel books you'll ever see. **Talking Bookshop** (zone 14; 11 Wigmore Street, W1; (0207) 491-4117; www.talkingbooks.co.uk; tube: Bond Street) has the best selection of books on tape—a huge wall of unabridged fiction from classics to this year's best-sellers—as well as books on CD. Theirs are not cheaper than those sold in the United States, but they offer an extraordinary range.

Antiquarian and Secondhand Books

Let us not forget the antiquarian and secondhand books. It would behoove anyone interested in browsing to take a walk down Charing Cross Road or around Soho to look in the many secondhand bookstores. The prices are very low, and you could get your hands on some very fine antique books for a couple of quid. Many of the secondhand bookstores listed below also have antiquarian books in locked glass cabinets. (Antiques neighborhoods, markets, and arcades, as listed in this book, will also have many shops and stalls featuring old and beautiful books.) Visit:

Any Amount of Books (zone 7; 62 Charing Cross Road, WC2; (0207) 240-8140; www.anyamountofbooks.com; tube: Leicester Square); **Gloucester Road Bookshop** (zone 11; 123 Gloucester Road, SW; (0207) 370-3503; www.gloucesterbooks.co.uk; tube: Gloucester Road); **Skoob Books** (zone 2;

15 Sicilian Avenue, WC1; (0207) 404-3063; www.skoob.com; tube: Holborn); and **Unsworths Booksellers** (zone 2; 15 Bloomsbury Street, WC1; (0207) 436-9836; www.unsworths.com; tube: Tottenham Court Road).

Decorative Home Accessories

Architectural Components (zone 11; 8 Exhibition Road, SW7; (0207) 581-2401; tube: South Kensington) has brass fittings for every possible household use with an emphasis on the bathroom. **The Conran Shop** (zone 11; Michelin House, 81 Fulham Road, SW3; (0207) 589-7401; tube: South Kensington) has a lot of interesting, though expensive, modern items for bed, bath, kitchen, and nursery. Very traditionally English in style are the wares at **General Trading Company** (zone 11; 144 Sloane Street, SW1; (0207) 730-0411; www.general-trading.co.uk; tube: Sloane Square), which offers everything you can imagine wanting for the home or tabletop. **India Jane** (zone 11; 140 Sloane Street, SW1; (0207) 730-1070; tube: Sloane Square) has some good buys in the way of Indian silver and picture frames.

The London Silver Vaults (zone 2; 53–64 Chancery Lane, WC2; (0207) 242-3844; tube: Chancery Lane) is actually 40 shops selling silver, old and new, and for every budget. **Past Times** is a store full of faux Olde English stuff from every period, from garden goods to desk accessories to books. The main branch is in zone 10, at 146 Brompton Road, SW3; (0207) 581-7616; tube: Knightsbridge); call for the locations of numerous other branches.

The Reject China Shop (zone 10; 183 Brompton Road, SW3; (0207) 581-0739; www.chinacraft.co.uk; tube: Knightsbridge) is a great place to replace missing Spode or Wedgwood plates or to pick up a cow creamer. It has numerous branches. Finally, don't miss **Thomas Goode** (zone 8; 19 South Audley Street, W1; (0207) 499-2823; tube: Green Park) for a genuine English shopping experience, with major china, silver, and crystal as well as knickknacks. Have a spot of tea there, too.

Designer Clothes

Below is a list of some of London's homegrown designers. They are certainly London's best-known designers, and not all sell their clothes in the United States. Some have their own boutiques, but unless you just want to see what they have to offer, you're better off buying in the department stores and boutiques that carry their clothes. If it's an internationally known designer, you're better off buying in the States, if possible.

Antoni & Alison, Hussein Chalayan, Caroline Charles, English Eccentrics, John Galliano, Ghost, Joseph, Katherine Hamnett, Justin Oh, Nicole Farhi, Bella Freud, Julian MacDonald, Alexander McQueen, Bruce

Oldfield, Red or Dead, Paul Smith, Pierce Fionda, Lainey Keogh, Zandra Rhodes, Paul Smith, Tomasz Starzewski, Phillip Treacy (hats only), Catherine Walker, Amanda Wakeley, Vivienne Westwood, and Matthew Williamson have stores here or can be found in Selfridges, Harvey Nichols, Harrods, or smaller designer boutiques (see below). Check the phone book for locations and phone numbers.

Designer Boutiques

Harvey Nichols, Harrods, Selfridges, and Liberty will likely carry some or all of the above designers' clothes (see the section "Department Stores," page 345). Here are a few smaller boutiques that carry many of England's designers:

Browns (zone 7; 23–27 South Moulton Street, W1; (0207) 491-7833; tube: Bond Street) has a huge selection of all the big names. Other stores are: **A La Mode** (zone 10; 36 Hans Cresents, SW1; (0207) 584-2133; tube: Knightsbridge); **Feathers** (zone 10; 40 Hans Crescent, SW1; (0207) 589-0356; tube: Knightsbridge); **Joanna's Tent** (zone 11; 289B King's Road, SW3; (0207) 352-1151; tube: Sloane Square); **Koh Samui** (zone 7; 50 Monmouth Street, WC2; (0207) 240-4280; tube: Covent Garden); **Question Air** (zone 7; 38 Floral Street, WC2; (0207) 836-8220; tube: Covent Garden); **Tokio** (zone 11; 309 Brompton Road, SW3; (0207) 823-7310; tube: South Kensignton); and **Whistles** (zone 14; 12 St. Christopher's Place, W1; (0207) 487-4484; tube: Bond Street).

Designer Resale Shops

Such a good idea, these shops. It's hit or miss, but you can get your hands on some very expensive designer threads and shoes for a fraction of what they'd cost new. Unfortunately, there tend to be more size 4s than 14s, but shoes and purses will work for anyone. Some good places to try are: **Bertie Golightly** (zone 10; 48 Beauchamp Place, SW3; (0207) 584-7270; tube: Knightsbridge); **Catwalk** (zone 14; 52 Blandford Street, W1; (0207) 935-1052; tube: Baker Street); **The Dresser** (zone 14; 10 Porchester Place, W2; (0207) 724-7212; tube: Marble Arch); **L'Homme Designer Exchange** (zone 14; 50 Blandford Street, W1; (0207) 224-3266; tube: Baker Street). For men's fashions, visit **The Loft** (zone 7; 35 Monmouth Street, WC2; (0207) 240-3807; tube: Covent Garden); and **Sign of the Times** (zone 11; 17 Elystan Street, SW3; (0207) 589-4774; tube: Sloane Square). When visitng **Pandora** (zone 10; 16–22 Cheval Place, SW7; (0207) 589-5289; tube: Knightsbridge), see also, along this same street, **The Dress Box** (8 Cheval Place; (0207) 589-2240) and **Salou** (6 Cheval Place; (0207) 581-2380).

Fabrics

Anna French (zone 11; 343 King's Road, SW3; (0207) 351-1126; tube: Sloane Square, then bus 11 or 22) sells children's room fabrics, as well as sheer, lacy, and flowery patterns. **Beaumont & Fletcher** (zone 11; 261 Fulham Road, SW3; (0207) 352-5594; tube: South Kensington, then bus 14) offers period (eighteenth- and nineteenth-century) and reproduction fabrics of a very high standard. **Colefax & Fowler** is one of the greats in traditional English decoration (zone 11; 110 Fulham Road, SW3; (0207) 244-7427; tube: South Kensington, then bus 14). **The Decorative Fabrics Gallery** (zone 11; 278–280 Brompton Road, SW3; (0207) 589-4778; www.decorativefabrics.com; tube: South Kensington) has a wide range of traditional and upscale fabrics, with good export service. **Osbourne & Little** (zone 11; 304–308 King's Road, SW3; (0207) 352-1456; www.osbourneandlittle.com; tube: Sloane Square) sells traditional and modern designs, all of high quality. **VV Rouleaux** (zone 11; 54 Sloane Square (Cliveden Place), SW1; (0207) 730-3125; tube: Sloane Square) has the best collection of ribbons, trimmings, and braids in London.

Linens

Irish Linen Company (zone 8; 35–36 Burlington Arcade, W1; (0207) 493-8949; tube: Piccadilly Circus) sells Irish linen and Egyptian cotton sheets and table clothes. **The Linen Merchant** (zone 10; 11 Montperlier Street, SW7; (0207) 584-3654; tube: Knightsbridge) sells bathrobes as well as bed linens. **Monogrammed Linen Shop** (zone 11; 168 Walton Street, SW3; (0207) 589-4033; tube: South Kensington) has a good stock of expensive, beautiful linen that can be monogrammed to order. **The White House** (zone 8; 40–41 Conduit Street, W1; (0207) 629-3521; tube: Bond Street) sells unbelievably lovely bedclothes at unthinkably extravagant prices.

Museum Shops

My favorite stores in London are the gift shops at museums. The **British Museum's** shop offers good gifts for old and young—reproductions of museum treasures such as the Lewis chess pieces and Roman coins or jewelry. **Hampton Palace's** shop has the best all-around selection of housewares, books, food, and decorative arts. **Museum of London's** shop has the best books on London. The **National Gallery** and **National Portrait Gallery** shops have the best postcards, calendars, and art books. The **Natural History Museum** shop has the best nature selection for kids, including tons of plastic and stuffed animals. The **Queen's Gallery** shop and the **Buckingham Palace** shop (open only in August and September) have the best royal-related items. The **Royal Academy** has art books and cool

T-shirts. The **Science Museum** has great gifts for children. Both **Tate Museums** have shops with good art books and postcards. The **Victoria and Albert Museum** has the best reproduction jewelry, decorative arts, and books on design and interior decoration. They all have excellent chocolate and souvenirs.

Perfumeries

One of the great things about London is its proximity to France, home of a thousand scents. The interest in aromas has wafted across the English Channel, and you can find some of the best perfumes in the world at the following stores. **L'Artisan Parfumeur** (zone 11; 17 Cale Street, SW3; (0207) 352-4196; tube: South Kensington) has scents for men, women, and children(!). Candles, too. **Crown Perfumery** (zone 8; 51 Burlington Arcade, W1; (0207) 493-1717; tube: Green Park), now also going by the name **Pure,** is a must-go place, where scents made specially for the likes of Queen Victoria, the duke and duchess of Windsor, Oscar Wilde, and Isadora Duncan can be sniffed. **Floris** (zone 8; 89 Jermyn Street, SW1; (0207) 930-2885; tube: Piccadilly Circus) is the classic English fragrance and soap maker, in business since 1730. Also offered are potpourri and candles. **Jo Malone** (zone 11; 150 Sloane Street, SW1; (0207) 730-2100; www.jomalone.co.uk; tube: Sloane Square) is a wildly popular store with remarkable, imaginative scents and creams. **Penhaligons** (zone 7; 41 Wellington Street, WC2; (0207) 836-2150; tube: Covent Garden) has been a lovely place with lovely smells since 1870. It's great for gifts and has numerous branches. **Les Senteurs** (zone 9; 71 Elizabeth Street, SW1; (0207) 730-2322; tube: Victoria or Sloane Square) has very unusual fragrances, straight from France, as well as fine skin-care products.

Shoes

Birkenstock (zone 7; 37 Neal Street, W2; (0207) 240-2783; www.birkenstock.co.uk; tube: Covent Garden), the hippy shoe from the 1960s, has never been so popular or mainstream. The real thing costs a bundle in the United States, but here you can get such styles as the Vegan, which contains no animal parts, or the Classic for slightly, and in some cases much, less. **Dr. Marten's Department Store** (zone 7; 1–4 King Street, WC2; (0207) 497-1460; www.drmartens.com; tube: Covent Garden) is five floors of Doc Marten shoes at prices that may be competitive with those in the States. Sale time is really the only time to find a bargain. **Emma Hope** (zone 11; 53 Sloane Square, SW1; (0207) 259-9566; tube: Sloane Square) offers amazingly elegant and quite expensive shoes. **Jimmy Choo** (zone 11; 169 Draycott Avenue; (0207) 584-6111; tube: South Kensington) is a very au courant shoemaker, beloved of the stylish young women of London and, increasingly, the world. **John Lobb** (zone 9; 9 St. James Street, SW1; (0207) 930-3664; tube: Green Park) is the oldest, grandest, and most expensive of the bespoke shoemakers; one of these classic pairs of English leather shoes will set you back about £1,500, and it will take months to get them, but they say it's well worth it. **Natural Shoe Store** (zone 11; 325 King's Road, SW3; (0207) 351-3721; ww.naturesko.com; tube: Sloane Square) has the best in comfort shoes: Ecco, Birkenstock, Arche, Krone Clogs, and American brands such as Bass, Dexter, and Rockport. Don't even think of getting the American brands, but check the prices on the Europeans. There's another branch at 21 Neal Street in Covent Garden.

Vintage Clothing

Steinberg and Tolkien (zone 11; 193 King's Road, SW3; (0207) 376-3660; tube: Sloane Square) has an astonishing, wonderful range of vintage clothing, from the Victorian period to that worn during the 1970s, and from Worth to Balmain to Schiaparelli to Biba to Halston. It's the place where costume designers from films come to dress their actors, where actors come to play, and where designers come for inspiration. Go for the fun of seeing the largest vintage clothing collection in London, and be sure to go downstairs. **The Antique Clothing Store** (zone 13; 282 Portobello RoaW10; (0208) 964-4830; tube: Ladbroke Grove) also has a large selection; you may even find antique christening gowns.

Wool and Cashmere

Wool and cashmere in London are from Scotland or Ireland and are more expensive and of better quality than the Chinese kind. The best time to buy is during sale times. Many of the wool stores will have sales during the summer to move the goods and take advantage of the influx of tourists, many of whom aren't prepared for the chilly London summer and will have need of woolens. Liberty, Harrods, Marks and Spencer, Debehams, and other big stores have good wool departments (see "Department Stores," page 345).

　Scotch House (zone 7; 191 Regent Street, W1; (0207) 734-4060; tube: Oxford Circus) has scarves, kilts, jackets, capes, gloves, and everything else that can be made from wool and cashmere. Call for information on branches. **Shirin Cashmere** (zone 11; 12 Beauchamp Place, SW3; (0207) 581-1936; tube: Knightsbridge) has a much more elegant (and expensive) selection than the Scotch House. **Westaway & Westaway** (zone 2; 64–65Great Russell Street, WC1; (0207) 405-4479; and 92–93 Great Russell Street, WC1; (0207) 636-1718; tube: Holborn) are two shops overflowing with sweaters in every color and size possible, at the best prices possible.

Part Eleven

Exercise and Recreation

Spectator Sports

Baseball and Softball

A wide variety of sporting events take place all over the country, with many organized softball teams based in London. For information on the times and places of games, contact Bob Fromer at the Baseball Softball UK Ariel House, 74 Charlotte Street, SW1T 4QJ (call (0207) 453-7055, or visit www.baseballsoftball.com).

Basketball

Basketball is becoming extremely popular in the UK. The season runs from September to May. The British Basketball League (BBL) Championships are hosted at Wembley Arena. For further detials, call the BBL at (0121) 749-1355, or visit www.bbl.org.uk. The following are considered the best London teams:

Haribo London Towers play at Crystal Palace National Sports Centre, Ledrington Toad, SE19 (outside zones). Take British Rail to Crystal Palace (phone (0208) 776-7755, or visit www.london-towers.co.uk). Tickets are £8 for adults and £6 for children.

Leopards Basketball at Brentwood Leisure Centre, Duddinghurst Road, Brentwood (outside zones). Take British Rail to Brentwood. Phone (01227) 230-231, or visit www.leopardsbasketball.com. Tickets are £7.50 for adults, £5 for children, and £22 for a family ticket.

Thames Valley Tigers at Bracknell Sports Centre, Bagshott Road. Take British Rail to Bracknell (outside zones). Phone (01344) 789-008) or visit www.tvtigers.co.uk. Tickets are £8 for adults and £6 for children.

Football

Soccer, or football as the English call it, is more than a national obsession—it is a religion with devotees and acolytes. The days when rival fans would do bloody battle in the streets are mostly gone due to CCTV, hi-tech detective work, well-organized policing at games, and reconstruction of the grounds themselves. However, the fever burns as strong as ever. There is huge money in football these days and the top teams, which belong to the Premiership league, are all locked into cable TV deals that have the exclusives on their matches. Consequently, tickets for these games are expensive (£12–50), whereas tickets for the teams further down the league are cheaper (£8–15). It is well worth a visit to a Premiership game, as the class (and price) of players these days is phenomenal. The spectators themselves are also worthy of close attention. Listen to their songs and chants and their sometimes venomous derision of the visiting team.

The football season runs from August to May. Games are 90 minutes long, with injury time and extra time if it is important that there be a winner (as in for a cup final). Most of the clubs will take credit-card bookings over the phone, which is crucial for Premiership games. They take place on Saturday afternoons and in the evenings on weekdays. Wrap up warm, and if the conclusion of the game is obvious ten minutes before the final whistle, leave early to avoid the crush and possible trouble. Avoid the standing seats at the clubs further down the league, as this is where trouble, if it breaks out, is more likely to occur. Premiership teams include:

Arsenal at Arsenal Stadium in zone 15, Avenall Road, N5 (phone (0207) 704-4000, or visit www.arsenal.co.uk). Take the tube to Arsenal. Tickets are £16.50–30.5; children are full price.

Chelsea at Stamford Bridge in zone 11, Fulham Road, SW6 (phone (0207) 385-5545) or visit www.chelseafc.co.uk). Take the tube to Fulham Broadway. Tickets are £25–33 for adults and £11 for children.

Charlton Athletic at The Valley (outside zones), Floyd Road, SE7 (phone (0208) 333-4010 or visit www.cafc.co.uk). Take British Rail to Charlton. Tickets are £20–25 for adults and £10 for children.

Tottenham Hotspurs at Whitehart Lane, High Road, N17 (phone (0208) 365-5000 or visit www.spurs.co.uk). Take British Rail to White Hart Lane. Tickets are £27–46 for adults and children.

West Ham United at Boleyn Ground (outside zones), Green Street, E13 (phone (0208) 548-2748, or visit www.westhamunited.co.uk). Take the tube to Upton Park. Adult tickets are £25–45 adults; those for children begin at £15.50.

All these teams, except Fulham, play outside our designated London zones.

Cricket

Despite the fact that it is a truly international sport (at which the Brits have not excelled for years), there is something quintessentially English about the game of cricket. It is sedate, difficult to understand, and full of quaint language. For example, a "maiden over" is a series of six balls, bowled in a swinging overarm motion, during which no runs are scored. The games sometimes last for days, interrupted frequently by rain and tea. It is considered vulgar to thrash one's opponent by too many runs; when it is clear the losing team cannot win, the winning side "declares" and gives the other team a chance to recover some of their dignity. You can see this game played on many a village green during the season, which runs from mid-April to early September, but there are two main venues in London, Lords and the Oval:

Lords at St. John's Wood Road (zone 14), NW8 (phone (0207) 289-1611 or visit www.lords.org.uk). Take the tube to St. John's Wood. This is the home of the Marylebone Cricket Club and often considered the home of cricket. Tickets range from £20–50; children are half price.

Foster's Oval at Kennington Oval, outside zones, SE11 (phone (0207) 582-6660 or visit www.surreyccc.co.uk). Take the tube to Oval. International cricket is often played here, tickets for which range from £30 to £50. Tickets for county matches are less expensive.

Tickets for international games need to be booked well in advance, but the league games, played between counties, are much easier to see.

Rugby

This is a brutal and violent game similar to American football, but without the padding. Again, the rules are characteristically British: the ball, shaped like an American football, is passed backward or sideways, never forward; during the scrum, the players crouch with their faces or shoulders between the thighs and against the buttocks of the player in front and push against a similarly tightly packed huddle of the opposition. The ball is thrown into this mass of steaming, muddy flesh, from which it is booted out. Whoever catches it then dashes along the field to score a try (touchdown), which is then converted by kicking it over the goal posts for extra points. Like cricket, it is a quintessentially British sport at which the natives no longer truly excel. The New Zealanders, French, South Africans, and Fijians are marvelous rugby players, but tickets for international games are hard to get. The season runs from September to May, and the game is enjoying something of a resurgence in popularity due to the amount of money it now attracts.

Rugby League is the professional form of rugby football. This is a fast-moving collision game with lots of open running, big hits and tackles (the closest thing to American football). There are 13 players on a team.

Rugby Union is traditionally the amateur form of rugby football, with the characteristic scrums, time-outs, and touch-downs, and 15 players per team. However, it now boasts a professional status, with the Allied Dunbar Premiership and the Jewson National League, which draw major crowds. The season runs from August to May. Watch out for the Harlequins, London Irish, Saracens, and the Wasps. Wrap up warmly if you go. The primary rugby venues are:

Athletic Ground at Kew Foot Road in zone 12, Richmond, Surrey (phone (0208) 940-0397; tube: Richmond). Here are played free amateur games.

Rosslyn Park on Upper Richmond Road in zone 12, Priory Lane, Roehampton, SW15 (phone (0208) 876-1879 or 876-6044). Take British Rail to Barnes. Tickets are £8 for adults, £4 for seniors, and £2 for children.

Twickenham Rugby House at 21 Rugby Road (outside zones), Twickenham Middlesex (phone (0208) 892-2000, or visit www.rfu.com). Tickets vary in price depending on the game. Tickets for the Six Nations series held here are almost impossible to get and are distributed to the faithful via the various clubs. You can see cup finals for the leagues here, too, for which tickets range between £15 and £35.

Clubs

Blackheath at Rectory Field (outside zones), Charlton Road, SE3 (phone (0208) 293-0853, or visit www.blackheathrugby.co.uk).

N.E.C.Harlequins at Stoop Memorial Ground, Langhorn Drive, Twickenham, Middlesex (phone (0208) 410-6000 or visit www.quins.co.uk).

London Welsh at Old Deer Park, Kew Road, Richmond, Surrey (phone (0208) 940-8155).

Saracens at Vicarage Road (outside zones), Watford (phone (0192) 347-5222 or visit www.saracens.com).

London Wasps at Loftus Road Stadium, South Africa Road, W12 (phone (0208) 743-0262 or visit www.wasps.co.uk).

Modejski Stadium on Junction 11 (off M4, outside zones). Phone (01932) 783034 or visit www.londonirish.com.

Boxing

Big fights happen in big venues, like Wembley Arena, Royal Albert Hall, London Arena, and Earl's Court. Publicity will be large scale, and tickets are always expensive. There are smaller venues for amateur or semiprofessional fights, and these will be advertised in local papers, *Time Out,* or on posters. You can catch a good pro or amateur fight at York Hall, Old Ford Road, E2 (phone (0208) 980-4171). This place has a serious East End vibe and has hosted amateur matches since 1929. Tickets are £10. Tickets for pro fights are priced by the promoters. Call Boxing News at (0207) 882-1040 for details on what's on, where, and when.

Tennis

In the build-up to the world-famous Wimbledon championships, the smaller but equally popular Stella Artois tournament takes place in mid-June at Queens Club, Palliser Road, W14. Call (0207) 385-3421 and take the tube to Barons Court. Tickets range from £24 to £57. Book early.

Wimbledon fortnight starts the last week in June, and demand for tickets always far exceeds the supply. For years, a ballot system has been operated. To get tickets for Centre Court or Number One Court you have to write, enclosing a self-addressed envelope, for an application form, between September 1 and December 31: The All England Tennis Club, P.O. Box 98, Church Road, London, SW19. Phone (0208) 946-2244. or visit www.wimbledon.com Tickets range from £26–66 for Centre Court and £24–47 for Number One Court. Take the tube to Wimbledon (District line). Bring a hat or umbrella and plenty of sunblock. There will be lots of queuing, so be prepared. The strawberries and cream are expensive (£1.85 for a punnet of no fewer than ten strawberries), but the museum is worth a visit.

Racing

Horse racing is very popular in Britain. You can see it almost every day on television, and every high street has at least one betting shop, or "turf accountant," as the Brits like to call them. Gambling is legal in Britain, and bookies will give odds on almost anything, from the gender of the next royal birth to whether it will snow on Christmas Day. A day at the races is as popular with the upper classes (members of which own the horses and can be seen at Ascot wearing ridiculous hats that are never worn anywhere else), as it is with the working classes.

The flat season runs from April to September, and the jumps or steeplechase runs from October to April. As well as branches of the major corporate bookies like William Hill and Coral, there are many trackside bookies with whom it is much more fun to bet. They usually take win-only bets, with a minimum stake of £5. Watch the extraordinary ballet of arm swinging and hand signaling as they establish the odds. More complicated bets (exactas, trifectas, accumulators, and so on) can be made at the corporate bookies, or tote, as mentioned before.

All the tracks are just outside London and are well serviced by rail. Take a coat and umbrella just in case. Most have bars and restaurants, which serve notoriously bad food, so be warned. A day at the races is exactly that, so be prepared for a longish haul. Racing venues include:

Ascot Race Course   High Street, Ascot, Berks (outside zones). Phone (0134) 462-2211 or visit www.ascot.co.uk. Take British Rail to Ascot rail. Admission is £10–40, depending on whether you sit in the grandstand or the silver ring. (The royal enclosure is closed to commoners!) You can catch Her Majesty in June having a punt. Good competitive racing can always be seen here. One of the highlights of the year is the Royal Meeting with Ladies Day on the Thursday of that week.

Epsom   Epsom Downs, Epsom, Surrey (outside zones). Phone (0137) 247-0047 or visit www.epsomderby.co.uk. Take British Rail to Epsom Downs. Admission is £11–20. This is where the Oaks and the Derby (pronounced Darby) are held in June. Derby Day is a big betting day in England and is something of a national mood lifter. The winner is always part of the headline news, and most people have a bet. Tickets in the Queen's Stand and Derby Day cost up to £95. Don't forget your top hat and tails.

Kempton Park   Staines Road East (outside zones). Phone (0137) 247-0047 or visit www.kempton.co.uk. Take British Rail to Sunbury on Thames or to Kempton Park. Admission is £11–17. This course hosts the King George VI stakes on Boxing Day. There is a new restaurant, but earlier warnings about the food hold true.

Sandown Park   The Racecourse, Portsmouth Road, Esher, Surrey (outside zones). Phone (0137) 247-0047 or visit www.sandown.co.uk. Take British Rail to Esher. Admission is £11–18. This track is supposed to be the best equipped in the London area. It hosts the Whitbread Gold cup in April and the Coral Eclipse Stakes in July.

Windsor   Maidenhead Road, Windsor, Berks (outside zones). Phone (0175) 386-5234 or visit www.windsor-racecourse.co.uk. Take British Rail to Windsor and Eton Riverside. Admission is £5–16. This is a pretty part of England and worth a visit in its own right. The castle (still very much in use by Her Majesty) can be visited and overlooks the course. The Thames is green and beautiful out here, and you can take a boat to and from the race track from the town, making a grand day out.

Greyhound Racing

These sleek animals tear round the track after a wooden hare on a rail. They run amazingly fast, and the race is over in a minute or less. The same deal with the horse-racing corporate and trackside bookies applies, as do the warnings about food. There is a lot of beer drinking at the dog races, and they make for a very entertaining evening out, featuring lots of characters and florid language. Again, all tracks are well serviced by public transport but are far from the center of London. Greyhound-racing venues include:

Catford Stadium   Adenmore Road, SE6 (outside zones). Phone (0208) 690-8000; take British Rail to Catford or Catford Bridge. Admission is £4 for adults, £2 for children. Races start at 7:20 p.m. on Mondays, Thursdays, and Saturdays.

Romford Stadium   London Road, Romford, Essex (outside zones). Phone (0170) 876-2345 or visit www.coraleurorbet.co.uk. Take British Rail to Romford. Admission is £1.50–5 and free on the popular side of the stadium on Mondays and Wednesdays. All races start at 7:30 p.m. and are held Mondays, Wednesdays, Fridays, and Saturdays. There are afternoon races on Thursday.

Walthamstow Stadium   Chingford Road, E4 (outside zones). Phone (0208) 498-3300 or visit www.wsgreyhound.co.uk. Take the tube to Walthamstow Central and then a minicab from there. Admission is £2.50–5, and races are held at 7:30 p.m. on Tuesdays, Thursdays, and Saturdays. Afternoon races are also held on Mondays.

Wimbledon Stadium   Plough Lane, SW17, in zone 12. Phone (0208) 946-8000 or visit www.wimbledonstadium.co.uk. Take the tube to Wimbledon. Admission is £3–5, and races start at 7:30 p.m. on Tuesdays, Fridays, and Saturdays.

Participation Sports

Gyms and Leisure Centers

Working out and staying in shape are as popular in Britain as in the United States, and gym culture flourishes. There are plenty of expensive and trendy gyms to work out or go posing at, but unless you have membership they can be expensive for a daily visit (£20–40). There are far too many to list here, so look in the Yellow Pages under Leisure Centres, or call Sportsline at (0207) 222-8000. Among the most popular is a chain of gyms called Holmes Place. These boast the usual extras like juice bars, saunas and steam rooms, Jacuzzis, and so on. Many hotels have their own facilities. What follows is a small list of sport and leisure in central London (please note that most of the leisure centers will expect you to do an "induction" to the gym (at a cost), irrespective of your experience):

Chelsea Sports Center in zone 11 Chelsea Manor Street, SW3. Phone (0207) 352-6985; take the tube to Sloane Square or South Kensington. Offers a 25-meter pool and the usual weights, aerobics classes, and so on.

Jubilee Hall Leisure Center in zone 7 at 30 The Piazza, Covent Garden, WC2 (phone (0207) 836-4835; www.jubileehallculbs.co.uk; tube: Covent Garden). This fully equipped gym, which has been refurbished recently, with a new cardio theater, free weights, and resistance machines, is in an excellent location. There are also yoga and various exercise classes.

London Central YMCA in zone 2, 112 Great Russell St., WC1 (phone (0207) 637-8131; tube: Tottenham Court Road). This is also very central, and totally comprehensive, with lots of classes.

Queen Mother Sports Center in zone 9 at 223 Vauxhall Bridge Rd., SW1. (phone (0207) 630-5522; tube: Victoria). Very central, this center has been modernized to the tune of over £1 million and has a complete range of facilities, equipment, and classes.

Porchester Center in Queensway, WZ (phone: (0207) 792-2919; www.cartneys.co.uk; tube: Queensway or Bayswater). Facilities include a 30-meter pool, gym, classes, and a wonderful health spa (Russian steam room, Turkish hot room, sauna, jacuzzi, and plunge pool). Gym, pool, and spa open daily.

Seymour Leisure Center in zone 14 at Seymour Place, W1 (phone (0207) 723-8019; take the tube to Marble Arch. This center has an Olympic-size pool, steam rooms, cardiovascular machines, and a snooker room (snooker is more complicated than pool and good fun).

Bicycling

You take your life into your hands bicycling around the streets of London, but there are parks to bike in that are wonderful. You can rent bikes by the golf driving range in Richmond Park; call (0208) 948-3209 for information. The London Bicycle Tour Company runs guided tours and also rents out bikes; call (0207) 928-6838 or visit www.londonbicycle.com.

Inline Skating

Inline skating is known as "rollerblading" in the UK. Hyde Park, by the Albert Memorial, is where you'll see the really good skaters and the hockey players. There are tracks all around Hyde Park that are excellent for skating. Good tracks can also be found in Battersea Park.

Horseback Riding

Though not exactly the sport of choice of the masses, there are beautiful places to ride in London. Hyde Park is an old favorite, with well-trodden riding paths like Rotten Row. Do not assume that riding in Hyde Park is without danger. You have to traverse a few streets and cross a busy main road to get into the park. The beasts are mostly of the warhorse variety, but you can occasionally get a bolter, and there's one place where they all want to canter. You can make arrangements to ride at the following:

Hyde Park Stables in zone 14, 63 Bathurst Mews, W2 (phone (0207) 723-2813; www.hydeparkstables.com; tube: Lancaster Gate or Paddington. Closed Mondays. The cost is £32 for experienced riders to ride in the park during the week and £35 on the weekend. Group lessons will set you back £34. The owners have recently opened another stable across the park, in South Kensington, in zone 11 at 11 Elversron Mews, SW7; (0207) 589-2299; tube: Gloucester Road. Here you can have individual lessons for £57.

Ross Nye Stables in zone 14 at 8 Bathurst Mews, W2; phone (0207) 262-3791; tube: Lancaster Gate or Paddingron. The price is £30 per hour and £40 for individual lessons. They won't take anyone under age six or anyone who weighs over 200 pounds. The stables are closed for a couple of months in the summer. Beginners and experienced riders are allowed, and children are encouraged.

Wimbledon Village Stables in zone 12 at 24 High Street, Wimbledon, SW19. Phone (0208) 946-8579 or visit www.wvstables.com; take the tube to Wimbledon. The price is £25 per hour during the week, £35 on weekends. Expect to pay £15 extra for an individual lesson. This is outside London but worth a trip if you want to avoid automobile traffic. They have small classes for beginners, and you will be taken on a rugged ride through Wimbledon Common, Putney Heath, and Richmond Park, all of which are semiwild expanses. Look out for deer. This is a much more beautiful experience than Hyde Park, though less convenient.

Ice Skating

Considering the fact that it never really gets cold enough for any of the natural bodies of water to freeze over, there is a surprising number of proficient skaters in London, some of whom can be seen whizzing around at breakneck speeds on London's many ice rinks. Admission and skate rental are cheap, and skating can be a fun night out. Try these rinks:

Broadgate Ice Rink in zone 3, Broadgate Circus, Eldon Street, EC2. Phone (0207) 505-4068; take the tube to Liverpool Street. Admission is £5; skate rental is £2. This tiny outdoor rink in the middle of London, among the glass castles of the financial district, is open October–April only. There's plenty of room to watch if you don't skate.

Leisurebox in zone 14, 17 Queensway, W2 (phone (0207) 229-0172; tube: Bayswater or Queensway). Admission is £6, including skate hire. A trendy joint; Friday and Saturday nights are disco nights. Good Chinese and Indian restaurants are in the immediate neighborhood for après skate. For those that find falling over again and again too painful, there is bowling at the same venue (see separate entry).

Swimming

Most of the leisure centers listed earlier have pools, but it is worth noting that almost every borough of London has at least one municipally run pool, some of which are more salubrious than others. To find your nearest pool, consult the Yellow Pages or call Sportsline on (0207) 222-8000. Following is a list of some of the better ones, and they're worth checking out when it's hot, although they get crowded:

Hampstead Heath Ponds in zone 1, Millfield Lane, NW3 (phone (0207) 485-3873; tube: Hampstead or Hampstead Heath or British Rail: Cospel Oak. Admission is free. These are three ponds in picturesque surroundings: one for men, one for women, and one for both. The segregated ponds are open all year. The mixed pond opens April–September only. There are no facilities except a basic changing area, so bring refreshments/picnics. The ponds are popular hangouts for gays.

The Lido at Hampstead Heath in zone 1 at Gordon House Road, NW3 (phone (0207) 485-3873; British Rail to Gospel Oak). Admission is £3.50, £1.50 for concessions. This is London's biggest outdoor pool and is only really worth going to on a hot day; it's open daily, April–September only

The Oasis zone 7, 32 Endell St., WC2 (phone (0207) 831-1804; tube: Covent Garden or Holborn). Admission is £2.90 for adults, £1.10 for children over age 5, and free for children under age 5. There is one indoor and one outdoor pool and a bathing deck for basking on those rare summer days!

Putney Leisure Center Dryburgh Road, SW15 (phone (0208) 785-0388; tube: Putney). Admission is £2.50. Here is an L-shaped indoor pool with a wave-making machine and a fully equipped gym with classes.

Richmond Pools in the Park in zone 12 at Old Deer Park, Twickenham Road, Richmond, Surrey; phone (0208) 940-0561; www.springhealth-leisure.com; tube: Richmond. Admission is £3 for adults, £2.40 for children, and free for kids under age 5. There are an indoor and an outdoor pool and a lush grassy area for flopping out on when it's hot.

Serpentine Lido in zone 14, Hyde Park (phone (0207) 298 2100; tube: Hyde Park Corner, Lancaster Gate, or Marble Arch). The Lido is open July–September only, from 10 a.m. to 6 p.m. daily. Admission is £2.70 for adults and 60p for children.

Karting

A very popular form of high-thrills entertainment, go-karting is catching on among laddish groups of young men. It's not cheap, but definitely exhilarating. The karts don't go all that fast, but it feels like they do. Venues are:

Daytona Raceway Atlas Road, NW10 (phone (0208) 749-2297 or (0500) 145155; www.daytone.co.uk; tube: Nolt Acron or Willesden Junction). You can race for £40 or have a practice session of 20 minutes for £20. You'll need to prebook.

Playscape Pro Racing Battersea Kart Raceway in zone 11, Hester Road, SW11 (phone (0207) 801-0110; www.playscape.co.uk/karting; take British Rail to Streatham or the tube to Sloane Square and then the Number 19 bus over the bridge. The cost is £42 for two hours. Special rares available for children on request. It's open daily.

Raceway in zone 15, Central Warehouse, North London Freight Terminal, York Way, N1 (phone (020) 7833 1000; www.theraceway.net; tube: Kings Cross).

Teamworks Karting in zone 3, Upper Level, Bishopsgate, Goods Yard, 33 Shordich High Street, E1 6PG (phone (0870) 900-3020; www.teamworkskarting.com; tube or British Rail to Liverpool Street). Teamworks is open Monday–Friday, 9 a.m.–11 p.m. and Sunday, 9 a.m.–6 p.m. In this brand-new center they run "arrive and drive" sessions from 10 a.m. to 6 p.m. The price is £25 for a 15-minute practice session, then £12.50 for every 15 minutes thereafter. Special events take place at lunchtimes on weekdays for £40.

For those with an appetite for more adrenalin, Silverstone Circuits in Northampton is an exciting day out. You can race carts or sign up for a day at the driving center where you can learn to drive Formula First (single searer) cars. Call the Silverstone Driving Center at (0132) 785-7271 or visit www.silverstone-circuit.co.uk. Prices range from £35 for a passenger ride to £150 for a 2-hour ride in either a Formula First car or Peugeot 30 racer.

Bungee Jumping

If you just can't get enough thrills with any of the above sports, you could try jumping off a crane at the **UK Bungee Club** (in Fairlop Waters, Forest Road, Barkingside, IG6; take the tube to Fairlop). The itinerant UK Bungee Club is based in Birmingham (in the Midlands) but roams the country setting up its cranes and making special appearances at major events. Phone (07000) 286433 to find out when they will next visit Fairlop Waters, the nearest spot to London, or visit www.ukbungee.com. A regular jump from 170 feet above water costs £50. Tandem jumps and cage rides are also available, and for an extra £15 they will video the ordeal. Enjoy!

Yoga, Etc.

In the past decade yoga has become as trendy as aerobics was in the 1980s, with new centers springing up, each cooler and more serene than the last. The added attraction could be that you may easily park your yoga mat up next to a famous rock star or actor. Whatever your reasons for going, fitness and serenity are also a strong possibility. The following is a list of the main yoga centers, although many leisure centers offer classes too:

Innergy Yoga Center in zone 13 at Acorn Hall, Kensal Road, W10 (phone (0208) 968-1178; www.innergy-yoga.com; tube: Ladbroke Grove). This place is so cool that they didn't want to give me any information. All I can tell you is that it's seriously trendy, that classes are predominantly Hatha yoga, and that Madonna once did a class here and caused a great frisson of excitement amongst the "Ladbroke Grovers" (the trendy patrons of the Ladbroke Grove/Notting Hill area).

Iyengar Yoga Institute in zone 14 at 223a Randolph Avenue, Maida Vale, W9 (phone (020) 764-3080; www.iyi.org.uk; tube: Maida Vale). Classes here are devoted exclusively to the Iyengar practice—precise and slow yoga, which aims at perfecting the postures. There are over 50 classes each week—from beginners to advanced, as well as those for pregnant women, seniors, and teenagers. The Institute is open daily from 9 a.m. to 9 p.m. A membership fee (£30) is payable if you attend more than twice. Classes for non-members range from £4.50 to £9.50.

The Life Centre in zone 13 at 15 Edge St., W8 (phone (0207) 221-4602; www.thelifecentre.org; tube: Notting Hill Gate). A 60-minute class costs £8, a 90-minute class costs £9.50. The Life Centre offers classes in Sivananda, Ashtanga, and Iyengar yoga, but Ashtanga classes predimonate; T'ai chi and Pilates are also available. Here you can get massages too, as well as a number of other alternative therapies.

Sivananda Yoga Vedanta Centre in zone 12 at 51 Felsham Rd., SW15 (phone (0208) 780-0160; www.sivanandayoga.org; tube: Putney Bridge or East Putney then the #14 bus). Daily yoga classes are offered for all levels; open classes are £7 or less; some are free. Satsang and lectures are offered.

Triyoga in zone 1 at 6 Erskine Road, Primrose Hill, NW3 (phone (0207) 483-3344; www.triyoga.com; tube: Chalk Farm). A very serene spot in the heart of Primrose Hill, Triyoga runs a plethora of classes: Ashtanga (a "flow-ing," dynamic form of yoga, set around a primary series of postures), Iyen-gar, and Okido (a Japanese-style yoga, which focuses on energy balancing and adopts different postures from those more widely practiced by Westerners). Tai Chi, Pilates, post- and prenatal yoga classes are also offered. The center opens at 6:30 a.m., and last classes are at 8 p.m. The cost is £8 for a one-hour class and £10 for a two-hour class. There are also treatment rooms offering a range of different massages, reflexology, facials, homeopathic treatments, and more.

Yoga Therapy Centre in zone 2, Homeopathic Hospital, 60 Great Ormond Street, WC1 (phone (0207) 419-7195; www.yogatherapy.org; tube: Russell Square). Classes are based on Hatha yoga. The center focuses on therpeutic classes to cope with ailments such as back pain, asthma, menstrual problems, and stress. It's open 9 a.m.–9:30 p.m. A 90-minute classe is £8.50, and a one-to-one therapy sessions last 60 minutes and costs £40.

Water Sports

For those who enjoy messing about on the river, there is plenty to do on the Thames and in the surrounding reservoirs and docklands. Experience water sports through the following:

Capital Rowing Center zone 12, Polytechnic Boathouse, Ibis Lane, W4 (phone (0208) 742-1997; www.capitalrowing.com; tube: Chiswick). For those who enjoy playing galley slave, £30 will buy you five hours of tortuous tuition.

Docklands Sailing and Watersports Centre in zone 5 at 235a Westferry Road, E14 (phone (0207) 537-2626; www.docklandswatersports.co.uk; British Rail: Crossharbour or London Arena DLR. The center offers sailing, Dragon-boat racing, rowing, and canoeing. Day membership costs £15 and it's open daily.

Docklands Watersports Club Gate 14, King George V Dock, Woolwich Manor Way, E16 (outside zones). Phone (0207) 511-7000 or visit www.teresa-joanne.com. Take Docklands Light Railway to Gallions Reach or North Woolwich. For jet-skiing enthusiasts, this club, which is based on a boat, the Tereza-Joanne, offers rental of craft, wetsuits, and use of the club. Prices start at £30 for 30 minutes and £55 for an hour.

Royal Docks Water-Ski Club Gate 16, King George V Dock, Woolwich Manor Way, E16 (outside zones). Phone (0207) 511-2000; visit www.waterskilondon.com. Take Docklands Light Railway to Gallions Reach or North Woolwich. Beginners are welcome; there are also courses and stunts for experienced skiers as well as speedboat driving and waterboarding. A 15-minute "row," which includes use of equipment and coaching, costs £16 for non-members and £10 for members.

Golf

As you would expect, there are no golf courses in the capital itself. The **English Golf Union** is an excellent resource for all golf information and can be reached at (0152) 635-4500. It would be worth the trip to the following courses based outside London if golf-withdrawal symptoms get bad! Courses outside the city include:

Brent Valley Church Road Cuckoo Lane, W7. Phone (0208) 567-1287; take the British Rail to Hanwell rail for18 holes at £9.25 per round, £14 on weekends.

Chingford Golf Course Bury Road, E4. Phone (0208) 529-5708; take British Rail to Chingford for18 holes. It's £11 weekdays and £15.25 on weekends.

Richmond Park in zone 12, Roehampton Gate, Richmond Park, SW15. Phone (0208) 876-3205; British Rail to Barnes. There are two 18-hole courses that cost £15 on weekdays and £18 on weekends. The price drops for games played late in the day.

Royal Mid-Surrey Golf Club in zone 12, Old Deer Park, Twickenham Road, Richmond, Surrey. Call (0208) 940-1894; take British Rail or the tube to Richmond. There are two 18-hole courses here, and whilst it is a private club, visitors are welcome. Admission is £68 for the day, £45 after 1 p.m., and £28 after 4:30 p.m.

In central London you can get lessons or do a bit of tee-ing off at the following spots:

Dukes Meadows Golf Club in zone 12, Dukes Meadows, Creat Chartsay Road, Chiswick, W4 (phone (0208) 994-3314; www.golflessons.co.uk; tube: Hammersmith, then 190 bus). The club is open daily 9 a.m.–10 p.m. There is something for everyone here: a 9-hole course, a 50-bay driving range, a 6-hole academy course (child-friendly), and a full teaching center. Golf-club hire is available. Wind down afterwards in the restaurant and bar. The cost to play the 9-hole course is £8.50 on weekdays, £10 on weekends. On the driving range, you'll pay £3 for a bucket of balls.

Regents Park Golf School in zone 14, Outer Circle, Regents Park, NW1 (phone (0207) 724-0643; www.rpgts.co.uk; tube: Baker Street). There is a driving range, a chipping and a bunker area, and lessons given by professionals. Membership is £75, although non-members are welcome. There is limited access to the facilites for non-members. Half-hour lessons are £24.

UK Driving Range in zone 15, Old Potato Yard, Kings Cross, N1 (phone: (0207) 837-1616; tube: Kings Cross). There are 24 floodlit bays and a putting green and bunker. The range is open weekdays, 10 a.m.–10 p.m. and weekends, 9 a.m.–9 p.m. You'll pay £3.50 for 60 balls; you can rent clubs for £1.

Tennis

Almost all London parks have tennis courts, which cost very little to play on. Bring your own racket and balls. There is usually a grass court or two and a few asphalt ones. It's very informal; just turn up on any weekday and you will almost certainly be able to play. For the serious player call the **Lawn Tennis Association** at the Queens Club in West Kensington (phone (0207) 381-7000). They will provide you with a booklet called "Where to Play Tennis in London."

Tenpin Bowling

Leisurebox in zone 14 at 17 Queensway, W2 (phone (0207) 229-0172; tube: Queensway or Bayswater). It's open 10 a.m.–10 p.m, and the cost for adults is £4.50; you'll pay £3.50 for children before 6 p.m. and £4.50 thereafter. Soft-shoe rental costs £1. There are 12 lanes.

Streatham Mega Bowl 142 Streatham Hill, SW2 (outside zones). Phone (0208) 671-5021 or visit www.megabowl.co.uk. Take British Rail to Streatham Hill. This alley has 36 lanes and is open Tuesday–Saturday, 10 –1:30 a.m. and Sunday–Monday, 10 a.m.–11:30 p.m.

Index

Accommodations. *See separate index,*
    Hotel Index
Air travel
    airport transportation, 128–31
    deals for, 38–39
    Gatwick Airport, 39, 128–29
    Heathrow Airport, 39, 129–30, 155
    London City Airport, 130
    Luton Airport, 130
    Stansted Airport, 130
Airbus, 129
Albert Memorial, 173–74
Alcoholics Anonymous, 52
Alfie's Antique Market, 347
All-Hallows-By-The-Tower, 250
Almeida (theater), 304
Ambulance, telephone numbers for,
    138
American Embassy, 49
Amphitheatre Bar and Restaurant, 310
Animals, quarantine laws for, 127
Antiquarius, 347
Antiques, shopping for, 333, 346–47
Apple Market, The, 343–44
Apsley House, 174–75
Aquariums, 198–99
Architecture museums, 229
Aromatic body stuff, 333
Arrival, 126–28
    by air, 128–31
    by car from continent, 131–32
    customs regulations, 47, 126–27
    immigration lines, 126
    by ship, 132

transportation to city, 128–32
Art museums
    Courtault Institute Gallery,
        220–21
    Gilbert Collection, 220–21
    Guildhall, 188–89
    Kenwood House, 195–96
    Leighton House, 197
    National Gallery, 205–6
    National Portrait Gallery, 207–8
    Queen's Gallery, 179–81, 211–12
    Royal Academy of Arts, 212–13
    Sir John Soane's Museum, 219–20
    Somerset House, 220–21
    Tate Britain, 223
    Tate Modern, 223–24
    Victoria and Albert Museum,
        226–28
    Wallace Collection, 228
Art shows, 55
Ascot Race Course, 55, 360
Astral Travels, 159
Astronomy, observatory for, 213–14,
    241
Atlas, street, 133, 144
ATMs, 41–42
Attractions. *See also* Churches;
    Museum(s)
    Albert Memorial, 173–74
    alphabetical listing of, 171–73
    Big Ben Clock Tower, 176
    British Library at St. Pancras,
        177–78
    Burgh House, 181

Hotel Index

Restaurant Index

Unofficial Guide **Reader Survey**

If you would like to express your opinion about London or this guide-book, complete the following survey and mail it to:

> *Unofficial Guide* Reader Survey
> PO Box 43673
> Birmingham AL 35243

Inclusive dates of your visit: _____

Members of your party: Person 1   Person 2   Person 3   Person 4   Person 5

Gender: M F   M F   M F   M F   M F

Age: _____

Have you ever been to Europe before? _____
Was this your first trip to London? _____
On your most recent trip, where did you stay? _____

Concerning your accommodations, on a scale of 100 as best and 0 as worst, how would you rate:

The quality of your room?   ____   The value of your room?   ____
The quietness of your room?   ____   The reservation process?   ____
Staff's relations with foreigners?   ____   Overall hotel satisfaction?   ____

Did you use public transportation? _____   What kind? _____

Concerning public transportation, on a scale of 100 as best and 0 as worst, how would you rate:

Ease of use?   ____   Value vs. rental cars?   ____
Cleanliness?   ____   Hours and areas serviced?   ____
Airport shuttle efficiency?   ____

Concerning your dining experiences:

Estimate the number of meals eaten in restaurants per day: _____
Approximately how much did your party spend on meals per day? ____
Favorite restaurants in London: _____
_____

Did you buy this guide before leaving? ☐   While on your trip? ☐

How did you hear about this guide? (check all that apply)

Loaned or recommended by a friend ☐   Radio or TV ☐
Newspaper or magazine ☐   Bookstore salesperson ☐
Just picked it out on my own ☐   Library ☐
Internet ☐

What other guidebooks did you use on this trip? _____

_____

_____

_____

On a scale of 100 as best and 0 as worst, how would you rate them?

_____

_____

_____

Using the same scale, how would you rate *The Unofficial Guide(s)?*

_____

Are *Unofficial Guides* readily available at bookstores in your area? _____

Have you used other *Unofficial Guides?* _____

Which one(s)? _____

_____

_____

_____

_____

_____

Comments about your London trip or *The Unofficial Guide(s):*

_____

_____

_____

_____

_____

_____

_____

_____

_____

_____

_____

_____

_____